SUCCEEDING IN THE World of Work

SUCCEEDING IN THE World of Work

GRADY KIMBRELL
Advisor
Career Development/Work Experience
Santa Barbara High School District
Santa Barbara, California

BEN S. VINEYARD, Ed. D
Professor and Chairman
Vocational Technical Education
Kansas State College
Pittsburg, Kansas

McKNIGHT PUBLISHING COMPANY
BLOOMINGTON, ILLINOIS

SECOND EDITION

Lithographed in U.S.A.

Copyright ©1975 by McKnight Publishing Company,
Bloomington, Illinois

Ronald E. Dale, Vice President-Editorial, wishes to acknowledge the skills and talents of the following people and organizations in the preparation of this publication.

Donna M. Faull
Production Editor

Ann Urban
Copy Editor

Elizabeth Purcell
Art Editor/Layout Artist

Willemina Knibbe
Production Assistance

Sue Whitsett
Proofreader

Scott Jones
Cover and Interior Designs

Ron Steege
Bloomington, Illinois
Cover Design

Raymond Glass
Cartoon Art

William McKnight, III
Manufacturing

Gorman's Typesetting
MR Typography
Composition

R. R. Donnelley & Sons
Chicago, Illinois
Preproduction/Printing

Library of Congress
Card Catalog Number: 74-21560

SBN: 87345-525-8

FOREWORD

There is a body of common knowledge needed by workers regardless of their particular occupations. For example, all workers need to understand how to apply for a job, how to get along with co-workers, and how to use a performance review and evaluation in improving occupational competence. All workers have need of the understandings that will help them move toward greater personal effectiveness; they need to understand their own values, interests, aptitudes and abilities as a basis for setting personal goals and planning ways to improve.

Performing in the occupational role in an effective, responsible, and rewarding manner requires not only a knowledge of the skills of the job and the knowledge and skills for general employability, but also understandings required for meeting one's adult responsibilities in such areas as money management, consumer buying, social security and retirement, and insurance. It requires an appreciation for and discriminating use of the resources for continued learning and development in relation to the occupation.

In Succeeding in the World of Work, the authors have presented in a clear and forthright manner a comprehensive discussion of the content which should be a part of the vocational education of all young people.

This common content, along with the knowledges and skills for occupational competency in a given field, constitute the program in vocational education. The common content serves as one basis for occupational mobility and for continued growth and development.

The authors of this book are well qualified through training and experience in both business and education for the task of developing a student text around the content common to all occupational fields. This book, which is a revision of an earlier text by the authors, is relevant to the needs of the young person preparing for a work role and should help him or her find success and personal rewards in employment.

Elizabeth J. Simpson, Dean
School of Family Resources
and Consumer Sciences,
University of Wisconsin

ACKNOWLEDGMENTS

The authors are grateful to all who assisted and cooperated in the preparation of this book. Special acknowledgment is made to the following:

American Express Travelers Cheques
BankAmericard
Bureau of Labor Statistics
General Electric Company
General Research Corporation, Systems Research Division
Kansas Employment Security Division
Kansas Motor Vehicle Division
Kansas State College of Pittsburg
Kellogg Company
Mutual of Omaha Insurance Company
National Bank of Pittsburg, Kansas
National Safety Council
Oklahoma State University Extension
Ray Glass
Sears, Roebuck and Company
Social Security Administration
State Farm Insurance Company
State of Kansas, Bureau in Brief, 1974
United States Coast Guard
United States Department of Health, Education, and Welfare
United States Department of Treasury, Internal Revenue Service
United States Government Printing Office
United States Marine Corps
United States Navy

Grady Kimbrell wishes to give special thanks to Cedric Betram Boeseke, who was the first coordinator to initiate an exploratory work experience program, who developed this innovation so successfully during its first two years that special authorization was written into the California Education Code, whose inspiration and tutelage caused him to devote his life to career development and relevant work experiences for young people, and whose leadership and enthusiasm has been of great significance in the proliferation of similar programs throughout the country in recent years.

TABLE OF CONTENTS

INTRODUCTION

Today the work you do to earn a living influences your **way of life**. It is a major factor in your identity. It affects your choice of friends and the way you spend your leisure time. Work gives you an opportunity to have impact on the culture in which you live. Work is the **central activity** around which people plan their lives. Successful work activity is necessary to achieve personal happiness.

In the past, the variety of work activity available to a young person was limited. Few women worked outside the home. Most young people followed in the same line of work as their parents. Many became farmers, having learned how to work at an early age by helping on their parents' farm. Others learned a trade by helping their parents or a friend of the family. There was not much choice about the kind of work a person could do.

During the past 50 years, our society has become much more complex. There are now more than 20,000 different jobs. Most women now work for at least 25 years of their lives outside the home. Women have become an important part of the work force. Most people no longer perform their work activities in the home — they travel to work. Thus, many young people never see their parents engaged in the work activity which earns the family livelihood. While there are several thousand **kinds** of work which are available to young people, there is less opportunity to closely observe work activity today than there was 50 years ago.

Psychologists tell us that one of the things which most disturb young people is the lack of an occupational identity. That is, too many young people have no picture of themselves some five or ten years in the future. They have no career goals. They don't know where they are going. Young people who know where they are going occupationally have a goal to pursue. They have a purpose.

How can you, as students, make career decisions which will determine the central activity of your daily lives for the next 40 or 50 years? Some say, "Sit at your desk, and you will be told about the world." Others say, "School won't help too much; you've got to **experience** the world." Most psychologists who have studied this problem agree that the two most important factors in gaining identity as a worker are the following:

1. Getting work experience to guide you in choosing a career.

2. Choosing and preparing for a career.

Thus, the best approach seems to be through cooperative work experience education.

Part I of this text deals with the meaning of work, and how part-time work experience provides an avenue for exploring careers in which you are interested. We shall discuss setting short-range and long-range goals which are realistic for you. You will learn how to locate, apply for, and progress on a job which will lead toward your long-range goal.

CHAPTER ONE
YOU AND WORK

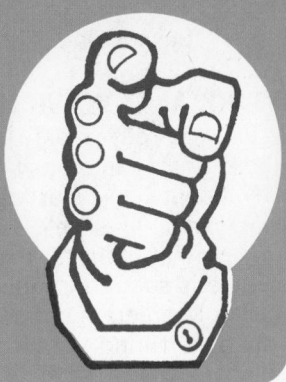

MEN AND WOMEN IN A WORLD OF WORK

After completion of high school, you can expect to live for about another fifty to sixty years.[1] As a student, have you considered how many of these years you will be working? Most high school students will be in the world of work for twenty-five to forty years. For men, this involvement has always been understood. Women have recently experienced a new involvement, because they are now becoming successful in careers that used to be open only to men. Despite the increasing role of women in the working world, too many high school girls still find it difficult to believe that they will be working for so long. Consider this as an example:

Ellen graduated from high school when she was eighteen and began working as a typist in an insurance office in her home town. Soon after she began working, she met Richard. They began dating regularly and were married shortly after Ellen's twentieth birthday. Richard was twenty-two and had a good job, but his income was barely enough to meet the expenses of a newly married couple. They decided that it would be best if Ellen continued working for awhile so that they could rent a nicer apartment, trade in Richard's five-year-old Chevrolet, and maybe even save a little money for a down payment on a house in a couple of years.

A month before their first child, Cathy, was born, Ellen quit her job. She did not begin working again until after their second child, Mark, was in the first grade. The family had moved to another city, and Ellen began working part time as a typist at the local high school. She was soon offered a better-paying job as a secretary in a real estate office, and Ellen was again a full-time member of the working world. Ellen changed jobs two more times to accept jobs with increasing responsibility. She continued to work until Mark had completed two years of college, moved to his own apartment, and begun his first full-time job.

Ellen has spent the last two years at home as a full-time housewife. But she is bored with inactivity after being employed for seventeen years. Ellen will go back to work as soon as she finds a job she likes and feels she can do well.

[1]The life expectancy for an 18-year-old boy is 73 years; for an 18-year-old girl, it is 76 years.

WORK AND YOUR LIFESTYLE

As you daydream (as everyone does) about your future, have you thought carefully about how your work affects you and your overall lifestyle? Did you know, for example, that half of the average person's lifetime is spent at or involved in work? Your work, or career, is **not** something that affects you only during working hours! If you are going to spend most of your waking hours involved in some kind of work activity for most of your adult life, you can see how important it is to spend some time planning this facet of your future.

Life is made up of relationships with people, places, and things. Your use of time in these relationships is called your **lifestyle**. These relationships may be grouped into five major facets of your life and diagrammed to show a "picture" of your lifestyle. Since everyone has a set of **values** (things that are important), lifestyle patterns are also different. One person may place about the same value on and give about the same amount of time to each of these five major facets. Such a lifestyle pattern would look something like this:

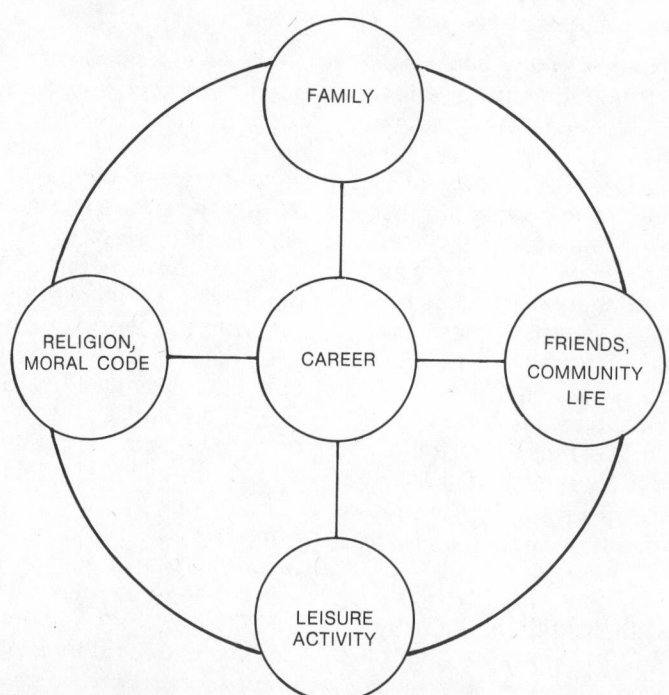

The Lifestyle Pattern of a Person Who Places Equal Value on Each Major Facet of Life

Most people, however, do not place equal value on or give equal time to each facet of their life relationships. More typical lifestyle patterns would be similar to these:

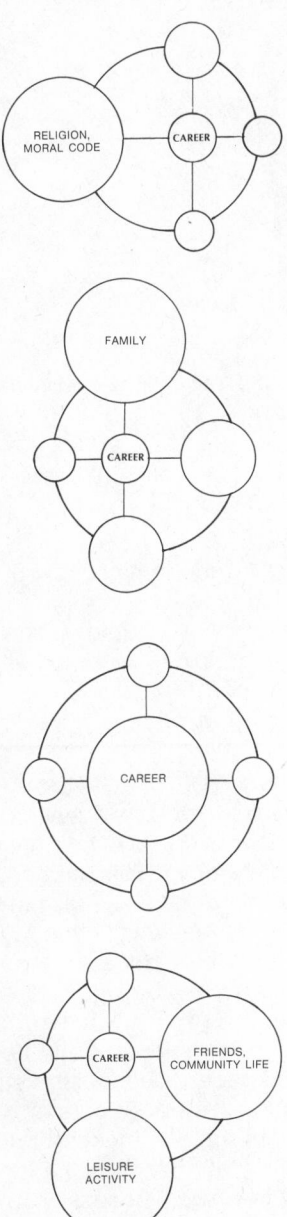

Lifestyle Patterns of People with Differing Values and Interests

WORK — LIFE'S CENTRAL ACTIVITY

Each major facet of your life in some way affects all of the others. Notice that **career** was placed at the center in each lifestyle pattern because it is the central activity around which we plan our daily lives. In America, work is our **way of life!**

As a Student, Your Lifestyle Is Determined Mainly by Your Different Student Activities

As a student, your lifestyle is determined mainly by your role as a student. It is the central activity around which you plan your daily life. **Your identity** is that of a **student.** When you are introduced to another person, you may be asked, "Where do you go to school?" or "What grade are you in?" As you approach adulthood, you will assume a new identity, and it will be determined mainly by the kind of work you do to earn a living. After being introduced to another person, you may be asked, "What do you do?" "What kind of work do you do?", or simply, "Where do you work?" While other things make up a part of your identity, the work you do is the chief ingredient! Even the work you plan to do is used to identify you. For example, college students are sometimes identified as prelaw or premed students. If you are concerned about your own identity — who you will become — remember that the work you do will largely identify you to others. For instance, by knowing the work people do, you can estimate:

1. What their incomes are.
2. What their educational backgrounds are.
3. Where they live.
4. Where they work.
5. What their political views are.
6. Who their friends are.
7. How they spend their leisure time.
8. What clubs they belong to.

Do you believe that your work can affect your life in so many ways? Consider these situations:

As an Adult, You Will Be Identified by Your Career

> Larry is a mechanic in a Ford agency. He moved to the community two years ago after being released from the Coast Guard. While in the Coast Guard, Larry's favorite form of recreation was bowling. When he heard that Ray, the agency's service manager, was on a bowling team, it was natural that Larry and Ray should become good friends. They had two common interests: their place of work and bowling, their leisure-time activity.
>
> Carol is a mechanical engineer. Her boss is very interested in politics and is on the city council. During the last election, Carol began to share her boss's political views and even became his campaign manager!

WHY WE WORK

You have now seen that working affects your total lifestyle and that almost all of us can expect to spend most of our adult lives working. Why do people work? Basically,

they work for three reasons, not necessarily in this order:

1. Money (economic) to provide for physical needs.
2. Contact with people (social) for the feeling of loving or belonging.
3. Self-esteem (psychological) for self-respect and pride.

YOU NEED $500,000!

If you were asked the question, "Why do you want to work?", your first answer might well be, "For money!" This, indeed, is a good reason. Based on the cost of living today and the outlook for the future, you will need at least half a million dollars to pay for the goods and services you will purchase during your lifetime! Some of these goods and services are necessary for your life and well-being. These necessities include such goods as food, clothing, and shelter (housing). Some services are also necessary. These include medical attention and education. An automobile is also a necessity if you must have one to get to work or to the places where necessary goods and services are purchased.

None of us is satisfied with only being able to purchase the goods and services which are necessary. Our **wants** exceed our **needs**! Whatever you desire in addition to the necessities of life is called a luxury. Of course, a **necessity** to one person may be a **luxury** to another.

Ways of handling your money so that you can get more goods and services for the amount of money you pay will be discussed in a later chapter. Money is **only one** reason for working. There are other important ones.

PEOPLE NEED PEOPLE

People need contact with others, although the amount of contact they need varies greatly from one person to another. One of the most hated forms of punishment is to be placed "in solitary." People are gregarious. They do not like to be alone. It is difficult to imagine a happy person without even one friend or at least someone with whom to talk. Work provides opportunities for contact with other people. You will find that your place of work will be a source of social contacts and possibly one or two close friends.

SELF-ESTEEM — EVERYBODY NEEDS IT

The famous social psychologist, Dr. A. H. Maslow, has identified the basic needs of all human beings. His list begins with the most basic needs — life, food, and water. After these needs are met, we become concerned about safety. Early man found shelter from the heat, cold, wind, and rain by living in caves or cliffs, or by building crude houses in trees. This protection also provided shelter from dangerous animals. Today people live in homes and apartments which provide protection from the elements. No one has to worry too much about being devoured by wild animals.

Once safety needs are met, we look for companionship and affection. Finally, when all these needs have been met, we seek status with others. This is known as **self-esteem.** It means that you feel good about yourself. Your outlook on life (your **satisfaction with life**) depends to a large extent upon how you feel about your work. This was illustrated when we discussed how each major facet of life relates to the other major facets of life to make up a person's lifestyle, see page 5. The importance of work is not the same for everyone. Some think work is important only because it provides the money to enjoy some leisure-time activity. To others, it is indeed a **way of life!**

How successful you are in life is largely measured by your success in your work. Being successful on a job which interests you helps you to develop a sense of pride. It gives you self-respect. Very often, those who are most interested in and successful in their careers are the people who are most satisfied with life. Job success is the chief way we measure our own usefulness, our worth. Naturally, this has a great effect upon one's personality. Without self-respect, you cannot accept yourself as being a person of worth. If you cannot accept **yourself** as a worthy person, you cannot accept **others** as worthy and be truly concerned about them.

If You Cannot Accept Yourself as a Worthy Person, You Will Not Accept Others as Being Worthy People Either

As you can see, you receive many benefits from working. As with anything else, however, you will not receive all this unless you **give** something. What you receive from working depends directly upon what you give to your work and to your employer. For example, if you expect a full day's pay, you must give a full day's work.

When you attend a movie, you must purchase a ticket and pay the full fare. If the theatre only showed you three-fourths of the film and turned off the projector, you would feel that you hadn't gotten your money's worth. Your attitude toward the theatre manager would be distrust, perhaps even anger.

Likewise, if your employer pays you for four hours' work and you have only worked three hours because of tardiness, a long coffee break, or time otherwise wasted, you are being unfair. Your employer will learn to distrust you. Those who cheat their employers this way are not likely to be promoted to a better-paying job. Many times they are fired! Remember that **you must make money for your employer's business in order for the business to be able to pay your salary.** When you begin work, or if you are working now, put in a day's work for a day's pay!

If You Expect a Full Day's Pay, You Must Give a Full Day's Work

In addition to giving your employer a fair day's work for your salary, you should also be loyal to the company. You should be **for** the organization. If you have minor complaints about your work or your company, do not discuss them with people outside the company. It is important to the welfare of the company (and to **you**) that it have a good name and a good **image**. This good name is partly what makes it possible for the company to make a profit so that it can meet its expenses, and this includes your salary!

WHAT'S AHEAD IN PART I

The search for identity in a rapidly changing world is what today's young people find most disturbing. They will find it only after setting (and making progress toward) some realistic goals. Achieving success in a carefully chosen career is one of the most significant goals which a young person can set, but there is a difference between **goals** and **realistic goals**!

Only you can decide upon a realistic goal for **you**, because no one knows you like you do. Even so, your decision will not be realistic unless you first make a careful study of your (1) values, (2) interests, (3) aptitudes and special talents, and (4) personality. In addition, you must give consideration to the occupational outlook.

In the next chapter you will learn the relationship between part-time student employment and a full-time career. You will learn how to choose a job rather than being chosen by it, and where and how to look for jobs.

There are certain techniques which improve your chances of getting the job you want. These techniques, along with how to make the best impression in an interview, are discussed in Chapter 3.

Although they are successful in obtaining a job, many young workers are not successful **on** the first job. Some are fired, others are laid off. Some employers tell these young workers the real reason for their failure, while others just say that the company must reduce the number of employees, or make some other excuse. The **real** reason for 90 percent of these failures is discussed in Chapter 4. You will have a chance to learn what the employer (boss) usually expects of a young worker. You will also learn what you can reasonably expect of your employer. You will gain some helpful ideas on getting along with those who work with you, since a friendly atmosphere makes your job much easier.

After you have worked for awhile, you may be given additional responsibility if you have done a good job. This is discussed in Chapter 5, along with promotions, salary increases, and procedures to take if you are fired!

In the remaining chapters of Part I, you will have an opportunity to learn how to better understand **yourself**, how to investigate careers, and how to relate these two sets of information to arrive at an appropriate long-term career goal. You will also learn how to find out what others think about you and how to become more effective in your personal and business relationships with others. You will learn new ways of getting others to do and see things **your way**!

STUDY AIDS

NEW TERMS

aesthetics	leisure activity
good will	lifestyle
gregarious	self-esteem

STUDY QUESTIONS

1. How many years will the average student in high school today work?
2. How are young people in school usually identified?
3. How are adults usually identified?
4. What kinds of things can you estimate about an individual by knowing the kind of work he or she does?
5. How much money do you think you will need during your lifetime?
6. What must you give your employer in return for a day's pay?

DISCUSSION PROBLEMS

1. How do people's careers affect their lifestyles?
2. What are three reasons for working? What is the importance of each?
3. What are the basic needs of all human beings? What is the relationship of a person's career to these needs?

CHAPTER TWO
EXPLORING CAREERS THROUGH PART-TIME JOBS

YOUR CAREER DEVELOPMENT

In Chapter 1, you learned that the work people do to earn a living affects their overall lifestyles; work is the central activity around which adults plan their daily lives. Adults are identified mainly by the responsibilities and benefits of the work that they choose.

Since the work you do will have a great influence upon your life, then **selecting an** appropriate career goal is one of your most important considerations. You need experiences which can prepare you for challenging and interesting work. Your life's work (your career) should match **your abilities, values, interests, personality, and overall lifestyle goals.** Success in your work influences all aspects of your life. People who have successful careers often find that their success is accompanied by happiness, satisfaction in life, and the ability to have closer personal relationships with family and friends.

Unfortunately, the majority of today's adults simply "fell into" the kind of work they do. A job that just **happened** to be available determines their career, and in large part, their lifestyle. The process ought to be just the opposite. Those who are most satisfied with life, their careers, and their specific jobs are those who had a plan and followed it. If the work you do is such an important part of your lifestyle, shouldn't you **choose** your work instead of being **chosen by it?** The first step in choosing your career is to set some lifestyle goals based on your values (things that are important to you). Through a process of **career development** you will be able to arrive at a career goal (or several possible career goals) and a plan to reach your goal. This process of career development has two parts. One part is learning to know and understand yourself and your needs. This will be covered in detail in Chapter 6. The second part is investigating career demands and opportunities through

Successful Work Activity Provides a Feeling of Enthusiasm At Any Age

experience and research. This will be covered in detail in Chapter 7.

In this chapter we will discuss the relationship between your part-time job and selecting (and progressing toward) a career goal. You may select one career goal or several possible ones, and you may change your mind several times before reaching your goal. However, if you have a goal in mind, you have something to work toward. It is then possible for you to write your own ''educational prescription'' — that is, you may select the courses in school which will help most in reaching your goal. If you control your experiences so that they are preparing you for a career in which you can succeed (yet offer enough of a challenge to be interesting) and which match your values and lifestyle goals, you will be on your way to **choosing a satisfying career**.

In order for a career to be satisfying, it must be **realistic**. A realistic goal is one which is **attainable**, one you can reach. A realistic career goal is one in which you will probably succeed because you have an aptitude, a **knack**, for a particular kind of work. If your career goal requires an expensive education, this must be considered realistically, too.

We mentioned that your career goal should be one that will be challenging to you, but not so great a challenge that you will be un-

able to meet it. More will be said later about general ability and aptitude tests. However, if you have difficulty learning in school, it would **not** be realistic to select a career goal which requires many years of college. It would probably result in disappointment for you, and it would delay your reaching a realistic goal. If your general learning ability is above average, you would probably not be challenged by many routine jobs which would seem quite easy for you. Of course, to prepare for many of the more complex jobs, some college study is necessary, and the first step toward college is a good high school record! Selecting a realistic career goal also depends upon your own personality. If you are the kind of person who likes to talk and who makes friends easily, you are an ''**outgoing**'' or enjoyable person. You may have the kind of personality it takes to be a salesperson. If you are usually quiet and find it difficult to make friends, you would probably not be as happy in sales. You would probably be a happier, more successful worker in a job where you work alone or with only a few other people.

YOUR PART-TIME JOB

If you have a part-time job, or if you are looking for one, this is your main job interest. You may find it difficult to look ahead to a full-time job or life career which may be

Many People Simply Fall into the Kind of Work They Do

several years away. While a detailed study of how to select an appropriate career will be delayed until Chapters 6 and 7, we have mentioned the importance of realistic career goals because of their relationship to your part-time job while you are still in school. Consider the benefits of a part-time job.

BENEFITS OF A PART-TIME JOB

1. The attitudes you develop toward your part-time job and toward your fellow workers will carry over to your full-time career.
2. If you can get a part-time job which is similar to your career goal, you can "test out" that field of work to discover how interesting it is to you and find out whether you have the aptitudes and personality which make for success.
3. If you are successful on your part-time job, you will have a valuable recommendation from your employer when you are ready for a full-time job.

WORK EXPERIENCE PROGRAMS

If your school has a career development or work experience education program, that office can be of great help to you in selecting realistic career goals and finding part-time employment which is related to your career goals. The program in your school may be called by another name, such as Cooperative Education, Cooperative Work Experience, Work Study, or Diversified Occupations. Some schools offer an "exploratory" work experience program on a non-payment basis. The advantages of this program are these: (1) Many more types of work opportunities are available, and you can choose one which is related to your career goal. (2) Because employers are not paying you for your services, they can take more time to let you observe and "try out" many work activities, instead of assigning

you just the duties you would perform as a paid worker.

If You Are an Enjoyable Person, You May Have the Kind of Personality It Takes to Influence Other People in Sales or Management

RELATIONSHIP TO CAREER GOALS

If your school does not have a work experience program, you can still profit by a part-time job after school or a summer job. In addition to the money, you will benefit from the experience in these ways:

1. You can still explore occupations which interest you and determine your suitability for them.
2. You can broaden your understanding of the working world and of working conditions, even if the job is not closely related to your long-range goal.
3. You can develop the kind of work habits which will help you succeed on a full-time job.
4. Your transition from school to work will be easier.

Look into Many Fields of Work Before Choosing Your Career

CAREER CLUSTERS

We mentioned two parts to the career development process:

(1) learning to know and understand yourself and your needs, and

(2) investigating career demands and opportunities through experience and research. Although most people do not give enough attention to either part, it is the second that is most neglected by young people. With this in mind, you may wish to take a look at the demands and opportunities of a **variety** of careers. The **Dictionary of Occupational Titles, Third Edition**[1] lists more than 20,000 separate occupations with their specific duties and responsibilities. It would, of course, be an impossible task to read through the more than 800 pages of fine print describing these occupations. To assist in the career development process, the U. S. Office of Education grouped occupations into 15 **career clusters**, as follows:

- Agri-Business and Natural Resources
- Business and Office Careers
- Communications and Media Careers
- Construction Careers

[1]**Dictionary of Occupational Titles,** Vol. I, Definitions of Titles, Third Edition (Washington: U. S. Government Printing Office, 1965.)

- Consumer and Homemaking-Related Careers
- Environmental Control Careers
- Fine Arts and Humanities Careers
- Health Careers
- Hospitality and Recreation Careers
- Manufacturing Careers
- Marketing and Distribution Careers
- Marine Science Careers
- Personal Services
- Public Services
- Transportation Careers

COMMON ENTERPRISE FUNCTIONS

Regardless of your career, you will be working in **some kind** of private enterprise (business) or public institution. You should know that every enterprise or institution has six common functions. These are:

1. Managing
2. Researching and Developing
3. Preparing to Produce a Product or Provide a Service
4. Producing a Product or Providing a Service
5. Selling, Delivering, and Servicing
6. Controlling the System

Every enterprise or institution must be managed. Thus, there must be **managers** at various levels in every establishment. These managers, particularly in a newly formed establishment, are often also the owners or part-owners of the firm. They make the decisions and direct the next common function, **researching and developing.**

Research and development is done for two reasons. **Market research** is done to gather information and estimate whether there will be enough people interested in buying the product or service the company plans to sell. **Product or service research** is done to design the product or service to be sold. After it has been decided that there will be a market for a product or service and that it can profitably be produced or provided, there are certain steps in getting ready to produce goods or provide services.

Preparing to produce a product or provide a service is the function that includes installing equipment, purchasing supplies, and hiring the workers necessary to either produce the product or provide the service.

Finally, the **product is produced or the service is provided** — after which, if the company is producing a product, it must be **sold, delivered, and serviced**. Appropriate records must be kept to guide management in **controlling** all other functions of the establishment. The control function is usually a management responsibility, and the accounting personnel usually gather the required information.

In the production of automobiles, for instance, management gives directions to workers who do research and development. Then equipment must be purchased and workers hired to produce a new model car. The car is then sold (with the help of extensive advertising programs), delivered, and serviced. Again, careful records must be kept in order to control the system. Market research and product design in manufacturing automobiles is a long process. It normally takes at least three years for a new model to go from the drawing board to the show room! Most American companies make slight changes in models every year with complete new models about every three years. A few companies, particularly foreign manufacturers, keep producing the same models for eight to ten years. Volkswagen kept the same basic body style for more than thirty years because it continued to satisfy consumer needs for low cost transportation.

When new products or models of a product are manufactured every few years, much money and many people are needed to **prepare to produce a product**. When the same product is manufactured for thirty years, it is not very expensive to **prepare** for production. Most of the costs are for the actual production of the product.

More and more companies today are involved in **providing a service**. An example of providing a service would be selling computer time (use) to companies which do not have their own automated equipment. Other services are provided by public stenographers, establishments which make photocopies of manuscripts, health clinics, all kinds of specialized training schools, and employment placement firms.

DIFFERENCES IN CAREER CLUSTERS

While all public institutions and private enterprises have common functions, there are differences between types of establishments. These can generally be described as differences in:

1. Where people work.
2. How people work.
3. How people communicate special knowledge or skills where they work.

Each establishment has its own environment. That is, the place of work, equipment, and supplies used are different in every company. Basically, the 15 career clusters listed on page 13 represent specific types of establishments. Each occupational cluster of work has a different environment. When you hear the word construction, what environment do you think of? What about environ-

Each Career Environment Has Its Own Special "Jargon"

ments for:

- Manufacturing?
- Agri-Business?
- Recreation?
- Marine Science
- Homemaking?

It is obvious that each career cluster has its own specific skills and its own special vocabulary (jargon or lingo). The specific skills and special vocabulary go together and must be learned for a person to succeed in any particular career. The skills and vocabulary of a construction worker, for example, are completely different from those of a health care worker.

CAREER ACTIVITIES AND INTERESTS

We have said that the main differences between the activities of workers in different career clusters are the special skills and vocabularies. It is the skills and vocabularies that are emphasized in all educational programs for any career. The person who plans to become an accountant (business and office careers cluster) studies the skills and terminology (vocabulary) of "journalizing," "posting," "calculating depreciation," "recording, adjusting, and closing entries," and "preparing financial statements." This is as meaningless to a cardiologist (heart specialist) as "coronary cineangiography" or "ventricular fibrillation" would be to an accountant. (These words are meant only to show that each career has its own vocabulary — you do not need to remember them!)

SAMPLE OCCUPATIONAL TITLES IN CAREER CLUSTERS

We previously listed and discussed the 15 career clusters outlined by the U. S. Office of Education. The following groups of occupational titles will give you some idea of the kinds of workers in each career cluster. Most schools organize their career education programs around the cluster concept, and some interest tests help indicate your preference for specific clusters.

AGRI-BUSINESS &
NATURAL RESOURCES

Agronomist
Animal Breeders
Botanist
Dairy Farmer
Fish and
   Game Warden
Forester
Grain Farmer
Miner
Nursery Gardeners
Soil Conservationist

BUSINESS & OFFICE CAREERS

Accountant
Bookkeeper
Computer
    Programmer
Data Processing
    Equipment
    Operator
File Clerk
Office Manager
Payroll Clerk
Receptionist
Secretary
Typist

COMMUNICATIONS & MEDIA CAREERS

Announcer
Author/Writer
Cinematographer
Editor (Films, TV,
    Publishing)
Layout Person
    (Advertising)
Newspaper Reporter
Printing Press
    Operator
Radio/TV Repairer
Telephone Installer
Telephone Operator

CONSTRUCTION CAREERS

Carpenter
Civil Engineer
Contractor
Electrician
Heavy Equipment
 Operator
Mason (Brick, Stone,
 Tile)
Painter
Plumber
Roofer
Surveyor

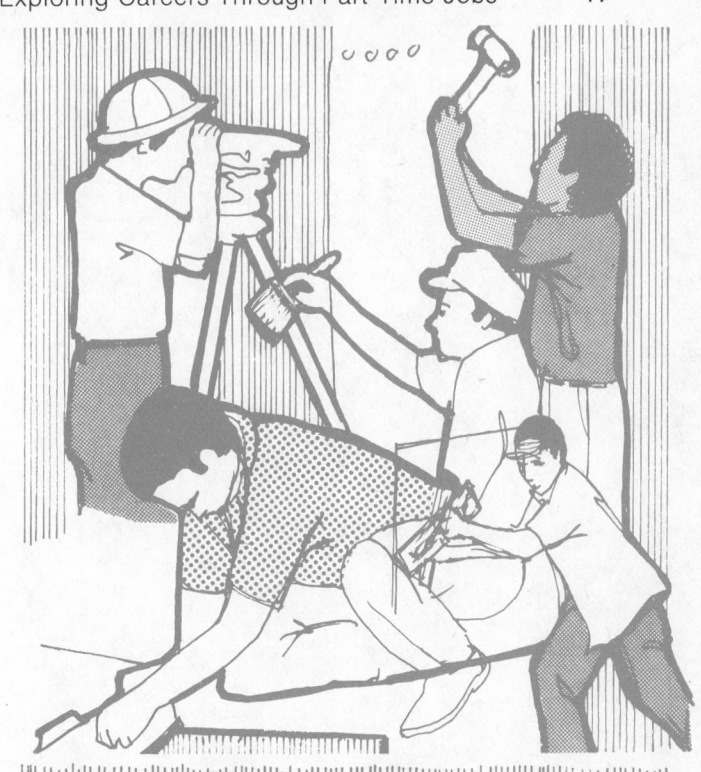

CONSUMER & HOMEMAKING CAREERS

Budget Consultant
Dietitian
Fashion Coordinator
Food Specialist
Four-H Club Agent
Home Economist
Interior Decorator
Maid
Nursery School
 Teacher
Seamstress/Tailor

ENVIRONMENTAL CONTROL CAREERS

Air Analyst
Fish and Game
  Conservationist
Hydrologist
Industrial Health
  Engineer
Landscape Architect
Pest-Control Worker
Sanitarian
Social Ecologist
Urban Planner
Wildlife Manager

FINE ARTS & HUMANITIES CAREERS

Actor/Actress
Composer
Conductor
  (Orchestra)
Dramatic Coach
Literary Writer
Musician
Philosopher
Photographer
Sculptor
Vocalist

HEALTH CAREERS

Dental Assistant
Dentist
EEG/EKG
   Technician
Laboratory
   Technician
Licensed
   Vocational Nurse
Nuclear Medical
   Technologist
Nurse's Aide
Physician
Registered Nurse
X-Ray Technologist

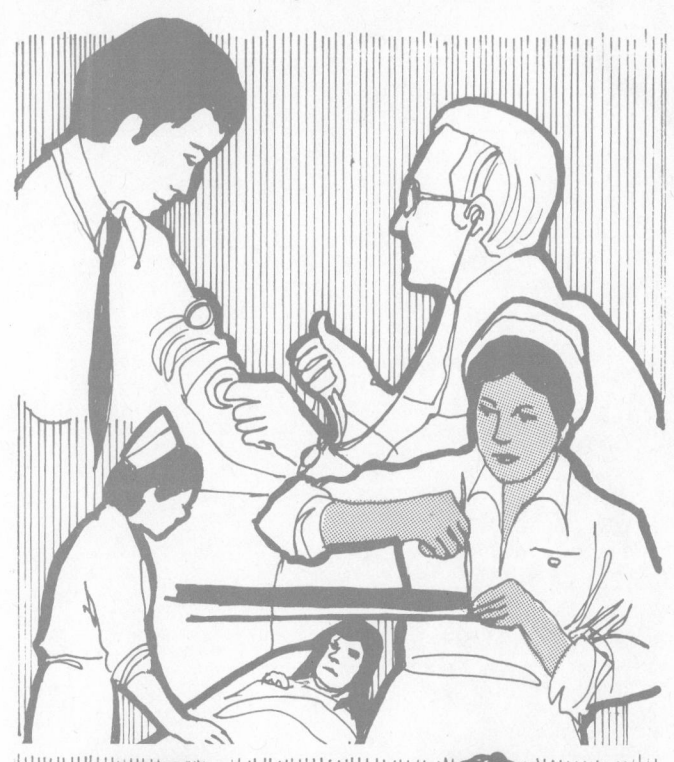

HOSPITALITY & RECREATION CAREERS

Athlete
   (Professional)
Bellhop
Flight Attendant
Host/Hostess
Hotel/Motel Clerk
Playground
   Supervisor
Recreational/
   Social Director
Travel Agent
Tour Guide
Waiter/Waitress

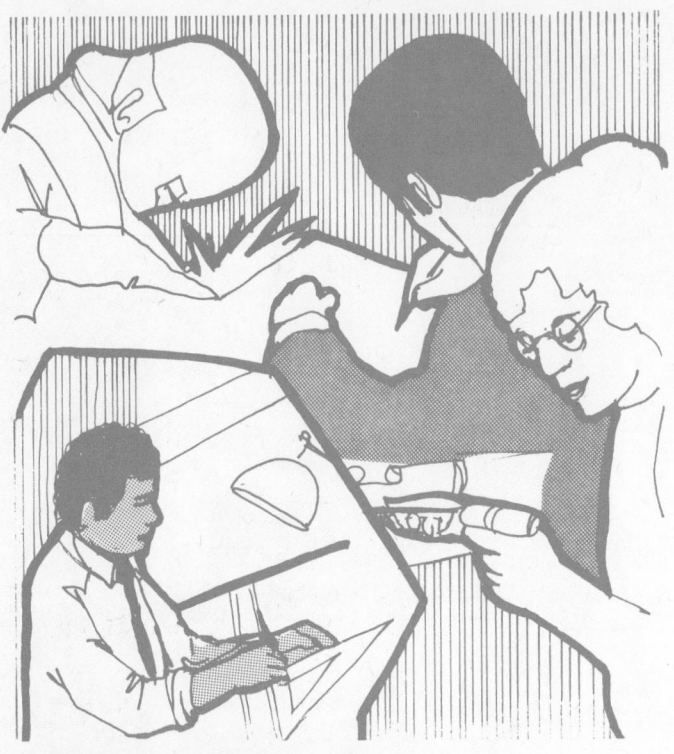

MANUFACTURING CAREERS

Assembler
Drafting Artist
Drill Press Operator
Expeditor
Inspector
Machinist
Punch Press
    Operator
Technical Writer
Tool-and-Die Maker
Welder

MARINE SCIENCE CAREERS

Diver
Diver Helper
Ichthyologist
Marine
    Bacteriologist
Marine Biologist
Marine Geologist
Marine Metalurgist
Marine Survey
    Technician
Marine Zoologist
Oceanographer

MARKETING AND DISTRIBUTION CAREERS

Buyer
Delivery Person
Gift Wrapper
Grocery Checker
Manager,
  Retail Store
Model
Order Clerk
Sales Clerk
Stock Boy/
  Stock Girl
Telephone Solicitor

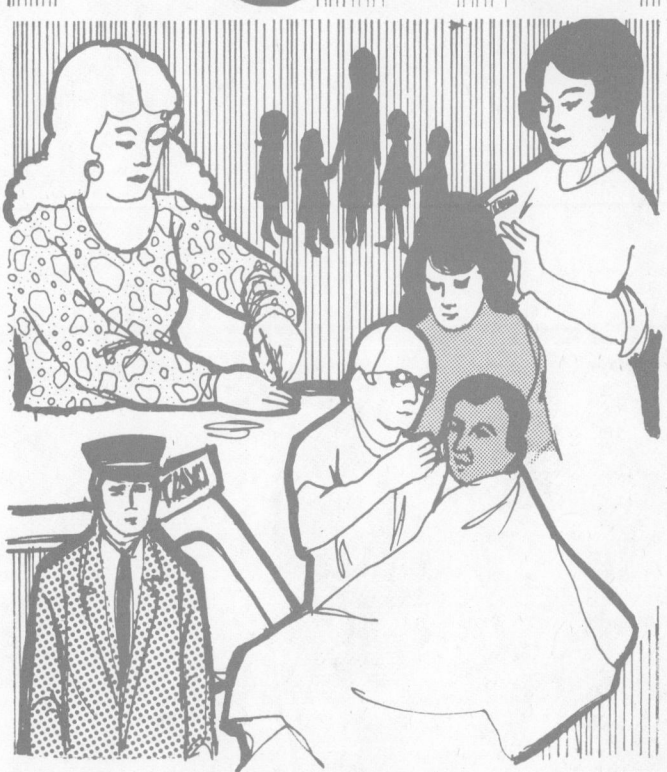

PERSONAL SERVICES CAREERS

Barber
Chauffeur
Cosmetologist
Escort
Children's
  Supervisor
Guide (Travel)
Manicurist
Masseur/Masseuse
Mortician
Valet

PUBLIC SERVICES CAREERS

Civil Defense
   Official
Fire Fighter
Immigration/
   Customs Officer
Mail Carrier
Police Officer
Politician
Public Health Officer
Social Worker
Teacher
Teacher Aide

TRANSPORTATION CAREERS

Aircraft Mechanic
Airplane Pilot
Air Traffic Controller
Automobile
   Mechanic
Bus Driver
Locomotive
   Engineer
Ship Captain
Taxi Driver
Ticket Agent
Truck Driver

The **best** way to learn about the demands and opportunities of a variety of careers, including the differences in environments, skills, and vocabularies, is to **experience them**! A summer or part-time job can lead in many directions, depending on your interests, aptitudes, and personality. The same job may be good training for several young people whose interests are quite different. Consider the case of Alan and Mark:

Between their junior and senior years in high school, Alan and Mark got jobs at Charter Motor Company, a local repair garage and service station. They were hired as service station attendants, and they worked full time until school began in the fall. They pumped gas, cleaned windshields, checked oil and water levels, checked tire pressure, wrote out credit slips, and made change for cash customers. When there were no gasoline customers, they helped the shop mechanics with servicing and minor repairs, such as lubrication, installation of fan belts and batteries, and occasionally assisted with brake overhauls.

When summer was over and school began, a full-time worker replaced them during school hours; but Alan and Mark continued working part time after school. By that time, however, Alan knew he didn't care much for the direct contact with the customers, which was part of being a service station attendant. He preferred helping the mechanics. He mentioned this to his boss, and because there was an increase in their repair business, he became an assistant to one of the shop mechanics. Mark enjoyed the contact with the customers more than any other part of his job. He liked talking with the customers, and was soon selling them tires, batteries, and other accessories.

After graduation from high school, Alan stayed with Charter Motor Company as a full-time mechanic. Mark began a training program for salesmen with the oil company whose products were sold by Charter Motor Company.

If you have difficulty in deciding whether a certain kind of work would be interesting to you and fit your personality, ask your school counselor or work experience coordinator to set up an appointment for you to visit someone who does that kind of work. In this way you may discuss with the professional the job qualifications, working conditions, salaries, and need for workers in that field.

LOCATING VACANCIES

If you have decided upon one or several possible career goals, and have considered your interests, aptitudes, skills, experience— if any — and your personality, **you are ready to choose a job**. You will not let it choose you! You may be looking for a part-time job

Visit with Someone Who Does the Kind of Work That Interests You

to support a car, buy some clothes, or save some money for a trip or college. You may already be looking for the full-time job you will begin after you are out of school. In either case, there are some proven sources and ways of locating vacancies.

In order for you to be able to choose the job that is right for you, it is necessary to organize a plan for locating vacancies. Of course you may have heard friends tell you how lucky they were, because they were offered a job as soon as they were out of school and didn't have to look for a job. If it turns out to be the right job for them, then they were lucky indeed! More often, those who take the first job that is available are among those who are chosen by their jobs. They may spend months or even years on a job which is not really suited to them before they break loose and begin an organized search for the job they might have had from the beginning — one that is right for them. This is a job in which they can be successful, are interested in and can take some pride in, yet is challenging to them. It just makes sense that the more job opportunities you have to choose from, the better your chances of finding this kind of job. Some of the sources of good job leads are discussed here.

SCHOOL WORK EXPERIENCE AND PLACEMENT OFFICES

Most schools have someone assigned the responsibility of assisting students in locating job vacancies. The larger high schools often have a well organized program of work experience education which provides both vocational counseling and job placement. Smaller schools may have a counselor or teacher who works with the community in locating jobs for students and graduates. The schools can be quite effective in placement because they know you well. They know your abilities, aptitudes, grades, attendance record, and they have information on your attitudes and personality. No one will be more interested in your getting the right job than the school from which you

Most Schools Assist Students in Locating Job Vacancies, But Don't Just Sit Back and Expect the School to Take Care of Everything

are graduating. However, don't just sit back and think that the school will take care of everything. It is usually necessary to refer several of the best applicants for each job, so you will have competition from others in your school. It is possible that the school could refer you to a number of jobs and yet you would not be hired. Your chances of getting a job that is right for you are good if you are willing to work hard at both locating and obtaining it. You should make a list of all job leads so that you will be able to follow up every possibility. When you are job hunting, your chances are better if you know exactly which places you will go to make application when you walk out of your front door. While the school work experience or placement office is an important source for job leads, there are other good sources.

There Is Nothing Wrong with Obtaining a Job through a Member of Your Family or a Friend — As Long As You Are Qualified to Do the Work

FAMILY AND FRIENDS

One of the best sources of job leads may be friends or members of your own family. They may not have jobs to offer you, but if they are working, then they are involved in the business world daily and may learn of job opportunities for which you are qualified. If you have a friend who has recently begun working, then he or she may have some job leads which are right for **you** even though they may not be right for your friend. Then too, leads often lead to other leads. Because of this, it is wise to follow up on every job lead even though it does not seem to be just what you are looking for.

Beginning with the members of your own family, make a list of those who might help you with job leads, and add to it the names of friends of your family. This should include those who are in business and might be able to hire you or know others who are looking for workers to fill job vacancies. You should also include those friends who work for companies where you think you might like to work. Add the names of your own school friends and your neighbors who are in any way related to business. A schoolmate's father may work for a company that is looking for someone with your qualifications. Some young people hesitate to ask their "influential friends" about job possibilities, saying that they do not want to get a job by using **pull**. However, there is nothing wrong with obtaining a job through a member of your family or a friend as long as you are qualified to do the work. Pressuring someone to hire you for a job for which you are not qualified is the kind of "pull" to be avoided, since both you and the company suffer. Many jobs, however, for which you are qualified are never listed with any placement agency or otherwise advertised, because they are filled by friends or present company employees.

EMPLOYMENT AGENCIES

Most larger cities have both public and private employment agencies. The public employment agencies are set up under federal and state laws and are known according to the name of the state in which the particular office is located, as **Minnesota State Employment Service** or **Texas State Employment Service.** By whatever name, their service is free; and in some cities, this is the only employment service offered. Many businesses list jobs with these state departments of employment, and you should fill out an application form in your local office. You will be interviewed to determine what your interests and qualifications are. When a job is listed which seems right for you, you will be called into the office and given a referral card to go for a personal interview.

Private employment agencies provide placement for a fee. They usually will not accept an application from people they think are not qualified for work in the field of their choice. When you make application with a private agency, you must sign an agreement to pay a certain amount or, more often, a percentage of your first few month's salary. Private agencies often know about jobs which are not listed with the state employment service. They should not be overlooked.

CITY, COUNTY, STATE, AND FEDERAL GOVERNMENT

City, county, state, and federal government agencies hire many kinds of workers. Such jobs have a number of advantages, as most are under a civil service or merit system which protects workers from unfair dismissal. The pay and working conditions are usually quite good. Since the U.S. Government is the largest employer in the country, thousands of new employees are hired each year for many kinds of jobs.

SCHOOLS

In most cities, another important source of jobs is the local school district. In addition to teachers, schools must hire many other kinds of workers. Among them are accountants, secretaries, stenographers, file clerks, PBX (switchboard) operators, library clerks, gardeners, custodians, cooks, nurses, and maintenance workers. Working conditions are usually very good. If you are interested in working in your local schools, check with the school district's personnel office or the superintendent's office.

COLLEGES AND UNIVERSITIES

Colleges, too, must hire many workers besides teachers and professors. Many people enjoy working on a college campus where they can be associated with those who are interested in learning and improving themselves. If there is a college in your city and this sounds interesting to you, apply at the personnel office of the college.

NEWSPAPER ADVERTISEMENTS

If you get into the habit of reading the **Help Wanted** advertisements in your local newspaper (or those in a city where you would like to work), you will learn quite a bit about the job market. You will have a good idea about what salaries are being offered for what kinds of work. It will also give you an idea about what the qualifications are for the kind of work which interests you. You should follow up every newspaper ad which looks like it might lead to the job you are seeking. However, you must be careful. Do not apply for a job which requires you to make a deposit of money. These are often not jobs at all, but attempts to sell goods. Other ads may require that you take a course for which you must pay a fee before you are hired. These are usually attempts to get you to enroll in a special school rather than an employer trying to hire someone to fill a job.

The More Possible Employers on Your List, the Better Your Chance of Getting the Job That Is Right for You

DIRECT CALLING

In addition to the sources of job leads which have been mentioned, you may find it necessary or desirable to do some direct contacting without the benefit of leads. If you do this, you will find it helpful to go through the yellow pages of the telephone directory for ideas of companies which you may call. Looking for a job in this way is difficult because you do not know whether there are any openings, and you do not know anyone connected with the company. However, if you contact enough businesses, you will probably find some who are looking for workers with your skills.

We have said that it is important to have as many job leads as you can so that you can **choose** the job that is right for you. Remember, too, that **there are lots of others looking for work**. You may not get the job you want most, and you may decide not to

Go through the Yellow Pages of the Telephone Directory to Identify Companies That Need a Person Like You

take some jobs offered to you. In such cases, you will simply follow up another lead. For this reason it is a very good idea to have a list of possible employers written down. Remember that:

1. The more possible employers you have written on your list, the better your chance of getting the job that is right for you.
2. A list of a number of possible employers will lessen the chance that you will jump at the first job offered even if it is not right for you.
3. If you are turned down several times, it is encouraging to have additional employers to whom you may apply.

In deciding which job to accept, you should consider one which:
1. Interests you
2. Fits your abilities
3. Fits your personality
4. Pays reasonably well
5. Provides opportunity for advancement
6. Provides good working conditions

CAREER PLANNING[2]

1. Most young people daydream about the kind of work or career they will do when they are adults. What career would you **most like** to follow if you had the opportunity and ability? Describe it.
2. Of course, there can be a big difference between a person's daydreams and what he or she really expects to do. A few students your age have made their minds up **definitely** on a choice of career or occupation, but not very many. Most students are thinking of possibilities rather than definite choices. What careers have you given serious thought to as your possible life work? (List three choices in order of preference.)
3. What are your parents' occupations?
4. Why do you think you would like the work you listed as your first choice?
5. Why do you think you would like the work you listed as your second choice?
6. Why do you think you would like the work you listed as your third choice?
7. What **facts** should you know about yourself **before** choosing a career?
8. How much education is required for the work you listed as your first choice? (High school, apprenticeship, trade school, business school, college or university, or special school?)
9. In your first choice for a career, what would your duties be?
10. How do your parents feel about your career choice?
11. Suppose your parents didn't agree with your plans. What would you do? (Consider that they are unwilling to support you in your plans.)
12. Who do you feel should be responsible for your career choice?
13. List some of your interests, hobbies, and activities both in school and outside of school.
14. Which of your interests would your career (first choice) satisfy and why?

[2]Adapted from material prepared by Covina-Valley Unified School District, Covina California.

15. Discuss your scholastic abilities. What are your strong points and weak points in school? How do you know this?
16. Which abilities do you have that will help you in the work you are planning?
17. Which scholastic ability do you **not** **have** that would help you in the work you are planning? Note: If you honestly feel you have no lack of ability for this work, say so.
18. List the grades you received at your last grading period.
19. Things that are important to us personally are called our values. List some of your values.
20. Which of your values would be satisfied by the work you are planning?
21. What do you plan to do after graduating from high school? (Such as working full time; enlisting in the military service; attending trade or business school; attending junior college, 4-year college; no plans, etc.)
22. After considering your interests, abilities, and values, is your career choice right for you? Why?
23. Are the courses that you are planning to take the right ones to help you in your career choice? If not, how do you know they are not?

Most Young People Daydream about the Kind of Work They Will Do As Adults

STUDY AIDS

NEW TERMS

aptitude	exploratory
attainable	work experience
career clusters	private enterprise
career development	realistic
educational prescription	values

STUDY QUESTIONS

1. How have most adults selected the work they do?
2. What are the two parts of career development?
3. What is the advantage of selecting a career goal, if you will probably change it later anyway?
4. What is the first step toward college?
5. Why did the United States Office of Education group occupations into fifteen career clusters?
6. What are the six common functions in every enterprise or institution?
7. What are the three basic differences between careers or career clusters?
8. What is the **best** way to learn about the demands and opportunities of a variety of careers?
9. Why is it a good idea to have a written list of possible employers?
10. If more than one job is offered, what should you consider when deciding which job to accept?

DISCUSSION PROBLEMS

1. How does a successful career affect your relationships with others?
2. How is a part-time job now related to a full-time career years from now?
3. What are some advantages of **exploratory** work experience education?
4. What are examples of (a) producing a product and (b) providing a service?
5. In which two or three career clusters do you think you would prefer to work, and why?
6. What are several sources of job leads, and what are the advantages of each?

7. Is it a good idea to accept the first job you are offered?

SUGGESTED ACTIVITIES FOR CHAPTER 2

1. **Career Consultations** — Arrange to visit someone who does the kind of work you think **might** be interesting. Be prepared to ask questions about the duties and responsibilities, required education, working conditions, salary, and special skills or aptitudes which are necessary for a beginning job and for advancement in that career.
2. **Career Speakers** — Arrange for several career speakers to talk with the class, each on a separate day. They may be workers in whatever kinds of work interest the class. Those who earn their living by doing a particular kind of work can provide a lot of information about how much education is required, what the salaries are, what the working conditions are like, and whether there is a need for more workers in a particular field of work.
3. **Field Trips** — Arrange for two field trips to businesses chosen according to the interests of the class. Actually seeing the conditions under which the employees work and watching them in their work activities can provide accurate, up-to-date information on many occupations.

CHAPTER THREE
APPLYING FOR A JOB

After you have decided what kind of job you are looking for and have made out a list of job leads, you are ready to apply for some of these jobs. You will be applying to employers who are shopping for the best person to fill the job. Their selections will be based upon about the same things that cause you to decide upon which car to buy. Before buying a car, you will want to know some facts about its condition, how it looks, and how it performs. The employer interviewing you will want to know:

1. Some facts about you, such as how much and what kind of education and experience you have.
2. How you look and behave.
3. How you perform.

This usually means filling out an **application form**. It may mean that you must write a **letter of application** and prepare a **personal data sheet**. Almost always it means that you must be interviewed before you will be hired. Sometimes you may be asked to take some kind of performance test. If you are applying for a job as a secretary, you will probably be given shorthand and typing tests. If you are applying for a job as a welder, you will be asked to do some welding to show how well you perform. Experience shows that employers look for certain things in each of these. If you present employers with the information they want, the way they want it, you have a much better chance of being hired!

Sometimes You May Have to Take Some Kind of Performance Test to Prove Your Ability to Do a Job

As soon as you are hired, you will need a Social Security card. Without it, you can't be paid. If you do not have a Social Security card, fill out an application and mail it now. An illustration of the form is shown below. These applications are available at your local Social Security Office (look up the address in the telephone directory), or they may be available in your school's work experience office.

APPLICATION FORMS

Since most employers will ask you to fill out an application form, following these suggestions will help **sell** you to the employer:

1. Fill out the application form in ink — or use a typewriter.
2. Answer every question that applies to you (if a question does not apply, you may write "NA", meaning **not applicable**, or draw a line through the space to show that you did not overlook the question).
3. Give your **complete address**, including your zip code.

4. The question on marital status simply means whether you are single, married, separated, divorced, or widowed.
5. Spell correctly. If you aren't sure about how to spell a word, try to use another word with the same meaning.
6. The question on place of birth means the city and state in which you were born, not the name of the hospital.
7. A question on job preference or "job for which you are applying" should be answered with a specific job title or type of work. Do not write "anything". Employers expect you to state clearly what kind of work you can do.
8. Try to have in mind all of the schools you have attended and the dates of your attendance. If there are several, it is a good idea to write them down before you apply for a job.
9. Be prepared to list several good references. It is much better to ask permission of those you plan to list. Those considered good references include (a) the pastor of your church, (b) a former employer, (c) a teacher who knows you well, (d) friends who are established in business.
10. When you write or sign your name on

APPLICATION FOR A SOCIAL SECURITY NUMBER
(Or Replacement of Lost Card)
Information Furnished On This Form Is CONFIDENTIAL

See Instructions on Back.   Print in Black or Dark Blue Ink or Use Typewriter.

─ DO NOT WRITE IN THE ABOVE SPACE ─

1 _Print_ FULL NAME YOU WILL USE IN WORK OR BUSINESS
(First Name) DONNA   (Middle Name or Initial – If none, draw line ___) M.   (Last Name) BENTON

2 _Print_ FULL NAME GIVEN YOU AT BIRTH   DONNA MARIE BENTON

6 YOUR DATE OF BIRTH   (Month) 6   (Day) 3   (Year) 58

3 PLACE OF BIRTH   (City) NORMAL   (County if known) McLEAN   (State) ILLINOIS

7 YOUR PRESENT AGE (Age on _last_ birthday)   16

4 MOTHER'S FULL NAME _AT HER BIRTH_ (Her maiden name)   ANN LESLIE STEWART

8 YOUR SEX   MALE ☐   FEMALE ☒

5 FATHER'S FULL NAME (Regardless of whether living or dead)   CHARLES VERN BENTON

9 YOUR COLOR OR RACE   WHITE ☒   NEGRO ☐   OTHER ☐

10 HAVE YOU EVER BEFORE APPLIED FOR OR HAD A SOCIAL SECURITY, RAILROAD, OR TAX ACCOUNT NUMBER?   NO ☒   DON'T KNOW ☐   YES ☐   (If "YES" Print STATE in which you applied and DATE you applied and SOCIAL SECURITY NUMBER if known)

11 YOUR MAILING ADDRESS   (Number and Street, Apt. No., P.O. Box, or Rural Route) 206 PROSPECT BOULEVARD   (City) NORMAL   (State) ILLINOIS   (Zip Code) 61761

12 TODAY'S DATE   8/28/74

13 TELEPHONE NUMBER   888-6241

14 Sign YOUR NAME HERE (Do Not Print)   Donna M. Benton

TREASURY DEPARTMENT Internal Revenue Service   Return completed application to nearest SOCIAL SECURITY ADMINISTRATION OFFICE

FORM SS-5 (7-00)   **HAVE YOU COMPLETED ALL 14 ITEMS?**

An Employer Will Want to See How You Look, Behave, and Perform

the application, use your correct name, not a nickname. Your first name, middle initial, and last name are usually preferred.

11. Be as neat as possible. The employer expects that your application will be an example of your **best** work.

An example of an application form appears on the following two pages. To prepare you to do your best on the application you will fill out for a real job, practice filling out one or two such forms. Your teacher can probably obtain a supply of these from local firms.

FF-75   (5-68) rev. (TEMPO)

INTERVIEWER'S SUMMARY

GENERAL ⓖⓔ ELECTRIC

APPLICATION FOR EMPLOYMENT

E & CR POSITION CODE

PRINT NAME_____				
LAST	FIRST	MIDDLE	(MAIDEN)	

SOC. SEC. NO.

TEMPORARY ADDRESS_____

PERMANENT ADDRESS_____

NO. & STREET   CITY   STATE   ZIP CODE   TELEPHONE

CHECK ALL THAT APPLY

☐ SINGLE   CITIZEN   ☐ YES
☐ MARRIED   OF   ☐ NO
☐ DIVORCED   U.S.A.?
☐ SEPARATED
☐ WIDOWED   ☐ MAN
☐ REMARRIED   ☐ WOMAN

HEIGHT_____ WEIGHT_____

BIRTH DATE_____
MONTH   DAY   YEAR

NAME, RELATIONSHIP & AGE OF HUSBAND OR WIFE, AND DEPENDENT CHILDREN

IF SINGLE, GIVE PARENTS' NAMES

NAME   RELATION & AGE   NAME   RELATION & AGE

(MAIDEN)

NOTIFY IN EMERGENCY_____
NAME   ADDRESS   TELEPHONE

HAVE YOU ANY DEFECTS OR LIMITATIONS? (Physical, Mental, other.)
☐ YES ☐ NO
IF YES, EXPLAIN FULLY

HAVE YOU EVER BEEN CONVICTED OF A MISDEMEANOR OR A FELONY?
☐ YES ☐ NO
IF YES, EXPLAIN FULLY

MIDDLE

POSITION DESIRED

WAGES OR SALARY EXPECTED $ PER { HR. WK. MO.

OTHER POSITIONS FOR WHICH YOU ARE QUALIFIED

DATE AVAILABLE

WHAT INTERESTED YOU IN G.E.?

LIST NAMES AND COMPANY LOCATIONS OF RELATIVES EMPLOYED BY G.E.

WERE YOU EVER EMPLOYED BY G.E.? IF YES, WHERE & WHEN?

HAVE YOU EVER APPLIED FOR WORK AT G.E.? IF YES, WHERE & WHEN?

FIRST

CIRCLE HIGHEST GRADE *COMPLETED* IN *EACH* SCHOOL CATEGORY	GRADE SCHOOL	HIGH SCHOOL	COLLEGE	GRAD. SCHOOL
	1 2 3 4 5 6 7 8	9 10 11 12	1 2 3 4	1 2 3 4

	NAME	LOCATION	COURSE–DEGREE	YEAR GRADUATED	CLASS STANDING
GRADE SCHOOL					
HIGH SCHOOL					
COLLEGE					
GRADUATE SCHOOL					
ADDITIONAL GRADUATE SCHOOL; BUSINESS OR VOCATIONAL SCHOOL					

LAST

OTHER TRAINING OR SKILLS (Special Courses, Office Machines Operated, Typing and/or Shorthand Speed, etc.)

HOBBIES

BRANCH OF U.S. SERVICE	DATE ENTERED	DATE DISCHARGED	FINAL RANK	SERVICE NO.
SERVICE SCHOOLS OR SPECIAL EXPERIENCE				TYPE DISCHARGE
SELECTIVE SERVICE NO. CLASSIFICATION & DATE		LOCAL BOARD NO. AND ADDRESS		
RESERVE OR NATIONAL GUARD STATUS		NAME & ADDRESS OF COMMANDING OFFICER		

NAME

PLEASE COMPLETE OTHER SIDE

EMPLOYMENT HISTORY

PLEASE LIST ALL EMPLOYMENT <u>STARTING</u> WITH PRESENT OR MOST RECENT EMPLOYER.

ACCOUNT FOR ALL PERIODS, INCLUDING UNEMPLOYMENT & SERVICE WITH U.S. ARMED FORCES. USE ADDITIONAL SHEET IF NECESSARY.

DATES	NAME & ADDRESS—EMPLOYER	1 JOB TITLE 2 DEPARTMENT 3 NAME OF SUPERVISOR	DESCRIBE MAJOR DUTIES	WAGES	REASON FOR LEAVING
FROM ....MONTH....YEAR.... TO ....MONTH....YEAR....		1 2 3		STARTING $ per FINAL $ per	
FROM ....MONTH....YEAR.... TO ....MONTH....YEAR....		1 2 3		STARTING $ per FINAL $ per	
FROM ....MONTH....YEAR.... TO ....MONTH....YEAR....		1 2 3		STARTING $ per FINAL $ per	
FROM ....MONTH....YEAR.... TO ....MONTH....YEAR....		1 2 3		STARTING $ per FINAL $ per	
FROM ....MONTH....YEAR.... TO ....MONTH....YEAR....		1 2 3		STARTING $ per FINAL $ per	
FROM ....MONTH....YEAR.... TO ....MONTH....YEAR....		1 2 3		STARTING $ per FINAL $ per	

INTERVIEWER'S COMMENTS

INTERVIEWED BY ....DATE............

PRE-EMPLOYMENT STATEMENT

I voluntarily give the General Electric Company the right to make a thorough investigation of my past employment and activities, agree to cooperate in such investigation, and release from all liability or responsibility all persons, companies or corporations supplying such information.

I consent to taking the pre-employment physical examination and such future physical examinations as may be required by the Company. I agree to wear or use protective clothing or devices as required by the Company and to comply with the safety rules.

I agree that the entire contents of this application form, as well as the report of any such examination, may be used by the Company in whatever manner it may wish.

If employed by the Company, I understand that such employment is subject to the security policies of the Company. I further understand that if the position for which I am hired requires access to classified information and I am not able to obtain a security clearance, I will not be allowed to work in this position. My employment with the Company in a position not requiring security clearance depends upon the existence of such a position for which I am qualified.

I further understand that any false answers or statements made by me on this application or any supplement thereto, or in connection with the above mentioned investigation, will be sufficient grounds for immediate discharge.

APPLICANT'S SIGNATURE ....DATE...............

LETTERS OF APPLICATION

We have discussed the importance of filling out the application form completely and neatly. This alone, of course, will not get you a job. Most often it is in the personal interview that the employer decides who will be hired. Both the application form and the letter of application (if well done) can get you into the employer's office for the interview. There are times when writing a letter of application is the only way of getting a personal interview. You should write a letter of application in these situations:

1. When you wish to apply for an out-of-town job (especially if it is a business or professional position).
2. When you answer a newspaper advertisement which asks that you apply by mail.

Telling the Employer How Badly You Need a Job Usually Does Not Help

3. When you wish to be interviewed by business friends of your family.
4. When an employer asks that you write a letter of application. Sometimes this is done to check your English usage and also to see how well you type or how neatly you write.

When you apply for a job, it is necessary to sell yourself to the employer. Telling the employer how badly you need a job will not get you the job. In fact, you shouldn't even mention this. Convince the employer that hiring you would benefit the company, but do not use pressure tactics in any way. A letter of application, then, is a sales letter. As with any kind of sales letter, you must make a good first impression. This means that you will type your letter unless you are answering an advertisement that asks you to apply in your own handwriting. (If you do not type, handwritten letters are acceptable.) If you are applying for a job as a typist, stenographer, or other clerical office worker, this is an excellent chance to show the employer how neatly you can set up and type a letter. No matter what job you apply for, a neatly typed letter with all words spelled correctly is impressive.

Here are some suggestions which will help you write a letter of application that will get attention:

1. Write a **first copy** so that you can develop what you should say the way you should say it. This will be rewritten or typed after you have polished it up. (You might ask a teacher or a friend in business to help you with this.)
2. In your first sentence, establish a point of contact. This should tell where or from whom you learned about the job. You might say, "At the suggestion of Mr. Benson (a mutual friend), I am writing regarding the job as messenger in your office." If you are writing in answer to a newspaper advertisement, you might begin, "Your advertisement in today's **Times** for a typist — clerk describes the work which I think I do best."

3. In the second sentence state that you are applying for the job. You might say, "Please consider me an applicant for this position." or "I should like to be considered an applicant for this job."

4. If you have little to say about how your education and experience qualifies you for the job, this can all go in the second paragraph. If you have no experience, don't mention it at all — just tell how your education (classes in typing, bookkeeping, auto shop, etc.) will help you in this job. If you have more to say about both your education and experience, separate paragraphs should be used for each.

5. If you include references in your letter, these should appear in the next paragraph. Be sure you get permission from those you wish to name as references.

6. In your last paragraph, ask for a personal interview at the employer's convenience; and tell how you may be reached by phone.

the applicant is qualified for the job and whose letters themselves are neat and well-written, with all words spelled correctly. This means that if you are very careful about how you write your letter, you will have a big advantage. After you have written one really good letter, you can make it the basis for letters of application for other jobs. Of course, you would have to change the first paragraph about what job you are applying for and where you learned about it. However, the paragraphs on your education and experience, references, and the last paragraph in which you ask for an interview would change very little.

After You Have Written One Really Good Application Letter, You Can Make It the Basis for Applications for Other Jobs

Before you rewrite or type your letter for mailing, carefully read the sample letters on pages 38 and 40. They may give you some additional ideas for polishing up your letter. These suggestions will help you in preparing your copy for mailing:

1. If you are typing your letter, clean your type before you begin. A letter typed on a dirty machine will show a's, e's, and p's with blackened areas which should be white. Set your margins

A Carefully Written Letter of Application Can Help Land the Job You Want

Some businesses receive dozens of application letters for each job. If they have advertised in the newspaper, they may receive hundreds of letters. Interviews are usually given only to those whose letters show that

about 1½″ on the left and right sides of your paper.

2. Type your street address 2″ from the top of the sheet. This can begin at the left margin or end even with the right margin. On the next line, type your city, state, and zip code. On the third line, type the date.

3. Begin the inside address (person or company to whom you are writing) about 1½″ down from the date line. If your letter is very short, you will need to leave several more spaces between the date and inside address so that your letter will be centered on the sheet when completed. Check to be certain you have spelled correctly the name of the person and company and that the address is correct. People are particular about how their names are spelled.

4. If you are addressing your letter to an individual, your salutation should be **Dear Mr. Fox:**, or **Dear Ms. York:**, **Dear Miss Doe:**, or **Dear Mrs. Winn:**. If you are writing to a company or to a personnel office and do not know the name of the person who will read and act upon your letter, you should use the salutation, Dear Sir or Madam:. The salutation should be followed by a **colon**.

5. Type the main part of your letter very carefully. It will make the best impression if there are no mistakes, but one or two careful erasures are acceptable.

6. Your closing should be **Yours truly,** **Yours very truly,** or **Very truly yours**. Only the first word of closing should begin with a capital, and the closing should be followed by a **comma**.

7. After the closing, space down four (4) spaces and type your name.

8. Before you remove the letter from your typewriter, read it carefully to see if there are any mistakes which could be more easily corrected while still in the machine.

9. Sign your name in ink above the type-written signature.

PERSONAL DATA SHEETS

We have said that the letter of application, if done well, can get you into the employer's office for an interview. However, it is to your advantage to give the employer some additional information about you which is not usually put into the letter of application. The best way to present this information is in the form of a personal data sheet. This information includes details about the courses you have taken in school; experience — if any; your age, height, weight, and general health; and hobbies which might be related to the job for which you are applying. It is generally better to list these details on a data sheet as they can be more easily referred to than if they were a part of your letter of application. Another name for a personal data sheet is **resume**.

Remember, if you have no experience, don't mention it! You should tell about the qualities you **do** have, not what you don't

You Should Make a Number of Copies of Your Resume' and Include One with Each Letter of Application

have! References, too, are often made a part of the resume' instead of the letter of application. You should make a number of copies of your resume and include one with each letter of application to employers.

In order to help you in making up your own personal data sheet, or resume', study the samples on pages 39 and 41.

---

714 Channel Drive
Santa Barbara, California 93105
May 10, 19

Mr. Kenneth Smith, Personnel Director
Electrophysics Incorporated
8462 Main Street
Santa Barbara, California 93105

Dear Mr. Smith:

    Mr. Charles Winfield, the Work Experience Counselor at Santa Barbara High School suggested that I contact you about the typist clerk job in your firm. Please consider me an applicant for this position.

    On June 12, I shall graduate from Santa Barbara High School where I have majored in business education. My courses have included two years of typewriting, two years of shorthand and transcription, business machines, and office practice. My typing speed is 65 words per minute, and I take shorthand at 100 words per minute.

    During my senior year in high school I participated in work experience education. My job assignment was in the accounting office of Radford Oil Company where I made use of and improved the skills I learned in school.

    I plan to continue my education in night school and hope someday to be a top secretary. May I have an interview? I shall be glad to call at your convenience. My home telephone is 769-1401.

                    Yours truly,

                    Ann Fisher

                    Ann Fisher

PERSONAL DATA

Personal

    Name--Ann Fisher
    Address--714 Channel Drive, Santa Barbara, California 93105, Phone--769-1401
    Age--18
    Height--5 feet, 6 inches
    Weight--120 pounds
    Health--excellent

Skills

    Typing--65 words a minute
    Shorthand--100 words a minute
    Filing
    Adding machine--10-key and full-key
    Key-driven calculator

Education

    Graduate of Santa Barbara High School, June 12, 19__

    Subjects studied--

        Typewriting, 2 years
        Shorthand, $1\frac{1}{2}$ years
        Transcription, $\frac{1}{2}$ year
        Business machines, $\frac{1}{2}$ year
        Office practice, $\frac{1}{2}$ year
        English, 4 years
        Math, 3 years
        Science, 2 years
        History, 3 years

Experience

    One year as part-time stenographer-clerk in the accounting office of
    Radford Oil Company.

Outside Interests and Hobbies

    Dramatic Arts, Tennis

References

    Mr. Louis Johnston, Personnel Manager, Radford Oil Company, 1726 Main
        Street, Santa Barbara, California 93101
    Mr. Charles Winfield, Work Experience Counselor, Santa Barbara High
        School, 700 East Anapamu, Santa Barbara, California 93103
    Miss MaryEllen Boxberger, Business Education Teacher, Santa Barbara
        High School, 700 East Anapamu, Santa Barbara, California 93103

516 Elm Street
Peabody, Kansas 51683
May 5, 19

Mr. James Duncan
Manager
First State Bank
715 Pine Street
Peabody, Kansas 51683

Dear Mr. Duncan:

My counselor at Peabody High School, Mr. Walter Smith, told me that you plan to hire a young man as a bank trainee. I would like to apply for this position.

On May 17, I shall graduate from Peabody High School. As you will see on the attached personal data sheet, I have taken some subjects in business education which should prove helpful in this job. I would also be willing to continue my education either in night school or part time if it would be helpful in my work.

Several months ago I was with a group which toured your bank, and I feel that it would be a very interesting place to work. Some day I would like to work up to the management level in banking.

May I have a personal interview? You may reach me any day after 3 p.m. at 846-6489.

Very truly yours,

John Grant

John Grant

PERSONAL DATA of
JOHN GRANT
516 Elm Street
Peabody, Kansas 51683
PHONE 846-6489

<u>Skills</u>

Typing--40 words a minute
Adding machine

<u>Education</u>

Graduate of Peabody High School, May 17, 19__

Subjects studied--

Typewriting, 1 year
Bookkeeping, 1 year
English, 3 years
Business math, 1 year
General science, 1 year
Band, 3 years
History, 2 years
Physical education, 4 years

<u>Outside Interests and Hobbies</u>

Play piano and trumpet
Photography
Tennis
Swimming

<u>References</u>

Mr. Walter Smith, Counselor, Peabody High School, 100 Walnut Street
Peabody, Kansas 61583

Mrs. George Lewis, Bookkeeping Teacher, Peabody High School, 100 Walnut
Street, Peabody, Kansas 61583

Mr. Robert Carson, Photographer, 614 Sycamore Street, Newton, Kansas 61543

Mr. Larry Williams, Assistant Manager, First National Bank, 1864 Main
Street, Newton, Kansas 61543

INTERVIEWS

We have studied the use of application forms, letters of application, and personal data sheets, but you will be hired only after you have been interviewed by the employer or the employer's representative. The employment interview can be one of your most important life experiences. What happens in this twenty or thirty minute period may direct your whole future career. Yet, some applicants for jobs give the impression that they might as well get interviewed for a job since they have nothing better to do at the moment. A personnel manager of a large corporation on the West Coast recently told about a young woman who came into the office seeking a job wearing a bathing suit. She was on her way home from the beach!

Some Applicants Give the Impression They Might As Well Be Interviewed for a Job, Since They Have Nothing Better to Do at the Moment

PREPARING FOR THE INTERVIEW

Before your first interview, you should look over your personal data so that you will be able to answer whatever questions may be asked of you. You will either be called by the employer's secretary and agree on a time for an interview or you will call to make an appointment. If you call for an appointment, you must clearly state your name and how you learned of the job opening. Be sure that you know the exact place and time of the interview — and write it down. Check the correct spelling of the interviewer's name and the correct pronunciation.

Usually, you will be interviewed by the employer or the personnel manager. It is normal to be a little nervous, but there is really nothing to be afraid of. It may help you to know that the purpose of the interview is to allow the employer to learn about: (1) your attitude toward people and work, (2) your education and work experience, and (3) your future career plans. It also gives you a chance to see whether you would like to work in a particular job or for a particular company. Since you want to make a good impression, find out something about the company before the interview. Try to learn what its products or services are, how large the company is, and whether it is a growing company. This will give you something besides yourself to talk about during the interview.

THE INTERVIEW

There are several things which you should take with you when you are going for an interview for a job. They are:
1. A pen and pencil.
2. Your Social Security card.
3. A work permit, if required (your school counselor or work experience coordinator can advise you).
4. If you have prepared a personal data sheet, take a copy with you to the interview.

Go alone! Do not take a parent or friend with you. One high school senior girl was referred to a job and decided that she would take her friend along. As her friend was also looking for work and her qualifications were better, the employer hired her friend for the job. Employers seldom hire people who cannot sell themselves in an interview without the help of another person.

Check your appearance. The employer's first impression of you when you arrive will be based on how you look. You must, therefore, be careful about your grooming and the clothes you choose for the interview. You should, of course, take a bath before dressing for the interview. You would think that it would not be necessary to mention this. Unfortunately, some young people do show up for a job interview with a body odor that immediately eliminates their chances of being hired. The strong smell of cigarettes, too, has prevented applicants from being hired. This odor is very annoying to those who do not smoke.

When You Choose the Clothes You Will Wear, Remember That You Are Looking for a Job, Not Going to a Party

The Employer's First Impression of You Will Be Based on Your Appearance

Boys should be very careful about their appearance. Their hair should be clean, trimmed, and well groomed. The fingernails, too, must be cleaned and trimmed if one is to make a good impression. Some boys in their upper teens do not shave as often as they should to make a good appearance. Girls should use only a small amount of makeup and should have a neat hair style.

When you choose the clothes that you wear, remember that you are looking for a job, not going to a party. The type of clothes you wear for the interview depends upon the kind of job you are applying for. If it is a factory or construction job, clean, unwrinkled work clothes are appropriate. Your clothes should be conservative, not faddish. They should be clean and unwrinkled. Well-shined shoes make a good impression. Take time to dress properly. Leather shoes are much preferred to tennis or canvas shoes for an interview. The employer will look at you as one who will represent the company if you are hired. If your working qualifications and another applicant's are about the same, the one that makes the best appearance will be hired.

Arrive five minutes early. If you are driving, allow some extra time in case traffic slows you up. If you are even **one minute** late or rush in at the last minute, it will look like you are a careless person. However, don't be too early. If you arrive about five minutes before the time set up for the interview, that is about right. When you arrive, the first people you speak with are usually the receptionist or the interviewer's secretary. You must be very cooperative with them. The employer may ask others their opinion of you.

When You Arrive for a Job Interview, Rushing in at the Last Minute May Not Give the Interviewer a Good Impression

You may have to introduce yourself. When you walk into the interviewer's office, you may be introduced by the receptionist or secretary — or the employer may introduce you and call you by name. If not then, you should introduce yourself by saying something like, "I'm Cathy Cooper, and I'm interested in the job as trainee in your bank." You should speak clearly and loudly enough to be heard, and you should smile. You should stand up straight, but do not offer to shake hands unless the interviewer offers to shake hands first. If a handshake is offered, then grasp it **firmly**. A handshake is a means of communication. A "limp fish" handshake may cause the interviewer to think that you have a weak personality. Of course you should not prove how strong you are by grabbing his hand and crushing it!

Stand until the interviewer asks you to sit. If you are not asked to sit down, then you must stand during the interview. When

you sit, sit properly. Don't slouch. Although you will feel nervous at the beginning, you will become more relaxed after the interview has begun. Your eyes should meet the interviewer's eyes regularly. Some people do not trust a person who can't look them in the eye. Perhaps the biggest mistake you could make at the beginning of an interview would be to place your purse or some other article on the edge of the interviewer's desk. If you are carrying a purse or a book with you, keep it beside you. Try to keep your hands quiet. Usually it is best to keep them in your lap. Do not lean on the interviewer's desk or try to read papers on the desk. You know, of course, that you should not chew gum or smoke.

Although You May Feel Nervous at the Beginning, You Will Become More Relaxed After the Interview Has Begun

There are two basic ways of interviewing. You may simply be asked to "tell about yourself." In this case you must do most of the talking, and include all of your qualifications for the job. The interviewer will be pleased if you also say why you would like to work for this particular company. This is why it is important to do some checking on the company before the interview. The other

Don't Prove Your Strength by Grabbing the Interviewer's Hand and Crushing It

thing.'' If you are asked about the salary you expect, it is best **not** to mention a specific amount. It may be too low. If you are hired, you could be paid less than others are getting for the same work. If you mention an amount too high, you may not be hired at all because the interviewer may feel that you would not be satisfied. You might say, ''I'm sure you know more about what a fair salary would be than I do — what do you pay for this kind of work?'' If you are pressed for an answer, you could mention the amount that you know others are getting for this kind of work. If the interviewer does not mention salary and you can tell that the interview is about over, it is all right to ask what you will

Apply for a Specific Job, Not ''Anything''

way in which the interviewer finds out about your qualifications is by asking questions. This is probably the way most interviewers learn about you. Some of the questions most often asked are (1) ''Why do you want to work for this company?'', (2) ''What do you plan to be doing five years from now?'', (3) ''Are you looking for permanent or temporary work?'', and (4) ''Which courses in school did you like best?''.

A more complete list of questions which may be asked of you appears on page 46. Be prepared to answer these questions completely. If you do not know the answer to a question, say that you don't know. If you try to ''fake it,'' the interviewer can usually tell. If so, you won't be hired, even if your other qualifications are good. There are two questions that we should give special attention to: (1) ''What kind of work would you like to do?'' and (2) ''What salary do you expect?''. Too many young people answer the first question by saying ''anything.'' This is irritating to many interviewers because they want to put you in a job for which you are applying. **There is no such job title as ''any-**

be paid if you are hired. If you bring it up too early in the interview, it will look like you are only interested in what you get out of the job. If you are applying for a permanent, full-time job, it is all right to ask whether you get a vacation — but only toward the end of the interview if it hasn't been mentioned by the interviewer. Part-time or temporary workers usually do not get vacations.

Show that you are interested in the company. This is easy if you have thought about two or three questions to ask about the company. These could be about a product or service, the number of employees, etc.

You may be asked to talk with someone in the company besides the interviewer. This might be a department head or someone with whom you would be working if you are hired. If so, it usually means that the interviewer thinks that you would be a good worker. Your chances of being hired are good.

When the interview is over, go! If you have given the interviewer your qualifications, and he or she seems to have run out of questions, the interview is over. If you do not leave at this time, you may lose your chance of being hired. If you have not been offered the job, it is all right to ask whether you will be called or if you may call back in a few days to learn the interviewer's decision. Say ''thank you,'' and leave. If you pass the receptionist or the secretary, thank her too.

QUESTIONS OFTEN ASKED DURING AN INTERVIEW

1. Why would you like to work for this company?
2. Are you looking for permanent or temporary work?
3. What job would you most like?
4. What do you want to be doing in five years? In ten years?
5. What qualifications do you have for this job?
6. What subjects in school did you like best? Least?
7. Do you prefer working alone or with others?
8. How do you spend your spare time?
9. What magazines do you read?
10. What is your main strength? Your main weakness?
11. What jobs have you had? Why did you leave?
12. What salary do you expect?
13. Do you have any debts?
14. Have you had any serious illnesses?

When the Interview Is Over, GO

15. Do you smoke?
16. How do you feel about working overtime?
17. Did you attend school regularly? How many days were you out last year?
18. What grades have you gotten in your school work?
19. When can you begin work?
20. How did you become interested in this company?

WHY PEOPLE AREN'T HIRED

Negative Factors Evaluated During the Employment Interview and which Frequently Lead to Rejection of the Applicant, in Order of Frequency (As Reported by 153 Companies Surveyed by Frank S. Endicott, Director of Placement, Northwestern University).

1. Poor personal appearance
2. Overbearing — overaggressive — conceited ''superiority complex''—''know-it-all''
3. Inability to communicate clearly — poor voice, diction, grammar
4. Lack of planning for career — no purpose and goals
5. Lack of interest and enthusiasm — passive, indifferent
6. Lack of confidence and poise — nervousness — ill-at-ease
7. Failure to participate in activities

8. Overemphasis on money — interest only in best dollar offer
9. Poor scholastic record — just got by
10. Unwilling to start at the bottom — expects too much too soon
11. Makes excuses — evasiveness — hedges on unfavorable factors in record
12. Lack of tact
13. Lack of maturity
14. Lack of courtesy — ill mannered
15. Condemnation of past employers
16. Lack of social understanding
17. Marked dislike for school work
18. Lack of vitality
19. Fails to look interviewer in the eye
20. Limp, fishy handshake
21. Indecision
22. Indefinite response to questions
23. Unhappy married life
24. Friction with parents
25. Sloppy application blank
26. Merely shopping around
27. Wants job only for short time
28. Little sense of humor
29. Lack of knowledge of field of specialization
30. Parents make applicant's decisions
31. No interest in company or in industry
32. Emphasis on whom he or she knows
33. Unwillingness to go where sent
34. Cynical
35. Low moral standards
36. Lazy
37. Intolerant — strong prejudices
38. Narrow interests
39. High-pressure type
40. Poor handling of personal finances
41. No interest in community activities
42. Inability to take criticism
43. Lack of appreciation of the value of experience
44. Radical ideas
45. Late to interview without good reason
46. Never heard of company
47. Failure to express appreciation for interviewer's time
48. Asks no questions about the job

WHY THE OTHER BOY WAS HIRED

There's a good deal of talk these days about teenage unemployment. Some of it makes sense and some of it does not.

Donald E. Wood wrote a letter to a teenage boy who had applied to him for a job. It represents a point of view shared by many employers. It is reprinted here to help you see how employers look at applicants.

Dear Kid:

Today you asked me for a job. From the look of your shoulders as you walked out, I suspect you've been turned down before, and maybe you believe by now that kids out of high school can't find work.

But, I hired a teenager today. You saw him. He was the one with the polished shoes and a necktie. What was so special about him? Not experience. Neither of you had any. It was his attitude that put him on the payroll instead of you. Attitude, son. A-T-T-I-T-U-D-E. He wanted that job badly enough to shuck the leather jacket, get a haircut, and look in the phone book to find out what this company makes. He did his best to impress me. That's where he edged you out.

You see, Kid, people who hire aren't "with" a lot of things, and we have some Stone-Age ideas about who owes whom a living. Maybe that makes us prehistoric, but there's nothing wrong with the checks we sign, and if you want one you'd better tune to our wave length.

Ever hear of "empathy?" It's the trick of seeing the other fellow's side of things. I couldn't have cared less that you're behind in your car payments. That's your problem and the President's. What I needed was someone who'd go out in the plant, keep his eyes open, and work for me like he'd work for himself. If you have even the vaguest idea of what I'm trying to say, let it show the next time you ask for a job. You'll be head and shoulders above the rest.

Look Kid: The only time jobs grew on trees was while most of the manpower was wearing G.I.'s and pulling K.P. For all the rest of history you've had to get a job like you get a girl: "Case the situation, wear a clean shirt, and try to appear reasonably willing."

Maybe jobs aren't as plentiful right now, but a lot of us can remember when master craftsmen walked the streets. By comparison, you don't know the meaning of "scarce."

You may not believe it, but all around you employers are looking for young men smart enough to go after a job in the old-fashioned way. When they find one, they can't wait to unload some of their worries on him. For both our sakes, get eager, will you?

Donald E. Wood

STUDY AIDS

NEW TERMS

application form	personal data sheet
interview	resume´
marital status	

STUDY QUESTIONS

1. Should an application for a job be written in pencil or ink, or completed on a typewriter?
2. On most application forms some questions will not apply to you. What should you do to show that you have not overlooked these questions?
3. What is meant by marital status?
4. How should you answer the question on place of birth?

5. Why do you think employers ask for an applicant's job preference? Is it a good idea to answer this question with "anything?"
6. Who do you think you should list as references?
7. How should you sign your application?
8. In what situations should you write a letter of application?
9. Should a letter of application be typed or handwritten?
10. Should you rewrite your letter of application or send the first copy? Why?
11. What is the purpose of the first paragraph of a letter of application?
12. What is the purpose of the last paragraph of a letter of application?
13. What kind of information should be presented in the resume´ or personal data sheet?
14. What does the employer hope to learn from interviewing an applicant?

DISCUSSION PROBLEMS

1. What will an employer interviewing you for a job want to know about you? Why?
2. Why is it important to go alone when being interviewed for a job?
3. If you were interviewing applicants for a variety of jobs, what questions would you ask?

SUGGESTED ACTIVITIES FOR CHAPTER 3

1. **Write a Letter of Application** — From the job leads you found in doing the suggested activities in Chapter 2 or from the advertisements in your local newspaper, select one job and write a letter of application. Carefully follow the instructions on writing application letters which are given in Chapter 3.
2. **Role-Playing the Interview** — Select someone to take the role of the interviewer and several other students to take the role of job applicant. The others in the class can listen and watch care-

fully to see which applicant would most likely be hired. After several have been interviewed, discuss the correct and incorrect behavior shown in the interviews.

CASES

The Wellington Company has an opening for a clerk typist. Suppose that you are the personnel manager and you have just interviewed three girls for the job:

Mary is an attractive girl and has a pleasing personality. She typed 50 words a minute on the typing test, and she has taken one year of shorthand in addition to two years of typing. Her grades in school were mostly B's and C's. She arrived five minutes late for the interview.

Just the idea of being interviewed was frightening to Karen so she brought her friend, Carol, along for support. They arrived five minutes early and, although nervous, Karen presented herself well. She was clean, neat, and well dressed. She typed 55 words a minute on the typing test, and took one year of bookkeeping in addition to two years of typing in high school. Her grades in school were mostly C's.

Vera arrived for the interview five minutes early. She answered each question accurately and pleasantly. On the typing test she scored 48 words per minute. Vera took one year of bookkeeping and two years of typing in high school. Her grades were mostly C's.

Who would you hire? Why? If you can't decide, what additional information is needed?

CHAPTER FOUR
YOU, YOUR EMPLOYER, AND YOUR CO-WORKERS

THE IMPORTANCE OF ATTITUDE

In the first three chapters we discussed the meaning of work and how to locate and apply for a job. After you have a job, there are certain things you must do to be successful on your job. The most important factor in job success is **attitude!** This is shown in the fact that the main reason young workers lose jobs is because they have a poor attitude. In fact, a recent study of beginning workers who had been fired showed that 80 percent lost their jobs because they couldn't get along well with other people. Getting along well with others does not just happen. It must be learned. Those who do learn to get along well with almost everyone are usually happier persons because people like them, they enjoy a greater feeling of job success, and they often receive higher salaries.

The study of physical anthropology has recently indicated that our behavior depends in part upon who our parents are. It is, to a degree, inherited. Much more important in the way we behave is what happens to us while we are growing up. The behavior we exhibit and the attitudes we develop up to graduation from high school usually carry over into adult life. They are with us both on the job and in social relationships. Basically, your attitude is your outlook on life. It is shown by the way you behave in the presence of other people. If you look at life as something exciting and worthwhile, and if you really enjoy life most of the time, your attitude toward other people will show this. You will be the kind of person who looks at the good side of things. If, on the other hand, you tend to see others — and life in general — as being unfair to you, then you probably don't like people very much. If this is you, you will be happy to learn that you **can** change. By practice, you can do a lot to become the kind of person who likes other people and whom others like. The younger we are when we begin to exercise some control over our own personalities, the more we can do toward becoming the kind of person we would like to be.

Your attitude can show up in many ways on the job. Consider Sara's attitude:

Sara, 18, is a waitress. She works in a restaurant known for its fine food and excellent service. She dresses neatly and is always well groomed. She has a good memory and never makes mistakes on orders. Her arithmetic is always correct on customer's checks. However, Sara does not smile easily. This, even though she is a good worker, makes her less popular with the customers; and her tips usually amount to less than that received by the other girls. The busiest day of the year for the restaurant where Sara works is Mother's Day. Every girl is expected to work on that day. However, Sara wanted to visit her own mother in Chicago on Mother's Day — so she begged the restaurant manager to let her off on the busiest day of the year. Although the manager gave Sara the day off, he and the other waitresses felt that Sara had let them down. Everyone else had to work that much harder. The manager has decided to fire Sara because she can't get along with the other employees and is irritable toward the customers.

Sara was an intelligent girl and a good worker, yet she was fired. Could she have done anything which would have saved her job?

Behavior characteristics of those who have healthy, desirable attitudes are compared in the following chart with those who have negative or poor attitudes. If your behavior is similar to that described on the negative side, you should know that such behavior causes others to react to you negatively. If you can work on just one or two areas so that your behavior shows a desirable, positive attitude instead of a negative attitude, the behavior of others toward you will change. People will like you better, and you will like them better. Study the chart to see where you fit in.

POSITIVE ATTITUDE	NEGATIVE ATTITUDE
1. Smiles easily	1. Rarely smiles
2. Willing to change ideas, dress, behavior when appropriate	2. Unwilling to change
3. Able to see the other person's point of view	3. Unable to see the other person's point of view
4. Almost never complains	4. Complains about nearly everything
5. Accepts responsibility for mistakes	5. Blames others for own mistakes or short-comings
6. Seldom criticizes others	6. Very critical of others
7. Considers what is good for or helpful to others	7. Thinks only of self, "What's in it for me?"
8. When talking with other people, looks them in the eye, but does not try to stare them down	8. Unwilling or unable to look the other person in the eye
9. Respects the ideas and opinions of others	9. Tries to force ideas and opinions on others
10. Never makes excuses	10. Often makes excuses
11. Has a variety of interests	11. Few interests, is often bored

WHAT YOUR EMPLOYER MAY EXPECT

We have said that you must make money for your employer's business in order for him or her to be able to pay your salary. In addition to a day's work for a day's pay, your employer will expect certain things from you. Most employers expect these things from their employees:

1. Cooperation
2. Honesty
3. Initiative
4. Willingness to learn
5. Willingness to follow directions
6. Dependability
7. Enthusiasm
8. Acceptance of criticism
9. Loyalty

There Are Tasks Nobody Likes to Do, but Those Who Do Them Make a Good Impression on the Boss

COOPERATION

The employer who pays your salary has a right to expect your full cooperation. This means that you will cooperate with everyone with whom you work — your boss and every-

one else with whom you come in contact. One of the best ways to show your cooperation is to offer to help other employees if your duties are completed. In many companies there are certain tasks that nobody likes to do. The employee who is willing to do these tasks will make a good impression on the boss and also gain the cooperation of fellow workers.

HONESTY

Employers will expect you to be honest with them and with the company. Being dishonest on the job can take many forms. One form of dishonesty is stealing time by coming to work a few minutes late every day. Some workers cheat their employers by stopping work before the end of the work day. If the hours of work are eight to five, you should be on the job a few minutes early so that you will be able to actually start at eight. Your employer will expect you to con-

Your Employer and Co-Workers Expect You to Work the Approved Number of Hours Each Day

tinue working, except for breaks and lunch, until five. Your time during working hours belongs to your employer. Stealing this time costs money — money that might be used in part to increase salaries or otherwise benefit you. Stealing time is probably the most costly form of dishonesty on the job.

Another form of dishonesty on the job is stealing company property. This is usually called pilfering. An employer may be aware of people who usually use company supplies for their personal benefit. An example of this would be that of using the office postage for personal letters. Although these people may not be fired, when it comes time for promotions, they are passed over, mainly because of the dishonesty they have shown. Other employees have been fired for stealing supplies or tools.

INITIATIVE

Employers have a right to expect you to complete whatever duties you are given and then, if you haven't been told what to do next, look around to see what needs to be done and do it. Of course, you must use good judgment. Don't attempt to do work that you are not qualified to do. Consider the example of Kathy Preston:

> Kathy was hired as the secretary to a personnel manager, Mr. O'Donnell, right after she graduated from high school. She was a charming girl and a good typist. However, she had never learned about initiative. When she completed whatever tasks Mr. O'Donnell gave her, she sat and read a magazine. There was other work that could have been done, but she didn't do it. She did nothing except when told directly each task to be done. Such constant supervision required so much of Mr. O'Donnell's time that he couldn't get his own work done. He discussed the problem with her on two occasions, but he had to let her go, because she was not able or willing to change. The next girl Mr. O'Donnell hired always kept busy and required little supervision.

WILLINGNESS TO LEARN

Your employer will expect you to learn the way things are done in the company. This is usually not so much of a problem for a young worker as with the people who have worked for years and developed their own ways of doing things. However, it is worth a special effort to show an eagerness to learn everything you can about your job and the company for which you work. Those who are promoted to jobs with greater responsibility and higher salaries are usually the workers who have taken the trouble to learn about more than just their own daily tasks.

WILLINGNESS TO FOLLOW DIRECTIONS

When you are given directions about how to do your work, you are expected to follow them **exactly**. That is why they are given. Sometimes you may not understand the reason for doing things a certain way, but

Don't Attempt to Do Work That You Are Not Qualified to Do

your employer or supervisor has a particular reason. Do the work as you are directed. After you have worked on the job for a while, you may suggest other ways of doing certain tasks if you think your ideas will be well received. Be careful about this, though. A new worker may be resented for making suggestions, even if they are good ones.

DEPENDABILITY

Your employer will count on you to be on the job every day and to arrive on time. Those who come to work late are resented by the other workers who do come to work on time. Thus, the worker who is not dependable will also find it difficult to work cooperatively with fellow workers. If you are ill, notify your employer of your absence as early as possible. This is usually before the time you would normally start work. Many workers lose their jobs because they do not take time to call their employers when they must be absent due to illness.

ENTHUSIASM

The best employees are those who like their work and show enthusiasm for it. You

Accept Comments That Help You with a Smile

are fortunate indeed if you find everything connected with your work interesting. Most likely, however, you will find certain things about the job which are interesting to you. When others ask you how you like your new job, tell them the things about it that you like. By concentrating on the positive — the things you like — you will find the total job more interesting. When you are interested in and enjoy your work, life itself is more interesting and enjoyable; and you will become a more interesting person because of it.

ACCEPTANCE OF CRITICISM

Nancy was a bookkeeper in a bank. She was a good worker, always arrived on time, and almost never missed a day of work. Nancy's problem was that she could not accept criticism and benefit from it. On several occasions she made incorrect entries on her records. She was told by her supervisor that she must give more careful attention to certain details of her job. Each time this happened Nancy would sulk — not speaking or smiling for the rest of the day. This placed the supervisor under a severe strain because it was difficult to criticize Nancy's work even though it was necessary. Nancy was "let go" because it took so much of the supervisor's time figuring out how to approach Nancy without hurting her feelings.

Criticism is necessary. It is the way in which employers let us know how they expect the job to be done. Your employer will expect you to accept criticism with a smile (not a smirk!) and to improve because of it. Regardless of how you may feel when another person criticizes you, you will be better off if you **appear** to take it good naturedly. When a friend's criticism is off base, it may be all right to laugh it off. If it is connected with your work, it is best to take your critic seriously and thank the person for attempting to help you. Accepting criticism means more than just listening politely. It means **making use** of the criticism. Think about your critic's remarks after you are alone and try to see how they can help you become a better worker. Of course, there are employers and supervisors who are unfairly critical; but there is nothing you can do about the boss's bad temper except quit if it is too difficult a work situation. You must be able to take it, but you can't lose your own temper. Regardless of how a criticism was meant, it will be constructive or destructive depending upon how you use it. It will give you an idea of what is expected of you.

You May Be Tempted to Be Critical of Your Employer When You Don't Understand His or Her Goals and Needs

LOYALTY

You have probably heard that you should not bite the hand that feeds you. This certainly applies to your relationship with your employer and the company for which you work. You must be **for** them. Just as none of us is perfect as a person, neither is any company perfect in every way. You may not agree with everything your employer does or with some of the policies of the company, but you must not complain to your friends or try to "run down" the company which pays your salary. Employers expect their workers to keep confidential those things that pertain to the business.

If you cannot be loyal to your employer and your company, look for another job. You will not be happy working for an employer of whom you cannot speak well; and while you are looking for a new job, resist the temptation to be critical of your present employer.

WHAT YOU, THE EMPLOYEE, MAY EXPECT

After reading what most employers expect of their employees, you may feel that you are expected to give a lot and not get much consideration from your employer in return. This is not so. You have a right to expect certain things from your employer. Of course, some employers are more considerate than others, but most will do these things for you as a worker.

1. Pay your salary.
2. Provide safe working conditions.
3. Provide training.
4. Introduce you to co-workers.
5. Explain policies, rules and regulations.
6. Explain changes in your duties.
7. Evaluate your work.
8. Discipline you if you break rules.
9. Encourage an honest relationship.

PAY YOUR SALARY

Your employer will pay you for the work you do. The amount you are paid will depend upon state and federal minimum wage laws, the "going" rate for the work you do, union contracts, and your ability to perform your job. As a part-time or beginning worker, your pay will be less than that paid other employees who have had more experience.

SAFE WORKING CONDITIONS

Your employer should provide reasonably safe working conditions. If you are under eighteen years of age, federal law prohibits your working in certain occupations considered dangerous, such as coal mining, logging, and jobs requiring the use of certain power machinery.

Federal Law Prohibits Those Under 18 from Working in Certain Dangerous Occupations

PROVIDE TRAINING

Your employer should provide whatever on-the-job training is necessary in order for you to do your job. The way this is done will differ from job to job and between companies. You may be asked simply to observe another worker performing the job you will be doing, or another worker may be assigned to teach you how to do a particular job.

INTRODUCTIONS

Your employer should introduce you to all of the workers with whom you will be working. This is a courtesy which is not always observed. If your employer does not show you this consideration, you will have to make your own introductions — or perhaps the other workers will do it for you.

EXPLANATIONS

Your employer should explain company policies, rules, and regulations so that you understand them. If you do not understand exactly how these affect you, ask for further explanation.

CHANGES

Your employer should tell you about changes in your duties, responsibilities, working relationships, rate of pay, vacation schedule, and anything else which affects you and your work.

EVALUATIONS

Your employer should evaluate your work by telling you what is both good and bad about how you do your job. A considerate employer will do this in private.

DISCIPLINE

If you do not follow the rules and regulations, or if you do not live up to the things mentioned in what the employer expects of employees, then you may be disciplined. Most employers are fair in penalizing their employees. If you have not fulfilled your responsibilities, you should not resent disciplinary action.

HONESTY

Most employees are honest with their employers, and you have as much right to expect honesty from your boss as he or she has to expect it from you.

OTHER RESPONSIBILITIES

Your employer is required by law to pay half the amount paid into your Social Security account — that is to match the amount you pay. In addition, your employer contributes to workman's compensation or your protection in case you are injured on the job.

Some employers' responsibilities are enforceable by law; others are not. If you become dissatisfied with your job because you feel that you are being treated unfairly, you may wish to talk things over with your employer. This will depend upon your own personality, your employer's personality, and how well you get along together and understand each other. If you decide to discuss your problem, remember that you will have a much better chance of getting your employer to see things your way if you are cooperative rather than if you simply lay the blame on others. If things cannot be worked out, look for another job — but don't quit until you have found a job you like better. Some workers quit a job they are dissatisfied with only to find that they cannot find another one they like as well.

Do Not Quit Your Present Job Until You Have Found Another One You Like Better

GETTING ALONG WITH CO-WORKERS

We have discussed what the employer, your boss, is likely to expect from you and what you can reasonably expect in return. Because almost everyone works with other people, it is necessary that we be able to get along well with these co-workers in addition to living up to the boss's expectations. There are many reasons why it is important that you get along well with your co-workers. If employees enjoy working with one another, they will get more work done — which will make the employer happy and may result in salary raises and promotions. In addition, if you are pleasant and fair to others with whom you work, they are more likely to be pleasant and fair to you. People can never attribute their success totally to themselves; it is through a combined effort by **everyone** that an individual can achieve success. An old saying in the business world is, "Make friends with those below you on your way up, for you'll meet the same people on the way down." Of course, as a beginning worker, you will be at the bottom of the ladder; but it is just as important to make friends of your co-workers from the beginning. When you are put in charge of other workers, you will probably have formed the habit of treating those around you with respect and courtesy.

Getting along well with co-workers is an art that is too often neglected. This is because it does not happen automatically. It takes work, but it is worth it. If you and your co-workers do not cooperate with one another on the job, it will be damaging to everyone involved. The amount and quality of work will be down, and so will be your chances for pay raises and promotions.

Every individual reacts differently in any given situation. The main reason for this is that all of us see things through the eyes of our own experiences. If you had a very unpleasant experience with dogs as a child, you will react toward all dogs quite differently from the person who grew up having dogs as family pets. The point is that each of us has had experiences which are different from those of every other person. Each of us, then, will see every situation a little differently from any other person. If you are to get along well in your working relationships with your co-workers, you must accept them as worthy individuals even though they are different in many ways from you. Nobody is perfect, but everyone has some good qualities. If you can accept those with whom you work as worthy persons and really try to understand them, you will be more apt to do your part in developing good working relationships.

You Must Learn to Get Along Well with Your Co-Workers, Even If They Are Different from You in Many Ways

If it seems to you that one of your co-workers is extremely difficult to get along with, don't judge the person too harshly. There are reasons for such behavior. Past experiences — or perhaps difficulties at home — are most often causes. It is your responsibility, as a co-worker and as a fellow human being, to do **more** than your share at such times to strive for a smoother working relationship. You may sometime need such understanding from those with whom you work

AS A BEGINNER

As a beginning worker you will be wise to keep your eyes and ears open and your mouth shut — except to ask questions about your work. After you have worked for a while, you will learn which employees are the better workers and which employees receive a paycheck but aren't going anywhere. You will probably find that those who have been working longer than you are happy to help you get started. The workers who tell you about a mistake you are making are doing you a favor. Accept it as a favor — and thank them. Some of your co-workers will offer suggestions for better ways of doing things. They have more experience than you. If their suggestions do not conflict with what your "boss" has told you, try them out. If they work well, adopt them. When help is offered by other workers, accept their suggestions pleasantly and with a smile. However, once you understand your job, do it yourself. Don't depend too much on others. They have their own jobs to do.

I have too often heard the phrase, "That's not my job; let someone else do it." This attitude is sure to create unhappy co-worker relationships. In every company there are tasks which must be performed that are not pleasant. But someone must do them. Don't say that you are "too busy" with other work to do the things you may not feel you were hired to do. Employers react most favorably toward those who are most willing to take on extra or unpleasant duties; and it is a fact that those who are most agreeable to performing these extra tasks are the first to be rewarded with salary increases.

FORMALITY IN BUSINESS RELATIONSHIPS

If you aren't sure about how friendly — or how formal you should be as a beginning worker, it is better to be too formal than to be too friendly. Of course, you should smile and be pleasant to everyone, as we have discussed. But don't get too "chummy" too soon. You may find that after you get to know all of your co-workers, you have become associated with those that you would not really like for your close friends, and it may be difficult to adjust your personal relationships with these persons and retain good working relationships.

It Is Better to Err in the Direction of Too Much Formality Than to Be Too Friendly

You may work where people are called by their first names, and it will seem natural for you to call your co-workers by their first names. In many companies, however, beginning workers are expected to call their older co-workers and especially their boss by their last names, such as Mr. Smith or Mrs. Jones. If you are not sure about how to address your co-workers, again it is better to be too formal than to be too friendly.

STAY NEUTRAL IN DISPUTES

One of the best ways to keep up a good working relationship with **all** of your co-workers is to mind your own business. No matter where you work, there will likely be disputes between some workers. If you get involved in such disagreements, you will be the loser every time. You may feel that you have strengthened your friendship with one person for the moment, but you will likely cause a strain on your working relationship with others for a long time. The best thing to do is remain neutral.

KEEP YOUR SENSE OF HUMOR

If you have or can develop, a good sense of humor, it will do more to make you a happy, well-adjusted worker than anything else. A sense of humor is the ability to laugh when the joke is on you. Not too many people can do this. If you can, your co-workers will accept you much more readily than they will the person who laughs only at others.

UNIONS AND PROFESSIONAL GROUPS

About 17 million workers in the United States belong to **labor unions**. About half of them are factory workers, such as those involved in the production of automobiles. Many others are carpenters, electricians, plumbers, or other skilled craftsmen. They pay dues to the union ranging from about $8 to more than $30 a month, in addition to an initiation fee that often runs more than $100 when they become members. Why do so many workers join unions? They join unions because it is beneficial for them to do so.

Today, Americans are paid higher salaries, work shorter hours, and work under safer and better conditions than any other people in the world. However, in the early days of manufacturing in the United States, workers labored long hours (often 12 hours a day, six days a week) under unsafe working conditions, and were paid only enough to buy the bare necessities of life. If workers complained, they were often fired, for there were plenty of others who were willing to take their jobs. This situation caused workers to organize into **labor unions**. In this way, instead of each worker trying to bargain with the employer, all or many of the workers joined together to bargain collectively with their employer. Wherever there are large numbers of employees working for one employer, there are certain to be disagreements over such things as salaries, fringe benefits, and hours of work. When representatives of organized labor and the employer or the employer's representatives (management) sit down together to try to settle such disagreements, each side knows that it must compromise. Negotiation between organized labor and management is known as **collective bargaining**. Under collective bargaining, labor and management discuss what they expect of each other concerning salaries (wages), hours of work, seniority rights, and other common concerns. When an agreement is reached, a **labor contract** is signed by representatives of labor and management. Such contracts usually are written for periods of one to five years, after which a new contract is negotiated.

The things most often covered in a labor contract include wages, fringe benefits, hours of work, seniority, and grievance procedures. The labor unions are, of course, mainly concerned with the welfare of the workers. Unions are constantly seeking higher wages, more fringe benefits, shorter hours of work, and greater benefits for their members. Fringe benefits are vacations, sick leave, retirement pensions, life and health insurance, coffee breaks, and other employee benefits other than wages. For every $100 paid in wages, most employers pay about $20 in fringe benefits for employees.

Management is also interested in the welfare of its employees, because happy workers produce more. However, the purpose of being in business is to make a profit. Profit is the money left from income after all expenses have been paid. In most businesses, wages paid to employees is the biggest expense of all. Management is therefore opposed to raising wages so high that a reasonable profit cannot be made. When this does happen, either the business fails (**goes broke**) or it raises the price of its product. If the prices are increased, then the higher wages of the workers do not buy any more than their old wages purchased before the price increase. This upward spiral of wages and prices, known as **inflation**, has been the pattern in recent years.

Collective bargaining requires that each side be willing to give a little. If one side refuses to compromise, agreement is impossible. In an effort to force management to agree to its demands, unions may strike. A strike is a refusal by employees to work, causing a loss in production and therefore a loss of profits to the company. Employees on strike receive no wages, but may receive some pay from the union called **strike benefits**. If employees strike without the approval of the union, they receive no strike benefits. This is known as a **wildcat strike**. Workers on strike usually picket the entrance of the business which has not met their demands. You have probably seen them carrying signs indicating that they consider the company "unfair" — or simply that the union is "on strike."

Unions must be given much of the credit for the high pay and good working conditions enjoyed by American workers. In addition, union-negotiated health and welfare funds provide medical care for employees and their families, regardless of the employees' income.

However, workers' demands for higher wages have resulted in price increases and lowered the purchasing power of the dollar. Much has been written about this constant increase in the cost of living since World War II. It is true that prices of food items, clothing, automobiles, and most other consumer goods have gone up in price each year. Many people are asking whether unions and management should have the right to make agreements which bring about higher prices.

Similar to unions are **professional organizations**. Certain occupational fields requiring four, five, six, or more years of college are known as **professions**. These include medicine, dentistry, law, teaching, and many others. Professional organizations, like unions, are mainly interested in the welfare of their members. Unlike unions, the professional organizations do not ordinarily strike to achieve their demands. The most widely known professional organizations are the

American Medical Association, the American Bar Association, and the National Education Association.

5-MINUTE TIMED TEST ON FOLLOWING DIRECTIONS

How well do you follow directions? You should be able to complete all the things required in five minutes by following the directions below. Your teacher may wish to time you to see who can finish first, second, etc., so close your book to show when you have completed all the work.

Do not begin until your teacher says "go," then follow directions **exactly** as given. You will need one sheet of notebook paper.

1. Read all directions before doing anything.
2. On a sheet of notebook paper, write your name in the upper right corner.
3. Number from 1 to 7, leaving three blank lines between each number.
4. Draw five small squares beside the number 1 on your paper.
5. Put an "X" in each square beside number 1.
6. Put a circle around the number 2 on your paper.
7. Count the number of pages in Chapter 4 of this book and write the answer beside number 3 on your paper.
8. Multiply the answer above by your age.
9. Say your name out loud.
10. Beside number 4, write today's date.
11. Beside number 5, write the city and state where you were born.
12. Count the number of persons in the room and write the answer beside number 6.
13. Say, "I have reached number 13, and I am following directions carefully."
14. Now that you have completed the reading, omit all directions except the first two.

STUDY AIDS

NEW TERMS

collective bargaining	labor contract
criticism	negative attitude
evaluations	positive attitude
inflation	strike
initiative	

STUDY QUESTIONS

1. What is the most important factor in job success?
2. Eighty percent of the beginning workers who lose their jobs are fired for the same reason. Why do you think this happens?
3. How can you tell if a person has a positive attitude?
4. In addition to a day's work for a day's pay, your employer has a right to expect certain things from you. What are they?
5. What can you reasonably expect from your employer?
6. Why is it important to get along with your co-workers?
7. Why is it a good idea to do some of the unpleasant tasks which you may not feel you were hired to do?
8. Is it best to become close friends with a co-worker during the first week or two on the job? Why?
9. Should you call your boss by his or her first name? Should you call your co-workers by their first names?
10. If two of your co-workers have a dispute, should you take sides? Should you try to settle it?

DISCUSSION PROBLEMS

1. In your opinion, is it a good idea to establish eye-to-eye contact? Why?
2. Do you think it is a good idea to criticize others? Why?
3. What do you consider the most important thing which your employer should expect of you as a worker?

4. What do you consider the most important things which you can expect from your employer?
5. If you were unhappy with your job or working situation, what would you do?
6. If your best friend at work got into an argument with another worker, what would you do?
7. Do you feel that unions and management should have the right to make agreements which result in higher prices?

YOUR SUCCESS AND ACHIEVEMENT

If you are presently working and have been doing what your employer expects of you and have learned to get along well with your co-workers, **you are on your way to success.** You can now begin thinking about plans for your future advancement. By carefully studying this chapter, you will know how to win that promotion or pay raise.

PROMOTIONS

The time to find out about opportunities for advancement in a company is during the interview for the job. You may ask, ''What are my chances for advancement if I do well?'' or ''What can this job lead to?'' After you have begun work, do not bother your supervisor by continually asking questions about promotions or pay raises.

Opportunities for advancement generally occur for the following reasons:

1. You are very talented and your employer specifies a job that utilizes your talents and meets a special goal for the company. This occurs when an employer creates a new job for you.
2. An employee leaves the company and the position must be filled to meet the goals of the company.
3. An employee does not perform well and must be demoted or reassigned

to another job. This leaves an opening for a competent employee.

When you think you should be given a promotion, ask yourself these questions: ''Have I learned everything there is to know about my present job?'' and ''Have I done my work in the best possible way?'' Promotions must be earned.

In working for a promotion, keep in mind the realistic, long-range career goal discussed in Chapter 2. That is, the kind of work you would like to be doing five or ten years from now. It is what you are working toward. It is important that long-range goals be kept flexible. Many young people set two or three possible long-range goals, knowing that it may be some time before they decide which is the most appropriate. By keeping your long-range goal flexible, you will be able to take advantage of more opportunities when they come your way. Suppose, for example, that you have decided to become a secretary and you begin work as a typist in an advertising firm. After you have worked for a year, you are asked to do some of the layout and design work for the advertising, and you find that this work is actually more interesting to you than your typing duties. Because your design work is good, you are offered a different job which would be mostly layout and design of advertising at a higher salary. Should you turn it down because it does not fit your long-range goal? Or do you change your long-range goal? In this case you would probably change your long-range goal. However, it was important to have a long-range goal as it led to something you enjoy doing even more than secretarial work.

In addition to your long-range career goal, you should have intermediate and immediate goals. Your intermediate goal in the example above might have been a stenographer because you would expect it to lead to your long-range goal of becoming a secretary. Your immediate goal was to perform your duties as a typist to the best of your ability.

Promotions may be of three kinds: (1) a better job in the department or plant where you are now working, (2) a job with greater responsibility in a different department or plant within the same company, and (3) a job with more responsibility with another company.

If you are thinking about quitting your present job to accept one with another company because you think chances for advancement are not good where you now work, make sure that this would bring you closer to your long-range career goal. We said that long-range goals should be flexible, but it is not wise to job-hop unless the new job is related to your long-range goal or you have decided to change your long-range goal. Would a new job with a new company really increase your chances for promotion? Does the new company usually give the more responsible jobs to its present employees or does it hire outsiders to fill the best jobs? Also, how well do you think you would fit in with the new set of co-workers? Sometimes taking a new job with another company is the best thing to do, sometimes it is not. However, it is always best to have the new job before quitting the old one. Those who quit their jobs to look for something better seldom find it, and they are without a paycheck all the time they are looking.

When you begin selecting a company to satisfy your career needs, it is important to ask these questions before making the decision:

1. What are my short- and long-range goals?
2. What are the short- and long-range goals of the company?
3. Can I help the company attain its goals?
4. Can the company help me attain my goals?

Everyone likes to be offered a promotion. It makes us feel important and shows us that we are appreciated by others — in this case, our employer. Promotions increase our personal feeling of worth and often give us a larger paycheck. In addition, promotions usually result in an increase in responsibility. Sometimes this means greater authority over other workers.

It Is Not Wise to Job-Hop Unless Your New Job Is a Step Toward Your Long-Range Goal

When the time comes to decide who will be promoted, your employer will give careful attention to all employees being considered, and to their past work. The things most often considered by employers in deciding who shall be promoted are these:

(Not in order of importance)
1. Seniority
2. Knowledge of job
3. Quality of work
4. Quantity of work

5. Initiative
6. Perseverance
7. Cooperativeness
8. Ability to think
9. Adaptability
10. Adequacy of training
11. Ability to get along with other people

Seniority is a privileged status attained by continuous service with a company. Those who have worked for the company the longest have the greatest seniority. Most companies take seniority into consideration when making promotions, but they usually don't give employees promotions simply because they have been with the company a long time.

The **quality of work** that you do is also carefully considered by your employer. If your work is done very well on the job you are now doing, you will probably perform well in another job with more responsibility.

Some employees do their work well but are slow. The **quantity of work** you turn out will be checked to see whether it is likely that you would turn out a greater than average amount of work on a more responsible job.

Your employer will learn how much **initiative** you have by observing how often you look around to see what tasks need to be done and then go ahead and do them without being told. If you are a person with initiative, you will require less supervision than the person who must be told about each task to be done. If you are able to perform your work without much supervision and then do whatever else needs to be done,

SENIORITY Is a Status Attained by Long and Continuous Service with an Organization

Your **knowledge of the job** you are presently doing is one of the things that employers notice when they are considering you for a promotion. If you know your present job well, they can expect that you will be able to learn to do a more responsible job.

Can You Stick to a Project Until It Is Completed?

your employer is likely to think that you would make a good supervisor yourself.

Once you begin a task, do you always carry it through to completion? Of course, you may have to leave it until something more urgent is done — but do you always come back to the unfinished task and complete it? If you are a person with **perseverance,** you will finish what you start. You probably have known people who begin many projects either at home or as a part of their jobs, but never finish them. Can you stick to a task or project until it is completed, even if it is tiresome or boring? Being able to do this is important to your future job success.

Cooperation with others was discussed in a previous chapter. We said that most of the beginning workers who lose their jobs lose them because they are not able to get along with their employers, supervisors, or co-workers. While cooperation with others is necessary simply to keep your job, an even greater degree of **cooperativeness** must be shown if you are looking for a promotion. As promotions usually mean that the new job will place greater responsibility on you, a special ability to get along well is required, even with those who are difficult to work with.

Very often a promotion will mean a job which requires you to make decisions. This means that your employer will consider your **ability to think for yourself.** If you are able to consider new situations and come up with the right answer most of the time, or the right way of doing particular tasks, then you are better able to think for yourself than the employee who must always ask someone else.

How **adaptable** are you? Can you learn to do many kinds of tasks? Are you willing to do things other than those for which you were originally hired? Since you are being paid to perform your job, your employer usually expects you to do whatever needs to be done, even if certain tasks were not mentioned when you were hired. Jobs and duties change. If you are adaptable, you are a more valuable employee than people who feel they should only do those things for which they were hired.

In considering you for a promotion, your employer will determine whether you have **adequate training** for the new job. Long before you have a chance for a promotion, think about what training you should have to bring you closer to your long-range career goal. You may find that there are several levels of training required for intermediate goals along the way. The **Occupational Outlook Handbook,** published by the U. S. Department of Labor, may help you decide what training is required by your intermediate and long-range goals. Your school work experience or counseling office probably has a copy. It is also in your public library. Suppose that your long-range career goal is to become a store manager, and your present job is a sales position in the automotive department. In planning your advancement toward this goal, you and your work must meet a high standard of excellence concerning items 2 through 9 on pages 64 and 65 which we have just discussed.

In addition, you will need to find out how much and what kind of training is required for each of the intermediate goals which may someday bring you to your long-range goal. You can learn this by asking your employer what training is required or suggested for various positions with the company. Most companies have an organizational chart which may help you to more clearly see some of your intermediate goals. You will find that the more education you have, the faster you will move along toward your long-range goal. If there are two employees who are otherwise equally well qualified, the promotion will always go to the one with more education. But how do you get this training if you are working full time? Some companies provide their own courses for employees, because they know that money for education is money well spent. Both the company and the employee benefit. If you live in a city where there is a college or university, there will probably be night classes available to you. Also, many public schools conduct adult evening classes. If no formal training is available in your area, you can still take correspondence courses and read trade magazines and books.

Your **ability to get along with friends, parents, and community members** is an indication of future human relationship skills. People who have difficulty associating with other people are usually more successful working alone. Since there are two major divisions of job responsibility, it is best to select the job environment that fits your ability to associate with people. These two divisions of responsibility are:

1. Responsibility to work with other people
2. Responsibility to work alone

Human relationships is a very important consideration when an employer selects employees for a more responsible job. How do you get along with people now? You should consider this factor very carefully if you want to succeed in the world of work.

If you are promoted, you will probably have greater responsibility. Many times this means responsibility over other employees. In this case, you must see that others perform their jobs well. This kind of promotion means that there will be a different kind of relationship between you and the employees you will be supervising. You are no longer their co-worker. You are the boss. If you can be the boss without being bossy, you will probably enjoy this new relationship. If not, you may be miserable. If you think that you will not be able to handle the responsibility or that you will be unhappy with it, perhaps you should turn down the promotion. This is not often done, but in rare cases it is better to wait until you are more ready to accept greater responsibility. For instance, if you are having problems at home which are very upsetting to you, it may not be wise to take on added responsibilities at work. Then too,

there are some people who can be happy with a job in which they have great responsibility for the performance of special duties, but simply don't like supervising other workers.

Suppose you have been offered a promotion which places you in charge of a number of other employees. What will your actions towards them be? What will their reactions be? Consider these ideas:

George worked as a gas station attendant at Walker's Auto Shop after school during his senior year in high school. When he graduated, Mr. Walker asked him if he would like to learn to be a mechanic. George was very interested in this work and quickly learned the many jobs that were required. He was a hard worker and willing to do something extra to help out a co-worker. After five years George was promoted to shop foreman. He was in charge of six mechanics. On the first day after his promotion, one of the other mechanics, Bob, arrived at work ten minutes late. George felt that he must let Bob know that this would not be permitted. "Hey you!" he yelled when Bob walked into the shop. "Where were you? You think we are paying you to sleep all morning?"

To Jack, another mechanic, George said, "If there is one thing I can't stand, it's somebody who leaves engine parts all over his bench. Where were you brought up? Learn to be neat and orderly if you want to keep working here!"

Perhaps George did need to say something to Bob and Jack. After all, he was responsible for their work. But the way in which he handled these situations might make Bob and Jack feel that they did not want to keep working under a supervisor like George.

Ellen began working for the Maddox Company as a typist after one year of college. After she had been with the company for a year, she was promoted to stenographer. Three years later she became secretary to one of the vice presidents of the company. She was an excellent worker and everyone liked her very much. When the office manager left the company to take another job, Ellen was asked to be the new manager. Company officials thought that she would make a good office manager, though she had never been placed in charge of other workers before. Ellen was placed in charge of an office staff of 16 men and women. When several workers started coming into work late and leaving early, she knew that she should do something; but she was afraid that she might make them angry with her. When some of the workers took a half-hour coffee break, Ellen didn't know what to do, so she did nothing — except worry about it.

Ellen wanted to be popular with the others in the office but felt she couldn't if she talked to them about their shortcomings. Soon the others in the office became disrespectful toward Ellen. Some talked back to her when she gave them work to do. Finally, in tears, Ellen went to the vice president and asked to be relieved of her responsibilities as office manager. Ellen was an excellent worker when she worked for someone else or as a co-worker, but she was afraid to accept the responsibilities of manager.

HANDLING RESPONSIBILITY

In the cases above, neither George nor Ellen made a good supervisor. George felt that he had to show those under his supervision who was boss, and he became "bossy." Ellen's need to be popular with all of the other employees kept her from being a good supervisor. She wanted everyone to like her but felt they wouldn't if she criticized them in any way. The other employees took advantage of Ellen's fears.

We have said that promotions often mean that you are given an increase in pay and are expected to handle greater responsibility. These responsibilities may be either of two types: (1) you may be performing a different set of duties not requiring supervision over other workers, or (2) you may supervise the work of one or more employees. Sometimes a promotion means both a change in your nonsupervisory tasks and also requires that you supervise the work of others. If you are promoted to a job which does not require that you supervise

New Workers Coming Under Your Supervision May Require Special Handling

the work of other employees, you will probably be given work which makes use of the training and experience that you have gained while on the job. Earning such a promotion will give you a real feeling of accomplishment. It will increase your feeling of worth as a person, and — if you can accept the new responsibility — you will be a happier person because of it. Probably you will be paid more for your work, too.

If your promotion carries responsibilities for the work of others, then you must learn to be a good supervisor. This is easy for some people and difficult for others. Of course, if you have no supervisory experience you are seldom placed in charge of a large number of workers. Your first promotion to a supervisory position may place you in charge of only one or two workers. If so, you will have a better chance to learn how to be a good supervisor, but you must work at it. The following list will give you an idea of what you should work on if you are to become a really effective supervisor:

1. Give directions clearly
2. Plan training for new workers
3. Be consistent
4. Treat workers fairly
5. Be firm when necessary
6. Be mindful of workers' welfare
7. Set a good example

If you directly supervise and are responsible for the work of others, you will find that your job will be a much easier one if you can give directions so that they are always understood. Communication is often the biggest problem supervisors have. If their workers cannot understand exactly what, and how the job is to be done, then even the best employee is useless. Too often, the supervisors are at fault because they give too little direction about the work to be done. Give all the direction needed for each particular job. If you are not sure that it was completely understood, ask the worker some questions about it until you are certain that he or she understands clearly.

New workers coming under your supervision require special handling. Of course, they are usually given a tour of the office or plant and introduced to the other workers. But to have really good workers, a plan of training is necessary. Teach them how to be good workers. This may be done by you as the supervisor, or you may assign them to someone else who knows the work and has a flair for teaching. New workers trained by good workers who are enthusiastic about their jobs are more apt to become good workers themselves.

Be consistent in handling your supervisory duties. For example, if you say that a certain duty must be performed a certain

If You Are the Supervisor, Don't Play Favorites

way, insist that it always be done that way and by every worker. Also, follow through on what you say. If you tell employees that you will deduct part of their salary if they are late to work, do it. If you don't follow through, your workers will not respect you and will tend to do as they please.

If you expect those under your supervision to do their best work for you, you must treat them fairly. Don't permit one worker to come to work late or get by with sloppy work while requiring others to arrive on time and perform well. Part of being fair with your workers is being reasonable. Don't set up requirements which cannot be met by the employees. If a worker feels that you are being unfair, listen to the complaint calmly and consider it. If the complaint is justified, you may wish to change your mind about the matter. If not, explain to the worker why a change cannot be made — that it would not be in the best interest of the workers, the company, etc.

As a person with supervisory responsibilities, you must sometimes be firm with your workers. Avoid yelling or losing your temper, but do not allow an employee to take unfair advantage of you, the company, or other workers. Just as every person dif-

Supervisors Must Control Their Emotions

Jack was a bright young man, but he always came to work 20 or 30 minutes late. He dressed well and made a good appearance, but his work was sloppy. His mind was on things other than his work. This example was followed by some of the other workers. Their work was also sloppy. When the supervisor was replaced by an ambitious young man whose work was a good example for other workers, the other employees' work also improved. One worker, who had regularly come to work 15 minutes late — just in time to beat the supervisor — also followed the example of the new boss and arrived at work at five minutes to eight.

fers, every situation dealing with workers will be different from every other. With some workers, a friendly suggestion is all that is required. To get others to perform as you require them to on the job, you may have to be a bit more firm: "Do it this way," and show them **how** the job is to be done. Sometimes a problem will come up because of the behavior of one or more employees toward other employees. Again, be firm when necessary. If it is too severe a problem to be corrected, it may be necessary to move employees to another office or section of the plant. If they fail to adjust to other workers and to the work after being moved, it will probably be necessary to let them go.

Be mindful of the workers' welfare. Consider what is best for them. This does not mean that you should put their desires above the interests of the company, but often think about whether they are getting a fair deal. Do what you can to make their work easier while keeping the amount of work done at a high level, or even increasing it. Be willing to go to your boss when necessary to request that changes be made for the benefit of your workers. Set a good example for your workers. Consider this example:

Just as you are responsible for the work of those under your supervision, someone else (your boss) is responsible for your work unless you own your own business. As the workers whom you supervise must account to you for their performance on the job, so must you account to your supervisor, or boss, for your own performance on the job. You must "answer to" the person who is responsible for your work. Your relationship with your supervisor or boss will be further discussed in the section on performance review and evaluation.

There are a number of advantages in holding a supervisory job. One advantage is that supervisors usually are paid more money than the workers they supervise. They should be, of course, since they have greater responsibilities. The job as a supervisor usually carries a certain amount of prestige, too. If they do their jobs well, supervisors are "looked up to" by other workers. Also, supervisors are often free from some of the more routine or even dull jobs. Their work may thus be more interesting. They have a greater chance to be creative than other workers, so they can try some things out that they feel will prove beneficial to the company. They have a greater "say" about how the company will be run. One of the most important advantages of being the supervisor is the chance to show leadership. If a supervisor does well, further advancement with the company is often likely.

There are disadvantages in being a supervisor, too. As a supervisor, you do not have the same kind of relationship with your employees that you had with your co-workers.

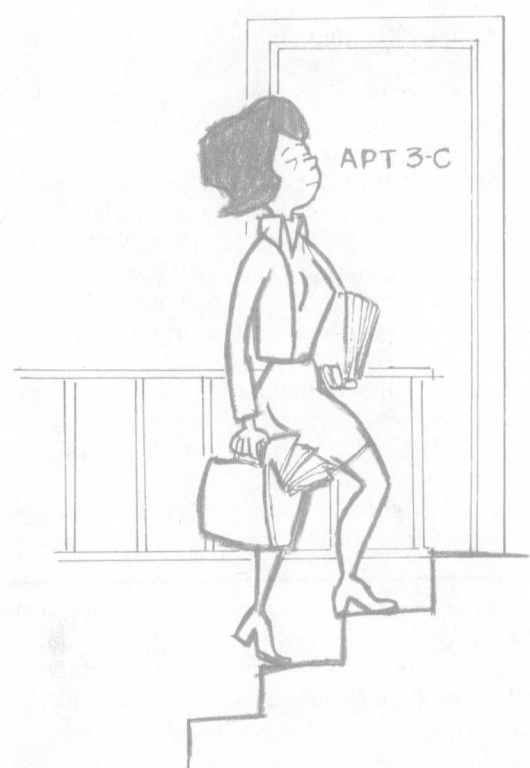

If You Are the Boss, Don't Try to Do Everything Yourself

You are the boss. People say different things to the boss than to their co-workers, and say them in different ways. They usually aren't quite so free in what they say. Some think this is a disadvantage, but others prefer this kind of relationship. As the boss, you are a target for criticism. Most of it you won't hear. You get a bigger paycheck than the other workers, and they must feel you earn

it. Another disadvantage is that when you do make a mistake, it is usually more costly to the company than the mistakes made by other workers. This is because your mistakes are made on the bigger things. Sometimes a supervisor errs in giving directions on how a job is to be done, and other workers make the same mistake.

Sometimes a person who is responsible for the entire output of work for a department or company tries to do too much. You may have known people who were so "overworked" that they had to take work home every night in order to keep up with it. Some people, of course, do have such a heavy burden of work that this is necessary. Often, however, the people who are so busy that they just never catch up with all the work to be done are themselves at fault. There may be others in the department, plant, or company who have a light schedule of work. The wise boss—whether a company executive, department manager, or job supervisor — will delegate some responsibilities to others. Why do some people try to keep all the responsibilities for themselves? Some do it because they are poor organizers. Some do it because **they think that they are the only ones able to handle the job.** Other people will not delegate responsibility because they want everyone else to depend upon them. This gives them a feeling of importance.

If you are the boss, don't try to do everything yourself. Organize the work responsibilities that go with it according to (1) who can handle these duties and responsibilities in the best manner, and (2) what is a fair work load for each worker. Of course, don't give away all of the work and responsibility. Doing this, you would lose the respect of your workers — and perhaps your job too. But by giving up some responsibilities to others who can handle them, you will be able to better handle the responsibilities left to you. In addition, those under your supervision will appreciate the opportunity to show that they, too, can be counted upon to handle important work.

SALARY INCREASES

If you receive a **salary,** you are paid a fixed sum each week, month, or perhaps twice a month. You may not even know how much you are paid for one hour's work. The word **wage** usually refers to the amount paid a worker for one hour's work. If you receive a wage, you will know how much you get per hour, but your paychecks will probably differ from payday to payday because the number of hours worked in one pay period differs from that worked in another. Those paid a wage, by the hour, usually are paid for overtime work. Those on salary usually are not. For the purpose of our discussion on salary increases, both wages and salaries will be considered as "salaries."

A millionaire was once asked if he thought he had enough money. "No, not until I get just a little more," was his answer. People would always like to have more than they have, but when they are given a raise, it's not enough. They want more.

If you get a raise in pay, you will be able to have a higher standard of living. Perhaps just as important is the feeling of increased worth you have about yourself. In some companies, employees are given a raise in salary after working for a certain length of time, usually six months or a year. If you work for such a firm, you are almost sure of a raise if you are a good worker and do the things expected by your employer. Before you get a raise in such a company, however, you will probably be evaluated in writing by your supervisor or some official of the company. This will be discussed in the next section.

In other companies, pay raises are not so automatic. If there is not a specified length of time employees must work before they are considered for a salary raise, then it is left completely up to the employer to decide when a worker deserves a raise. In such companies, the best workers are given raises fairly often; others may work for years without a raise at all.

PERFORMANCE REVIEW AND EVALUATION

In addition to seeing you perform your duties on the job daily and noticing how you get along with the other workers, your employer may make a written report on your effectiveness. This, of course, will be used in deciding whether you will be promoted, given a raise, allowed to continue working at the same job and salary, or fired.

Employers gain much useful information about their workers from employee evaluations. Individual strengths and weaknesses of workers show up more clearly when the supervisor is taking a close look at each employee. It may be found that a particular employee would do better work if transferred to another plant or to another type of job within the company. It gives the company, and the workers, a better chance to make use of individual strengths. Employees are most valuable to the company when they are doing those things they can do really well. The evaluation may show a need for special training programs for workers with common weaknesses. In addition, the employee evaluation usually causes workers to improve their own work.

Employees generally are allowed to see how their supervisors evaluated them. This is, of course, best. Otherwise the evaluation could hardly cause employees to improve their work. Evaluation reports which are not shown to the workers can still serve as a basis for promotion and dismissal. After rating the employee according to whatever form is used by the company, the supervisor will most often discuss the results with the employee rated. This is done in private to avoid unnecessary embarrassment.

During the evaluation interview, the supervisor — or boss — may discuss both strengths and weaknesses of the worker. Some supervisors try to save time by discussing **only the weaknesses.** This is not a good way to conduct evaluation interviews, but if your boss does it this way, you must still try to profit from the criticism. The only purpose of pointing out your weaknesses to you is so that you will be able to become a better worker by improving in certain things. It is to your advantage as well as to the company's that you improve in your job. If you follow the recommendations made by your supervisor for the continued improvement of your work, you will receive more pay raises. Even more important, you will take greater pride in your work, which helps to make you a happier person. If you are truly pleased with your work efforts, often your happiness will influence your relationships with friends, family, and co-workers.

If your supervisor points out your weaknesses but does not make any recommendations about how you can improve, ask for some suggestions. Your boss will probably be able to help you, and you will show that you are genuinely interested in improving your work.

Study each item in the employee evaluations on the following pages. By knowing in advance what you will be "tested on," you will be better prepared for advancement in the world of work.

GENERAL RESEARCH CORPORATION
SYSTEMS RESEARCH DIVISION

Support Staff
PERFORMANCE EVALUATION REVIEW

Name _____ Employee No._____ Date _____

Position _____ Date Hired _____ Date of Last Review _____

To be filled out by immediate supervisor and department head as appropriate. On the basis of your personal contact with this employee, your opinion and analysis of the employee's performance on the job is requested. Please evaluate by checking the square which best describes the employee's performance. If you have not observed the factor well enough to evaluate it, please leave blank.

	Unsatisfactory		GRC Norm		Excellent
JOB KNOWLEDGE	☐	☐	☐	☐	☐

Consider the employee's fundamental understanding of basic techniques and procedures relating to his position.

Does not have enough understanding to handle present work properly.

Well-informed on all aspects of job.

Expert in his job, and has good knowledge of related jobs.

Comments:_____
_____

	Unsatisfactory		GRC Norm		Excellent
WORK OUTPUT	☐	☐	☐	☐	☐

Consider the volume of work consistently done in relation to the volume required for fully proficient performance of the job.

Work output consistently falls below the daily requirements of the job.

Work output is consistently good.

Work output is always above the standard requirements of the job.

Comments:_____
_____

	Unsatisfactory		GRC Norm		Excellent
QUALITY OF WORK	☐	☐	☐	☐	☐

Disregard volume. Consider accuracy, thoroughness and related characteristics of work.

Careless. Time required for revisions noted to be excessive.

Does a good job. Seldom has errors. Checks quality frequently.

All work performed is exceptionally accurate, and thorough. Catches errors in the work of others.

Comments: _____

	Unsatisfactory	GRC Norm	Excellent

JUDGMENT ▮ ▬▬▬▬▬▬▬▬▬▬ □ ▬▬ □ ▬▬ □ ▬▬ □ ▬▬▬ □ ▬

Consider the ability to think through a problem, select pertinent factors and arrive at a sound course of action.

| Jumps to con- clusions. Judg- ment is not dependable. | Judgment is dependable | Sound judg- ment. Decisions always based on thorough analysis. |

Comments: _____

	Unsatisfactory	GRC Norm	Excellent

RELIABILITY ▮ ▬▬▬▬▬▬▬▬ □ ▬▬ □ ▬▬ □ ▬▬ □ ▬▬▬ □ ▬

Consider the responsibility assumed by employee for his own actions.

| Can rarely be counted on to carry out work as directed. | Can be re- lied upon | Never any doubt about his carry- ing out duties with a minimum of supervision. |

Comments: _____

	Unsatisfactory	GRC Norm	Excellent

COOPERATION ▮ ▬▬▬▬▬▬▬ □ ▬▬ □ ▬▬ □ ▬▬ □ ▬▬▬ □ ▬

Consider employee's attitude toward his work, associates, company, and its effect on others. Also consider his willingness to work with and for others.

| Shows reluctance to cooperate. Constant friction with others. Antagonistic. | Gets along well with associates. Meets others halfway. | Good team worker, always helpful. Goes out of way to cooperate. |

Comments: _____

INITIATIVE

Consider ability to originate actions and take necessary steps in attacking new problems.

Unsatisfactory	GRC Norm	Excellent
☐	☐	☐
Relies on others. Must be told what to do and consistently needs help in getting started.	Solves problems pertaining to his own work on his own and occasionally offers suggestions for improvement.	Outstandingly active in making new suggestions.

Comments: _____

COMMUNICATION (expression)

Consider the ability to transmit knowledge and ideas orally and in writing with effectiveness and clarity.

Unsatisfactory	GRC Norm	Excellent
☐	☐	☐
Inarticulate.	Transmits information well both verbally and in writing.	Speaks and writes exceptionally well.

Comments: _____

JOB PLANNING

Consider success in planning and organizing work.

Unsatisfactory	GRC Norm	Excellent
☐	☐	☐
Work shows serious lack of proper planning.	Plans effectively.	Effective under the most difficult circumstances.

Comments: _____

For Evaluation of Supervisors Only

DEVELOPMENT OF OTHERS

Consider the extent to which the supervisor recognizes and develops the aptitudes, abilities and capacities of others.

Unsatisfactory	GRC Norm	Excellent
☐	☐	☐
Contributes very little to the development of his subordinates.	Successful in recognizing and developing the potential of others.	Extremely capable and active in developing his subordinates.

Comments: _____

LEADERSHIP

	Unsatisfactory		GRC Norm		Excellent
Consider the supervisor's ability to inspire in others the willingness and desire to achieve.	☐ ☐		☐	☐	☐
	Ineffective as a leader.		Obtains satisfactory results.		Inspirational and effective leader.

Comments: _____

_____

_____

OVERALL PERFORMANCE

	Unsatisfactory		GRC Norm		Excellent
	☐ ☐		☐	☐	☐

1. Does this employee's present position place him in the line of endeavor best suited to his temperament and ability? Please comment:_____

_____

_____

_____

2. What are the employee's particular strong points?_____

_____

_____

3. In what areas is improvement needed? (If applicable)_____

_____

_____

4. General Comments:_____

_____

_____

_____

_____

_____

Employee's Signature _____ Date _____ Evaluated by _____ Date _____

Employee's Comments _____

_____

_____

_____

_____

Reviewed by _____ Date _____

TERMINATING THE JOB

Ann Winfield was a high school senior who worked part time as a typist in a law firm. She assisted a legal secretary by typing letters and memoranda from a transcribing machine. One day Ann had difficulty adjusting the machine properly and asked Mrs. Allen, her supervisor, for help. Mrs. Allen was upset over the illness of her mother and, although she quickly made the simple adjustment of the machine, she spoke sharply to Ann about her not being able to do anything herself. Ann was crushed. She soon developed a dislike for both Mrs. Allen and everything about her job. Three weeks before school was out, Ann called Mrs. Allen on the phone and "told her off." Ann quit her job without giving any advance notice of her intention to do so. In the weeks following graduation, Ann looked everywhere for a job. It seemed that word had gotten around town about her behavior in quitting her part-time job. Nobody wanted to take a chance on getting an employee like that. She did finally get a job in another city.

Hopefully, Ann learned from this experience that if you have a problem on the job it is best to at least try to see the good things about the work and the employer. You may get interested in your work and find that the boss isn't so bad after all. Sometimes workers forget that the boss has problems, too. Often, the boss spends many more hours on the job than the employees. Many business owners and company executives, for instance, work 50 to 60 hours per week. The extra time your boss is working may increase company profits — thus helping to pay your salary.

GIVING NOTICE OF TERMINATION

There are, of course, good reasons to quit a job. If you have accepted a better job with another company or if you must quit your job because you are attending college in another city, you have good reason to terminate employment. In this case, there are certain courtesies which should be observed.

Notice of your intent to leave your job should be given to your immediate supervisor unless company policy states that it should be given to someone else. It is often necessary to notify the personnel office in larger firms. You may be asked to make written notification. If this is the policy, follow it.

You should give notice of termination soon enough for the company to find a replacement by the time you leave. Courtesy requires that you give at least two weeks' notice. If you are paid once a month, then it is customary to give at least a month's notice. Failure to do this may make it difficult to find suitable work in other firms.

IF YOU'RE FIRED . . .

If business is off and you are one of the last employees hired by the company, you may be one of the first to be "laid off." When this happens, you are not really "fired." That is, your loss of the job was not due to your being an unsatisfactory employee. If your boss feels that you are unsatisfactory either in your performance on your job or in your ability to work well with the other employees, then you may indeed be fired! Then what happens? If you are wise, you will think about what happened and how you could have prevented it. You will learn from your mistakes. If you place all the blame on your employer, you probably won't learn much. If you can see what **you** did wrong, then you will be more able to avoid being fired from another job. Then begin immediately to look for the job which you think will be "right for you." The places to go and the methods to use are the same as when looking for your first job. These were discussed in Chapter 3.

We said that if you are paid once a month, it is customary to give your employer at least a month's notice if you plan to quit your job. If you are paid once a week, you should give at least a week's notice. It is customary for the employer to give similar notice if you are to be laid off. If you are not given any advance notice, you are entitled to **severance pay.** That is, because you are **severed** (cut off) from your job without notice, you are entitled to receive a check for one week's work if you are paid each week, two week's work if you are paid every two weeks, etc.

If you are laid off or fired from a job on which you have been working for some time, you may be eligible for some **unemployment compensation.** Unemployment compensation checks are provided for a limited time to those who are able to work, available to accept work, and actively seeking work. Students working part time do not usually qualify because their yearly earnings do not meet the minimum required.

STUDY AIDS

NEW TERMS

adaptability
perseverance
promotions
seniority
severance pay

supervisor
termination
unemployment
   compensation

STUDY QUESTIONS

1. When is the best time to find out about opportunities for advancement with a company?
2. What questions should you ask yourself about whether you deserve a promotion?
3. What are long-range goals? What are **your** long-range goals?

4. Three kinds of promotions were discussed. What were they?
5. What things will your employer consider in deciding who will be promoted?
6. If you are working full time, can you still continue your education? How?
7. Do you think you would like to have a job in which you would be responsible for the work of others?
8. In relationship to workers, what qualities does the good supervisor have?
9. What disadvantages are there in being a supervisor?
10. Why do some people refuse to delegate work, keeping all responsibilities for themselves?
11. Why do most companies use a written evaluation of employee's work?
12. If you decide to quit a job, what do you tell your employer?
13. What should you do if you are fired?

DISCUSSION PROBLEMS

1. Would you prefer to stick with one company for years or change jobs whenever you could get one with higher pay? Why?
2. Do you think that you would like the responsibility of supervising other workers? Why?
3. If you were a supervisor and one of your employees came to work late almost every day, how would you handle the situation?
4. What do you consider the most important traits of a supervisor?
5. If your boss evaluated your performance on the job and told you only about your **weaknesses,** how would you feel? How would you behave?

PART TWO
AWARENESS OF PERSONAL RESPONSIBILITIES

INTRODUCTION

As you read Part I of this book, you became aware that your lifestyle will be determined by a number of factors, including the work you do to earn a living. Part II will deal with the responsibilities which you must personally accept if you are to become a happy adult, satisfied with your overall lifestyle.

Part II deals mainly with a study of **you,** of **careers,** of **human relationships,** and of your **personal safety.**

You will receive guidance in understanding those things about you that are relevant to making a career decision and on how to search out information on careers so that you will be able to "match up" your own evaluation of yourself with an appropriate career goal.

Human relationships, or how we get along with others, is the single most important factor in success both in social situations and in your career. By following the suggestions for good human relationships presented in Part II, you will be more effective in **making things happen.** You won't have to wait for something to happen to you!

Part II also will make you aware of the personal safety needs in every facet of your life.

CHAPTER SIX
UNDERSTANDING YOURSELF

YOUR SELF-CONCEPT

Your career development is the **implementation of your self-concept.** That is, the way you see yourself greatly affects your choice of a career and your overall lifestyle. Your **self-concept,** or how you feel about yourself, is not always the same. We see ourselves differently at different times in our lives, sometimes clearly and sometimes not clearly at all! This is based mainly upon how other people react toward us.

Traditionally, men have seen their role primarily in the world of work while women have seen themselves primarily in the role of a housewife. Women who did aspire to careers in the world of work often felt limited to careers which **society** felt were appropriate — it was "all right" for a girl to become a nurse, a teacher, or a secretary.

Now society's role expectations of men and women are changing. Today there is an emphasis on equality of opportunity for employment and education. Many state governments have adopted policies guaranteeing rights for both sexes and all races. There is no reason why any man or woman, regardless of race, color, or creed, should not

Society's Role Expectations of Men and Women Are Changing

aspire to any career he or she desires — so long as that person is qualified to perform well in that career!

We have already discussed the importance of having one or several career goals, and we said that our long-range goals must be kept flexible to take advantage of appropriate opportunities. But which opportunities will be the appropriate ones — the right ones — for you? You probably won't know unless you learn to understand yourself better than you do now. In discussing careers, we said that each career goal considered should be **realistic.** That is, it should be one that you can reach, and it must be one that will give you satisfaction after you reach it. If you are anything like the average person and will be changing the **kind** of work you do several times during your life, then you must learn all you can about yourself — your lifestyle goals, interests, aptitudes and abilities, personality, and other influences upon your lifestyle.

LIFESTYLE GOALS

DREAMS

In Chapter 2, we discussed how many young people simply "fall into" some occupation. They take whatever job happens to be available when they are ready to take a job. As adults, many of them do find themselves and begin a career which fits their lifestyle goals. However, many continue working in a career which is not really satisfying and which **dictates a lifestyle** different than they would like. Don't let a job dictate a lifestyle pattern for you! Like most young people, you probably do some day dreaming about your future. This is good. It is an important part of your career development. In fact, it's the first step. Lyrics from **South Pacific** included the words, "If you don't have a dream, how you gonna have a dream come true?" So do some dreaming! Consider the lifestyle you would like to have five, ten, even fifteen years from now.

Like Most Young People, You Probably Do Some Daydreaming about Your Future

VALUES

Values are those things that you think are important. Up to the age of about 15 or 16, your values are very much like those of your parents. If your parents consider taking part in religious activities important, so do you. It is one of your values. If they feel that taking a daily bath and being neatly dressed are important, so do you. When you are in about the tenth or eleventh grade in high school, you begin to set your own values. You keep some of the values of your parents and reject others. You take a look at life and try to decide how you want to fit into it. You think about the importance of the values listed below and your answers have a great deal to do with the career you should pursue. Consider the importance of each listed value to you — which are most important?

> 1. Being famous.
> 2. Earning a lot of money.
> 3. Having power over others.
> 4. Being active in a religion.
> 5. Being helpful to others.
> 6. Having a happy home life.
> 7. Good health.
> 8. Appreciation of fine arts.
> 9. Being creative.
> 10. Having lots of friends.

What other things are important to you? Can you see how your values can affect your satisfaction with the work you do?

CAREER ACTIVITY PREFERENCES

Part of getting to know and understand yourself is surveying your interests. This can be done informally by thinking about and perhaps taking some notes on the things you most enjoy doing. Activities which interest you the most are those in which you feel comfortable, those in which you perform well, and those which are exciting to you. Think about your hobbies. How do you like to spend your spare time? Many successful photographers were once interested in taking pictures only as a hobby. What classes in school have been your favorites? If you have taken some vocational classes, you may have developed an interest in a particular career field. If you have been involved in many school and social activities, you may have **many** interests. If your activities have been few, you may need to be exposed to new ones. You may not know whether you will have an interest in something until you have tried it. The more interests you can develop, the better your chances of finding a career which will be satisfying to you.

If you feel that you won't know enough about your likes and dislikes to profit from an informal survey, perhaps the formal approach is best for you. There are career activities preference inventories which can be taken much like you would take a test — except that there are no right or wrong answers. You may have already taken one at your school. If not, your school counselor or work experience coordinator can probably arrange for you to take one.

DATA-PEOPLE-THINGS PREFERENCES

Besides the work activity which seems interesting to you, think about whether you would prefer to work mainly with data, people, things, or combinations of these. If you like working with numbers, symbols, and ideas, you might enjoy a career in which you would work with **data** (information). If you enjoy the company of others and tend to feel lonely and unhappy when left alone for more than an hour or two, you would probably prefer to work where you are in the company of other people. You probably

If You Prefer to Work with People, Some Jobs Will Not Appeal to You

would not enjoy being a forest ranger or a lighthouse keeper! If you would rather spend an evening alone building a model than go to a party with friends, you might like a job where you work alone. You might enjoy working with "things."

In some kinds of work, you would deal with only one of these — data, people, **or** things. In many careers, you would deal with a combination of data and people, data and things, or people and things. Some careers involve all three: data, people, **and** things.

> If you enjoy working with data but also like working with people, you might like such occupations as:
> - Advertising copy writer
> - Lawyer
> - Play director

> If you like working with data and things, but prefer to work alone or with only one or two others, these occupations might appeal to you:
> - Research biologist
> - Interior decorator
> - Engineer

> If you like to be in the company of or come in contact with people, and you also like working with things, you might enjoy such jobs as:
> - Salesperson
> - Dental hygienist
> - Public relations representative

> If you like working with data, people, **and** things, these jobs might interest you:
> - Office manager
> - Teacher
> - Librarian

The above occupations are only examples of the relationship of data, people, and things. You must select your interests and your own career from thousands of opportunities available in the world of work.

APTITUDES AND ABILITIES

Having an interest in a career is not all that is necessary to successfully pursue it. You must have the necessary aptitude or ability, too. Jane wanted more than anything in the world to be a singer. Her parents arranged for her to take singing lessons, which she did for several years, but her voice simply wouldn't cooperate. Becoming a singer was not a realistic goal for her. She didn't have the natural talent for it.

When we say that people have **ability** to do something, we mean that they are **able** to do it. We usually mean that they are rather skillful at it, too. They may have this ability because they have worked very hard to develop it or because they have a natural talent for it. When people seem to be born with natural talent which makes it easy to learn certain things, we say that they have an **aptitude** for these things. It is much easier to learn those things for which we have an aptitude. For instance, you may have known someone who learned to play the piano with little or no instruction, while others develop little ability after years of study. In some careers, such as music, a fair share of natural talent (aptitude) is necessary in order to be successful.

If you are to set and work toward realistic career goals, you must know something about your abilities. Otherwise, you wouldn't know whether a particular goal were realistic for you or not. How do you learn about your abilities — and perhaps more important, your aptitudes, since these can be developed into abilities? It isn't too difficult if you know where to look. We will talk about two kinds of aptitudes and abilities: (1) those which are mainly mental and (2) those which are mainly physical.

MENTAL APTITUDES AND ABILITIES

Your mental abilities are indicated by the grades you achieve in your classes in school. If you try to do all the work asked by your teachers, your grades can be a fairly accurate measurement of your aptitudes and abilities. If your efforts are not very great, you may have more aptitude than your grades indicate. However, to develop these aptitudes into useful abilities may be difficult for you until you decide to make greater effort.

Your teachers can provide information about your ability to do certain kinds of work. If you are taking shorthand, your shorthand teacher will be able to give you an idea about how useful your shorthand ability would be to a business manager. The same goes for other skill courses, such as auto mechanics, electronics, drafting, typing, bookkeeping, etc.

A school counselor can help you learn what your strengths and weaknesses are. You have probably already taken one or perhaps several tests which give a good indication of your general ability. You may have taken an aptitude test. Your counselor can give you information about your aptitudes and abilities as shown by the results of these tests. If you have not taken any aptitude or ability tests, ask your counselor to arrange for some.

Your general intelligence can be measured by a variety of tests which usually measure three different kinds of intelligence. They are (1) verbal ability, (2) arithmetic ability, and (3) reasoning.

Your verbal ability is measured by how well you understand the meaning of words — your reading vocabulary. This is considered a most important part of general intelligence because so much learning depends upon your ability to understand written material in instructions, articles, the newspaper, and books. Your verbal ability can be increased by working on your vocabulary. Develop the practice of using the dictionary to look up the meaning of words you do not understand.

Your arithmetic ability is measured by how fast and how accurately you can solve arithmetic problems. This part of most intelligence tests usually begins with simple arithmetic problems, then goes on to more difficult problems for those who can do them. Your arithmetic ability, too, can be increased by practice. If you do not know how to add, subtract, multiply, and divide accurately and with fair speed, it will show up in intelligence tests.

Reasoning is the ability to see how things do or do not fit together and then find the reasons why. Reasoning may also involve looking at past experiences and coming up with logical plans. It is difficult to improve your score on this part of an intelligence test.

There are other kinds of tests which can measure your aptitude for certain kinds of mental activities. Tests can show whether it would be easy or difficult to develop ability in special fields. These tests are used successfully to determine a person's ability to learn clerical skills, radio code, to play a musical instrument, etc.

Special Aptitude Tests Can Determine Your Potential for Success in Certain Careers

PHYSICAL APTITUDES AND ABILITIES

Some of the aptitudes measured by aptitude tests are more physical than mental. The General Aptitude Test Battery (GATB), developed by the United States Employment Service, measures 12 kinds of aptitudes, some mainly physical. Two of these are finger dexterity and manual dexterity. Your finger dexterity is how well you can use your fingers to move small articles rapidly and accurately. Manual dexterity is the ability to move your hands easily and skillfully. Finger and manual dexterity are necessary in many kinds of work. Assemblers, sewing machine operators, and welders must have at least good finger and manual dexterity.

You may have other physical abilities which are not so easily measured. Or, you may lack some physical ability which is necessary to succeed in certain kinds of work. We mentioned the girl who wanted to become a singer but whose voice wouldn't cooperate. Many boys would like to become professional baseball players, but they lack the natural talent to play the game well — even if they practiced for a hundred years! If you are considering a career which requires special talent, try to be realistic. A goal is worthwhile only if there is a possibility of reaching it. Each of us has shortcomings, but each of us has some strengths too. As you look toward the future and plan your career, do so with a positive attitude. Do the best you can with what you have, and you will find that you are a happier worker and a more satisfied human being than the person who had more talent but did little with it.

PERSONAL QUALITIES

Employers often look for job applicants with "pleasing personalities." For several years, I was in charge of the student employment office of a large high school on the West Coast. Employers regularly called me to discuss the kind of student workers they wished to hire. Their remarks went like this:

"Send me someone with a nice personality; he or she will be the first person my clients will see when they come into the office, and I want them to make a good impression."

"Send me a person with a clean-cut personality."

"I want a person who can type and who has a good personality."

After referring several students for each job vacancy, I would call the employer to see which student was hired and why the others were rejected. Their comments often were similar to these:

"I hired Ann because she has such a nice smile and a pleasing personality. She'll make a great first impression on my clients."

"Lorna was a whiz at typing, but she didn't have much personality."

"I hired Ruben because he had more personality than the others you sent."

Personality is the one most important thing which causes people to like you. What is this thing called personality? Webster defines it as "the complex of characteristics that distinguishes an individual." It is the combination of personal traits that make you different from every other person. It is the set of habits which you develop in reacting to people and situations. Because your personality is shown to others through these habits, it is not something you can put on and take off. It is always with you. It is through your personality that you show others what kind of a person you are. Earlier in this chapter, we discussed values — those things which are important to you. Your values are shown to others through your **personality traits**. These personality traits are generally considered to be among those which make up your personality:

1. Attitude
2. Courtesy
3. Dependability
4. Desire to succeed
5. Enthusiasm
6. Foresight
7. Friendliness
8. Health
9. Honesty
10. Initiative
11. Loyalty

12. Morality
13. Neatness
14. Open-mindedness
15. Personal appearance
16. Punctuality
17. Self-control
18. Sense of humor
19. Tact
20. Use of voice

The **value** which has the greatest effect upon your personality is shown in your **attitude toward other people.** The person whose list of values is topped by a real concern for and desire to be of help to other

Those Who Are Least Satisfied with Life May Be Too Pessimistic

people is the unselfish person. Unselfish persons accept every person as a worthy human being. **They care for people.** To them, people are the important things in the world. Selfish people do not really care about what happens to others. This is shown in their attitude toward others. We mentioned

earlier that most of the beginning workers who lose their jobs are those whose attitudes show little concern for others. They are uncooperative. Those who are most satisfied with life are those who have a positive attitude. They look for the good in others. They are **optimists.** Those who are least satisfied with life are **pessimists.** A pessimist can see all of another person's faults but none of his or her virtues. Pessimists can only see the bad things in life. No wonder they are usually unhappy.

In Chapter 8 we shall discuss ways in which you can improve your personality and become a more effective person in all of your relationships. To do that, you must take a rather complete inventory of your personality. You probably have a pretty good idea about what is meant by attitude, and you may have learned of some areas in which you will need improvement. We haven't said much about other personality traits.

COURTESY

The attitude you have toward other people is shown in how you behave in every situation. One of the most obvious ways it shows up is in how courteous you are. The people I have known who were most lacking in courtesy showed it to everyone with whom they talked. They were only interested in what they had to say. They interrupted another person at any time because they didn't care what anybody else had to say. Have you known people who wouldn't let you finish a sentence? If you have, you probably didn't tell them about it.

Courtesy means having two things — good manners and a true concern for the comfort of others. Do you say please and thank you? If you are late arriving at a friend's house, do you call so that he or she will not be expecting you momentarily? Thinking about and doing what you can to make others comfortable is worth more than gold in making others like you. Nothing so valuable costs so little as courtesy. It's free.

Some People Are ONLY Interested in What THEY Have to Say

DEPENDABILITY

A dependable person can be "counted on." The player on football teams who always blocks the opposition is dependable. Dependable people get the job done every time. Nobody else has to worry about it. People who always complete the work given them on the job are dependable. The person who sometimes does not complete work as assigned can't be counted upon and isn't worth much to an employer. Someone else must be ready to take over. If this happens very often, of course, the employee doesn't have a job at all.

DESIRE TO SUCCEED

Everyone wants to be happy and satisfied with life, and we have learned that satisfaction in life depends a great deal upon how satisfied you are in your work. If you are successful in an interesting job that is challenging to you, then you will gain a great amount of satisfaction from it. But becoming a success in your work doesn't just happen

to you, like waking up one morning with measles. In a recent survey, the most successful young men and women were asked, "What is the one most important thing that led to your success?" Their answers were very similar. It was **desire.** They simply wanted it more than those who were not so successful. You know that the members of a football or basketball team have to have a strong desire to do their best, to win. If you have watched them practice, you know how hard they work to succeed. Those who are the most successful on the field or court are those who want it the most. It's like that in your career too.

The Player on a Football Team Who Always Does the Job Is Dependable

ENTHUSIASM

The people who are enthusiastic about life are optimists. They are happy and excited about the good things that are happening to them. If their jobs are "right for them," they are especially enthusiastic about their work. Enthusiasm is a personality trait that makes it a pleasure to work with or be around people who have it.

FORESIGHT

Foresight means to look ahead, to plan

ahead. It means that you don't just let things happen to you. You plan things. When you apply for a job, you have thought about what questions may be asked of you — and you have the answers. During a job interview, you find out what the opportunities are for advancement. On a job, your employer may not remind you of the time when certain assignments must be completed. You must plan your work so that deadlines will be met. People with foresight are **alive.** They don't just let things happen, **they make things happen.** How well do you plan the use of your time and money? Are you broke before each payday? Do you plan the use of your time so that your school assignments are always completed on time?

You Must Plan Your Work to Meet Company Deadlines

FRIENDLINESS

If you find that most people are friendly toward you, you are probably friendly yourself. The person who is most liked has many friends because of a sincere interest in others. The friendly person has a nice smile and smiles often. To have more friends, give your friendship to more people.

HEALTH

Some people with poor health have been very successful because of their talent and desire to succeed. Many healthy people have not been successful because they lacked ability, desire, or certain personal qualities. However, other things being equal, good health is very important to success. When you feel good, your work is easier. It may even be fun. Healthy workers are more productive too, and employers often consider health when hiring new employees and giving promotions. Young people are often careless about their eating and sleeping habits. They punish their bodies by trying to get along on improper foods and too little sleep. They get by with it for awhile, but they don't know what their limit is until they have gone past it. Good health habits help you to feel, act, and look your best.

HONESTY

Whether you are an honest person or a dishonest person is your choice. You can be whichever you choose to be. Because of the peace of mind you will have and the trust others will have in you, it will be to your advantage to be an honest person. Wherever you work, there will be opportunities to be honest or to be dishonest. Your employer pays you for your time. Show that you are honest by your willingness to give a day's work for a day's pay. Do not fake sickness and stay away from work. This is not fair to your employer or to the other workers who must do at least part of your work. When you give your word for something, make it good. If you are given credit for something someone else did, place the credit where it is due. Do not steal time, money, supplies, or ideas. To do so will cause others to distrust you.

INITIATIVE

If you can see that things need to be done and do them, you have initiative. As a beginning worker, you will do your work exactly as your employer directs you. Your suggestions in the beginning would probably not be too well thought out and might make your employer think that you don't respect his experience. After you have been on the job for a while, you can begin to take a bit more initiative. After your assigned duties are completed, look around to see what else needs to be done. If you are sure that you can do this "extra work," do it. Start with small things. In this way, you will learn just how much initiative your boss likes you to take. If you do a really outstanding job on the little jobs in which you show initiative, your employer will probably allow you to take more and more responsibility. If you are able to handle these additional responsibilities well, you will probably be promoted.

LOYALTY

You are loyal to your company and to your employer if you think well and speak well of them. You will respect the men and women who run the company. You will be happy about company successes. To be loyal to your company also means that you will not tell those who do not work for the company about things which should be kept confidential. To do so might result in an advantage to another company and lower profits for your own company. If you are truly loyal to your work and the company for which you work, they become of great interest and importance in your life. If you find that you cannot be loyal to your employer and to the company for which you work, it is best to look for another job.

MORALITY

People are societal creatures. That is, they set up certain patterns of behavior which guides the lives of all men and women in their society. This is true everywhere, and it was true long before people learned to speak, read, and write. In our society, the ideals of honesty, fair play and justice are important. Therefore, if we are to be happy in this society, if we are to make a good adjustment to it, we must accept these moral principles. We may add other standards to our own moral code. These may or may not involve belief in a certain religious faith. Regardless of your feelings toward religion, the rule of doing for others as you would like them to do for you is a good one.

NEATNESS

If you are a neat person, it shows up in many ways. You are probably a neat dresser and always personally well-groomed. In addition, you will do the necessary house-cleaning to keep your work area tidied up. If you make out reports, they will be done neatly. If you are a typist, you will regularly clean the type on your machine; and when you erase, you will move the typewriter carriage all the way to one side so that the erasure crumbs will not fall into the machine. If you are not a neat person, this will show up in many ways too.

OPEN-MINDEDNESS

Open-mindedness means being able to see both sides of a question or argument.

If You Close Your Mind to New Approaches, Thoughts, or Information, You Cannot Be Better Than Your Present Beliefs or Knowledge

It means considering, carefully, what the other person has to say even when you don't agree. It is very much to your advantage to keep an open mind in all things. The moment you close your mind to something, you can no longer learn anything which is not in agreement with your belief. Thus, to close your mind prevents you from becoming a more intelligent person. Such people are sometimes referred to as being dogmatic and opinionated. They think that their beliefs and opinions are correct and will never change. Open-minded people freely allow others to question their beliefs and opinions. Open-minded people tend to be happy workers. They accept criticism of their work without feeling that their personal worth is being questioned. They take the criticism seriously and try to see how they can improve because of it. If they decide that criticism of their work is inaccurate, they are not hostile toward those who are making the criticism. The open-minded person **always** gives the other person the benefit of any doubt in a situation.

PERSONAL APPEARANCE

Your personal appearance was discussed in Chapter 3. Of course, it is just as important to keep your good appearance every day on the job as it is during an interview for a job. Wear clothes which are appropriate for the kind of work you are doing, and have them regularly cleaned or washed. Polish your shoes regularly. Personal cleanliness is important to your health and the impression you leave with other people.

PUNCTUALITY

Time is money. In an earlier chapter we said that if you went to a movie and paid the full price, you probably would be unhappy if the theatre projectionist switched off the projector before the movie was over. You would expect to see the full movie for the full price. Your employer also expects a full day's work for a full day's pay. If you get into the habit of arriving late to work, you are

cheating your employer, who will be unhappy with you about it. If you go to a movie and you get to see it all, but it starts twenty minutes late, you won't be quite so angry as if they switched off the projector. But you still wouldn't be very happy about their not starting on time. In some companies, if you are late to work, they will take the time out of your paycheck. Even so, your employer wouldn't be very happy about your being late. Just as it would be an inconvenience to you if the movie started late, it would be an inconvenience to your employer if you are late. Being punctual is more than simply arriving at work on time. It means **starting** work on time. If it takes you 15 minutes to get settled and begin work, you are still not being punctual. Punctuality is a habit. You are forming your habit of punctuality right now. Are you always on time to each class in school?

SELF-CONTROL

Self-control means how well you can control (1) your emotions and (2) your efforts. People who often lose their tempers have little control over their emotions. They would do well to try very hard to (A) see the other side of whatever makes them angry, giving the other person the benefit of the doubt, and (B) hold back their anger until they can let it off in a way that is not damaging to their relationship with another person. People who take out their anger by whacking a golf ball around the course will probably have more friends than the people who allow their anger to explode in the presence of others. Almost everyone wishes to accomplish something, to reach some kind of goal. But it takes work to do it. If the boss is looking over your shoulder, you will probably get the job done. But what if you are not supervised? Getting the job done when working on your own requires self control. Self-control, too, becomes a habit. If you have a great deal of self-control, you will be able to answer "yes" to most of these questions:

1.   Do I sit down and complete my school

assignments when I would rather watch a television program?

2. Do I set up a schedule of work and stick to it?
3. Do I avoid "telling off" another person who makes me angry?
4. Do I work well when tired?
5. Do I take criticism without becoming upset?
6. Am I patient with other people?

If you had several "no" answers, you had better spend some time thinking about the kind of person you would like to become.

SENSE OF HUMOR

If you can see the funny side of life, you have a sense of humor. Being able to enjoy the humorous makes life a lot easier and much more interesting. Having a good sense of humor is healthy both physically and mentally. The person whose thoughts are always serious ones will seldom laugh. Don't take life seriously **all the time.** Look for and enjoy the funny side of life, and learn to laugh even when the joke is on you.

TACT

Can you say the right thing at the right time? Can you handle situations so that no one becomes offended? If so, you are tactful. Being tactful does not require that you be dishonest. If a co-worker wears a dress which you do not like, you do not have to say that you like it. If you can see something about it that you like, mention that. You might like the color or texture of the material. Part of being tactful is knowing **how** and **when** to discuss things with your friends, your co-workers, and your boss. Try to sense the **feelings** of those around you. Once you discover what pleases them, what their moods are, and when they are happiest and most agreeable, you will find that they will be cooperative.

USE OF VOICE

Your voice and the way you speak are just as important as your personal appear-

ance in attracting or repelling others. Your voice and speech habits are very revealing. A person trained to do so can tell what kind of an attitude you have toward your family and friends, about how much education you have, how much self control you have over your emotions, and how mentally and physically healthy you are. Even so, you can control the use of your voice considerably. By practicing, you can develop the habit of speaking in the tonal range that

An Attractive Voice Will Go a Long Way Toward Developing a Satisfying Relationship with Others

is most pleasant. However, it must not sound artificial. A speaking voice which is attractive involves these qualities:

1. A medium to low tonal range.
2. Relaxed rather than tense.
3. Loud enough to be heard, but not booming. (A booming voice — too loud — will cause others to resist you.)
4. Clearly and properly enunciated words.

5. Correct pronunciation.
6. Variation in talking speed but not too fast nor too slow.
7. Inflections properly used. (What you say will be more interesting if you raise and lower the inflection to accent meanings.)

An attractive voice will go a long way in developing a satisfying relationship with others. When you speak on the telephone, your voice becomes even more important than in a face-to-face conversation. The person with whom you are speaking on the telephone cannot see you, and can only form an impression of you by listening to your voice. When your phone rings, answer it promptly. In business, the full cooperation of the other person often depends upon this. Usually, the name of the company or department is given first and then the name of the person answering. "Maddox Company, Miss Jones speaking." However, this varies; ask your employer how you should answer the phone. Speak clearly and di-rectly into the mouthpiece. Speak loud enough that the other person does not have to strain to hear you, but don't yell! Develop the habit of being courteous, **never interrupting** the other person.

The kind of work you choose to go into as your career will depend, in part, upon your personality; and the degree to which you are satisfied with life in general will depend a great deal upon your adjustment to your work. Recent surveys show that many people, as many as 90 percent in some occupations, are **not** satisfied with their work situation. Often it is because their work does not fit their personalities. While you **can** change your personality — and even improve it — you should also choose your work to suit your basic personality insofar as possible.

You now know what traits make up your personality. Rate your own personality according to the traits in the chart on page 95. Do not write in this book, but list these traits and your rating on a separate sheet of paper.

Personality Rating					
Trait	Excellent	Good	Fair	Poor	Very Poor
ATTITUDE					
COURTESY					
DEPENDABILITY					
DESIRE TO SUCCEED					
ENTHUSIASM					
FORESIGHT					
FRIENDLINESS					
HEALTH					
HONESTY					
INITIATIVE					
LOYALTY					
MORALITY					
NEATNESS					
OPEN-MINDEDNESS					
PERSONAL APPEARANCE					
PUNCTUALITY					
SELF CONTROL					
SENSE OF HUMOR					
TACT					
USE OF VOICE					

EDUCATION AND TRAINING ACCEPTABLE

If you have done some "dreaming" about your lifestyle goals, considered what is important to you (your values), pondered your general interests and career activity preferences, thought about your preferences for working with data, people, and things, and have taken an objective look at your overall personality, you have come a long way toward understanding yourself! You probably know whether you are willing to spend more years of education and training after graduation from high school. The amount of education and training you consider acceptable will limit or expand the number and kinds of careers which will be open to you.

OTHER INFLUENCES

There are other factors which affect you, but parental, teacher, and peer pressures; economic resources; marital status; and chance seem to have great influence upon making you the kind of person you are. In turn, they affect your selection of and success in your career.

PARENTAL, TEACHER, AND PEER PRESSURES

Your parents began influencing your life the day you were born. This is hardly open to question since most young people operate on their parents' set of values until they are well into their teens. A few, of course, rebel against their parents' values because of undersirable home-life experiences. Teachers who are understanding can influence young people, providing a sense of direction even when students' home environment is emotionally unhealthy.

Your peers (classmates), your teachers, and your parents have been influencing you each year. As you approach graduation, you may find that you are being influenced by the plans of your peers. Sometimes this is desirable, but too often it is not. Since each person is unique, your lifestyle goals, career goals, and educational plans should be your own, **based upon what is most appropriate for you.**

ECONOMIC RESOURCES

Whether you have the money to pursue continued education and training must be considered in the career development process earlier described as "implementing your self-concept." While there are cases in which it is simply not financially possible to continue your education, **it is usually possible if you want it badly enough.** In recent years the number of scholarships, grants, student loans, and on-campus jobs has increased greatly. This will be discussed further in Chapter 19.

MARITAL STATUS

If you are married now or have plans to be married soon, this will naturally affect your future greatly. Young married couples have many more responsibilities than their single friends. The young married person must have a somewhat different set of values, a different lifestyle, and a different self-concept. These differences affect the feasibility of certain career goals and educational plans.

CHANCE

At the beginning of this chapter you read that your self-concept is based mainly on how others react toward you. This allows the element of **chance** to partially determine the way you feel about yourself. All human relationships involve the element of chance! Sometimes you are lucky and find yourself in the right place at the right time. Sometimes you aren't so fortunate and a negative reaction from someone else may cause you to question your self-concept. Sometimes the reaction you receive from others is not accurate. Nevertheless, you may be influenced by it. You will explore the nature of human relationships and how to be more effective in your social and business relationships in Chapter 8.

STUDY AIDS

NEW TERMS

data	open-mindedness
economic resources	optimist
feasibility	personality
finger dexterity	pessimist
foresight	role expectations
manual dexterity	self-concept

STUDY QUESTIONS

1. What is your self-concept?
2. Why should career goals be kept flexible?
3. How can a career dictate a lifestyle?
4. Do you daydream about your future? How do you picture yourself ten years from now?
5. How do your **values** compare with those of your parents?
6. What values are most important to you?
7. What kind of career activities would you like to sample?
8. Would you prefer to work with data, people, or things?
9. What do you consider your strong apti-

tudes and abilities?

10. What do you consider your best personality traits?

11. Which of your personality traits need improvement, and how do you plan to improve them?

12. How long do you think you will be able to continue your education after you graduate from high school?

13. How much are you influenced by a) your parents, b) your teachers or counselor, and c) your friends?

14. Will you have enough money to continue your education so that you will be able to qualify for a career you will enjoy?

15. Do you have plans for marriage within two years after high school graduation?

DISCUSSION PROBLEMS

1. In what ways do you consider a person's self-concept important?

2. How are the role expectations of men and women changing?

3. What are some of your values (things important to you)? Why do you think they are important?

4. Why are your interests important in selecting a career?

5. Do you prefer working with data, people, things, or combinations of these? Why?

6. What do you consider your best abilities? What careers are related to these abilities?

7. What are some of the things that make up your personality?

CHAPTER SEVEN
RESEARCHING CAREERS

METHODS OF RESEARCHING

After you have learned to understand the many facets about yourself which relate to your career development, the next step toward reaching a realistic career decision is to **research careers**. Researching a career means carefully studying all of the relevant information about a variety of careers. This research, or investigation, of careers can be best accomplished by:

1. Carefully investigating all available information in the form of books, pamphlets, magazine articles, resource directories, and films.

2. Consulting directly with practitioners (workers) in careers which interest you.

3. Broadening your base of experience by actually working in one or several career fields which appeal to you as appropriate future careers.

REVIEW CURRENT LITERATURE

You will find that it is easier today to research careers than ever before, because there is so much more information available. You can conduct your investigation entirely on your own, or in libraries that have organized files of career information.

Career Information Centers. Many schools today have career information centers to assist students in locating information on hundreds, even thousands of careers. Although this is a relatively new trend, some well-equipped career information centers have information in the following forms:

It Is Easier to Research Careers Today Because There Is More Available Information

1. Career resource directories, such as the **Occupational Outlook Handbook** and the **Dictionary of Occupational Titles**.
2. Books which provide information on specific careers or career clusters.
3. Pamphlets and brochures which give information on specific careers.
4. Filmstrips and cassette tapes which provide a visual and sound presentation on specific careers or career clusters.
5. Motion pictures or video tapes which provide information on activities in specified careers.

Check to see whether your school has a career information center. If it does, use it! Interest and aptitude testing may also be available through the career information center.

Individual Research. If your school does not have a career information center, you can still research careers. The **Occupational Outlook Handbook** is probably available in your school library, counseling office, or career development office. Both your counselor and work experience coordinator will assist you in locating career information materials.

CAREER CONSULTATIONS

A **career consultation** is simply a meeting with someone who is successful in a field of work. Such meetings, or consultations, should take place in the job environment of your consultant. By taking part in a career consultation, you will have an opportunity to both observe the working environment and ask questions of the consultant about the work tasks performed and opportunities of a career in which you are interested. Career consultations provide up-to-date information on specific careers by those who are best qualified to give it — the successful worker in that career.

WORK EXPERIENCE

After you have researched careers by other methods and arrived at one, or perhaps several, tentative career choices, you may wish to do some **reality testing**. This is best done through actual **on-the-job work experience**.

Reality Testing Is Best Done Through Actual "On-the-Job" Work Experience

School-Sponsored Programs. Basically, there are three types of work experience programs: (1) exploratory, (2) vocational, and (3) general. As there are dozens of names for work experience programs, chances are that your school has such a program but calls it by another name. The purposes of these basic school-sponsored programs are:

Exploratory Work Experience Education

Exploratory work experience education is primarily a career guidance program. It provides opportunities to systematically sample conditions of work in a variety of career fields. This provides a basis, through observation and supervised participation, for an informed career choice. The student receives school credit on most programs.

Vocational Work Experience Education

Vocational work experience education provides specific career preparation. The employment is related to the career for which your school program is preparing you. Many such programs are called **cooperative programs** because a teacher-coordinator both teaches a vocational class and supervises students on their jobs. Employers of students in this program pay at least the minimum wage, and the school usually grants credit for time spent on the job.

General Work Experience Education

General work experience education provides maturing experiences for young people through school-supervised part-time employment as a part of the total school program. The goal of this program is to develop desirable attitudes and promote understanding of the relationship between formal education and job success. This part-time work need not be related to your specific career goal. Employers pay at least the minimum wage, and school credit is awarded students who successfully complete the program.

Work Experience On Your Own. If there is not a work experience program available at your school, or if you are not enrolled in it, you can still gain valuable experience and test the reality of the world of work by getting a part-time job which is related to your tentative career goal.

RELEVANT DATA

We have discussed several methods of researching careers, but we have not talked much about the **kind** of information you should seek. The most relevant information includes the following:

1. Value priorities of the career.
2. Job activities of workers in the career.
3. Need for relationships with data, people, and things.
4. Aptitudes and abilities needed.
5. Personal qualities required.
6. Educational and training requirements.
7. Salaries and fringe benefits of the career.

VALUE PRIORITIES

Some careers, by their very nature, require that those who enter them hold certain values. For example, the pastor of a church would surely place religion high on a list of personal values. The artist would rank aesthetic appreciation and creativity very high.

In Chapter 6, you considered your own values. By studying the demands of any career you will be able to determine whether they are compatible with your own set of values.

CAREER ACTIVITIES

In your research of current literature, career consultations, and work experience, you will be able to determine whether the actual duties which must be performed in each career are enjoyable, tolerable, or maybe even boring. It is **vital** that you enjoy what you do, since you will be spending a large portion of your life carrying out the activities necessary to the purpose of your career.

DATA — PEOPLE — THINGS RELATIONSHIPS

You will be able to get a good idea of whether a career requires primary relationships with data, people, things, or combinations of these through the use of the research methods described at the beginning of this chapter. Of particular assistance in discovering the kinds of relationships which normally exist in each occupation is Volume 2 of the **Dictionary of Occupational Titles** (DOT). Pages 649 and 650 provide a complete explanation of how worker relationships with data, people, and things for any occupation can be interpreted from the last three digits of the DOT numbers.

Actual work experience in any given career, of course, provides real life situations in which you can experience these relationships.

APTITUDES AND ABILITIES

In Chapter 6, we discussed aptitudes and abilities as they relate to you as an individual. Each career has need for individuals with special combinations of abilities — or aptitudes which make it possible to develop useful skills. If you took inventory of your abilities and identified your aptitudes in the previous chapter on understanding yourself, you can see how you "measure up" to the career demands by researching the literature on careers which interest you, consulting with those who are successful in these careers, and trying out your skills and ability to learn through on-the-job work experience.

PERSONAL QUALITIES REQUIREMENTS

Success on most jobs depends more on human relationships than anything else. Your success in human relationships, in turn, depends primarily on your personal qualities. You assessed your own personal qualities in Chapter 6. The best way to research the personal qualities requirements of any career is to talk with those successful in the field and get some first-hand work experience.

EDUCATION AND TRAINING REQUIREMENTS

There are two kinds of educational requirements. The first is called **entry level** which simply means the minimum amount of

education necessary to begin work in any career or on any job. The second kind of educational requirement determines, in part, whether and how far you will be able to advance in your selected career. In Chapter 6, you considered how long you are willing to continue your education and training. By researching the education and training requirements of the careers which interest you, you will be in a better position to make an appropriate career choice. This information is available in the **Occupational Outlook Handbook** and through consultation with those who are presently succeeding in their chosen careers.

There Is a Difference between Entry Level Requirements and Requirements for Advancement

SALARIES AND FRINGE BENEFITS

Naturally, you will be interested in the amount workers are paid and what other benefits are available if you should select certain careers. This is a very important consideration, one that is too often overlooked by young people who have not yet had to provide the financial support for a family. You will need to keep your lifestyle goals in mind as you research the salaries and benefits of each career. Your best information on salaries and fringe benefits will probably be the **Occupational Outlook Handbook,** the **Occupational Outlook Quarterly,** and consultations with local practitioners.

YOUR CAREER DECISION

After you have had an opportunity to study yourself as outlined in Chapter 6 so that you do indeed understand yourself — and have done an in-depth study of those careers which seemed as if they **could be** appropriate for you, you are ready to make a tentative career choice. This means a choice that you may later change, but for now it looks like it is right for you. Maybe you won't be able to narrow it down to only one career. You may find that there are two or three possible careers that all seem to be equally appealing.

As you compare your needs with what you have learned while researching careers, remember that your career fulfills three kinds of needs: (1) economic, (2) social, and (3) psychological. Keep in mind that more than anything else, your career determines your lifestyle.

In comparing your needs with career demands and opportunities, consider how well each possible career would match the "real you" in these areas.

1. Would this career be in keeping with my set of values?
2. Would the actual on-the-job work activities of this career be interesting and enjoyable?
3. Would this career satisfy my preference for working with data, people, or things?
4. Do I have the skills or aptitudes to learn the skills which would assure my success in this career?
5. Do my personal qualities match those necessary for successful relationships with others in this career?
6. Am I willing to delay full-time employment until I can complete the education and training necessary for success in this career?

7. Is there anything about this career which would make it a poor choice considering the other influences upon my life (parents, friends, available finances, marital status, etc.)?

YOUR PLAN TO REACH YOUR GOAL

Your career development is a long process. It began sometime during your preschool years as you observed others in productive work situations in the home, through the medium of television or motion pictures, and outside the home as you accompanied your parents. It will continue throughout your lifetime. The average person in America changes careers five times during his or her lifetime. Those who plan well to begin with don't change so often. They waste less time working toward the wrong goals.

Too many people spend less time seriously planning their lives (including their career development) than they do planning a summer vacation! If you have carefully followed the guidance provided for your benefit in Chapters 6 and 7, you will surely have **some idea** of what one, two, or several career goals would be appropriate for you. The next step is to begin planning how you can reach your goal. This will involve further research into the **specific** education and training you plan (discussed in Chapter 19); how to locate vacancies; and how to apply for and make progress in the career of your choice.

STUDY AIDS

NEW TERMS

career consultation   practitioner
entry level   relevant data
environment   researching

STUDY QUESTIONS

1. What is meant by researching careers?
2. What is a career information center?
3. What is available in a career information center?
4. If your school does not have a career

information center, where can you find information on careers?

5. What is the best way to do reality testing?

6. What are some benefits of exploratory work experience?

7. What is the importance of value priorities in selecting a career?

8. If you have made a career decision, what is it? If not, what information do you need in order to make your career decision?

DISCUSSION PROBLEMS

1. What are some methods of researching careers?

2. How would you go about arranging for a career consultation?

3. What value do you see in on-the-job work experience?

4. What are some of the relevant data in researching careers?

5. Why is it important to have a plan to reach your career goal?

CHAPTER EIGHT
HUMAN RELATIONSHIPS

The words **human relationships** simply mean how you get along with others. We have already discussed the fact that your success in your career — indeed much of your satisfaction with life — will be determined chiefly by **how you get along with other people**.

We mentioned earlier that most people simply drift into an occupation by accident. We said that those who plan ahead and **choose their work** are often more satisfied with their work and happier with their lifestyles than those who do not plan this important part of their lives. The ability to make things happen is important both in your social life and in your career. This ability is called **personal effectiveness**. How effective you are in making things happen depends largely upon the degree to which you can get others to see things your way — to **influence** them. This, in turn, depends upon your personality — how others know you, and how well you are able to understand others.

UNDERSTANDING OTHERS

Everything a person does is done for a reason. Many times a person doesn't even know the reason for his or her own behavior. To understand others, and thus be more effective in our human relationships, we must know something about why others behave as they do. First of all, we must recognize that every human being is unique, different from every other. Of course, we cannot make a complete, in-depth study of every person with whom we have a social or career relationship. There are, however, certain things that we can say that are generally true about most human beings that help us understand their behavior in many situations. There are also ways of "reading" others which help us understand their behavior. Certain clues to personality traits can often provide an insight into what a person thinks about you or an idea or product on which you would like approval.

BEHAVIORAL MOTIVES

Everything we do is done because **we want something**. As small children, we are all self-centered human beings. Our own wants are all that matter. By the time we are three or four, we normally have had enough "give-and-take" human relationships with others our own age that we begin to learn something about sharing. In elementary school the idea of sharing is emphasized as a means of developing good human relationships. One definition of maturity is how far we have progressed from the self-centered nature that was our entire world as young children. We all have needs and wants that we consider more important than the needs and wants of anybody else. Sometimes, however, these needs and wants are disguised and difficult to identify.

Some People Define Maturity in Terms of How Far an Individual Has Progressed Emotionally Since Childhood

The most successful people in our society are those that have learned that human beings do not behave on the basis of what is logical. It is a fact that people generally react to others based on their emotions. Why do we react to others on the basis of our emotions in the face of factual information which would logically lead us to behave differently? We do so primarily because of a basic need in all human beings to feel important. If our need to feel important is satisfied, **then** we are free to behave logically. If not, then we are insecure and will react to others based upon how important they make us feel. If you are honest with yourself, you will admit that you feel insecure in some ways. There are some ways in which you are not entirely satisfied with yourself. The teen years cover the time in our lives when we all have feelings of insecurity. This is because we are still trying to determine our own identity, a time when we are especially conscious of human relationships. Take some comfort in knowing that **everyone** has these feelings. This, in itself, should help you to feel more secure.

READING OTHERS

There are times when it is important to convince others to see things your way. This ability is especially important to company executives and to sales personnel whose success may depend on their ability to make others agree to their suggestions. Can you usually get others to do things your way, when yours is a good way? If you wish to influence someone to accept your way of thinking, it is first necessary to understand how that person thinks and to make use of certain psychological advantages. In this way you will be able to approach people in the manner which will most likely cause them to go along with your wishes.

Since each person is different, the right approach with one may be the worst possible approach with someone else. Learn all you can about the person you wish to influence. Consider each of the personality traits discussed in Chapter 6 — they are important to your understanding of others. Be careful, though, not to condemn someone because you see many personality faults. The idea is simply to **understand** the person. You should consider hobbies and leisure-time activities in trying to understand other people. A person's range of interests often gives clues to his or her values.

Additional ways of sizing up a person include observations about his or her physical motions and habits. The expression of inner emotions by a visible physical action is known as **body language**. For example, a girl who walks with her shoulders slouched, her head down, and her eyes to the ground would convey a dejected image. A girl who is sauntering, shoulders back, head up, with her arms swinging freely conveys a carefree, happy image. In the same way, when people "fidget" in their chairs, their actions are often interpreted as dissatisfaction or boredom.

Facial expressions often indicate a person's emotions or feelings on a subject — eyes opened wide can usually be interpreted to mean surprise. When a person has

The Driving Habits of Some People May Tell You a Great Deal About Their Personalities

"pursed" lips, you can usually interpret this as disapproval.

By observing people's habits, you learn certain characteristics about others. While we need to learn more about a person before making judgment, these first impressions are also important.

INFLUENCING OTHERS

We have discussed the importance of understanding other people if you hope to convince them to see things your way. Now you are ready for the "recipe" for influencing others. It is not guaranteed to work **every time**, because we are dealing with human beings, and each one is different from every other. However, if you are sincere in your approach, you will find that your relationships with others will be rewarding in every facet of your lifestyle.

SHOW GENUINE INTEREST

Most people can spot a "phony" a mile away. The only way to influence other human beings is to be **sincerely** interested in them and in what interests them. Dale Carnegie wrote a book in 1936 which has been reprinted nearly a hundred times and sold nearly ten million copies. It is called **How to Win Friends and Influence People**. Dr. Carnegie learned the techniques of getting other human beings to react the way **he wanted** them to. Dr. Carnegie states that "you can make more friends in two months by becoming interested in other people than you can in two years by trying to get other people interested in you." But remember, your interest must be genuine!

SMILE

The lyrics of an old song were, "When you're smiling, the whole world smiles with you." The writer of that song must have known something about human relationships. It's true that others react to you more favorably if you smile than if you don't. In fact, the expression on your face says more than the clothes you wear — and a smile is a lot less expensive than a new wardrobe! When you smile at a person, you are saying, "I like you." A smile brings forth a desirable emotional response and smoothes the way if you are trying to influence another person to see or do something your way. Thus, a pleasant smile is one of the most valuable assets one can possess.

MAKE THE OTHER PERSON FEEL IMPORTANT

In Chapter 1, we discussed Dr. Maslow's list of basic human needs. You may recall

Other People React to You More Favorably When You Smile

that the list began with the most basic needs for maintaining life — food and water. The next levels of human needs included shelter and safety, companionship and affection, and self-esteem. Most people have all of these needs met except the last, self-esteem. Self-esteem means achieving **status** among others. This is the **desire to be important**. Think about your own feelings. When someone says something that makes you feel important, you have a warm feeling toward that person. Think about your friends; they would far rather talk about their own achievements than yours!

Since human beings react on the basis of their emotions, you can readily see that it is to your advantage to create a warm feeling toward you in those you wish to influence. One way of creating a feeling of warmth toward you is to know and to use the other person's name correctly. Someone said that "the sweetest sound in all the world is the sound of one's own name." Take advantage of this knowledge and use the other person's name in your conversations.

Everyone likes to feel important. Indeed, **needs** to feel important. A feeling of importance is created in other people when you give them your attention. You can make

people love you, do almost anything for you, by giving them your attention and making them feel important. It is such a basic need that some people take extreme, unusual action to gain the attention of others. An example of this is the hypochondriac who places great emphasis on imaginary illnesses in order to gain attention, a feeling of importance, and sympathy.

Some People Take Extreme and Unusual Actions to Gain the Attention of Others

BE SYMPATHETIC

Causing others to react to you in your human relationships as you would like them to do does **not** mean that you must be a fast, convincing talker. **Listening** is more important in achieving your goal than talking! Listen to the other person's problems and be sympathetic. Respect the other person's point of view, even if you don't agree with it. While you can never **really** see things through the eyes of the other person, it is essential to try to see things from his or her point of view. Unless you can do this, how can you possibly be sympathetic to someone else's interests? Henry Ford, who founded the Ford Motor Company and fathered "mass production," was asked the secret of his success. His answer:

"If there is any one secret of success, it lies in the ability to get the other person's point of view and see things from his angle as well as your own."

GIVE AWAY CREDIT FOR YOUR IDEAS

Sometimes it is better to give up some of the things which make **you** feel important in order to achieve your goal in human relationships. Let's say you have an idea. It is an idea which you believe is a new and better way to do something at your place of work. If you try to promote a new procedure as your own idea you may be successful and you may not. Remember, your supervisor or boss is another human being with needs for attention and a feeling of importance. If your supervisor has a secure feeling (self-esteem), he or she will perhaps assist you in implementing your idea. However, if your supervisor has **not** received an adequate portion of attention and feeling of importance to have reached a high level of self-esteem, you will be more likely to achieve your purpose by manipulating things so that he or she can **discover** the need for and answer to the **new way**. It is your decision. You can work for months, even years, trying to get something done which is your own idea; but if you give away your idea — or the credit for it — it may be achieved almost immediately. And you will have gained a friend by providing a feeling of importance for another human being.

AVOID ARGUMENTS

Have you ever tried to convince someone to see things your way by engaging in an argument? Chances are that if the other person did finally agree with you, he or she

wasn't **really** convinced. Not only that, to some extent, you alienated that human being, and it will surely be more difficult to deal harmoniously with that person in the future.

Janet Sylvester sells recording equipment for one of the largest producers in the world. She is a very successful salesperson and **never** gets trapped into an argument. One day she walked into an insurance firm in Southern California where she hoped to sell a complete system of recording equipment for dictation and transcription. As she walked into the office of the vice-president to make her sales presentation, she was greeted with, "Oh yes, I should have canceled our appointment. I've decided to purchase the system from the Brand X Corporation."

It was obvious that the company vice-president was expecting an argument or at least some negative comment about the other firm's recording equipment. Janet simply remarked, "Brand X is an excellent product. I am sure you will be happy with it." The vice-president didn't know what to say. No argument here! Janet, who has an attractive smile, showed a genuine interest in the welfare of the insurance firm and complimented the vice-president on the leadership of its executives. Within twenty minutes the vice president **asked** for a demonstration of her dictating and transcribing equipment. The sale was made the same day!

If you have observed people who argue frequently, you may have noticed that neither person is really the winner. The more they argue, the less likely they will be able to work well together. **The only way to win in an argument is to avoid it.**

ALLOW "FACE SAVING"

When people are wrong about something and know it, the result is a temporary loss of self-esteem. If not pushed, they may admit their error, even take pride in doing so. However, it won't happen if someone is trying to force them. To make reference to the error, to say how wrong they were, or to say, "I told you so" is an excellent way to alienate people. This sort of "backing another into a corner" is cruel and will cause the other person to fight you at every opportunity. It **never** pays to talk about others' mistakes. Let them "save face." Ignore the situation and talk about something else, and you will keep a friend.

ADMIT YOUR OWN ERRORS

Just as it is to your advantage **not** to point out the errors of others, you will gain the respect and confidence of others by admitting your own errors. In the long run, there is absolutely no advantage in being defensive about being wrong. There is something noble in quickly admitting when you are wrong. When you admit a mistake, the other person has no emotional need to **prove** you wrong. In fact, you will often gain sympathy from the other people, which, in turn, makes it easier to get them to take whatever action you desire.

PRAISE LAVISHLY BUT SINCERELY

If you wish to influence others, to cause some change in their behavior, do not begin with criticism. Such an approach naturally places most people in a defensive frame of mind. Instead, begin by looking for the things you **sincerely** feel are worthy of praise.

Everyone is affected by praise, but it must be sincere.

ACCENTUATE THE POSITIVE

Have you ever listened to a chronic complainer — someone who has nothing good to say about the world or the people in it but can go on for hours talking about the bad things? Such a person has a **negative attitude** toward life. (Negative and positive attitudes were discussed in Chapter 4.) Can you imagine a person with a negative outlook on life putting **you** into a receptive mood? Happy people are more receptive to suggestions for change. Therefore, if you want

to change someone's behavior — influence him or her to act as you would like — then it is to your advantage to place that person in a happy mood. An effective way of doing this is to always emphasize the good things about the world and the people in it.

Let us analyze different ways to accentuate a message and the ways it influences you.

Example 1

"Hello! You don't want to buy this broom, do you?

Example 2

"Hello! I would like to interest you in the unique features of this broom."

Example 3

"Hello! I have two unique brooms. Broom A is designed for heavy-duty work. Broom B is designed for sweeping small particles such as sugar, sand, etc. Which broom would best meet your needs?"

Notice that Example 1 makes it easy for you to say no. Example 2 invites you to listen, and your answer could be yes or no. Example 3 does not ask for a yes or no, but it **accentuates** a choice between Broom A and Broom B. Watch out, because you might purchase a broom, since the sales person in Example 3 **accentuated the positive**.

CATCH THE MOOD

Another important factor in influencing others is catching the person in the right mood. People are much more likely to agree to whatever ideas you present if they are in a good mood. How can you tell when people are in a good mood? You can tell by their answers to a greeting. Listen to their voices. When you say, "Good morning. How are you?" their reply will likely be something like, "Fine, thank you." If the "Fine, thank you" is said with a rising inflection, the person is probably in a good mood. If it is said with a lowering of pitch, the person is probably **not** in a good mood — and it may be wise to wait until later to discuss an important issue.

Executives and top sales personnel know that the best time to talk anybody into anything is during a good meal. We are more susceptible to influence from others while eating something we especially like. But this period lasts only a short time; it starts with the first bite and ends shortly after it has all been eaten. If you wish to persuade someone to see things your way, it may be worth the price of a steak!

IMPROVING YOUR EFFECTIVENESS

No one is as effective in human relationships as he or she **can** be. There is always room for improvement. Most people, though, simply don't make the effort to improve their effectiveness in human relationships. If you are interested, you can increase your effectiveness and learn how to make things happen instead of just letting things happen to you. In the beginning of this chapter you learned some things about understanding others — why they behave as they do and how to "read" them. Now, review the eleven ways we discussed which will help you to influence others to do things **your way**:

1. Show genuine interest.
2. Smile.
3. Make the other person feel important.
4. Be sympathetic.
5. Give away credit for your ideas.
6. Avoid arguments.
7. Allow "face saving."
8. Admit your own errors.
9. Praise lavishly but sincerely.
10. Accentuate the positive.
11. Catch the mood.

PERSONALITY IMPROVEMENT

None of us is perfect, and none can expect to develop a perfect personality. Yet, each of us **can improve**. Many schools are now teaching classes in personal improvement and personality development. Correcting those things that irritate others and improving your personality are possible, but these things are not easy. Your personality has been developing since you were born. The reason you act the way you do in a given situation may be partly due to your

relationship with other people before you entered school. Habits which were formed years ago are difficult to break, but it is easier to change them this year than it will be next year or five years from now. If you feel that improving your personality is really important to you, it can be done. The procedure outlined here can help you:

(1) **Find out what your shortcomings are, and admit them.** On page 95 you were asked to rate yourself on 20 personality traits. If you were honest, you probably found some traits which can stand some improvement. If you are not satisfied that you really know enough about your personality to begin a meaningful plan of improvement, ask your school counselor to give you a personality inventory.

(2) **Decide on one habit or trait for improvement.** If you try to improve on many traits at once, you will not be able to follow through on any of them. By concentrating all your effort on just one trait, you will develop new — and more satisfying — ways of thinking and behaving.

(3) **Develop a plan for improvement.** Make a plan and stick to it, without exception! If you wish to correct an undesirable habit, such as biting your fingernails, try to develop a habit which is opposite. Begin taking pride in how your fingernails look — or how they are going to look. Then, to use up the nervous energy formerly expended in biting your nails, try some new activity which is more acceptable — perhaps doodling.

(4) **Check your progress.** Check yourself regularly and often at first. If the trait you wish to improve is something that gives you opportunity for improvement every day, check yourself every day. After you have followed a plan for improvement for several weeks, you may find that you have indeed made progress; but keep checking yourself for weeks or even months so that you will not slip back into the old ways! If you feel that friends will be honest in their judgment, it is a good idea to ask them how they think you are progressing.

(5) **When you feel that improvement is**

permanent, begin working on another trait or habit.

"You **can** improve your personality, but you must want very much to do so. If it is not really important to you, if you don't have a **good reason** to improve, then you will probably go right on being your old self. Some good reasons to improve your personality might be to become more popular, to be happier and have more satisfying relationships with others, or to become a better salesperson. It can be done **if you want it**. One final word about personality improvement. Psychologists tell us that, in general, doing things **with** and **for others** tends to improve our personalities.

STUDY AIDS

NEW TERMS

human relationships	personal
influence	effectiveness
body language	receptive
insecure	self-centered
	sympathetic

STUDY QUESTIONS

1. Why might you wish to **influence** another person in your work situation?
2. Do you think that most people have feelings of insecurity?
3. What are some of the ways which help you size up a person?
4. What are the eleven ways which can help you influence others?
5. How can you go about improving your personality so that you can become personally more **effective**?

DISCUSSION PROBLEMS

1. Why are human relationships important to your career?
2. What is the importance of the ability to "make things happen?"
3. Why do most people react, at least in part, based upon their emotions?
4. What do you consider the most important factors in influencing others?

CHAPTER NINE
PERSONAL SAFETY

THE IMPORTANCE OF SAFETY

The technical society of the twentieth century demands that particular attention be given to safety. The speed of travel, the powerful machines we use in our work, the complexity of industrial life, and the recreational activities we enjoy require special safety instructions and individual awareness for everyone.

Have you ever thought about the possibility of your living to age seventy without a disabling accident? The probability of anyone's living to age seventy without an accident is quite low. In 1972, over three times as many more disabling accidents occurred than the number of births in the United States. We are grimly reminded of accidents when we walk down the street and see people who have been handicapped by accidents. The skilled people in the medical profession are able to restore many of the accident victims to good health, but many others are partially or permanently disabled for life.

In 1972, more than eleven million disabling injuries and 117,000 deaths due to accidents were reported.[1] These figures do not include painful injuries which did not result in personal activity restriction.

Accidental death rates per 100,000 population have been reduced from 85.9 to 56.2 since 1912.[2] However, the total of 117,000 accidental deaths is much too high for 1972, the most recent year on which statistics are available. With regulations, controls, education, and most important — individual awareness, the number of accidents can be reduced. An example is the record of scheduled, domestic commercial air transport planes, which had no passenger fatalities in 1970.[3] This was an amazing feat, for millions of persons traveled billions of miles at high altitudes and speeds, all with no accidental death of a passenger. It is a good example of safety awareness on the part of employees of the commercial aviation industry. Safety starts with each individual, and safety awareness is important to you and to those around you.

THE HISTORY OF ACCIDENT PREVENTION

Much progress has been made in industrial accident prevention in the twentieth century. Improvement has been achieved through education and a gradual change in the philosophy of responsibility for accident

[1]National Safety Council, **Accident Facts 1973**, p. 3.

[2]National Safety Council, **Accident Facts 1973**, p. 14.
[3]**Ibid.**, p. 75.

Leading causes of all deaths

	No. of Deaths	Death Rate*
All Ages	1,921,990	954
Heart disease	739,265	367
Cancer	323,092	160
Stroke**	207,179	103
Accidents	**116,385**	**58**
Motor-vehicle	55,791	28
Falls	17,827	9
Drowning	7,699	4
Fires, burns	7,163	4
Other	27,905	13
Under 1 Year	75,073	2,206
Anoxia	19,315	568
Congenital anomalies	11,309	332
Immaturity	8,946	263
Pneumonia	7,015	206
Complications of pregnancy, childbirth	5,320	156
Conditions of placenta	2,520	74
Accidents	**2,425**	**71**
Ingestion of food, object	768	23
Mech. suffocation	620	18
Motor-vehicle	370	11
Fires, burns	182	5
Other	485	14
1 to 4 Years	12,290	88
Accidents	**4,548**	**33**
Motor-vehicle	1,707	12
Fires, burns	830	6
Drowning	730†	5
Poison (solid, liquid)	211	2
Other	1,070	8
Congenital anomalies	1,428	10
Pneumonia	1,134	8
5 to 14 Years	17,431	43
Accidents	**8,186**	**20**
Motor-vehicle	4,045	10
Drowning	1,560†	4
Fires, burns	655	1
Other	1,926	5
Cancer	2,524	6
Congenital anomalies	1,021	2
15 to 24 Years	44,422	129
Accidents	**24,668**	**72**
Motor-vehicle	17,443	51
Drowning	2,190†	6
Firearms	777	2
Poison (solid, liquid)	676	2
Other	3,582	11
Homicide	3,779	11
Suicide	2,731	8
Cancer	2,730	8

	No. of Deaths	Death Rate*
25 to 44 Years	113,434	238
Accidents	**24,410**	**51**
Motor-vehicle	13,868	29
Drowning	1,540†	3
Falls	1,162	3
Fires, burns	1,055	2
Other	6,785	14
Heart disease	18,907	40
Cancer	18,352	39
45 to 64 Years	474,128	1,145
Heart disease	177,687	429
Cancer	117,842	284
Stroke**	30,936	75
Accidents	**24,192**	**58**
Motor-vehicle	11,012	27
Falls	2,907	7
Fires, burns	1,953	4
Drowning	1,130†	3
Other	7,190	17
Cirrhosis of liver	17,138	41
Pneumonia	9,987	24
65 to 74 Years	446,864	3,636
Heart disease	195,383	1,590
Cancer	91,971	748
Stroke**	48,591	395
Diabetes mellitus	11,564	94
Pneumonia	10,814	88
Accidents	**10,643**	**87**
Motor-vehicle	4,210	34
Falls	2,635	22
Fires, burns	898	7
Surg. complications	615	5
Other	2,285	19
Emphysema	8,496	69
Cirrhosis of liver	4,891	40
75 Years and over	738,348	9,892
Heart disease	345,261	4,626
Stroke**	121,636	1,630
Cancer	88,448	1,185
Pneumonia	29,146	390
Arteriosclerosis	26,750	358
Accidents	**17,313**	**232**
Falls	10,225	137
Motor-vehicle	3,136	42
Fires, burns	1,194	16
Surg. complications	681	9
Ingestion of food, object	538	7
Other	1,539	21
Diabetes mellitus	14,963	200
Emphysema	7,330	98

Source: Deaths are for 1969, latest official figures from National Center for Health Statistics, Health Services and Mental Health Administration, U.S. Department of Health, Education and Welfare.

*Deaths per 100,000 population in each age group. Rates are averages for age groups not individual ages.

**Cerebrovascular disease.

†Partly estimated.

prevention. The industrial worker in the nineteenth century faced many hazards — especially in railroads, steel mills, and mines — that have been reduced today. The passage of employers' liability laws and mandatory insurance coverage of workers made it necessary for industrial management to reduce accidents of workers. Many mechanical safeguards were installed to reduce hazards, and safety education programs were initiated, especially by the larger industries. The National Safety Council (a nongovernmental, privately supported public service organization) has contributed sixty years of service providing safety education and leadership in accident prevention. The Council was chartered in 1912 by an act of Congress and has rendered continuous service since that date. One of its important contributions is the publication each year of **Accident Facts,** which contains a detailed analysis of accident statistics.

Many other organizations are active participants in providing vital statistics on accidents and related areas of health. These organizations include a number of federal agencies which publish reports each year. The U. S. Bureau of the Census; National Center for Health Statistics; Federal Aviation Agency; National Transportation Safety Board; Bureau of Mines; Bureau of Labor Statistics; Federal Highway Administration; and the Department of Health, Education and Welfare are some of the important contributors.

Many private organizations also cooperate in supplying accident information. The insurance companies are especially interested in maintaining statistical information and are helpful in promoting safety. A number of private social welfare organizations assist in accident prevention and provide rehabilitation for those who are injured.

Many local and state agencies cooperate by making statistics available to national agencies. These include schools and public safety agencies.

Laws have been passed on the local, state, and national levels to enforce safety regulations and prohibit unsafe acts. The latest law on the national level is the Williams-Steiger Occupational Safety and Health Act of 1970. It is referred to as OSHA, and it requires all employers covered under the regulations to keep up-to-date records and have these records available for inspection by government representatives when requested. A summary of all recorded cases is to be posted at the end of the year.

CAUSES OF ACCIDENTS

The causes of accidents have been researched for many years, but unanswered questions still remain. Accident prevention programs have been very successful when the causes are known and can be controlled. However, in many areas of prevention, the reasons are not fully understood, so positive controls cannot be applied.

Most Accidents Are Caused By Unsafe Behavior

Persons working in accident prevention research generally divide accident causes into two groups. The first can be identified as **human failure** or unsafe behavior by individuals. The second cause can be identified as **unsafe environment.** Much greater success in accident prevention can be achieved by making the work area or environment safe.

It is estimated that most accidents are caused by unsafe behavior. Therefore, it is important that we develop a better safety awareness. It is possible to discipline ourselves and help others develop better habits and attitudes by studying accidents in which the cause was definitely the result of unsafe behavior.

As a cause of accidents, unsafe behavior can also be divided into several categories. This division makes unsafe behavior easier for study. A number of the categories overlap, so several human failures may be involved in unsafe behavior which result in a single accident. The categories include the following: (1) attitudes of the individual, (2) lack of knowledge of the individual, (3) physical limitations of the individual, and (4) lack of skill on the part of the individual. By studying an accident, one can identify the cause of the accident within one or more of the above four categories.

Perhaps the least understood and most difficult to accomplish is the development of positive attitudes toward safety. Many motor vehicle accidents can be attributed to poor safety attitudes of the driver. Although much research has been conducted to determine the human element in the cause of automobile accidents, it is not possible to accurately identify persons prone to accidents. A number of events must happen at the same time to set up an accident situation. There is general agreement that a positive relationship exists between people's personal adjustment to society and their attitude toward safety. Some individuals are willing to take chances, while others act cautiously. Poor judgment is often cited as a cause of accidents, and

poor judgment may be related to the driver's temporary emotional state.

LACK OF KNOWLEDGE

The individual's lack of knowledge is responsible for accidents, because the lack

Many Automobile Accidents Are Caused by Careless Driving Habits

Many Fires and Injuries Occur When People Do Not Realize the Danger Involved in Using Flammable Liquids

of knowledge on the job, at home, or on the road can be dangerous to persons and property. Today many people are required to use many complicated pieces of equipment that they may not fully understand. Many fires are caused in homes and industry by the use of electrical fuses with too high an amperage rating; many fires and injuries occur when people do not realize the danger involved in using flammable liquids close to open flames. These are only two of many examples.

PHYSICAL LIMITATIONS

Physical limitations are closely related to lack of skill. However, there is enough difference to separate the two in terms of accident causes. Drowning ranks second as a cause of accidental death for persons in the 5-45 age range. No doubt many people are drowning victims because they lack the strength to swim to safety. Many other types of accidents may also be attributed to physical limitations. The lack of vision or the lack of hearing are serious causes of accidents for older people. Many are injured in industry because of physical limitations in lifting objects. It is very important to know your physical limitation at work and at play.

LACK OF SKILL

Probably the lack of skill as the contributing cause of accidents appears more in emergency situations. Emergencies on the job or on the road can become an accident unless the person is trained to cope with the situation. For example, a tire blowing out at a high rate of speed may cause an unskilled operator to lose control. Because they lack skill, many people have serious falls when skiing. Airplane pilots have crashed during the landing procedure due to lack of skill in handling the airplane when a sudden change in wind direction and velocity occurred. Young persons riding bicycles often lack skill and must be given more traffic attention than experienced riders. Since it can be developed, everyone should develop as much

Lack of Skill Can Cause Serious Accidents

skill as possible in driving a car on in a work situation.

UNSAFE ENVIRONMENT

Accidents are more likely to occur in an unsafe environment. However, despite the potential dangers involved in using more power and traveling at higher speeds, accident rates have been reduced. Engineering science can be credited with providing better design and predicting possible failures in equipment, thus reducing accidents. Only about 15 percent of all accidents can be attributed to an unsafe environment. Safety engineers study accidents to discover special ways of designing or redesigning equipment to protect the user. The use of head protection for workers in construction and in other potentially dangerous work has reduced death and injury. Safety glasses reduce the chance of eye injury, and auto seat belts and padded interiors are the result of safety engineering. These are common examples of efforts to reduce the accident rate.

Special training is required of certain employees, giving them skills and abilities to identify accident-causing conditions in machines, on construction sites, and in transportation facilities. For example, inspection and preventive maintenance on airplanes reduce the chance of failure; elevators in buildings receive regular inspection; pressure containers and boilers receive inspection at regular intervals. Inspection of this nature (and these are only three of many, many types of inspection) is done by individuals specifically trained with knowledge of defective equipment which could fail, causing death and injury to many.

Today most products are manufactured to meet standards of safety and performance. However, the safest of products must be used safely, and that is where the element of human behavior enters the picture.

Full control of the environment is expensive and may inconvenience people in their activities. Such environmental controls would very likely require changes in design and in the horsepower of automobiles and trucks. Periodic inspection of all transportation equipment — cars, trucks, buses, bicycles, and motorcycles — would be re-quired. Other requirements would include the closing of roads when safe driving vision is reduced by fog and rain and the closing of streets and highways during times of ice and snow accumulation.

Making our environment a safe one is everyone's responsibility. It is very important that young people develop their attitudes and habits of safety before they take on the responsibilities of adult life.

WHERE ACCIDENTS OCCUR

In its latest report, the National Center for Health Statistics stated that for the year 1969 there were 1,921,990 deaths in the United States. This was a rate of 954 deaths per 100,000 population. Accidents rated fourth in the cause of deaths. There were 116,385 accidental deaths (58 per 100,000 population).

Accidents vs other causes of death

Accidents are the leading cause of death among all persons aged 1 to 38. Among persons of all ages, accidents are the fourth leading cause of death. The following table shows for all ages the number of deaths by leading causes in 1969 (latest official figures available) and the death rates, separately for male and female.

Cause	Number of Deaths			Death Rates*		
	Total	Male	Female	Total	Male	Female
All Causes	1,921,990	1,080,926	841,064	954	1,103	814
Heart disease	739,265	421,845	317,420	367	430	307
Cancer	323,092	176,142	146,950	160	180	142
Stroke (cerebrovascular disease)	207,179	94,227	112,952	103	96	109
Accidents	**116,385**	**80,706**	**35,679**	**58**	**82**	**35**
Motor-vehicle	55,791	40,213	15,578	28	41	15
Pneumonia	62,394	34,852	27,542	31	36	27
Diabetes mellitus	38,541	15,689	22,852	19	16	22
Arteriosclerosis	33,063	14,346	18,717	16	15	18

Source: National Center for Health Statistics.   *Deaths per 100,000 population.

11,500,000 disabling† injuries in 1972

	Deaths	Change from 1971	Disabling Injuries†
	117,000	+2%	11,500,000

The death total in 1972 was about 2,000 more than in 1971. Motor-vehicle and public deaths increased, while home and work deaths decreased. See page 12 for effect of ICD Eighth Revision. The death rate per 100,000 persons was 56.2, up 1 per cent from 55.8 in 1971.

Principal classes of accidents:

	Deaths	Change from 1971	Disabling Injuries†
Motor-Vehicle	56,600	+3%	2,100,000
Public non-work	52,400		2,000,000
Work	4,000		100,000
Home	200		10,000
Work	14,100	−1%	2,400,000
Non-motor-vehicle	10,100		2,300,000
Motor-vehicle	4,000		100,000
Home	27,000	−2%	4,200,000
Non-motor-vehicle	26,800		4,200,000
Motor-vehicle	200		10,000
Public††	23,500	+4%	2,900,000

NOTE: Deaths and injuries shown for the four separate classifications total more than national figures shown at the top of the page because some deaths and injuries are included in more than one classification. For example, 4,000 work deaths involved motor vehicles and are in both the work and motor-vehicle classifications; and 200 motor-vehicle deaths occurred on home premises and are in both the home and motor-vehicle classifications. The total of such duplication amounted to about 4,200 deaths and more than 100,000 injuries in 1972.

†**Disabling beyond the day of accident.** Injuries are not reported on a national basis, so the totals shown are approximations based on ratios of disabling injuries to deaths developed from special studies. The totals are the best estimates for the current year; however, they should not be compared with totals shown in previous editions of ACCIDENT FACTS to indicate either year-to-year changes or trends.

††Excludes motor-vehicle and work accidents in public places. Includes recreation (swimming, hunting, etc.), transportation except motor-vehicle, public building accidents, etc.

The total number of persons killed in accidents (116,385) during 1972 could be represented in number relationship as the population of Huntington Beach, California or of Albany, New York. An additional 11,500,000 persons were injured in accidents during the same year, and this number would represent a population equal to New York City.[4]

MOTOR VEHICLE ACCIDENTS

An analysis of accidental deaths and injuries reveals that 56,600 persons were killed and 2,100,000 were injured as the result of motor vehicle accidents during 1972.[5] The 15-24 year age group is most susceptible to auto accidents. In this age group, 24,668 young persons were killed — a death rate of 72 per 100,000 population. Children of ages 1-14 are also victims of motor vehicle accidents, with 5,752 deaths reported. Accidents of all types claim more young lives than the six leading diseases combined. All types of accidents were responsible for the deaths of 15,159 children between the ages of 1-14 years in 1971.[6]

1. **Speed.** Since young people of ages 15-24 are more likely to be in danger from motor vehicle accidents, a further analysis of where, how, and why these accidents happen is important. Speed is considered one cause of accidents for this group. Of the 56,600 fatal motor vehicle accidents in 1972, driving too fast was a factor in approximately 16,000 of them. A further breakdown indicates 5,000 occurred in urban areas and 11,000 in rural areas.[7] Driving too fast is clearly seen to be a definite, extreme danger for this age group. Young men have the highest rate of accident fatalities of any group.

2. **Alcohol and Drugs.** Recent studies indicate that alcohol was involved in

Your Automobile Should Be Periodically Inspected by a Qualified Mechanic

at least one-half of all fatal auto deaths in 1972. Drugs have also become a problem in auto accidents, according to a study in which 24 percent of the fatally injured drivers tested indicated presence of drugs.[8]

3. **Other Facts.** Other statistics and facts for young drivers to remember include the following:

- Collisions between motor vehicles account for the largest number of fatal accidents. The chances of survival are very, very low when two cars, both going fifty miles per hour, collide head-on.

- The time of day and the day of the week that you are on the road may also change your chances of being involved in an accident. The percentage of accidents and deaths increases between the hours of 4-7 P.M. and is highest during these hours on Friday and Sunday. However, more accidents occur on Saturday (accidents not resulting in deaths), and this is true during most months of the year. More motor

[4]**Ibid.**   [5]**Ibid.**   [6]**Ibid.**   [7]**Op. Cit.,** p. 49.   [8]**Ibid.,** p. 52.

Deaths and death rates by day and night

Motor-vehicle deaths at night total only a few thousand more than during the day, but deaths related to travel are sharply higher at night, as noted in the table below. In urban places, the mileage death rate at night is nearly three times the day rate; in rural places, the night rate is about two and one-half times the day rate.

		PER CENT OF DEATHS	DEATH RATES*
TOTAL	DAY	47%	3.0
	NIGHT	53%	8.0
URBAN	DAY	48%	1.9
	NIGHT	52%	4.9
RURAL	DAY	47%	4.3
	NIGHT	53%	11.3

● Source: State traffic authorities and the Federal Highway Administration.

∗ Deaths per 100,000,000 vehicle miles.

Accidents by hour by day

Accidents by hour of day vary importantly by day of week. As noted in the table below, fatal accidents occur most frequently during the following hours: weekdays, except Friday—evening rush; Friday—late night; Saturday—late afternoon and night; Sunday—early morning. See page 51 for number of deaths by day of week.

Hourly Distribution of Accidents by Day of Week

Hour of Day*	Fatal Accidents					All Accidents				
	Total	Mon.-Thurs.	Fri.	Sat.	Sun.	Total	Mon.-Thurs.	Fri.	Sat.	Sun.
Total	100.0%	100.0%	100.0%	100.0%	100.0%	100.0%	100.0%	100.0%	100.0%	100.0%
Midnight	5.3	4.2	3.6	7.1	7.7	2.7	1.9	1.8	4.2	5.3
1:00 a.m.	5.1	3.5	3.3	7.1	9.1	2.4	1.4	1.4	4.0	5.5
2:00 a.m.	4.2	2.8	2.8	6.1	7.2	1.9	1.1	1.1	3.1	4.5
3:00 a.m.	2.6	1.9	1.7	3.5	4.5	1.2	0.7	0.6	2.0	3.0
4:00 a.m.	1.8	1.2	1.1	2.6	3.1	0.8	0.5	0.4	1.3	1.8
5:00 a.m.	1.5	1.4	0.8	2.2	1.7	0.7	0.6	0.5	1.0	1.2
6:00 a.m.	2.2	2.6	2.2	1.7	1.8	1.6	1.8	1.5	1.2	1.1
7:00 a.m.	2.5	3.4	2.7	1.6	1.3	4.1	5.5	4.4	1.8	1.2
8:00 a.m.	2.5	3.1	2.7	1.7	1.6	4.5	5.9	4.7	2.3	1.5
9:00 a.m.	2.5	2.8	2.9	1.8	1.9	3.5	4.0	3.4	3.2	2.5
10:00 a.m.	3.0	3.4	2.7	2.7	2.4	4.0	4.2	3.6	4.3	3.4
11:00 a.m.	3.3	3.9	2.9	3.2	2.5	4.9	5.1	4.5	5.5	4.1
Noon	3.4	3.8	3.3	2.8	3.1	5.6	5.8	5.3	5.8	5.2
1:00 p.m.	3.9	4.1	4.2	3.4	3.3	5.5	5.4	5.0	6.0	5.5
2:00 p.m.	4.6	4.5	4.1	4.2	4.1	6.1	6.1	5.7	6.1	6.2
3:00 p.m.	5.7	6.6	5.8	4.6	4.8	7.9	8.4	8.2	6.6	6.7
4:00 p.m.	6.1	7.1	5.7	4.7	5.3	8.7	9.6	9.3	6.8	6.9
5:00 p.m.	6.4	6.9	6.4	5.6	5.7	8.2	8.9	9.0	6.3	6.9
6:00 p.m.	6.2	6.2	6.5	6.0	5.8	5.9	5.7	6.2	5.7	6.2
7:00 p.m.	6.2	6.3	6.9	5.7	5.9	5.1	4.7	5.6	5.3	5.5
8:00 p.m.	5.4	5.3	6.1	5.2	5.3	4.1	3.7	4.5	4.5	4.7
9:00 p.m.	5.3	5.5	5.9	4.9	4.5	3.8	3.4	4.3	4.2	4.2
10:00 p.m.	5.1	4.7	7.1	5.5	4.0	3.5	3.0	4.4	4.2	3.7
11:00 p.m.	5.2	4.2	8.6	6.1	3.4	3.3	2.6	4.6	4.6	3.2

Source: Based on reports from 18 state traffic authorities. *Hour beginning.

vehicle deaths were reported in July in the year 1972 than any other month that year.

- Deaths and death rates are higher during the holidays than during comparable nonholiday periods. During these periods more cars are on the highways, and the accident rate per car also increases. During recent holidays, the increase in traffic was 4 percent, but the death rate was 22 percent higher.[9]

4. **Mechanical Condition of Vehicle at Time of Accident.** Defective cars are also responsible for accidents. Many accidents are the result of tire and brake failures. Lights are also a factor at night. The danger of carbon monoxide gas overcoming the driver is always possible, especially when air conditioning is used and when the heater is used in cold weather. A periodic inspection of the exhaust system by a **qualified** person is highly recommended.

DROWNING ACCIDENTS

Drownings rank third in the causes of accidental deaths for all ages in the population. However, a closer study of statistics reveals that drownings rank second in cause of deaths from accidental causes for persons in the 5-14, the 15-24, and the 25-44 age groups. On the average, more than 7,200 drowning deaths occurred each year since 1968. The largest number occurs in the age group of 15-24 years. In 1972, a total of 2,190 persons in this group were drowned. Nearly one-third of the persons drowned were teenagers, and 85 percent were males.[10]

Teenagers need to exercise the best possible judgment while enjoying water sports and recreation. It is most important to be alert and to learn all information about water safety. This is especially true for the active

The Highest Rate of Work-Related Accidents Occurs in Construction and Mining Occupations

high school age group, which could possibly have the lowest accidental drowning rate. Many water accidents occur when persons cannot swim, although just about everyone can and should learn to swim before high school. It is reported that all physically fit boys and girls in the country of Iceland must learn to swim during high school.

Good judgment and alertness to water safety not only apply to swimming but to boating as well. Boating safety should be learned and practiced by anyone before going on the water in any type of boat.

ACCIDENTS AT WORK

The chances of death or injury on the job have gradually been reduced since 1912. However, too many workers are involved in accidents on the job today. In 1972, about 80 million persons were employed in the United States. During that year, 14,100

[9]**Ibid.,** p. 57   [10]**Ibid.,** p. 14.

Accidental Deaths by States, 1972 and Rate Changes from 1971

State	Deaths		Death Rates		State	Deaths		Death Rates	
	1972	1971	1972**	Change from 1971††		1972	1971	1972**	Change from 1971††
Total U.S.....	117,000	115,000	56.2	+ 1%	Missouri.........	2,800	2,932	58.9	− 5%
					Montana........	691	643	96.1	+ 6%
Alabama........	2,532	2,580	72.1	− 3%	Nebraska.......	983	968	64.5	+ 1%
Alaska.........	...	345†	122.3†	...	Nevada.........	492	488	93.4	− 3%
Arizona.........	1,515	1,405	77.9	+ 3%	N. Hampshire....	348	373	45.1	− 8%
Arkansas........	1,485	1,275	75.1	+14%					
California........	...	11,665†	60.0†	...	New Jersey......	2,761	3,043	37.5	−10%
					New Mexico.....	1,034	1,010	97.1	− 1%
Colorado........	1,484	1,415	63.0	+ 2%	New York........	6,629	6,680	36.1	− 1%
Conn. (10 mos.)..	902	1,118	35.1	− 3%	N. Carolina......	3,972	3,680	76.2	+ 7%
Delaware........	248	262	43.9	− 7%	N. Dakota.......	443	444	70.1	− 1%
Dist. of Col......	307	330	41.0	− 8%					
Florida..........	4,727	4,218	65.1	+ 9%	Ohio............	4,950	4,860	45.9	+ 2%
					Oklahoma.......	...	1,603	61.4*	...
Georgia.........	2,648	2,829	56.1	− 8%	Oregon.........	1,384	1,385	63.4	− 1%
Hawaii..........	284	297	35.1	− 7%	Pennsylvania....	5,116	5,326	42.9	− 4%
Idaho...........	728	628	96.3	+12%	Rhode Island....	340	320	35.1	+ 5%
Illinois..........	4,524	4,787	40.2	− 6%					
Indiana.........	...	3,185†	62.2†	...	S. Carolina......	2,026	2,007	76.0	− 1%
					S. Dakota.......	758§	533	111.6	+40%
Iowa...........	1,606	1,667	55.7	− 5%	Tennessee......	2,746	2,664	68.1	+ 2%
Kansas.........	1,211	1,267	53.6	− 4%	Texas..........	6,486	6,240	55.7	+ 2%
Kentucky........	2,062	2,098	62.5	− 2%	Utah...........	707	616	62.8	+12%
Louisiana........	2,439	2,337	65.6	+ 3%					
Maine...........	596	574	57.9	+ 1%	Vermont........	258	220	55.8	+16%
					Virginia.........	2,786	2,646	58.5	+ 4%
Maryland........	1,562	1,576	38.5	− 2%	Washington.....	1,961	1,918	57.0	+ 3%
Massachusetts...	...	2,681†	49.0†	...	W. Virginia......	1,274	1,188	71.5	+ 5%
Michigan........	...	4,426	49.2*	...	Wisconsin......	2,284	2,141	50.5	+ 6%
Minnesota.......	2,125	2,183	54.5	− 3%	Wyoming.......	368	331	106.7	+10%
Mississippi......	1,911	2,031	84.4	− 7%	Puerto Rico‡....	...	...	...	...
					Virgin Islands‡...	39	61	70.1	−36%

Source: State registrars of vital statistics. *1971. **Rates are deaths per 100,000 population.
†1969−National Center for Health Statistics. ‡Not included in Total U.S.
††Some changes may reflect revised population figures. §Includes 237 deaths from flash floods.

Accidental death rates, by states, 1972

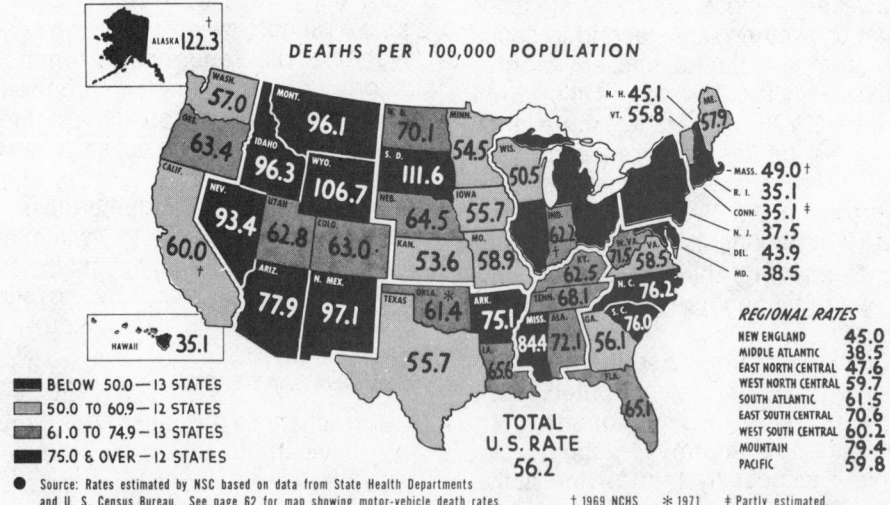

DEATHS PER 100,000 POPULATION

ALASKA 122.3†

REGIONAL RATES
NEW ENGLAND	45.0
MIDDLE ATLANTIC	38.5
EAST NORTH CENTRAL	47.6
WEST NORTH CENTRAL	59.7
SOUTH ATLANTIC	61.5
EAST SOUTH CENTRAL	70.6
WEST SOUTH CENTRAL	60.2
MOUNTAIN	79.4
PACIFIC	59.8

BELOW 50.0—13 STATES
50.0 TO 60.9—12 STATES
61.0 TO 74.9—13 STATES
75.0 & OVER—12 STATES

TOTAL U.S. RATE 56.2

● Source: Rates estimated by NSC based on data from State Health Departments and U. S. Census Bureau. See page 62 for map showing motor-vehicle death rates. † 1969 NCHS * 1971 ‡ Partly estimated.

ALL ACCIDENTS   19

WORK ACCIDENTS, 1972

(See also page 2 for National Health Survey totals)

Between 1912 and 1972, accidental work deaths per 100,000 population were reduced 67 per cent, from 21 to 7. In 1912, an estimated 18,000 to 21,000 workers' lives were lost. In 1972, in a work force double in size and producing more than seven times as much, there were only 14,100 work deaths.

Industry Group	Workers (000)	Deaths		Death Rates*			Disabling Injuries** 1972
		1972	Change from 1971	1972	1962	% Change	
ALL INDUSTRIES	82,300	14,100†	−100	17	21	−19%	2,400,000†
Trade	18,700	1,300	0	7	9	−22%	420,000
Manufacturing	19,200	1,700	−100	9	11	−18%	530,000
Service	18,100	1,900	−200	10	13	−23%	420,000
Government	13,400	1,800	+100	13	13	0%	330,000
Transportation and public utilities	4,700	1,700	0	36	43	−16%	200,000
Agriculture	3,600	2,200	−100	61	60	+ 2%	200,000
Construction	4,000	2,800	+100	70	74	− 5%	260,000
Mining, quarrying	600	700	+100	117	108	+ 8%	40,000

*Deaths per 100,000 workers in each group.
**Disabling beyond the day of the accident. Totals include deaths.
†About 4,000 of the deaths and 100,000 of the injuries involved motor vehicles.

Accidental work deaths in 1972 totalled about 14,100, a decrease of 100 from the 1971 count. See page 12 for effect of ICD Eighth Revision. Disabling injuries totalled 2,400,000, an increase of 100,000 from the 1971 figure. The number of workers employed and average hours worked per week each increased about 3 per cent.

Deaths and death rate trends

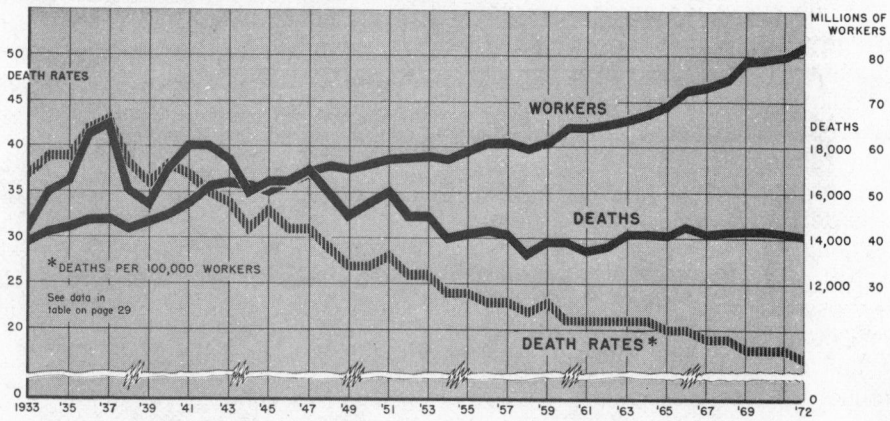

work-associated accidental deaths occurred, and 2,400,000 persons were involved in disabling accidents. Between 1912 and 1972, the 67 percent reduction rate of work-related accidents was made possible by responsible action by the workers, supervisors, and safety engineers. More people suffer injuries or death in manufacturing jobs, but the highest rates are still in construction and mining, where numbers of persons employed are considerable.

It is very important for all young workers to develop good safety habits and attitudes before starting to work. They should also learn the hazards of the work environment before going on the job. More attention is given to safety apparel and accident prevention devices in industry, and the workers' cooperation is sought in prevention of accidents.

ACCIDENTS AT HOME

The popular saying "in the safety of one's home" is not true for all members of the family. More accidents occur in the home than in any other place. In 1972, more than four million disabling accidents occurred in the home, and 27,500 of these resulted in death. The very young and the old are more accident prone than the teenager. Falls in the home cause more deaths than any other accident. Persons 75 years old and over are most likely to fall, but young persons in the 15-24 year age group suffered 2,500 home accident deaths in 1972. Poisoning by solids and liquids — including drugs, medicines, mushrooms, and shellfish — as well as commonly recognized poisons, was the chief cause of accidental death in this group. [11] The death rate in this category has increased significantly in recent years. The increase is related to accidents involving overdoses of psychotropic drugs. Reduction of accidental deaths is the responsibility of persons in this age group. Another hazard in and around the home is poisoning by gases and vapors, especially from auto-

More Accidents Occur in the Home Than in Any Other Place

mobile exhaust gas. Sitting in a parked car with the engine running in cold weather is particularly dangerous.

Data on home-related disability accidents is not available. Cuts and lacerations are caused by a number of tools, instruments and machines. Injuries in the use of lawn mowers are increasing — this should serve as a warning to teenagers who use the machines.

PUBLIC ACCIDENTS

Accidents in public places caused 23,500 deaths in 1972. Accidental death listed in this category includes accidents involving public transportation, firearms, drowning, and falls in places other than at work, in the home, or at school. Swimming is the most dangerous to young persons.[12]

[11]**Ibid.,** p. 7.

[12]**Ibid.,** p. 3.

ACCIDENT PREVENTION

All people have a responsibility to protect themselves and others from accidents. Perhaps the first step is to get everyone to **think** about the results of accidents. Knowing where, when, and how accidents are likely to occur will go a long way in the prevention of accidents.

There are other factors of a personal nature which are difficult for the young person to control. These factors include overconfidence, inadequate sense of responsibility, insecurity, poor morale, emotional tension, over-excitement, and fear.

If young workers and students can identify any of the factors as a part of their behavior, a start on safety awareness is made. A continuous attempt to develop good safety attitudes is another good step. There is no honor in being a victim of an accident. The real hero and citizen is the young person who can prevent accidents.

All young people can protect themselves and their friends and families by developing safe habits and thus producing safety. The saying, "The life you save may be your own," points out the reason to develop yourself into a safe individual and a responsible citizen.

COST OF ACCIDENTS

A study of accident statistics indicates that the cost of accidents reached $37 billion in 1971.[13] Accident losses listed in monetary amounts give us only one part of the true loss. It is not possible to estimate the cost of human suffering and crushed dreams which are the results of an accident.

What was the cost to the 17-year-old high school junior who dived into a stream and received a broken neck that paralyzed him for the rest of his life?

What was the cost to a young college student who received a broken back in an auto collision and must live the rest of his life as a paraplegic?

One month of assisting in the emergency rooms of a large hospital will impress upon anyone the need for accident prevention. The cost of accidents is shocking — physically as well as financially.

What was the cost to a young mother who was permanently blinded by an explosion of a gas stove? The above examples of cost cannot be estimated, but thousands of sad experiences happen every day.

[13]Ibid., p. 4.

Costs of accidents in 1972*

The accidents in which the deaths and injuries occurred, together with non-injury motor-vehicle accidents and fires, cost the nation in 1972, at least

$37.0 billion

These costs include: (billion)

Wage losses due to temporary inability to work, lower wages after returning to work due to permanent impairment, present value of future earnings lost by those totally incapacitated or killed **$12.0**

Medical fees, hospital expenses .... **$ 3.9**

Insurance administrative and claim settlement costs (claims are not identified separately but losses for which claim payments are made are included in other items in this table—see note below) .... **$ 7.6**

Property damage in motor-vehicle accidents .... **$ 6.0**

Property destroyed by fire .... **$ 2.3**

Money value of time lost by workers other than those with disabling injuries, who are directly or indirectly involved in accidents .... **$ 5.2**

Notes on certain accident costs

There are alternative ways of identifying certain costs of accidents. The items in the table above represent one of the ways. All measurable costs have been included, and none have been included twice. See comments below under insurance costs.

Wage losses. Loss of productivity by injured or killed workers is a loss to the nation. Since, theoretically, a worker's contribution to the wealth of the nation is measured in terms of wages, then the sum total of wages lost due to accidents provides a measure of this lost productivity. For nonfatal injuries, actual wage losses are used; for fatalities and permanently disabling injuries, the figure used is the present value of all future earnings lost.

Insurance administrative and claim settlement costs. This is the difference between premiums paid *to* insurance companies and claims paid *by* them; it is their cost of doing business and is a part of the accident cost total. *Claims* paid by insurance companies are not identified separately in the total. Since every claim is paid to a claimant for such losses as wages, medical and hospital expense, etc., losses for which claims are paid are already included in various items in the table.

---

*Costs are not comparable with previous years. As additional or more precise data become available they are used from that year forward, but previously estimated figures are not revised.

STUDY AIDS

NEW TERMS

accident facts
safety attitudes
unsafe environment
accident rates
public accidents
Williams-Steiger Occupational Safety
  and Health Act (OSHA)
human failure
National Safety Council

STUDY QUESTIONS

1. How many American citizens were injured in accidents in 1972?
2. What was the chief cause of all deaths of persons 5-14 years of age reported by the National Safety Council?
3. With reference to accident prevention in the United States, what is the significance of the year 1912?
4. What is the most recently enacted federal safety law for the United States?
5. What is the number one cause of accidental deaths in the United States?
6. How do environmental factors contribute to accidents?
7. Why do young men have more automobile accidents than young women?
8. What are the most dangerous hours of the day to be driving an automobile?
9. Which States have the highest accidental death rates per 100,000 population? Do you have an explanation?
10. Which age group is most likely to be the victim of a drowning accident?

DISCUSSION PROBLEMS

1. What can young men and women do to protect themselves from accidents?
2. Why are young men more likely to be involved in accidents than men in other age groups?
3. Can you identify an unsafe environment in your home, at school, or in your city?
4. Who should be responsible for accident victims unable to care for themselves?

PART THREE
AWARENESS OF CONSUMER RESPONSIBILITIES

INTRODUCTION

One of the most thrilling and exciting experiences of your lifetime is securing and starting work on **your first full-time job.** The transition from school to work is more than finding a job. It means becoming independent of your parents' support. It is the beginning of full adulthood when you accept adult responsibility and citizenship.

Becoming a good citizen requires more than holding a job and making a contribution with your skill and energy at work. You must join other consumers and use your earnings to achieve the most happiness for yourself and those you care about.

Learning to become a wise consumer is not easy. The well-being of a family depends to a great extent on learning and using good buying habits. In the last few years, much has been done to assist Americans to become better consumers. Programs on radio and television have been designed to assist consumers in getting the most for their money. The federal government and state governments have recently passed laws to assist and protect the consumer. Many government agencies now perform services which assist the public in becoming wise consumers. However, you must be alert to good buying procedures — and make them a habit!

In Parts I and II of this book, you learned about selecting a career and preparing for employment, succeeding on the job, and advancing in your career.

The purpose of Part III is to assist you in becoming a better consumer and a well-informed citizen. As an independent consumer in a complex and competitive industrial society, you will need to learn how to receive the most benefits from your money. Learning good habits in management of your money and learning the art of spending will greatly increase your chances of achieving your long-range goals.

In Part III you will have an opportunity to learn of budgeting your money for wise spending. You will learn ways of making the best choices and selecting the best quality of products for your particular needs. Everyone needs to learn how to use banking services and when to use credit to an advantage.

Many young people are victims of fraud, or are deceived by persons who misrepresent either products or services. Some of the most common types of frauds are described to help you avoid being victimized by high-pressure sales personnel or others.

A knowledge of social security benefits

is important to the young family as well as to the retired workers. All citizens are expected to know the cost of government; thus, an understanding of the tax system is important. Part III will be both useful and interesting. As a worker on your first job, you can apply much of the consumer information that is provided.

CHAPTER TEN
MANAGING YOUR MONEY

WISE USE OF MONEY

Most of us have problems in managing our money. One problem is that few of us have enough money to buy all the things we would like to buy and do all the things we would like to do. Another problem is that we do not **plan** the use of our money well enough to receive the full value of each dollar. Often, it is wasted. Some people waste money without even knowing it.

Learning to use money wisely isn't easy. It takes some knowledge on how to use your money and a lot of **careful planning.** Since few people have a lot of money to spend, it is good business to learn how to use what we have wisely.

Learning to manage money is like learning to drive a car, because it gets easier as you become more experienced. Managing your money, like driving your car, requires that you develop good habits. Good drivers or good managers need not work any harder than the poor drivers or poor managers. They know what to do and do it consistently with the confidence that comes from developing competency in driving — or in managing money. Good driving will save you costly repairs, and court fines as well. Good money management will help you get the most out of the money you have.

Have you ever noticed two people who earn about the same amount of money each month, but one seems to have more to show for the earnings? Is this because one does a better job in managing money?

You may know a family who seems to have more of a money problem than the average family. This family is always behind in paying bills. Even though the head of the family makes a good salary, this family is never quite able to catch up in paying bills. Such a family is not living within its means. What is meant by "Living within your means?" It means the wise use of the money you earn. Also, it means spending

Manage Your Money for Things You Want

no more than you earn, or not buying things for which you cannot pay.

Learning to live within your means is very important when you start on **your** first job, just as it is to the head of a family. Many family problems can be avoided by carefully planning and controlling money.

All workers have certain financial responsibilities to themselves, to their families, and to their communities. Just as poor drivers wreck their cars and injure others, poor financial managers waste their money, lessen their chances of economic success, and create problems for their families.

LEVELS OF RESPONSIBILITY

The level of responsibility for the use of money may vary from individual to individual. The use of money is probably more important to young people today than it was 100 years ago. In 1870 about 53 percent of the population was engaged in farming. Today less than 7 percent of our population is engaged directly in agriculture. The family income in 1870 was low, and consumer goods were not available in the quality and quantity they are in the 1970's. The median family income has increased, and many more consumer items are available today. Life has become more complex for everyone.

To better understand some of the problems of the young consumers and their level of financial responsibility, let us look at a few case studies involving young people.

CONNIE MARTIN

Connie Martin is 16 years old and a junior at Washington High School. She lives within a few blocks of the school with her father and mother, Fred and Marjorie Martin; her brother, Larry; and her sister, Linda. Larry is 14 years old and a freshman at Washington. Both Connie and Larry walk to school each day. Linda attends Lincoln School which is eight blocks from their home on West Sycamore Street.

Fred Martin is a carpenter. Bad weather and strikes have caused Fred to lose considerable work time the last three years, and the family has found it necessary to adjust the budget several times.

Connie has been given a small allowance for school supplies and clothing. Any extra money Connie has for luxuries and entertainment must come from her own earnings. She has been earning and saving some of her money for the last two years. Connie understands that the family financial picture is not too bright at the present time and that she will need to be responsible for herself after she graduates from high school.

Connie has studied the occupations that are available to young women, and she has found cosmetology very interesting. Connie's friend, Jane, has an older sister who is a licensed cosmetologist, and Connie enjoys visiting her shop and watching her work.

After discussing future goals with her school counselor, her mother and father, and with friends, Connie has decided to take a cosmetology course after graduating from high school.

The cost of a cosmetology course is about $500. Connie has started saving one-half of the money she earns working at the public library three hours after school each day. With the additional money Connie makes baby-sitting, she expects to have the $500 saved before graduation. Is this a realistic goal?

JOSEPH THOMPSON

Joe Thompson is 6 feet tall, 190 pounds, 18 years old, and a senior at East High School. He is interested in sports and has made the varsity football team the last three years. Joe is a good worker and a jolly fellow, but has not been too successful in his business ventures.

Joe's father and his older brother, Bill, are sales representatives for the Johnson Wholesale Plumbing Supply Company. Both have rather high gross earnings from their salaries and commissions. However, they have a lot of expenses since they must furnish a car for travel and entertain customers out of expense accounts which are not adequate.

Joe has two brothers and three sisters younger than he, all in school. Even though Joe's mother shops wisely, it is quite a task to meet the expenses of a large family living in an expensive section of Waynesville, a city of 125,000 people.

Last summer, Joe decided he would help the family by going to work as a hardware salesperson. He purchased a three-year-old automobile for $1200 and spent $500 for clothing needed to meet his customers. Joe worked very hard during June, July, and August selling a special aluminum kitchenware. His earnings were high, but he was not able to make enough money to pay for his car and clothes.

Joe has a different level of financial responsibility than most of his friends; but rather than admit defeat, he is determined to pay for his car and go to work full time as a hardware salesperson upon graduation from high school.

It Is Important to Live within Your Means

MILDRED AND STANLEY WOODWARD

Mildred Sharp had known Stanley Woodward since they started to Lincoln School in Mount Vernon eight years ago. They seemed to be fond of each other since their first year in school together.

Mildred lived with her father and mother, Dennis and Marie Sharp, in a large house on Elm Street. Dennis owned and operated the Main Street Garage where he had developed a good business during the last 15 years. Mildred's mother helped keep the accounts in the garage for her husband.

Stanley Woodward lived 10 blocks north of the Sharp's. His father, John Woodward, was a plumber and worked for the Mount Vernon Plumbing Company, where he had been employed for the last 10 years. Stanley was the oldest of four children in the Woodward family. His sister, Mary, was 15 years old, and brothers, Keith and Bruce, were 12 and 10 years old. Stanley's mother, Gladys, was always busy keeping their clothes clean and repaired and doing all the jobs needed for a busy family of six.

Mildred and Stanley had dated since the ninth grade in high school, and it was taken for granted that they would be married later. Last fall Mildred and Stanley were both seniors at Jackson High School and were both enrolled in the distributive education class. Mildred applied for a job at Bradley's, a children's clothing store, and was employed in the dress department. She was very happy with her work and was making a good salary while learning to be skilled in selling.

Stanley had worked in the Kroger store for the last three summers and liked the grocery business. Thus, the first place he made application was at the Tenth Street Kroger store. He was employed as a trainee to work in all areas of the store.

In October, Mildred and Stanley decided to get married. Both had saved some money and had enough clothing to last them the rest of the year. If they both worked, they thought they could manage to get married and still finish their senior year in high school. Neither was interested in going to college. Stanley was hopeful that some day he could become a store manager and Mr. Kyser, the store manager, had promised him full time work when he graduated from high school. Mildred was happy working in retailing, and she agreed with Stanley that retailing would be a good life's work.

Mildred and Stanley were married during the Christmas holidays with the blessings of both the Sharp and Woodward families. Knowing that Mildred and Stanley would have to budget carefully the money they earned, the Sharps asked Stanley and Mildred to live with them until both were through high school. A financial agreement was reached between the Sharps and the newlywed Woodwards. Stanley and Mildred agreed to take over specific responsibilities around the home and to contribute a percentage of the cost of maintaining the home.

In this case, the arrangement worked very well. Mildred and Stanley were, for the most part, independent. Both were employed and taking their places in the adult world, as well as completing the last year of high school. Their level of responsibility had been well defined and they were able to handle their financial, employment, and school responsibilities. The study of consumer education in the distributive education class also provided them with additional knowledge and skill to manage their affairs.

HELEN LANE

Helen Lane had always wanted to become a secretary. Even as a high school freshman, she had informed her typing teacher of plans to become a legal secretary. Helen lived with her parents on a large ranch in Kansas. Helen's mother encouraged her to prepare for secretarial work by attending the Northern Area Vocational School.

The idea of leaving the ranch where she had lived all her life to live in a small apartment was frightening to Helen, who had graduated from the small Madison County Rural High School last June. Only Helen's strong determination could force her into this new level of responsibility where she would have to be completely independent.

Helen found a small apartment about five blocks from the school. She selected the apartment on Maple Street because it was about equal distance to the shopping center and to the school. It was very important to live near the shopping center since Helen didn't want to be bothered with a car. A shopping center with a bank, a number of stores, and a restaurant would serve her needs quite well. The apartment was furnished with just about everything a student would need in furniture and appliances. Helen enjoyed entertaining the students in her class by cooking special dishes.

After four months of managing her affairs, Helen found she was quite capable at managing a budget, buying food and clothing, and maintaining the apartment. Her mother and father were proud of the ability she displayed.

Managing for herself was easy for Helen because she had practice. Her mother and father had encouraged self-reliance. Helen had also received instruction which built her confidence. The study of consumer education in homemaking classes had been very useful, as was the study of budgeting in high school business courses. Helen's success was partly because she knew how to plan. Helen not only knew how to keep accounts, she knew how to be a good consumer. The allowance Helen's father sent her each month was more than adequate.

PHIL AND MARY KIRBY

Phil and Mary Kirby had wanted to buy their own home for several years. Only recently had they been able to save enough money for a down payment on a new home in the North Hill addition. Phil and Mary had been married for six years. Phil, who is 29, liked to live in the three room apartment on Tenth Street because it was close to the plant where he worked.

Mary, who is a nurse, had worked at the Memorial Hospital for the first three years after marriage. Now that Bruce, their two-year-old son, needed more room to play, they were anxious to find a small home. Six months ago they found a small, three bedroom home on Kennedy Street in North Hills. The planning for selecting, financing, and contracting for the house was done over a number of months. With Phil's latest raise in salary, they were sure that they could pay off the mortgage in twenty years.

After Phil and Mary had reviewed their budget plan several times, they visited Mr. Jones at the First National Bank. He reviewed their financial situation and recommended that they pay no more than $225 per month on house payments. He also recommended that they be given a loan and promised to help in appraising the property selected.

The little house on Kennedy Street was the best they could find to fit their particular needs and still be within their financial range. A check list to be used in buying a house was furnished by their bank. According to the check list, it appeared the house had a good location for their needs. A school was within

five blocks, and the neighborhood appeared to be quiet, with few busy streets. Most of the houses in the addition were less than three years old and were occupied by young families. The exterior of the house was in good condition, newly painted, and well landscaped.

The interior of the house also was in good condition, but a little painting was needed before occupancy. The room arrangement was satisfactory; all the equipment and appliances were a good brand and were nearly new.

Phil and Mary liked the house even more after moving in four months ago. The payments of $210 per month were not easy to make; so a number of cuts in spending had to be made. The family budget for recreation was reduced by dropping their membership in the country club. It would not be easy to pay dues each month as they had done before. After three monthly payments were paid, it seemed that by using savings for a 20% down payment and using 25 percent of their earnings based on an average of the last three years, Phil and Mary would not be overburdened with their payments. They had shown considerable responsibility in the planning and buying of their first home.

Phil and Mary acted wisely in managing their money. First, they saved enough money to make a good down payment. Second, they planned their spending and selected a house within their financial ability. Responsibility in financial matters is extremely important to the young family.

PLANNING YOUR PROGRAM OF SPENDING

A spending plan, or budget, is most important for managing your money. At the end of the week have you ever thought, "Just look at the money I have spent this week. How did I spend so much with so little to show for it?" The secret of knowing where your money is spent is to develop a good budget. If you are paid at the end of each week, perhaps a weekly plan could be used; but such planning offers no continuation from week to week. Therefore, long-range plans with some flexibility appear to be the best.

A family budget should be planned on a yearly basis. Your spending plan should be based on what you wish to do with the money you earn. Planning a budget has certain advantages to you whether you are a student in a work experience program or the head of a family.

(1) It will force you to establish goals in using your money.
(2) It will help you live on the money you earn.
(3) It will help you eliminate wasteful habits of spending your money.
(4) It can help you achieve long-range goals.
(5) It can give you valuable experience and develop competency in money management.

Budgets can be simple or complex. The budget of the federal government is a document that requires the work of thousands of people and is a major document when printed. The budget of a student working part time can be written on a single sheet.
Your budget may not look like a major automobile manufacturer's budget, yet the two are basically the same. Two steps are involved in planning your budget.

1. First you must estimate how much money you will earn for the week, month, or year. In estimating your income, all sources should be included in your budget.
2. Then you must estimate expenses for the year.

In preparing an estimate of income for the year, it is helpful to review income for the last year. A city manager will use figures from the last year's budget and the present year's spending to estimate the amount of money needed for the next year.

The second step in planning your budget is to determine how to use the money you earn. This may be difficult because you will be deciding what things you must buy, how much you will save, how much you will spend on recreation, etc. This part of the planning can be fun as well as difficult. At this point you must set goals and make some compromises in spending money. You will need to make cuts in different items to balance your expenses with income.

The experiences of John Smith, a recent high school graduate, will help you understand the principles of making a simple budget.

A Realistic Budget Can Help You Achieve Your Long-Range Goals

PLANNING A BUDGET

John Smith enjoyed working in his first full-time job as a lathe operator. He had worked part time last year for the Acme Tool Company as a student learner. The part-time work was a part of his high school work in the cooperative work experience program. Wages paid for the part-time work were not high, but he learned to operate the lathe. Mr. Jones, his foreman, promoted him to a lathe operator.

John had learned about consumer education in his high school program and was anxious to make plans and set goals for the year. He decided to use the budget plan developed by the Household Finance Corporation as his guide in making a budget for the year. The booklet titled, "Money Management — Your Budget," had been very helpful to him in completing one of his school assignments in consumer education.[1]

John remembered from his studies that a successful money manager uses goals as a guide for planning the use of money. This part of the planning was not difficult for him. He had always wanted a more stylish wardrobe, and since it would soon be football weather, sport clothing was listed first. The old car his uncle had given him last year was needing repair, but would probably last for another year without too much trouble. A good car was a definite need and something to budget money for next year.

There was no steady girl friend, but John wanted to start saving money for a home when the right girl came along. Thus, he listed money for getting married and starting a home as number one for future expenses.

Ingredients for a Spending Plan

Estimating Income. Estimating income for the year is quite a challenge for most people. No one knows what the coming year will bring! It is wise to begin by listing the minimum income you expect to receive for the coming year.

John was hopeful that he would receive a raise before the end of the year. However, since he could not be sure, he decided to use the amount of his weekly check as a basis for estimating income. Only "take home" pay was listed as income. Federal and state income taxes were deducted by the company along with his social security tax.

[1]Household Finance Corporation, "Money Management-Your Budget,"(Leone Ann Heuer), Chicago, 1950.

The "take home" amount of his check was $125 per week which totals approximately $500 per month and $6,000 per year. The monthly and total amounts were listed on page 1 of his budget form.

Future Fixed Expenses. Everyone has bills which fall due at certain times during the year. Some of the bills may be paid out of the weekly pay check. The larger bills which fall due monthly, quarterly, semi-annually, or annually are special problems to those who do not have a spending plan. A good way to pay such bills is to plan a chart with names and the dates they are due. John reviewed a list of possible future expenses and planned his fixed expenses in the categories that applied to him. He listed all fixed expenses on page two of his budget form. The total was $1,540.

FIXED EXPENSES
(Omit items already deducted from paycheck)

TAXES
  Federal income tax
  State income tax
  Property taxes

MONTHLY RENT OR MORTGAGE
PAYMENTS

UTILITIES
  Telephone   Electricity
  Gas   Water

INSURANCE
  Life   Automobile
  Health and accident   Personal property
  Hospitalization   Social security
  Fire and theft   Others

ANNUITIES and other investments toward retirement

FUEL for home heating

UNION DUES

PROFESSIONAL ASSOCIATION DUES

INTEREST on loans where principal is not being repaid along with interest

REGULAR PAYMENTS — may include
  interest on loans
  on furniture or equipment
  on car
  Christmas Club

SAFETY DEPOSIT BOX

CAR LICENSES — state and city

SCHOOL TUITION, TEXTBOOKS and FEES

Future Fixed Expenses

ITEM	Amount Due	Date Due	In Top of Columns List Budget Periods											
			Jan.	Feb.	March	April	May	June	July	Aug.	Sept.	Oct.	Nov.	Dec.
Taxes														
Property	$50.00													$50.00
Rent														
Apartment	$900.00		$75.00	$75.00	$75.00	$75.00	$75.00	$75.00	$75.00	$75.00	$75.00	$75.00	$75.00	$75.00
Safety Dep. Box	$10.00													$10.00
Telephone	$80.00		$6.66	$6.66	$6.66	$6.66	$6.66	$6.66	$6.66	$6.66	$6.66	$6.66	$6.66	$6.66
Union Dues	$150.00		$12.50	$12.50	$12.50	$12.50	$12.50	$12.50	$12.50	$12.50	$12.50	$12.50	$12.50	$12.50
Insurance														
Hospital	$150.00		$50.00				$50.00				$50.00			
Car	$100.00							$50.00						$50.00
Life	$150.00							$75.00						$75.00
	$1,590.00		$144.16	$94.16	$94.16	$94.16	$144.16	$219.16	$94.16	$94.16	$144.16	$94.16	$94.16	$279.16

Future Flexible Expenses

ITEM	Amount Needed	In Top of Columns List Budget Periods											
		Jan.	Feb.	March	April	May	June	July	Aug.	Sept.	Oct.	Nov.	Dec.
Clothing	$ 500.00												
Contributions													
Church	$ 20.00												
Charities	$ 20.00												
Civic Group	$ 20.00												
Annual Subs.													
Local Paper	$ 15.00												
Magazines	$ 15.00												
Medical Care	$ 100.00												
Recreation	$ 640.00												
Emergencies	$ 500.00												
TOTALS	$1,830.00												

Future Flexible Expenses. The flexible expenses which are certain to appear offer an opportunity for making budget adjustments in order to meet unexpected changes in spending. Many items listed in this group will vary in cost and will occur at different times during the year.

John examined the list of suggested items which appear as possible expenses in the budget. He budgeted for clothing, charities, subscriptions, recreation, and gifts. He also budgeted a part of his income for emergencies. His budget items are listed on page three of his budget form in the flexible expense section. The total amount in this section of the budget was $1,830.

FUTURE FLEXIBLE BUDGET ITEMS

CLOTHING

HOME FURNISHINGS AND

HOUSEHOLD EQUIPMENT
  Including repairs
HOME IMPROVEMENT
  Including equipment and repairs

CONTRIBUTIONS
  Church   Professional Groups
  Charities   Fraternal Groups
  Civic Groups   Social Groups

ANNUAL SUBSCRIPTIONS
  Papers
  Magazines

MEDICAL AND DENTAL CARE
  Not covered by insurance,
  including medicines

RECREATION
  Including hobbies unless included under
  personal allowances or day-to-day
  expenses

GIFTS AND ENTERTAINMENT
  Birthdays
  Weddings and Anniversaries
  Christmas
  Babies
  Graduation

A CUSHION for the unexpected
and emergencies

Day-To-Day Costs

ITEM	Four Week Period				Total for Four Weeks	Total for Year	Monthly Costs
	1	2	3	4			
Food	$20.00	$20.00	$20.00	$20.00	$ 80.00	$1,040.00	$ 86.00
Laundry,							
Dry Cleaning,							
Clothing Repair	$ 4.00	$ 4.00	$ 4.00	$ 4.00	$ 16.00	$ 208.00	$ 17.33
Personal Supplies	$ 3.00	$ 3.00	$ 3.00	$ 3.00	$ 12.00	$ 156.00	$ 13.00
Household Supplies,							
Soap & Cleaners	$ 2.00	$ 2.00	$ 2.00	$ 2.00	$ 8.00	$ 104.00	$ 8.67
Car Expense	$10.00	$10.00	$10.00	$10.00	$ 40.00	$ 520.00	$ 43.33
TOTAL	$39.00	$39.00	$39.00	$39.00	$156.00	$2,028.00	$168.33

Day-to-Day Living Costs. The amount of money used for day-to-day living costs makes up a sizeable percentage of your expenses. These expenses are flexible. Budgeting for expenses in this area helps to control spending and provide information on how money is used.

John examined the possible expense items below and made estimates of expenses in the categories which applied to his budget. The total expense for day-to-day cost of living was $1,592. John purchased a special record book to record daily expenses to compare with the amount budgeted.

CAR UPKEEP AND TRANSPORTATION

ENTERTAINMENT — extra food; candies; flowers

FAMILY PERSONALS — toothpaste; first aid; shaving supplies; cosmetics

FOOD — meals eaten at home; meals eaten out

HOUSEHOLD HELP — care of house; yard; baby

HOUSEHOLD SUPPLIES — soaps and cleansers; small items for the home

LAUNDRY; DRY CLEANING; CLOTHING REPAIRS

STATIONERY; POSTAGE; NEWSPAPERS

A Trial Plan

	For One Budget Period	For One Year
INCOME Subtract FUTURE FIXED EXPENSES	$500.00 $120.83	$6,000.00 $1,540.00
Balance: Subtract FUTURE FLEXIBLE EXPENSES	$379.17 $152.50	$4,460.00 $1,830.00
Balance: Subtract PAST-DUE BILLS	$226.67 None	$2,630.00 None
Balance: Subtract DAY-TO-DAY LIVING COSTS	$226.67 $156.00	$2,630.00 $1,592.00
SAVINGS FOR GOALS	$ 70.67	$1,038.00

The Trial Plan. After John had completed estimates of all the expenses which were likely to occur, he made a total of all the expenses in each category. The totals were brought forward and listed in the trial plan which appears on page four of his budget form. If John can live on the $4,962 budgeted for the year, he will have made considerable progress toward his long-range goals. Saving $1,038 or 15 percent of the take-home-pay may be very difficult for most young people.

PUTTING A BUDGET INTO USE

Do you remember the first time you tried to drive a car? It took patience and practice before driving was easy and fun for you. Making and using a budget is difficult at first, but with patience and practice, you will be able to use a budget as a tool for managing your money. Once you have developed good habits in money matters, you have built a good foundation for success. It may take several budget periods before your actual expenses match the budgeted amounts. However, this does not mean that your budget was a failure. Most budgets need to be adjusted at the end of the period.

A budget cannot provide an immediate cure for serious financial problems. It may take a long time to recover from some unexpected expense. A good budget plan should alert those not living within their

Ask for Financial Advice If You Have Trouble Living Within Your Budget

means and help them adjust their expenses to their income.

Here are some suggestions to keep your plan running smoothly:

1. Keep your plan for managing money simple. The more convenient the system is to use, the easier it will be to get it going and to stick to it.
2. Be realistic in setting up your plan. If your income or that of the entire family is balanced against a complete and accurate list of expenses, any problems that come up may be faced squarely.
3. Make your spending plan adjustable to changing circumstances. If fixed expenses are grouped together, the family has a clear picture of what must be paid and when. Flexible expenses may offer opportunities for adjustment if there is need for re-arranging or refiguring.
4. Develop a system for handling the details of budgeting — keeping necessary records . . . paying bills . . . setting aside money for future expenses.
5. Decide on a place to keep materials and information: YOUR BUDGET booklet . . . incoming bills . . . receipts . . . cancelled checks . . . account book or ledger. A desk drawer, small filing case or even a sturdy box will serve to keep necessary information together.
6. Find a safe place for valuable papers and records such as insurance policies, savings bonds, receipts for stock purchases, personal records, automobile receipts and title, tax records. A safety deposit box in your bank is the safest place for valuable papers. A fireproof container should be used if these things are kept in the home.[2]

WHERE TO GET ADDITIONAL HELP

Practically everyone will need expert help on money matters sometime during adult life. Much general information can be obtained by reading various publications, especially those published by the Household Finance Corporation. Government publications are available describing most of the agencies which federal government controls. However, many personal problems require professional help.

An attorney who specializes in money matters should be consulted when a legal opinion is needed. This is especially true in making contracts, selling real property, and collecting bad debts. Additional information in this area of study is discussed in Chapters 11 and 12.

Many banks employ people who will provide free information to customers. Information is available on investments and on bank loans for purchase of homes, equipment, cars, and other property.

Additional help in money matters may be obtained by discussing the problem with your supervisor. A few companies have people employed who will provide legal and financial information for their employees. University extension classes dealing with a number of consumer problems are scheduled in the large cities. Classes are also offered by high school and junior college adult education departments. Individual and group instruction on consumer problems can be furnished by the county agricultural agent and the county home demonstration agent.

High school students should remember that their teachers can help them in this area. Teachers in agriculture, business, homemaking and industrial arts specialize in consumer education.

[2]Household Finance Corporation, "Money Management-Your Budget," (Leone Ann Heuer), Chicago, 1950.

The wise management of money has a vital bearing on the success and happiness of individuals and their families. It is important that young people join the world of work with a high level of skill and knowledge in the wise use of money. With the help which is available today, no one should permit the future to be jeopardized by lack of skill in the use of money.

STUDY AIDS

NEW TERMS

economic problems   competency
financial responsibility   estimate
money management   categories
budget   safety deposit box
flexibility

STUDY QUESTIONS

1. What is a "budget"?
2. List five reasons for planning a budget.
3. What are the two basic steps involved in planning your budget?
4. What must you decide in order to estimate expenses?
5. What four groups of expenses should be listed in your budget?

6. How do you decide the amount to be saved for your future goals?

DISCUSSION PROBLEMS

1. Why should you plan a budget while you are attending school? Should you keep the same budget after you are employed?
2. How would you estimate your income? How would you estimate your expenses?
3. Why is it sometimes difficult to follow the budget you have planned? What should be done if you cannot follow your budget?
4. Imagine you and your friend are discussing making a budget. Your friend thinks making a budget is just too much trouble. Try to convince your friend that the budget will really help and that it is worth the time required to prepare and keep within the estimated budget.
5. Was budgeting as important to the young person in 1870 as it is today? Explain the problems encountered by both groups.
6. What would be a good goal for saving your money earned from summer work?

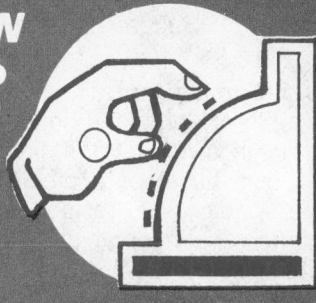

CHAPTER ELEVEN
CONSUMER RESPONSIBILITIES AND PRACTICES

WHY YOU BUY

Answers to the question, "Why you buy?" may be quite simple or very complex. One simple answer would probably be, "I buy to satisfy my needs." However, when one considers those needs limited to things which are indispensable to maintain life, it is apparent that buying to satisfy needs is only a part of the reason for buying. People buy to satisfy their wants as well as their needs. Thus, the answer becomes more complicated. Most consumers want many things that are not needed to sustain life, but make life more comfortable and enjoyable. Human wants are no doubt greater than essential needs to maintain life.

People's wants stem in part from their individual philosophies and that of their homes and their neighborhoods. Persons who adhere to the materialistic philosophy consider the acquisition and use of materials and services of great value and importance to happiness and satisfaction of wants. A second philosophy could be related to that of **economic conservatism** with considerable self-denial in the use of goods and services. There are different levels of adherence to either of these philosophies and most of us could be considered to hold a philosophical role someplace between the two extremes.

Human material wants may be classified in two general groups which include indi-vidual wants and group wants. Individual wants include food, shelter, and clothing. Also included in individual material wants is equipment with which to travel and to engage in sports and recreation.

Group wants can be classified as more service-oriented than material wants. They include participation in various community and civic activities, clubs, and religious and fraternal organizations.

The wants of people and their families and the ability to satisfy these wants tend to establish a dominant lifestyle, but a number of other factors may also influence the lifestyle of an individual or a family.

Our Wants Are Often Greater Than Our Needs

1. Employment. The type of work in which people are engaged has a definite effect on their lifestyles and indirectly their buying habits. A person's employment may limit the choice of residence, clothing, and home. The economic resources which are obtained from work limit the satisfaction of material wants and have a great effect on the choice of friends. For example, one person may wish to enjoy golf after work, while another may want to go home and watch a television program. The time for vacation and travel is also influenced by the type of employment. Persons with seasonal work may have more time for vacation trips with their families while others may only have time to relax on the weekend. Thus, occupation and employment influence buying habits and lifestyles.

2. Leisure. The way in which workers spend their leisure time also affects their lifestyles and buying habits. The younger workers may like water sports and purchase boats and skis; an older worker may prefer travel and buy travel equipment, a tent, and other camping needs. Some workers may take vacations at resorts or visit foreign countries, so they will need to purchase travel tickets, luggage, travel accessories, and special types of clothing. Thus the use of leisure time exerts a significant pressure on lifestyle and buying habits.

3. Personal Attributes. Personal attributes include physical, mental, and social characteristics of an individual. The attributes a person possesses influence his or her lifestyle and behavior at the marketplace.

Heredity is a factor in the development of certain attributes and to a great extent determines physical size, build, endurance, and strength. **Aptitudes and special abilities** are also closely related to heredity. Personality, interest, and motivation are related to hereditary factors and environmental factors. A person with strength and physical agility may have a natural inclination to be interested in and to participate in sports and physical exercise activities. Even the selection of friends and type of work are closely related to hereditary and environmental factors.

Environmental factors include the groups with which individuals associate. They may be encouraged to accept certain customs and values of the group. The clothes people wear, the place they live, and the things they buy are all related to their personal attributes, although the relationships may be complex and difficult to chart. The political, social, and religious philosophies adhered to reflect the influence of one's social or work group.

Thus, in sometimes unnoticed associations, the individual's personal attributes do influence his or her opportunities, selection of employment, and manner of spending leisure time. All are directly related to lifestyle and "why you buy."

AVAILABILITY OF MERCHANDISE

The principle of economics, known as the **law of supply and demand,** operates in all selling and buying procedures. This "law" states that if the supply of a product is balanced by the demand, the price is a true one directly related to value of the product. But if the supply is less than the demand, the price rises above true value; or if the supply exceeds the demand, the price falls below true value. This balance between supply and demand is a very important consideration in buying food, clothing, and services.

In order to shop most economically, you will need to purchase food or clothing when the supply is most plentiful. Low supply and demand limits production and usually results in increased selling price.

Shopping is usually more economically done in large stores where the supply of merchandise is greater than in small neighborhood stores or from door-to-door salesmen. The large store is able to buy in quantity, thus receiving a lower wholesale price than the neighborhood salesman. Stores in several locations or towns operating under a central management have the opportunity to buy in quantity when the supply is greatest and retail to customers at a lower price. Thus, the discount store or so called "chain" store can be an economical place to purchase high quality merchandise.

Outguessing the markets for goods and services is difficult and sometimes impossible. However, there are general guidelines that may be helpful in the purchase of food and clothing. Seasonal changes in supply and demand are accompanied by changes in prices. For example, the demand for winter coats is greatest at the start of the fall and winter season. Thus, the prices are highest at that time. Reduced prices can be expected near the end of the season. However, the best selections will probably not be available.

Certain food prices are known to fluctuate during the year. Better prices can be found on fruits and vegetables when the supply is great in the spring and summer. A good shopper will take time to study the markets.

PEER GROUP INFLUENCE ON BUYING

Peer group pressure is a powerful force to establish conformity. This is especially true during high school. Everyone wants to be accepted by his or her peers. There is often a strong influence to "follow the leader" when you wish to be identified with a group. For example, if group leaders tend to buy new style clothes, many of the group members may also buy the same style. In recent years many new clothing styles have been introduced to group leaders in a community to influence other buyers.

The need to stay in good standing with a peer group is important to people. Sometimes clothes or sporting goods are bought to gain a person membership in the group. For members of other groups it may be cars, jewelry, or other articles.

It is important for each young person to stop and analyze the situation, answering this question, "Am I planning my budget according to my own income and expenditures, or am I overlooking my personal wishes in order to be 'one of the group'?"

The Desire to Be Accepted by Your Peers May Cause You to Play "Follow the Leader"

It is not wise to attempt to "keep up with the Jones's" when your income is not adequate. Only by adapting your budget to your own income and expenditures can you become an intelligent consumer.

SPECIALISTS' INFLUENCE ON BUYING

An analysis of buying practices by individuals and groups indicates that a number of factors may be present in motivating the person to make a purchase. The influence in this situation is more than peer pressure and involves the status, prestige, and values of the individual. The desire to achieve recognition by buying goods and services is almost universal among individuals and groups. It is not limited to one economic class but can be observed among all economic levels.

Many possible examples can be cited to illustrate this idea. Supervisors of a large department store may all drive the same make of cars because they feel this is the type of car they are expected to drive, since it was recommended by the president of the store. The president of a company recommends a particular country club and all of his junior executives feel an obligation to join.

The styles of clothes individuals buy and wear are to meet the expectations of a

Plan Your Spending According to Your Income, Not the Joneses'

group or identify with a group. In the West, ranchers wear a special type of boot that may have been a useful style at one time but no longer has the same usefulness today. Among professional men and women, the personal library in the home and foreign travel have been accepted as marks of culture and are expected. The schools and colleges to which parents send their children no doubt reflect the influence of specialists or leaders in setting patterns of action.

These illustrations serve to point out the far-reaching influence of specialists in various areas as they shape the values and buying habits of many individuals associated with them.

HOW TO BUY

LONG-RANGE PLANNING

Having a well-planned budget for the year is helpful in developing a long-range buying plan. An approximate dollar amount should be designated for each expense. Few families or individuals can purchase everything needed at one time; the budget

allowance is just not enough. Thus, things needed first will be purchased first. Long-range planning applies especially to goods that will be used for some time, and must also take into consideration the relationship of what is purchased first and last.

Buying clothing for the second year is a good example. Your entire wardrobe is more important than one individual garment. When your clothing budget is limited, a long-range purchase plan for clothing should include the colors you like and what fits your personality. Additional purchases should fit into your particular color and style scheme. It would be very foolish to buy a brown suit when all of your other garments and accessories are gray or black.

Every purchase of clothing needs to fit into your master plan for the year. Two factors are important to your long-range plan. First, take inventory of what you have at the present time. Second, plan what you need and hope to buy during the year.

MAKING AN INVENTORY

Making an inventory of your wardrobe is quite simple. All that is needed is a list of garments and the condition of each one. Probably a mental list is all that is needed. What do you have for work, school, and formal occasions? In which area do you need the most replacement? Should you consider a new color combination? Will the styles change much? The problem here is to think in terms of what you have, what you will need, and then decide what your shopping should include.

PLANNING FOR QUALITY SHOPPING

After you have completed your inventory, the next step is to make tentative shopping plans. Here compromises will have to be made. Few people have enough money to buy everything desired. Planning for your future shopping is not as easy as making an inventory. Here judgment and knowledge are important. Careful study on how to buy will include:

1. Consideration of which items receive heavy use and therefore need to be durably constructed;
2. Knowledge of what makes one article more durable than another article; and
3. Knowledge of what difference in cost is appropriate for various qualities of merchandise.

Most of us will make mistakes from time to time. However, careful study will prevent many errors and help develop good buying habits.

Understanding the difference in cost of various qualities of merchandise requires further consideration of prices and quality of goods. The price of goods is not always a good guideline for quality. Price is determined in several ways. You may wonder why a pair of shoes priced at $25 at a downtown store may be listed at $18 in a discount store located at the edge of the city. Is quality involved here? The answer, of course, is no. The difference in pricing is most likely based on the cost of distribution. The cost of distribution is more in the city.

Rent costs more; the store is more centrally located; and there are more sales personnel to serve you. Therefore, quality of the shoes is not the only factor in pricing. The service and convenience given by the city store make it necessary to charge more for the shoes. Thus, quality is not the entire basis for the difference in price between the downtown shoe store and a discount store.

The difference in pricing may be based on factors other than good service and convenience. Supply and demand enter the picture. A limited supply of needed merchandise in demand will sell for a higher price. When food products are scarce, the prices are higher. A shortage of milk will result in higher prices, for agricultural products are particularly affected by supply and demand.

WHERE TO BUY

When one company is the only manufacturer of a needed item, that company may be able to hold a monopoly and charge prices much higher than production costs. Federal and state laws have been passed to prevent groups of firms from holding down production and raising prices. However, some firms still have a monopoly on certain products. The price of these items may not be based on supply and demand.

Determining the quality of merchandise is not easy, and deciding on the level of quality which you will need is more difficult. It has been said that the quality of a product can be assured when buying well-known brands of merchandise. In most cases this is probably true. However, it may be possible to get the same product sold under a retail store brand for less. For example, Whirlpool manufactures appliances for Sears, which sells them under the Kenmore brand name. Montgomery Ward's brand name for appliances is **Signature,** but the appliances are made by a number of well-known manufacturers of appliances. The smart shopper learns that it is possible to get high quality products under different brand names.[1] Much information on the quality of appliances is available through consumer reports.

WHAT TO AVOID WHEN BUYING— CONSUMER FRAUD

Fraud in business and industry has been a matter of national concern for a number of years. Recently, new authority has been given the U. S. Food and Drug Administration to protect the consumer from abuse. The Federal Trade Commission (FTC) has been given additional authority to control deceptive advertising. Both organizations have certain regulatory functions which are closely related. In the area of labelling of products, the authority of the Food and Drug Administration often brings its functions close to that of the Federal Trade Commis-

sion. The Federal Trade Commission is responsible for the enforcement of regulations dealing with misleading advertisement of food and drugs.

The **"truth in packaging"** law and the **"truth in lending"** law provides the government agency with more authority to protect the consumer.

FRAUD IN BUSINESS AND INDUSTRY.

The federal government has also been active in consumer protection in an area related to fraud. Many products on the market are unsafe under certain conditions. To protect the consumer from faulty machines and devices, the Consumer Product Safety Act was signed into law by President Nixon in October of 1972. The purpose of the act is stated below.

1. To protect the public from injuries associated with consumer products.

A Dishonest Scheme That Takes Advantage of Another Person Is Fraud

[1]"A hotpoint by any other name would be a": **Everybody's Money.** (Winter 1968-69), Vol. VIII, No. 4, pp. 8-9.

2. To assist the consumer in evaluating the safety of the product.
3. To provide leadership in standardization of products.
4. To promote investigation into cause and prevention of product-related injury and death of consumer.

The act provides for the establishment of a Consumer Product Safety Commission with the **power to develop and enforce uniform safety standards for products.** The Commission has the **power to ban products from the market that are proven to be dangerous to the user.**

Governmental agencies have only recently moved forward to protect consumers. However, private organizations have fought the fraudulent practices and unethical businesses for a number of years. One of the most effective has been the Better Business Bureau, an organization that started in 1912 by the Associated Advertising Clubs of America. The purpose of the organization then was to establish a vigilance committee to reduce deceptive advertising. In 1921, the National Better Business Bureau was organized to deal with operating problems involving national business establishments. The Association of Better Business Bureau, which developed later, had as its objective to improve business practices on the local level. In 1973, a total of 150 local offices served people in the United States, Canada, Puerto Rico, and Israel.

As a result of recent attacks on the Bureaus by members of the press, elected governmental officials, and consumer groups, the Better Business Bureaus have initiated reorganization of their activities. Charges made include complaints of consumers that the local offices of the Bureaus lacked staff, maintained inadequate records, and demonstrated little interest in processing the complaints. One congressman charged that the employees of the Better Business Bureaus served as agents of business and tended to support business organization against the consumer movement both in government and in the private sector. It was also indicated that the Bureaus often continued to keep business firms on the membership roll although the firms had fraudulent practices proved against them.

The reorganization of the Better Business Bureaus started in 1970, when the Council for Better Business Bureaus (CBBB) set up new goals. The organization has established a fourteen-point program for improvement. Five of the fourteen points were given immediate priority for a five-point plan. The first part of the plan was to improve and expand local services of the Better Business Bureaus. The second was to set up consumer arbitration panels to hear and judge disputes. To help local offices improve their services, a third point was to set up a computer center in the National Headquarters Office, located in Washington, D. C. The fourth priority was given to development of a consumer education program to better inform the consumer. The fifth, and last, priority of the plan was to create a National Advertising Board of Review to eliminate or reduce false advertising of national organizations.

A consumer rebellion is being led by national leaders and groups forcing local, state, and federal elected officials to enact more and more legislation to protect the consumers' rights. It will be interesting to watch what private organizations funded by local and national business firms can do to improve consumer protection.

There is no doubt that the combined efforts of all the agencies will force the business community to respect the rights of the consumer. At the same time, product quality will need to be described in detail, and the consumer fully informed of what can be expected. Consumers can expect better treatment, but they may experience an increase in cost of quality products.

An example of this better treatment is the new requirements for textile manufacturers. Since 1972, textile manufacturers are required to meet the F.T.C. regulation of "Care Labelling" of textile wearing apparel. The labels give specific laundering and dry

PERMANENT CARE INSTRUCTIONS
WASHING — HAND OR MACHINE WASH
USING PERMANENT PRESS OR WASH
AND WEAR CYCLES AT MEDIUM SETTING.
DRIP OR TUMBLE DRY AT MEDIUM
SETTING. REMOVE QUICKLY FOR BEST
PERMANENT PRESS RESULTS. DO NOT
BLEACH. MAY BE DRY CLEANED.

CARE INSTRUCTIONS
Machine Wash
using mild soap
at medium setting.
Tumble dry at
low heat or
hang dry after
complete spin cycle.
Press with warm
(Never Hot) iron.

WARM WASH
Normal Cycle
TUMBLE DRY
Medium Heat
Wash and dry reds
and dark colors
separately
Avoid Bleach

Proper Care for Knit Garment.
Dry Clean **only,** Soft **press**
Maximum temperature 320° F
Use **press cloth** for **hard**
pressing.

Textile Wearing Apparel Labelling May Save You Money

cleaning instructions that may save you money.

Care labelling is also tagged to bolt fabrics. Since July, 1972, a colored triangle on the bolt with a code number is attached to each bolt indicating the method of cleaning that should be used for long wear.

To help consumers get better wear from textile garments "Care Labelling" is required.

Most business firms operate on the theory that honesty is the best policy and provide the best service and products possible. However, there is plenty of evidence that there are some establishments who practice fraud in most of their operations. One needs only to read the records of court cases to soon learn to be alert for fraud.

FRAUD IN AUTOMOBILE SERVICE AND REPAIR

Since there are millions of automobiles and trucks on the roads and millions of people involved in service and repair, it is not surprising to find some fraud. Recent research in the auto repair services clearly shows that the consumer is being victimized by fraudulent practices on the part of some garages. Fraud occurs when a mechanic in a garage replaces many parts which are not defective. The cost of labor for a job may also be padded by a few unscrupulous garage owners. Not all cases involve fraud, for some of the abuse can be the result of untrained auto mechanics who make incorrect diagnoses of the auto malfunction.

Take the case of operators of a transmission repair shop in a large Midwestern city. After many complaints, the Attorney General sent his agents to investigate. The operators were asked to repair the transmission of a new car that had purposely been made to malfunction by installing a defective switch. The operator of the repair shop installed another transmission and charged the agent several hundred dollars for the repair job. The operators were arrested, and the shop was closed. The operators were waiting for their day in court while their victims were waiting to file lawsuits to recover the money lost in the fraud.

Service station operators and their employees have been charged with fraud and unlawful business practices. Charges include high-pressure sales tactics in replacement of parts. One sales pitch was for the attendant to remove the air filter from the engine and attempt to sell the customer a new one. The same sales pitch is used to sell car batteries, radiator hoses, shock absorbers, fan belts, windshield wiper blades, and tires. In some cases, actual damage to the customer's car was done to sell parts and do repairs.

Such operations have been called the "fifty-percenters." The operator and attendant split the money on a fifty-fifty basis. Often the victims are motorists from out of state, people who lack experience with the English language, or women traveling alone.

Premium gasoline mixed with regular gasoline can be sold as premium with a higher percent of profit. A less expensive oil can be substituted for premium oil and go unnoticed by the customer.

The consumer is being given some protection today by enforcement of laws related to highway safety. Cars have been recalled to repair defects and automobile tires have been recalled because of failure to withstand highway tests. The National Highway Safety Administration has forced the recall of tires when there was conclusive evidence that the tires were defective. Some of the largest and most prestigious tire manufacturers have been involved in recall. The law requires all purchasers' names and addresses to be recorded with the type and serial number of tires purchased. In case the tires are found to be unsafe, a recall can be made.

Without the present consumer legislation, few (if any) tires would be recalled. Some defective tires are stamped (for farm use only) and should not be used on high-speed automobiles and trucks.

The following suggestions are made to help you protect yourself from dishonest auto services.

1. Select a reputable service station operator who will feel responsible to you as a regular customer.

Fraud Occurs When a Service Worker Replaces Parts Which Are Not Defective

2. Keep your car properly serviced to avoid stalls and breakdowns on the road. It is especially important to have the tires, batteries, hoses, and belts checked regularly.
3. Have your car serviced and checked before long trips.
4. Be alert when stopping at service stations other than the one you patronize. Don't leave your car while it is being serviced at a service station.
5. Be suspicious when a number of attendants are servicing your car and start to remove the air filter, check the battery with a tester, or inspect the shocks and other parts of the car.
6. Don't be pressured into buying parts for your car when a situation develops which is similar to the one described in item above.
7. When major repairs and tune-ups are due, take the car to a dealership with a good service department.
8. Be sure you discuss the list of the work before signing the authorization form. Don't permit additional work done on the car without an estimate on the cost.
9. Most service station operators and garage mechanics are honest, but you will be wise to let them know you are interested in knowing what work is being done.
10. A little praise and courtesy for the people who service your car may also help you get the best service.

FRAUD IN SALES

Many schemes to deceive the consumer in sales of products and services have been tried on consumers of all ages. Many times the schemes work and the unwary consumers never know they have been victims.

One common fraudulent practice is known as "bait and switch." The merchant baits the consumer into the store with bargains, but when the customer tries to buy the bargain, the salesperson downgrades the product and recommends a more expensive product from which more profit can be made.

This scheme is used in many types of stores. Men's suits may be advertised at $50.00, but when you try to buy one, the sales representative tries to sell you a more expensive one to increase the sales commission at your expense.

The "contest winner" game is another scheme to deceive the consumer. One pitch is to call you on the telephone and ask you a simple question that anyone can answer. When you answer the question, you are informed that you are a winner and can purchase a $100.00 clothing certificate for $75.00. The limited things that can be purchased may be worth no more than $75.00 in the first place. The scheme is to make you think you are a winner, when in fact you are not.

One of the oldest schemes is the magazine subscription fraud. Certain misrepresentations are made by door-to-door sales representatives. You should be suspicious if you hear the old stories of people working their way through college, selling for a "charitable" organization, or earning points for a promotion. Beware of the door-to-door magazine sales representatives.

The encyclopedia game is another deceptive way to sell the unwary consumer. Sometimes the sales representatives will offer you a big discount for the new edition if you will permit the company to use your name as one who recommends the books. In order to accept the generous offer, you are requested to make a $50.00 advance payment. Many times the salesperson and

Sometimes a Salesperson Will Downgrade Advertised Bargains in Order to Sell a Higher-Priced Product ("Bait and Switch")

One Must Be Wary of Purchasing Articles from Door-to-Door Sales Personnel Who Do Not Have a City License to Sell Their Products

the $50.00 are never seen again. It is not wise to buy from door-to-door sales representatives unless they have a city license to sell or can produce good identification.

Persons wanting to purchase a used car may find classified advertisements listed as "For sale by owner." Be alert to such schemes. The sellers are sometimes part-time sales personnel who tell you that they are selling their second car as a sacrifice because they are ill.

FRAUD IN HOME IMPROVEMENT

Beware of solicitors offering free inspection or free estimates for home improvement. Just about every time a free inspection is made, the home owner is told that repairs are badly needed. Local and state law enforcement agencies are in a much better position to deal with fraudulent practices today. However, a wise consumer will be alert to any free inspection schemes provided by persons from another city. Fraud has occurred in termite control, furnace and air conditioning inspection, electrical wiring inspection, roof inspection, and other areas of home repair and improvement.

FRAUD IN OTHER AREAS

The young person graduating from high school or college is the target of many schemes to sell insurance, additional education, and business opportunities. Operators and representatives of correspondence schools make impossible promises to prospective students and many times misrepresent the actual job opportunities in the occupation.

High school diplomas and college degrees are offered by many nonaccredited schools and offer little more than an impressive bit of art work indicating you have been awarded a degree by the particular school. Unless the school is accredited or approved, the diploma may be of little value.

Older people who are lonely are the target of many fraudulent schemes. Lonely Hearts Clubs may charge higher rates than

Many People Have Been Dissatisfied with Computer Dating Programs

the service is worth and may set up the wealthy members for unscrupulous people to take advantage of the situation. Computer dating is another service in which many complaints have been recently publicized. Organizations providing this type of service may be unable to find dates for persons living outside of the larger cities.

Lawsuits have resulted when older people have been swindled by various dance studio organizations which sell expensive dancing lessons. The studio gives a couple of free dance lessons and then high-pressures people to sign up for more lessons. Before they realize that they have been "taken," they may have signed a contract that could cost thousands of dollars.

FRAUD IN GOODS AND SERVICES

Many industries serve the needs of our population. A small deception by a large company may cost the consumers billions of dollars. A fraud on the consumer of one-half of one percent of the sale produces great profit and may go undetected for years.

In large-scale fraud, the traditional economic theory is that consumers are protected from fraudulent practices by the force of competition. Customers will search the marketplace for the best quality and prices that can be obtained. If they should discover that they have been cheated, they will not return to the place for further purchases. Thus, the particular marketplace will be forced out of business.

FRAUD IN FOODS

However, in the purchase of processed foods, a chemical analysis is needed to determine whether the food purchased was adulterated. The theory that the consumer is protected by the force of competition is not valid. For example, if the processor of cream of mushroom soup should purposely reduce the mushroom content by 10 percent in every fourth can processed, the consumer would probably not learn of the deception.

Buyers of food items today cannot be fully aware of the quality and quantity they are getting, and the idea of "let the buyer beware" may not hold for all. Fraud occurs in the sale of food if the food is adulterated, misrepresented, given short weight or short measure, or mislabelled.

To prevent large-scale frauds in food sales, legislation has recently been enacted to give the Food and Drug Administration more authority in setting up labelling rules for food advertising of nutritional additives. It is a twelve-point program and should help consumers get their money's worth at the marketplace.

All nutritional labelling of foods is voluntary at the present time, unless the food is fortified with a nutrient or is advertised as having a nutritional labelling on the product. Fats and cholesterol are to be listed on the product to help the consumer who needs to

The Labelling of the Contents of a Package Helps the Consumer Make Better Selections

limit intake of these substances. It is also required that artificial flavoring be indicated on the package. Under the provisions of the law, the word "imitation" is used when the food is inferior to the imitated foods. Frozen desert made to imitate ice cream is required to carry full labelling and also fortified to a level of favorable comparison to ice cream. The new labelling system is already in use by some companies. Other companies were required to comply during 1974. The law, when enforced, aids the consumer in getting the best possible food.

In the past, many frauds have been exposed in the sale of foods. A few of the most flagrant violations are reviewed here.

In a large Midwestern city a few years ago, hamburger meat was made of horse meat and mixed with pure beef which was more expensive. The fraudulent dealers were reported to have made millions of dollars in tricking the public, mostly low-income people who could least afford expensive meats. The addition of a soybean substitute in ground meat has also been practiced by different meat processors. Under the labelling laws, this type of ground meat must be labelled. The content of sausage and frankfurters has been questioned because of various ingredients mixed and sold as edible food. The artificial coloring of sausage and frankfurters has also been under investigation by the Food and Drug Administration inspectors. The coloring and addition of many other foods have been prohibited after the danger to human health was proved.

Although it may not necessarily be considered fraud, the sale of contaminated food has resulted in lawsuits and action by the Federal Trade Commission. Contamination—through carelessness—of candies, peanut butter, and other foods has resulted in fines and jail sentences for those responsible.

One area of possible food fraud is in the sale of "natural foods." Natural foods are processed with no chemical preservative, no stabilizers, emulsifiers, or artificial coloring. The foods are grown without the use of commercial fertilizers, pesticides, or herbicides. Natural foods are more expensive than regularly processed foods, with the price sometimes as much as 100 percent above that of regular foods.

It is difficult, or perhaps impossible, for the consumer to identify organic foods. Inspectors of the New York State Food Laboratory tested advertised organic foods from a number of stores and found that many contained traces of pesticides in amounts equal to regular foods.

Since no clear definitions of organic, natural health foods exist, fraud may have not been involved. However, if customers purchasing foods expected foods free of pesticide residue, they were being cheated on many items.[2]

[2](Public Hearings in the Matter of Organic Foods) — Before Louis J. Lefkowity. Attorney General in charge of the Bureau of Consumer Frauds and Protection, December 1, 1972, New York.

Kellogg's® RICE KRISPIES®

Nutritive Values
Product Information

A one-ounce serving of Kellogg's Rice Krispies cereal with four ounces of whole milk provides vitamins, minerals, and protein, plus food energy needed to build a nutritionally sound breakfast.

These toasted puffs of rice are fortified with eight important vitamins and restored with iron.

Nutritionally, one ounce of Kellogg's Rice Krispies supplies these percentages of an adult's officially established minimum daily requirement (MDR):

NUTRIENT	Percent MDR in— Rice Krispies 1 oz. (1 cup)	Rice Krispies with ½ cup Whole Milk*
VITAMIN A	33%	37%
VITAMIN D	33%	45%**
VITAMIN C	33%	37%
NIACIN	33%	34%
THIA-MINE (B₁)	33%	37%
RIBO-FLAVIN (B₂)	33%	50%
IRON	7%	7%
PHOSPHORUS	3%	18%
CALCIUM	—	19%
***VITAMIN B₆	0.6 mg	0.65 mg
***VITAMIN B₁₂	1.6 mcg	2.1 mcg
***MAGNESIUM	15.2 mg	31.1 mg

TYPICAL NUTRITIONAL COMPOSITION

	RICE KRISPIES % of Total Weight	Amount in 1 oz.	RICE KRISPIES with ½ cup Whole Milk*
Protein	6.5%	1.8 gm	6.1 gm
Fat	1.3%	0.4 gm	4.7 gm
Carbo-hydrates	86.5%	24.5 gm	30.5 gm
Calories		109 calories	189 calories

*Whole milk values derived from USDA Handbook No. 8 and USDA Report No. 36.
**Vitamin D fortified milk at 400 USP units/quart.
***Minimum daily adult requirements have not been established.

INGREDIENTS: Milled rice, sugar, salt and malt flavoring with vitamins A and D in vegetable oil, sodium ascorbate, niacinamide, thiamine (B₁), riboflavin (B₂), pyridoxine (B₆), vitamin B₁₂ and iron phosphate added. BHA and BHT added to preserve product freshness.

Rice Krispies is a trade mark (Reg. U.S. Pat. Off.) of Kellogg Company, for its delicious brand of oven-toasted rice cereal.

MADE BY KELLOGG COMPANY
BATTLE CREEK, MICHIGAN 49016, U.S.A.
© 1967 BY KELLOGG COMPANY
® KELLOGG COMPANY

THIS PACKAGE IS SOLD BY WEIGHT, NOT VOLUME. SOME SETTLING OF CONTENTS MAY HAVE OCCURRED DURING SHIPMENT AND HANDLING.

Ctn. No. K-0050H

With the consumer revolution of the 1960's and 1970's and action by many consumer groups and the Food and Drug Administration, efforts to reduce fraud in the sale of foods have made significant progress. Nevertheless, more progress can be made if the consumer takes an attitude of "Buyer beware and be alert" in all purchases. A continuous study of food prices, labelling laws, and state standards is needed for protection.

FRAUD IN DRUGS

The days of the traveling medicine show and ridiculous claims for medicines are gone. Most rural residents and persons living in small towns enjoyed the medicine show's music and entertainment. A few were tricked by the purchase of medicine, which was sometimes herbs and a high content of alcohol. This combination made the user feel the medicine was helpful. In some cases people were poisoned by the drugs which were concocted by quacks with no knowledge of chemistry.

Today many drugs and patent medicines are sold by national advertising on radio and television and in publications. A number of these medicines are produced by drug companies which have made claims that have been proven to be false. In some cases the advertising claims have been fraudulent and the manufacturers have been stopped from using false claims through court action. The Food and Drug Administration has the legal authority to intervene if there are false or misleading claims in labelling the product. The Federal Trade Commission has authority to take action in cases where the advertising is false or misleading. The United States Post Office Department can also act in cases when the mail system is used for fraudulent purposes. Only recently, after consumer groups became more aggressive, has there been increased action by the three governmental agencies. Many companies selling nationally known and used drugs were forced to change their advertisement claims. For-

Manufacturers Have Been Forced to Advertise Accurate Claims of What Patent Medicine Will Do

tunately, the F.T.C. and the F.D.A. can take more positive action today with more and better laws and with more agents and inspectors. Private groups and state agencies are also more active in the reduction of deceptive advertising.

High fines result if a company violates the F.T.C. order to stop advertising claims for a product. One example occurred when the makers of a patent medicine were fined for failing to stop advertising the product as being a remedy for tiredness, loss of strength, a run-down feeling, nervousness, and irritability.

FRAUD IN HEALTH SERVICES

Today consumers of health services face many uncertainties in securing needed health care. In the first place, they have little information to judge the ability, dedication, or ethics of a physician. In the second place, they may have no time or choice in case of an emergency when they must take what is available at the particular time.

The public attitude toward health is changing rapidly. For many years, adequate medical services were considered as a privilege limited to those who could pay. Today health care is considered as a basic right of all people. Yet still we have disagreement on the basic concepts of health service.

Fraud in the medical profession is difficult to spot and to prove. It is difficult to prove that certain expensive tests and treatments were needed, or that they were not needed. Some tests and treatments are done for added caution, while others may be done to collect fees. Some surgery, no doubt, is unnecessary and therefore fraudulent. Many operations are done when the real worth of such an operation is very doubtful. The American Medical Association and the American College of Surgeons have continuously urged the ethical practices of those in the medical profession. The Judicial Council of the Medical Association has recommended expulsion of members proved guilty of unethical and illegal practice. Unfortunately, fraudulent practices — such as fee splitting, unnecessary operations, and rebates from clinical laboratories — have been reported. Malpractice suits have been won against members of the medical profession. The cost of insurance protection against malpractice lawsuits is at an all-time high.

Hospitals and nursing homes have been charged with fraudulent practices by different groups. Sometimes the charges grow out of bills for medicine not used and services not provided. In some nursing homes, charges for doctor calls have been made when the doctor does little more than read the patients' charts.

People in desperate need of medical attention are more likely to be victimized by quacks. Young women, unwed and pregnant, in desperation may visit an unskilled quack for an abortion. Many have lost their lives in such practices. Medical doctors have also been convicted and imprisoned for illegal abortions.

In the field of psychology and psychiatry "phonies" have been able to set up an office without detection and hand out dangerous advice for big fees. Some have certificates of having completed doctor degrees which are also fictitious.

Protecting yourself from fraud in the health service area is important to you and your family. The following suggestions are made to help you get the best service and avoid fraud.

1. Keep up to date on current medical costs and practices in your area.
2. Learn the reputation, competency, and dedication of the physician you select. In a large city this may be more difficult. The local hospital has a list of doctors on its staff and will generally help you find a physician to fit your needs. Your friends or business associates can help you, too.
3. It is wise to have selected a hospital before you need one. The hospital may be judged on the basis of accreditation, if it is a teaching hospital, and on who owns the hospital. Accreditation of the hospital is the minimum safeguard against an unsafe physical plant and substandard medical care.

   Hospitals with training programs and medical school affiliations have more attending physicians on their staff. The ownership of the hospital may be less important. However, suggestions are that best service will most likely be found in a voluntary non-profit hospital.
4. It is not unethical to discuss cost of the hospital or fees charged by a physician before service is rendered. Compare rates and fees with others.
5. When your health insurance pays for the service, be sure the charges aren't padded, for this practice will eventually cost you more in insurance premiums.

6. Refuse to be rushed into surgery or expensive tests. Insist on an explanation of the reasons and the risks involved. A good physician will tell you without your asking and will invite you to get a second opinion.

Unethical behavior by persons in the health service should be reported to the local and state medical societies.

ADVERTISING

Just as the peer group affects buying practices, advertising also has great influence on the individuals and their groups. Advertisement is so much a part of our lives that we are seldom aware of its real effect on us. We hear it and see it on television in the morning; we hear it on our car radio, and we see it on the billboards and in newspapers and magazines that we read.

In 1970, about 20 billion dollars were spent on all types of advertising in the United States. During the same year retail sales were about 364.5 billion dollars. These figures provide some comparison for the cost of advertising.[3]

The success of those in the advertising business in directing the consumer in the buying of goods and services cannot be doubted. Major advertising agencies employing thousands of writers, artists, announcers, program directors, printers, and sales representatives have been established to do the advertising job. Professionals using psychological and sociological techniques in mass persuasion have been very successful in helping the consumers decide what styles they will wear, what food they will eat, and what music they will hear. Researchers in advertising can also assist the business organization in selecting the type of program that will attract the most viewers. Advertising is very influential in the United States and in most of the world.

[3]United States Department of Commerce.

AVAILABILITY OF PRODUCTS

Through advertising, buyers are kept informed as to which products are available and where they can be bought. Many times information concerning where to buy a particular product or service is needed. The Yellow Pages provide such information in their classified listing of services offered and products for sale along with business addresses and telephone numbers. The names, addresses, and telephone numbers of lawyers, physicians, engineers, and other professionals you may wish to contact are also printed in the Yellow Pages.

Advertising also provides consumers with information on new products which may be very useful to them. In such advertising, the emphasis is placed on the newness of the product, not the availability of the product.

Advertising also tells the customer where to get the best price on goods and services. Comparing the prices of foods advertised in the local newspaper makes it easier for the shopper to save time and money on

Advertising Can Be Helpful to the Consumer

certain foods when quality is the same or can be compared.

It is also claimed that advertising by different companies makes competition more effective. The economic theory is that the buyer is protected from overpriced and inferior merchandise when there is competition, which is partly the result of advertising. No doubt the theory can be accepted that some advertising tends to increase competition and reduce prices for buyers by making them aware of the difference in the firm with lowest prices and best quality goods.

The slogan, "It pays to advertise," can usually be interpreted to mean that the business firm and the consumer profit from advertisement. Cost of advertising, although useful to the consumers in many cases, add to the cost of the product and must be charged to the buyer. Sometimes industrial firms may advertise much more than is needed to acquaint the consumer with the product. Many national television programs are sponsored by firms whose products are common household words. However, the firms advertise to keep their product in the limelight. Illustrations are the various soaps, washing powders, breakfast foods, soft drinks, and razor blades advertised by firms who have national distribution. In many instances the consumers pay for national telecasts of sporting events and other telecasts of national interest. It is quite possible that the large firms would not need to make the large outlay of money for advertising to retain the level of sales. However, some executives may feel it is a matter of pride and prestige for the firm to provide national telecasts. The cost of such advertising must eventually be paid for by the consumers who may or may not object.

DECEPTIVE AND MISLEADING ADVERTISING

The objective of advertising agencies is to help the client make a profit and in so doing make a profit for the agency. The

JULY CLEARANCE
All Major Appliances To Be Sold
(Appliances in stock—only)

10% ABOVE DEALERS COST

- Air Conditioners
- Refrigerators
- Freezers
- Color & B&W TV's
- Dishwashers
- Stereos
- Gas & Electric Ranges

Here is a sporty new 19... may win

CONGRATULATIONS! YOU ARE A WINNER

Advertising Can Be Deceptive

interest and welfare of the consumer may sometimes be over-looked by the advertising agency and the producer.

Deceptive and misleading advertising was not controlled until 1938. Before that date, the only control attempted was that of the advertising industry, which was ineffective. Advertising claims were considered to be "trade puffing" and could not be considered as a product warranty. Thus, no legal action could be initiated. The passage of the Pure Food and Drug Act introduced some governmental control of advertising.

Recently the Federal Trade Commission has been given more power to prevent deceptive advertising. State laws have also been enacted to protect the consumer against false claims by advertisers. Publishers of magazines and newspapers presently are assuming more responsibility to the consumer by screening advertisements accepted for their publications.

THE SEVEN FORMS OF PROPAGANDA

Advertising methods and techniques have changed much in the last sixty years. Advertisers must get the best possible results from a one-minute spot of time on national telecasts, since as many as seventy million viewers may be reached. The principles of psychology applied in selling goods and services are much better understood today. Research in human motivation and buyer behavior makes it possible for persons skilled in this area to capitalize on consumer weaknesses that can be used in persuading individuals and groups to buy certain products. Some of the advertisements presented on television may insult the intelligence of the average viewer, but at the same time reach their objective in a very subtle way. One or more of the seven well-known forms of propaganda can be identified in programs today.

Propaganda is a term used to identify a unique method for the purpose of getting people to think or act in a particular way. The purpose is to get people to accept both products and ideas. It is a process to acquire ready-made thinking for a group and may be applied through all means of communication. Propaganda has been classified in the following terms.

1. "Name-calling" is a device used in advertising and politics in which the person, product, or organization is called a name. The name is emotionally negative to the people to be influenced. The idea is to have the people follow an emotional appeal rather than a rational approach to a situation. Today the management of one company would not dare to refer to another company as "the gyp company" or the "Big Polluter" in an advertisement for fear of a lawsuit. How-

ever, some consumer groups do label the products of a company unsafe or inferior, and that label may be more fiction than actual fact. Real name-calling occurs on some of the national radio networks where certain individuals and groups are identified with broad derogatory names. Examples include calling college professors "pinks" or "intellectual socialists;" calling politicians "big spenders;" and labelling all welfare recipients "lazy people."

2. "Glittering Generalities" is a propaganda method in which general terms are used to influence people emotionally to be favorable toward a product or cause. A number of words, including "the American way," "fair play," "square deal," "truth," "liberty," "jus-

Good Consumers Should Not Be Misled by Advertising

tice," or "democracy" are used to influence buyers. Many examples of this type of propaganda can be identified in advertising.

3. "Transfer" is a technique in which advertisers attempt to associate their product or purpose with a symbol people accept as good. The basic idea is that a warm feeling of good will will be emotionally transferred to the idea that the advertiser wants the consumer to accept. Many words and slogans do have emotional effects on people. The use of a picture of the Rock of Gibraltar by an insurance company is one. The use of the black clenched fist is another symbol. Nations of the world, religious organizations, fraternal organizations, and professional organizations use the transfer technique for continued acceptance.

4. One of the most widely used propaganda techniques is the "Testimonial." The great line-backer, Bill Block, uses only Heavenly Shaving Cream and Saber Razor Blades. Lovely Gay Green uses only Angel's Soap to keep that creamy complexion. These are fictitious examples of how this technique is used.

5. The "Plain-Folk" device is used to get prospective customers to feel favorably toward a product. Television advertising uses the proper dress, language, and action to get the Plain-Folk idea to work. This type of propaganda is considered very effective and is used in political campaigns as well as in advertising.

6. "Card Stacking" is a technique in which every conceivable argument and supporting view, real or imaginary, is used to create a favorable position for one who is advocating the use of a product or accepting an idea. Only the supporting arguments are used, and the unfavorable are not considered. This presentation gives

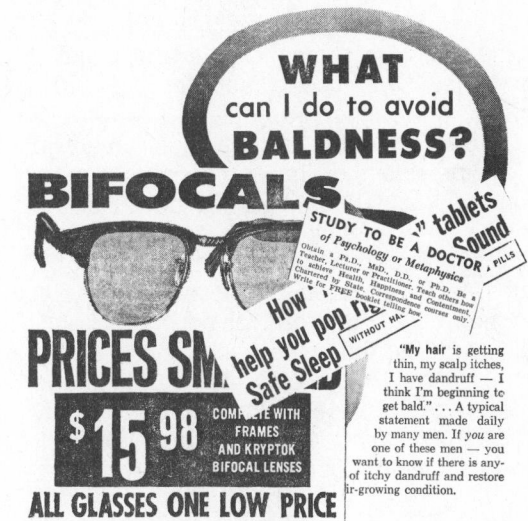

Some Advertisers Attempt to Influence Consumers with Endorsements from Other People

the consumer a one-sided picture or story.

7. "Band Wagon" propaganda uses a technique which implies that **everyone** is using a particular product. The name is derived from the expression "Hop on the bandwagon."

Most of us have been fooled by propaganda techniques, because we allow an emotional bias to overcome judgment and reason. Some of the propaganda used today is very subtle and is designed and presented by experts who go to great expense to get favorable reaction from the consumer.

REPORTING FRAUD

Today many governmental agencies and consumer organizations are working to prevent fraud in all areas of economic activity. However, the agencies and organizations need the help of persons who have been victims of fraudulent activities. Fraud can happen to anyone and is not something to be ashamed of, but it is a citizen's responsibility to report the fraud to the proper authorities.

When you have been hit by fraud, go first to the business representative and make a complaint. Give all the facts, and give the company a chance to settle your claim. If you don't get action on the local level, go to the president of the company.

In many situations it will be necessary to write a letter outlining your complaints. Be sure to describe the complaint and give dates, facts, and details that are necessary.

When contracts are involved in the fraud, include in the letter the name of the salesperson and the company. List the place and date of the transaction. Your complaint may be stronger when a copy of the contract, advertisements, labels, and other printed materials related to the problem are included with the letter. **The original copies should be retained by the person MAKING THE COMPLAINT.**

If no action is taken by the company within fifteen days after your letter has been mailed, a second letter should be written with copies sent to the State Attorney General, county attorney, local newspapers, radio and television stations, and consumer organizations.

Businesses operate to make a profit, and they must serve the public to exist. However, the consumer must sometimes make special effort to receive justice at the marketplace.

IT PAYS TO UNDERSTAND ADVERTISING

Advertising can help you improve your buying decisions. Although most advertising today is honest, the buyer must remember that the purpose of advertising is to sell and to inform. The seller's purpose is to design advertising that will persuade you to buy goods and services. Thus, it is important for the buyer to understand the seller's appeals. Some of the appeals to look for and not be over-influenced by are listed below.

- Beauty, glamour, sex, vanity (clothing, cosmetics, etc.)
- Recognition (status, group acceptance)
- Self-esteem (skill, ability, knowledge, independence)
- Financial gain
- Fear and Anxiety (insurance, safety devices, medicine, recreation)

Learn to use advertising by:

- Knowing federal and state regulations on control of advertising.
- Being alert to deceptive schemes.
- Being sure your information is complete and accurate.
- Not becoming emotionally involved by the appeal.

STUDY AIDS

NEW TERMS

advertisements
bait
care labelling
cost of distribution
comparative prices
consumer fraud
consumer product
  safety law
fraud

inflation
inventory
life style
monopoly
persuasive influence
peer group
prey
propaganda
quality

STUDY QUESTIONS

1. What influences a person's lifestyle?
2. Can you think of any times when peer groups have influenced your buying?
3. What three steps should be followed for good shopping?
4. What does long-range planning mean in buying goods and services?
5. What are the two steps required for a long-range plan?
6. What are the three points to study in order to do quality shopping?
7. What was the purpose of the Consumer Product Safety Act of 1972?
8. Under what conditions can the contest winner scheme be considered as fraud?
9. How does the supply and demand of goods and services affect prices?
10. What is the public attitude toward making health services available to all?

DISCUSSION PROBLEMS

1. Make an inventory of your clothing, writing beside each item the approximate cost. Add to find total value of your clothing. At your present salary, how long would it take you to replace your wardrobe?
2. Why should you decide what you need to purchase before shopping for needed articles?
3. How do employees decide what kind of clothing is needed for a particular job if they are not required to wear a uniform?
4. Should the United States Government establish a socialized medicine program for the citizens of the country?
5. What additional controls should be placed on advertising which are not in effect at the present time?

CHAPTER TWELVE
USING CONSUMER CREDIT

ESTABLISHING AND MAINTAINING CREDIT

You may have gone to a local store to make a purchase, and, instead of paying cash, said "Put it on our bill." You were using credit. Each year credit purchases account for over $5,000,000,000 worth of merchandise in the United States. Some predict that **we will become a moneyless society** with different forms of credit to purchase all goods and services. This may never happen, but more and more credit cards are available for making purchases. The most recent addition is the use of **bank cards.**

Credit is extended to a greater number of people each year because, as responsible citizens, they have earned "the right to receive credit." You and your family have probably gone through a formal process of applying for credit. Generally, the process is repeated each time you apply for credit with a different business.

The person granting credit wants to know a great deal about the person applying for credit. Business organizations have different procedures. However, most retail businesses belong to credit bureaus which provide them with information about people who have been bad credit risks in the past. **Poor credit risks** are people that are slow to pay their bills, or never pay their bills, or have been sued for not paying their bills.

Good credit is a personal asset. **Asset** means sufficient property to pay debts. The credit bureaus only records your performance. You must maintain it by using credit wisely and not using credit beyond your ability to pay.

Credit has been defined in a number of ways. An acceptable definition for credit is "a transaction where there is present an exchange of goods, services, or money with a promise to pay at a future time." Most people and business organizations use credit in some form. Consumer credit is an economic tool used by most of us to buy

Some Predict That We Will Become a Moneyless Society

what we need today and pay for it when we are paid at the end of the month.

Credit is also important to big and small businesses, as well as local, state, and the federal governments. The federal government probably uses more credit than any other organization. When you purchase a government bond, you are extending your government credit as well as making an investment.

PURPOSE OF CREDIT

Credit is an economic tool that serves not only the individual but also business, industry, and government. Consumer credit makes it possible for the family to make purchases and pay for them over a period of time. For example, practically every family who enjoys a nice home must pay for it over a long period of time. It is difficult for an individual to buy a car without credit. Credit also provides a convenient way to buy by paying for all purchases with a check at the end of each month.

The use of consumer credit means much more to the manufacturer of consumer goods. By having credit available to the customers, it may be possible to sell them much more. With sales assured, the manufacturer can take advantage of mass production techniques and produce goods at less cost which can be sold to the consumer at a saving. With low cost and good distribution, the average American family can enjoy the products of a productive economy.

The credit that a government offers makes many services and improvements possible. It is almost impossible for a city to install a new water system, develop new streets, or build a school without credit.

Credit is necessary for most businesses to operate. A business uses commercial credit to cover the cost of **producing and selling the product, to buy raw materials, to enlarge facilities, and make improvements.** The farmer uses credit to purchase farm equipment, seed, and perhaps more land. Without a system of credit, people could not start, operate, or improve a business enterprise.

These 6 C's Count for Credit
CHARACTER — a sincere attitude toward paying your bills.
CAPACITY — ability to repay loan from money coming in.
CAPITAL — owning property or things worth more than your debt.
CONDITIONS — agreements made in advance between lender and person borrowing.
COLLATERAL — the possessions of any kind, which are set aside or deposited as security for the debt.
COMMON SENSE — ability to use credit wisely.

WHERE TO GET CREDIT

Charging your purchases at the local grocery store is only one form of consumer credit. There are several others. **Service credit** is a good example of another form of consumer credit.

When Bill Smith picks up his telephone receiver and dials a long distance call to his mother, he is using **service credit.** The cost of the call is automatically recorded, and Bill will receive a bill for services at the end of the month. Even when he turns on an electric light, he is using service credit. **Service credit** is extended to practically everyone who is provided a utility such as gas, water, electricity, and telephone service. Utility service is granted on the basis of confidence that the user will pay for the service.

Another type of credit mentioned previously is **charge account credit.** This type of credit is offered to millions of persons to purchase gasoline for the car, pay for motel and hotel services, buy clothing, and other articles. Modern data processing techniques make it possible to use credit cards in handling billings and payment. Bank Ameri-card, Master Charge, and Bankmark Card credit services have many additional purchases and services available through charge account credit.

This service demonstrates the confidence placed in the consumers as well as their responsibility in meeting financial obligations.

Consumer credit is used to a large extent in buying more expensive things such as cars, furniture, and appliances. This type of credit is known as "installment credit." More than three-fourths of all purchases of durable goods are on an installment plan.

Many times it is necessary for a family to meet unforeseen expenses by borrowing money. This type of credit is known as personal loan credit and may be obtained at a number of places. Banks provide small personal loan services at a reasonable interest rate. Those with a good credit rating have little difficulty getting small loans from banks. Credit unions lend money only to members. Interest is charged as a monthly rate on the unpaid balance. To join some credit unions, a person may pay as little as 25¢ per month. After depositing $5, the consumer has a full share.

Personal finance and small loan companies require little or no collateral. **Interest rates are higher** since they must take a greater risk. Many states regulate the amount of interest that can be charged.

The **truth-in-lending legislation** passed by the U. S. Congress in 1967 requires that the lender tell the borrower the total cost of the loan. This information will make it easier to compare cost of loan company services.

Pawnshop operators loan money on items of value, such as radios, watches, musical instruments, etc. Most pawnshop operators charge a high rate of interest for their services. If the loan is not paid at a stated time, the owner of the pawnshop may sell the item you leave.

Some lenders operate outside the law. **It is illegal to charge more interest than the maximum set by laws of the state.**

Stop Careless Spending

All family members old enough should watch their spending. Are dollars buying what the family wants most?

Are you spending more than you planned to? Are you spending too much on—
- daily needs such as food and clothing
- rent
- transportation—car or bus
- recreation

Do you have too many—
- insurance payments
- time payments.

THE WISE USE OF CREDIT

A good money management plan includes guidelines for the wise use of credit. Making good judgments in buying and the wise use of credit are closely related. Too much credit may bankrupt a business or ruin a family's credit rating. Consumers can use credit wisely when they understand and follow three guidelines.

1. Use credit **only when necessary** or when the cost and risk can be justified.
2. Using your budget as a guide, **assume no debt that you can not repay from your present income.**
3. Find the **least expensive and most advantageous** credit available.

Credit is always a risky thing to use. Should the head of a family lose his or her job, become ill, or be injured in an accident, it would probably not be possible to overcome a large debt. Credit should be **used, not abused.**

The average person is not cautious enough in reading contracts and making judgments when using credit or installment buying. We usually think of the down payment price and of the amount of weekly or monthly payments. What we fail to do is to multiply and add quickly enough so we can determine the price of an article both with and without the installment purchase charges. Always add the total credit finance charges to the price of the merchandise **before making a credit purchase decision.**

All family members should watch their spending.

Are dollars buying what the family wants and needs the most?

Are you spending more than your budget can pay for? Are you spending too much on —

- daily needs such as food and clothing?
- rent?
- transportation — car or bus?
- recreation?

Do you have too many —
- time payments?
- luxury payments?
- unnecessary payments?

The federal government has issued the following information as a guide to credit buying:

BUYING ON CREDIT

DO . . .

1. Read **each page** of contract or agreement. Be sure it says exactly what the salesperson says. If it does not, DO NOT SIGN IT!
2. **Know what the total cost will be** to you when the payments are finished. That is, cost of item, carrying charges, cost of credit, and any other added charges.
3. Know that the price tag on an item is the price of the item alone. It does **not** include cost of credit, delivery charges, installation costs or any other added charges.
4. Be sure to **compare prices.** This means going to different stores comparing brands and prices.
5. Inform a legal authority for assistance **immediately** when you are told that there was a mistake on the contract and you are asked to sign again. DO NOT SIGN!
6. Know that interest rates are very deceiving and hard to understand. **Demand** a full explanation of the interest rates before making any purchase.

DON'T . . .

1. Sign your name to any contract or papers until you have talked with legal services.
2. Buy any item until you know the total amount it will cost you including credit and other charges.
3. Borrow money unless you have to. If you must borrow, try to borrow from a credit union or a bank. These two places charge less interest.
4. Allow fast-talking sales personnel to talk you into buying anything you don't particularly want or need or cannot afford to pay for.
5. Allow sales representative to leave anything at your house to "try out" if you do not want it. If they insist, tell them you will not be responsible for it and don't sign your name to anything.
6. Ever tell a salesperson you **can't** afford an item. He will show you **how** you can afford it. Tell the salesperson you **don't want** the item.
7. Buy from sales people who tell you that you don't have to read the contract.
8. Buy anything on credit thinking you can pay for it by getting new customers for the salesperson.
9. Be afraid to say **no** to a salesperson.

ESTIMATING COST OF CREDIT

CREDIT FINANCING

When payment on purchases extends over a long period of time, the purchaser is charged for this time. This is expected, because the purchaser is actually using the property of others while making payments. When a salesperson needs a car to do sales work, it may be necessary to use the bank's money to finance part of the cost. The salesperson pays interest on the loan. Practically any type of credit will cost the user. The cost may not be noticeable, but it is added to the cost of the product. For example, when you buy gasoline using a credit card, the company must go to extra expense for billing and mailing. This costs money and the added cost must be passed on to you, the consumer.

When merchants extend credit, they may experience costs other than bookkeeping and billing. A few customers may be unable to pay their debts. Thus, the merchant will have reduced profits. A business expects a certain percent of profit. It also expects loss from bad debts but the loss must be recovered by passing it on to the consumer. Your credit cost in this case may be slightly higher prices.

Many merchants operate on a cash basis. However, to be competitive today and to stimulate sales for a larger business volume, many merchants provide credit for their customers. An open charge account may not be expensive if the total charge is paid on a monthly basis. Should the sales items be appliances, furniture, or automobiles, payment may extend over several months and a different sales plan is used.

When buying large items, such as television sets, radios, refrigerators, and furniture, you must make payments monthly. This type of credit is granted on a time payment basis and is referred to as **installment credit**. In this situation, the merchant may be unable to finance time payments and will seek assistance from a bank or other financial institution. The customer is expected to pay a carrying charge for purchases made on time.

TYPICAL CREDIT CHARGES

The charge for credit may be added to the beginning balance and the total repaid in 12 equal monthly payments.

When They Say	You Pay Annually
$6 per $100 or 6% per year	11.1%
$8 per $100 or 8% per year	14.8%
$10 per $100 or 10% per year	18.5%
1% per month	22.2%

When contract is paid in installments, the average amount owed is about one-half of the beginning balance. Thus, actual rate is approximately twice the stated rate.

The charge for credit may be based on unpaid balance.

Rate Per Month on Unpaid Balance	Annual Rate
⅚ of 1%	= 10%
1%	= 12%
1½%	= 18%
3%	= 36%

EXAMPLE OF INSTALLMENT CREDIT

Suppose Bill Smith buys a color television set for $511.95. He pays $100.00 down and signs a sales contract to pay the remaining $411.95 over a period of 33 months, with payments of $16.25 for 32 months, and a final payment of $15.95. Under the terms of this sales agreement, finance charges (which total $124.00) are added to the unpaid amount of $411.95 for a total of $535.95. The cost of Bill's television set will total $635.95 with down payment, unpaid balance, and finance charges.

What Credit Really Costs?

FIGURING THE COST OF CREDIT

When Bill Smith buys a television set on the installment plan, he will pay more than if he pays cash. The extra expense is a total of three extra costs:

1. Pure interest must be made on the unpaid balance of $411.95.
2. Losses from bad debts must be added to the cost of credit.
3. Administrative cost of bookkeeping, billing, and mailing must be also added.

Pure interest charged on the unpaid balance is regulated by laws of the various states. However, the charges made by department stores, finance companies, and banks may vary within a city or state.

The $411.95 unpaid part of the sale will cost Bill interest plus carrying charges. To figure how much it will cost Bill to use time payment instead of cash, use the following formula:

TO FIGURE THE COST OF CREDIT

1. Multiply the amount of each payment by the number of payments to be made on the television set.
2. Add the down payment to the total sum of the monthly payments.
3. Subtract the cash sale price of the television set from the sum of the down payment plus the total monthly payments. The amount will be the carrying charges Bill is paying.

Step I

Multiply the amount of each payment by the number of payments.

$$32 \times \$16.25 = \$520.00$$
$$1 \times \$15.95 = \underline{15.95}$$
$$\$535.95$$

Step II

Add the down payment.

$$\$535.95$$
$$\underline{\$100.00}$$
$$\$635.95$$

Step III

Subtract the cash price from the cost of the installment plan.

$$\$635.95$$
$$\underline{511.95}$$
$$\$124.00$$

The cost of installment payments is $124.00.

When Bill Smith uses this simple formula, he finds the cost of his carrying charges. However, he needs to figure a constant rate of charge to compare cost with other financing plans.

The largest part of the financing charge occurs in the administration of installment sales. Such costs include investigating the credit records of credit applicants, collecting the monthly payments, bookkeeping costs, and mailing. Automobiles 'sold on time payment must have the cost of insurance added, which increases the administrative cost.

CALCULATING THE INTEREST RATE

It is simple to compare the cash price of a TV set with the cost using installment credit. However, Bill still is unable to calculate the actual interest rate he will be paying for the use of credit. The annual percentage rate is needed if he is to compare the cost of the credit he is using with other types of credit. It is important to know how to figure the rate of interest if you plan to use installment credit or borrow money. Interest rate statements may be confusing to most people. Do not be embarrassed to ask enough questions to help you understand any business transaction.

When you charge the dollar cost of installment credit to an annual interest rate, you can compare interest rates charged by different business organizations. The following is one method to figure the annual interest rates.

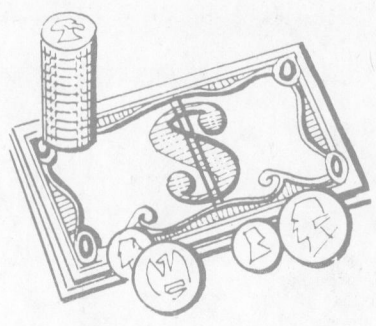

TO CALCULATE THE INTEREST RATE

Step I

Multiply two (2) times the dollar cost of credit ($124.00):

$$2 \times 124 = 248$$

Step II

Multiply the (248) by the number of payments to be made in one year (12):

$$248 \times 12 = 2976$$

Step III

Multiply the amount financed ($411.95) by the total number of payments (33) plus 1 (34):

$$411.95 \times 34 = 14,006.30$$

Step IV

Divide the results in step II (2976) by the results in step III (14,006.30). The answer is the annual rate of interest:

$$14,006.30 \overline{)\ 2976} \quad .21 \text{ percent annual rate}$$

Bill Smith is paying $124.00 installment credit charge for the use of $411.95 for 33 months. The annual rate is about 21 percent.

The percentage rates charged for installment credit by different companies may not reflect a true situation. The rates charged by some companies seem quite high. One reason can be attributed to the large number of installment contracts with small sales. The administrative cost is the same for large or small accounts. Since the accounts vary in size, it is difficult to compare rates from company to company unless their credit granting situation is about the same. In Bill Smith's purchase of $511.95 with a balance of $411.95, the cost of administration was probably as expensive as if he had purchased a $4,000.00 automobile. Thus, in comparing percentage rates charged, it is necessary to know something of the service provided by the company making the sale. In the next sections we will examine ways in which costs may be compared.

COMPARING CREDIT CHARGES AND INTEREST RATES

In order to get the best rates on credit, it is necessary to know the sources of credit available. Rates may vary with the risk the company is willing to take in extending credit. Those with good credit ratings generally are able to get the best rates.

The sources of installment credit can be grouped under three classifications:

1. Retailers who finance and operate their own credit plans. This includes department stores, mail order houses, appliance dealers, and others.
2. Retailers who sell their customers' contracts to finance companies. This group includes auto dealers, farm

machinery dealers, and appliance dealers.

3. Institutions which make loans directly to customers. These include banks, finance companies, credit unions, and others offering installment credit.

Rates vary among the sources making rates comparable. However, it is necessary to reduce all the rates to a common basis; that is, to compare the rates plus any other charge that is added to the contract. First, determine the complete cost. Some companies advertise low rates and add many other charges which should be added on before the percentage rate is computed for the credit. Second, it is important to learn if a full payment before maturity of the contract will result in reduction of interest and charges. A saving should be made if early payment is made.

After rates have been compared, services provided should also be considered. Some of the services to be considered are:

1. The ease of obtaining credit
2. The ease in making payments
3. Careful bookkeeping
4. The methods used in collecting
5. Whether the company provides low cost insurance on the automobile

After you have compared the rates of all sources of credit and the service provided by each, you are ready to decide if it is wise to use credit for the purpose you desire. You can buy for cash or buy on credit.

When you buy on credit, you pay an extra charge. Whether the extra charge is called "service charge," "interest," "carrying charge," or "finance charge," it raises the cost of what you buy. This extra charge can keep you from buying other things you need. For example:

1. An appliance store advertises a refrigerator for $329.95. You can buy it on a 24-month installment contract with a $10 down payment, and you may pay as much as $65 extra for credit — enough to buy 130 quarts of milk.
2. A wool rug, including sales tax, sells for $420.00. Credit charges on a 24-month contract can cost you $180 — enough to pay cash for a clothes dryer.

USING CREDIT

Before signing an installment contract or a note, it is wise to compare the benefits you will get from credit with the extra money it will cost.

Should Bill Smith pay the extra $124.00 for a television set now, or wait one year and pay cash? Of course no one can answer for Bill. Is a color television set worth an extra $124.00 cost?

Deciding when to use installment credit is easier when one looks at the following benefits. These benefits can be listed in five general categories.

Comparisons on Cost of Credit to Finance Purchase of a $420 Rug for 24 Months

You may want to make similar comparisons before you buy.
Costs vary with the institution, business, and State laws.

Item	Bank	Consumer Loan Co.	Dealer	Credit Union	Mail Order Store
Amount financed	$420.00	$420.00	$420.00	$420.00	$420.00
Monthly payments	19.95	25.00	19.60	19.75	20.44
Total time price	478.00	600.00	470.40	474.00	490.50
Finance charge	58.80	180.00	50.40	54.00	70.50
Actual annual rate	13.4%	36% to $300; 10% above	11.5%	12% on unpaid balance	16.1%

Kinds of Credit

1. There are benefits from increased earning power. Many businesses started by getting a loan and paying off the loan from monthly earnings from the business. Tom Jones, a high school student, bought a lawnmower on the installment plan after he had contracted with a number of homeowners to keep their lawns cut for the summer. Loans and installment purchases which increase earnings are considered worthwhile. Borrowing for educational purposes is also in this category.

2. Lowering expenses is beneficial and may make a loan worthwhile. If Bill Smith finds that a better car will reduce his car expenses, it may be wise to purchase a better car. He can enjoy driving a safer and more dependable car at the same expense.

3. It may be necessary to use installment credit in emergencies. Suppose the furnace suddenly burns out, or your car breaks down and it must be used to get to work. Many installment purchases are made under emergency conditions. When emergencies such as sickness, accident, or failure of car or equipment occur, it is worthwhile to use installment credit.

4. Many times it is wise to leave your savings invested and make short-term installment purchases. For example, if Mary Smith had to use her savings in government bonds to replace a dryer in her beauty shop, she would save money by paying installment credit charges rather than lose interest on bonds. Stocks and bonds can be used for security in getting a short-term loan.

5. The final category of benefits to consider is earlier enjoyment of purchases. Generally, earlier enjoyment will be considered in terms of labor saving, time saving, greater convenience, and better family living conditions. Home appliances usually save

labor and time. The purchase of a home for greater convenience and family comfort can generally be justified when compared with the expense of paying rent.

In general, a person receives some benefit from installment credit. The worth of the benefit received must be judged on an individual basis. You will be using installment credit and should be familiar with the costs and problems involved. If you decide that the benefits are worth the extra cost of an installment purchase, find the best terms available. Ask yourself the following questions before using credit:

1. Is having something now worth the extra cost?
2. Do I need it now?
3. What will I gain from it?
4. Can I meet the payments?
5. Is it worth the risk?
6. Will it help me make more money?
7. What will I give up while paying for it?

COLLATERAL NOTE

Pittsburg, Kansas, _____ 19_____ No._____

$_____

FOR VALUE RECEIVED, _____ promise to pay to the order of THE NATIONAL BANK OF PITTSBURG, Pittsburg, Kansas, (hereinafter called the Bank)

the sum of _____ DOLLARS

at THE NATIONAL BANK OF PITTSBURG, Pittsburg, Kansas, payable as follows:

$_____ on the _____ day of _____ 19_____ and $_____ on the same day of each succeeding month

until the _____ day of _____ 19_____ on which last mentioned date the entire balance of the principal then unpaid shall become due and payable.

With interest from _____ until paid at the rate of _____ per cent per annum, payable at said bank.

The interest on each installment, and the interest on the unpaid balance of the principal sum are to be paid at the maturity of each installment. The delinquency charge is **10%** interest per annum on the unpaid balance after maturity of each installment.

If default is made in the payment of any installment or in any payment of the principal of this note or any interest when due, then all the remaining installments and the entire unpaid principal of this note shall become due and payable at once. All signers, endorsers, and parties to this instrument hereby waive demand, protest and notice of non-payment, and agree to all extensions and partial payments before or after maturity. Appraisement waived or not, at option of holder.

As collateral security for the payment of and to secure the payment of this note and any note given in extension or renewal thereof and also of any other note, obligation, indebtedness or liability, direct or contingent, of the undersigned, or any of them, to the bank, due or to become due, whether now existing or hereafter arising, the undersigned has deposited and hereby assigns, transfers, sets over and delivers to said bank the following property:

_____

_____

_____

And the undersigned further gives the bank a lien to secure the payment of all of such obligations and liabilities upon the deposit balances, credits, securities or other property now or at any time hereafter given to or left in possession of the bank by the undersigned, whether for the express purpose of being used by the bank as collateral security or for any other or different purpose, with full authority to said bank to apply any such deposits or credits upon any of said obligations by way of set off or otherwise, whether said credits or said obligations are due or not.

In the event of default in the payment of any installment or in any payment of the principal of this note or any note given in extension or renewal thereof or any other note, obligation, indebtedness or liability, direct or contingent, of the undersigned, or any of them, to the bank, or of depreciation in the value or in the market value of the securities above described, or in case of the insolvency or bankruptcy or receivership of the undersigned, or any of the undersigned, or other parties liable for the payment of any of said indebtedness or obligation or when the bank deems itself insecure the bank may at its option, with or without notice, declare this or any other note or obligation of the undersigned due and also may, but is not required to and with or without declaring the same due, as aforesaid, sell said securities or property or any part thereof, at public or private sale, and if sold at public sale such sale shall be advertised the same as a sale under chattel mortgage; said bank may become a purchaser at either public or private sale of said property. The proceeds of said sale shall first be applied to the payment of all charges and expenses, and second to the payment of interest and third to the payment of the principal of this note and any other note, debt or liability of the undersigned to said bank whether due or not. Any overplus to be paid to the undersigned, and the undersigned agrees to pay any deficiency on demand. The said bank is further authorized to surrender, compromise, release or exchange collateral, and/or may apply any deposit balance by way of set off or otherwise. The undersigned and endorsers and guarantors hereof hereby expressly consent to the renewal or extension of and authorize and empower the bank to make exchanges, compromises and releases for valuable consideration, of any or all choses in action or other securities which it may at any time hold as security for the payment of this note or any other note, debt or liability owed by the undersigned to the bank, and all sureties, endorsers and guarantors of such obligation, including this note or any other note, debt or liability owed by the undersigned to the bank, or owners of collateral security therefore, agree and consent that after maturity thereof extension and renewals of this note or any other note, debt or liability owed by the undersigned to the bank, may at the option of the bank be made. The undersigned hereby authorize said bank to use their names to enforce collection of said securities or property by suit or otherwise or in assigning or transfering the same.

The undersigned borrower acknowledges receipt of a copy of this note on the date hereof.

1. Amount Financed $_____
2. **FINANCE CHARGE** $_____
3. Total of Payments $_____

   ANNUAL PERCENTAGE RATE_____%

   Due_____

Address _____

KANSAS MOTOR VEHICLE RETAIL INSTALLMENT CONTRACT PURCHASE MONEY SECURITY AGREEMENT

Form Kansas 300A

(In compliance with provisions of the Kansas Sales Finance Act, The "Truth in Lending" Act and the Uniform Commercial Code)

Date_____

_____
(Seller-Secured Party)

_____
(Buyer-Debtor)

_____
(Street Address)

_____
(Street Address)

_____, Kansas
(City)

_____
(City)   (County)   (State)

WITNESSETH: That the above Buyer-Debtor being justly indebted to the above Seller-Secured Party, for which a note, secured hereby, has been executed on even date hereof, payable as set out below, because of the purchase on this date by Buyer-Debtor from Seller-Secured Party of the personal property and/or services described in the following schedule:

CLASS	NEW or USED	YEAR MODEL	TRADE NAME	NO. CYLS.	MODEL LETTER OR NUMBER	BODY TYPE OR TRUCK TONNAGE	SERIAL NO.	MOTOR NO.

Check Equip. ☛ ☐ Auto. Trans.   ☐ Over-drive   ☐ Radio   ☐ Heater   ☐ Power Steering   ☐ Power Windows   ☐ Power Brakes   ☐ Power Seats   ☐ Air Conditioning

Other Equipment or Additional Collateral: _____

the same having been purchased from Secured Party for a total deferred payment price and according to the terms and conditions as to cash price, down payment, insurance, fees, finance charges and total of payments as set out in the following schedule:

(CHECK AND INSERT AMOUNT INCLUDED FOR INSURANCE)

☐ Comprehensive
   OR
☐ Fire, Theft, Combined Additional Coverage
☐ $_____deductible Collision
☐ Towing and Road Service

Buyer may choose the person through which this insurance is to be obtained.

TOTAL PHYSICAL DAMAGE . . . . $_____
Items Checked Above Effective:

_____, 19____, to_____, 19____
☐ Disability (Health and Accident) . . . . . $_____
☐ Credit Life (Cancellations of balance) . . . . $_____
   For Terms of Contract
☐ Other Coverages (described below)

Insurance against liability for bodily injury or property damage not included unless specifically described as "Other Coverages."

_____
                                    $_____
_____
                                    $_____

Effective_____19____ to_____19____

TOTAL AMOUNT (Item 7 in Computation) . . . . $_____

If the cost of any insurance, other than insurance on the Cars, is included in the Deferred Payment Price, Buyer designates the buyer whose signature first appears below as the person to be covered thereby.

1. CASH PRICE (Selling Price if this were a cash sale, including Accessories) . . . . $_____

2. TRADE IN: Make_____
   Year Model_____Body_____
   Other_____

   $_____ − $_____ =
   (A) Gross   (B) Owing
                  (C) Net Trade $_____

3. CASH DOWN PAYMENT . . . . $_____

4. TOTAL DOWN PAYMENT (Item 2(C) plus Item 3) . . . $_____

5. UNPAID BALANCE OF CASH PRICE . . . . $_____

6. SALES TAX (Item 1 Minus Item 2(A) x 3%) . . . . . $_____

7. INSURANCE—TOTAL AMOUNT (included in block at left) $_____

8. OFFICIAL FEES . . . . $_____

9. AMOUNT FINANCED (5 plus 6 plus 7 plus 8) . . . . $_____

10. FINANCE CHARGE . . . . $_____

ANNUAL PERCENTAGE RATE	%

11. TOTAL OF PAYMENTS (9 plus 10) $_____

12. DEFERRED PAYMENT PRICE $_____
    (4 plus 11)

PAYMENT SCHEDULE: _____monthly installments of $_____each beginning on the_____day of_____, 19____, and continuing on the same day of each month thereafter and a final installment of $_____. The Finance Charge applies from_____19____.

CREDIT LIFE AND DISABILITY INSURANCE Is not required to obtain this extension of credit. If borrower desires such coverage he should sign on the appropriate space to the right hereof.	**1. The cost for Credit Life Insurance alone** will be $_____for the term of the credit. I desire Credit Life Insurance only. Date_____Signature_____	**2. The cost for Credit Life and Disability Insurance** will be $_____for the term of the credit. I desire Credit Life and Disability Insurance. Date_____Signature_____

READ REVERSE SIDE BEFORE SIGNING: The conditions of this security agreement other than amount and terms of payment are set out on the reverse side of this page, under "SECURITY AGREEMENT CONDITIONS," and are made a part and included within the contractural obligation of Debtor and Secured Party herein.

NOTICE TO BUYER:
1. Do not sign this contract before you read it or if it contains any blank spaces.
2. You are entitled to an exact copy of the contract you sign.
3. You have the right to pay in advance the unpaid balance of this contract and obtain a partial refund of the finance charge based on the "Rule of 78's."

Undersigned Debtor-Buyer acknowledges that he received, at the time of execution of the above contract an exact copy thereof, completely filled in.

_____
Seller-Secured Party

_____
Buyer-Debtor (Person to be Insured)

By_____Title_____

_____
Co-Debtor

Except for instructions, the smallest type contained hereon is 8-point.

Installment Contracts Must Be Written in Compliance with Provisions of State and Federal Acts

SECURITY AGREEMENT CONDITIONS

Now therefore, in consideration of the sale of the property described on the reverse side hereof, and to further secure the payment of the note executed on even date hereof, any future advances of money or credit made to or on behalf of the Debtor, and any extensions or renewals hereof, the Debtors hereby convey, give and grant to the Secured Party, a security interest in the collateral described on the reverse side hereof; and in addition thereto, any collateral of like description or classification as that described on the reverse side hereof, or substituted therefor, that is or may be acquired by the Debtor subsequent hereto; provided however, if the Debtors well and truly pay said note according to the terms thereof, then this Security Agreement shall cease and be void. The personal property hereby secured may remain in the possession of Debtor as long as all the conditions of this Security Agreement are performed.

The personal property hereby secured may remain in the possession of Debtor as long as all the conditions of this Security Agreement are performed.

Debtor agrees to pay for each installment delinquent not less than ten days, one delinquency charge of 5% of the installment or $2.50, whichever is the lesser. Debtor may prepay this obligation in whole or in part at anytime during the Secured Party's regular business hours. The amount of such refund shall represent at least as great a proportion of the finance charges as the sum of the periodic balances scheduled to follow the first scheduled payment after the date of prepayment bears to the sum of all of the periodic balances under the schedule of payments in the contract. If the amount of the credit is less than one dollar, no refund need be made.

Debtor agrees as follows: to keep said property free and clear of all taxes, liens and encumbrances; to keep same in good repair, to keep same insured in some insurance company satisfactory to Secured Party, against loss by fire, theft, accidental damage to the property in an amount equal to the amount of indebtedness hereby secured, with the policy thereof also protecting and delivered to Secured Party, with full power in Secured Party to receive, receipt for and collect all money that may become due and payable thereunder, whether by reason of loss, damage, return premium or otherwise and apply same toward the replacement of said property or the repayment of said indebtedness and all other sums payable hereunder, at the option of the Secured Party; that if Debtor shall fail to keep said property free of taxes, liens or encumbrances, or to keep same insured as stated then Secured Party at his (its) option may do so (but shall not be obligated to do so), and if not reimbursed by Debtor for same upon demand the cost or expense of so doing shall be added to the indebtedness secured by this Security Agreement and any sum so advanced shall draw interest at the highest lawful rate.

Debtor does hereby constitute Secured Party his attorney in fact to sign proofs of loss in his name wherein claim against any insurance company or companies or otherwise shall arise and to sign and receipt for any and all moneys that may be due hereunder.

In the event of any default under this agreement, the Secured party is authorized to cancel said insurance and to receive and return premiums, if any, which shall be either credited to the unpaid balance due under this contract, or used to purchase insurance protecting the interest of Secured Party alone, or used for both, whichever Secured Party elects.

Debtor further agrees as follows: Not to use said property illegally, not to use or permit same to be used for hire, not to dispose of same, or any interest therein, or permit it to be removed from the state in which the collateral is to be kept as indicated in this Security Agreement, except for its temporary removal in connection with its ordinary use, without first obtaining written consent of the Secured Party; and that no transfer, renewal, extension or assignment of this Security Agreement or any interest hereunder, or loss, injury or destruction of said property shall release Debtor from the obligations hereof.

The Debtor shall be in default under this agreement upon the death, dissolution or termination of existence of the Debtor, or by the loss, theft, substantial damage, destruction, sale or encumbrance of any of the collateral, or the making of any levy, seizure or attachment upon the collateral, or if by reasonable determination by Secured Party that any representation made herein was false when made.

In the event Debtor shall default on any payment of indebtedness secured hereby, or fails to comply with any other condition of this Security Agreement, or if any bankruptcy, wage earner, receivership or insolvency proceeding, shall be instituted by or against Debtor or his said property covered hereby, or if any execution, attachment, sequestration, or other writ shall be levied on same, or if any suit or lien shall be instituted against Debtor affecting same, or if Secured Party deems said personal property in danger of misuse or confiscation, or if it is misused or confiscated or if Secured Party for reasonable cause shall at any time deem said secured property, or said debt, unsafe or insecure, Secured Party may declare the entire balance of indebtedness immediately due and payable and may require the Debtors to assemble the collateral and make it available to the Secured Party at a designated place, or take immediate possession of said property without demand and without notice, including any and all equipment and accessories thereto, possession by Debtor thereafter being unlawful; and for such purpose Secured Party may enter upon the premises where said property may be and remove same. The Secured Party may also exercise all of the rights and remedies given a Secured Party under the UNIFORM COMMERCIAL CODE as enacted by the State of Kansas in addition to the rights and remedies contained herein.

At the same time of such repossession Secured Party may take possession of any other property in or on said secured property, including the license plates, and hold the same temporarily for delivery to Debtor upon demand, without any responsibility or liability whatever for so doing on the part of Secured Party, his (its) servants and employees; provided, that if Debtor fails to make a written demand upon the Secured Party within 48 hours after the repossession of the vehicle, such failure shall be deemed to constitute a waiver of any claim for any personality that may have been contained in said repossessed vehicle.

Debtor hereby exonerates and fully releases from all damages or charges any person or corporation from whom said property may be taken under the terms hereof, and further authorizes any person in whose possession it may be to turn over to Secured Party upon demand for same, any statement by Secured Party being prima facie evidence of the right of Secured Party to take possession thereof hereunder.

Acceptance by Secured Party of any installment or payment hereunder, in full or in part, shall not be deemed to waiver of any breach or default in Debtor under the terms hereof, or to alter Debtor's obligation or Secured Party's rights with respect to subsequent payments or default therein.

Buyer-Debtor agrees that if this Security Agreement is assigned to an assignee in good faith, without notice of a claim or defense, that he will settle all claims against the Seller directly with him, and agrees not to set up any such claim, as a defense, counterclaim, set-off, cross complaint or otherwise to any action for the purchase price or possession of the collateral described in this Security Agreement brought by the owner hereof, except defenses of a type which may be asserted against a holder in due course of a negotiable instrument.

This is the entire agreement between the parties and there are and can be no oral understanding concerning this agreement not covered hereby or endorsed hereon in writing. The terms and conditions hereof are and shall be binding upon both Debtor and Secured Party, their heirs, executors, administrators, successors and assigns. Words in the singular include the plural, the masculine includes the feminine, and the neuter and vice versa.

ASSIGNMENT

For value received, the within Security Agreement and all the right, title, and interest of the undersigned Seller-Secured Party therein and thereunder, and the property therein described and secured, herewith submitted for purchase by it, and hereby sold, transferred, conveyed and assigned to:

_____

its successors and assigns, with full authority to do every act and thing necessary to collect and discharge same. The undersigned expressly warrants that the within Security Agreement arose from a bona fide Deferred Payment sale to Debtor-Purchaser of the property described therein and secured thereby; that the title to said property at the time of said sale was vested in the undersigned free and clear of all liens and encumbrances that the undersigned had the legal right to and did properly deliver said Property to Debtor-Purchaser at the time of the sale thereof; that said property was not misrepresented in any way to Debtor-Purchaser, and that the statements of Debtor-Purchaser in his credit statement are true to the best of the knowledge and belief of the undersigned. The undersigned further warrants that the security interest of the within Security Agreement is the first and prior thereon; that the undersigned is the owner of said Security Agreement and has the right to sell and assign the same; that DEBTOR-PURCHASER VOLUNTARILY PURCHASED SAID PROPERTY FOR THE DEFERRED PAYMENT PRICE RATHER THAN FOR THE CASH PRICE BOTH INDICATED THEREON; that the down payment received as mentioned in said Security Agreement was paid in full by Debtor-Purchaser in cash and/or trade-in, as stated therein, and that no part of said down payment consisted of notes or post-dated checks unless specifically shown therein; that the Debtor-Purchaser is of lawful age; that the property is correctly described therein; that the signature(s) of the Debtor-Purchaser is (are) genuine; THAT THE SECURITY AGREEMENT WAS COMPLETELY EXECUTED PRIOR TO DEBTOR-PURCHASER SIGNING SAME.

Assignor further warrants that the existence of this Security Agreement is noted on the Motor Vehicle Certificate of Title and that if the cost of insurance is not included in the Security Agreement that he will furnish the Assignee the name of the Insurer carrying the coverage on the property covered by this transaction.

That in the event that any of the above warranties are held to be false, causing monetary loss to the assignee, the undersigned agrees to save harmless the assignee herein. Dated this_____day of_____, 19_____

State of Kansas, County of_____, ss.
Subscribed to before me, a Notary Public, this

_____day of_____, 19_____

_____
Notary Public

My commission expires_____

_____
Dealer

By_____

C&L Forms Division—Couts Printers, Inc.—AC 913 321-2050—1503 Central—Kansas City, Kansas 66102

8. Am I paying too much in interest and carrying charges?
9. Am I dealing with a fair and honest lender?

If your answers to the questions are yes, you are most likely prepared to use credit.

TYPES OF CREDIT

Most of us, at one time or another need to borrow money in the form of cash. The need for cash may come as a result of an emergency. It is wise to know how to borrow money when you need it.

Institutions which loan money include banks, credit unions, and small-loan companies. Banks have a simple method of making loans with little "red tape" involved. It may be possible to borrow up to $500 on your personal signature. You sign a single-signature promissory note for the amount loaned plus the interest you are requested to pay. The interest is deducted in advance in personal loans.

BANK CREDIT

In obtaining a bank loan, it may be necessary to have a second person, or co-signer, sign the note. This provides the bank additional assurance that the loan will be repaid. In all other ways the co-maker loan and the single signature are the same. Both are promissory notes.

It is also possible to obtain a **collateral loan.** This is a loan in which you furnish stocks, bonds, and/or savings of equal value for security.

Interest rates paid on bank loans are generally lower than percentage rates paid on installment credit purchases or on installment loans.

INSTALLMENT LOANS

Small loan companies operate to provide loans from $20 up to $5000. The money may be repaid on the installment plan. This is the same as installment buying except the borrower receives cash instead of merchandise.

Many small loan companies advertise installment loans to consolidate the debts of the borrower. If people are unemployed or have other difficulties, they may borrow enough to pay all their bills and extend payments to the finance company as installments.

Small loan companies are licensed lenders and may charge up to 2½ or 3 percent a month for $300 or less. Rates vary from state to state. Those who need to borrow money on installment should apply the annual rate formula to compare prices charged for the service.

CREDIT UNION LOANS

As mentioned earlier in this unit, credit unions provide credit for members only. Members may borrow small amounts without a co-signer or collateral. Rates vary, but generally an interest rate of 1 percent per month is charged on the actual balance of the debt.

AUTO LOANS

Loans to purchase automobiles may be secured at a number of places including banks, finance companies, and credit unions. Loans are made under the provisions of the uniform commercial code. Most people purchase their cars on the installment plan. It is important to carefully check the interest rates, insurance costs and other costs involved.

Study the Kansas Motor Vehicle Installment Contract agreement as an example. Also study the copy of the Security agreement conditions which the purchaser should read before signing the contract.

REVOLVING CHARGE ACCOUNTS

The revolving charge account credit plan offered by large department stores, mail order companies, and other retailers is popular with consumers today. Plans used by different companies vary in rates and agreements, but all follow the same general plan.

| ACCOUNT NUMBER | 7 | | | |

This order is subject to the approval of the Credit Sales Dept. of Sears, Roebuck and Co. There are to be no agreements regarding it, other than those mentioned below or attached hereto in writing.

Retail Installment Contract and Security Agreement

SEARS, ROEBUCK and CO. _____

Address of Store (Street Number, City, State and Zip Code)

By _____
(Interviewer)

Date *March 13* 19*70*

I hereby order the following merchandise:

DIVISION	DESCRIPTION	PRICE	
46	*Kenmore Refrigerator*	411	95

OFFICE USE ONLY

☐ DEFERRED PAYMENT DATE
☐ EMPLOYE SALE

TERMS CODE *3*   C. LIFE

CASH PRICE	411	95	411	95
CASH DOWN PAYMENT			
AMOUNT FINANCED			411	95
FINANCE CHARGE	124	00	124	00
DEFERRED PAYMENT PRICE	535	95	

	TOTAL OF PYMTS.	THIS SALE >	535	95
	EXISTING OUTSTANDING BALANCE		—	
	TOTAL OF PYMTS.	NEW BAL. >	535	95

Beginning *April 8, 1970*, I will pay $ *16.25* per month for *32* month(s), and
beginning _____, I will pay $ ——— per month for ——— months and a
final monthly payment of $ *15.95* until the amount financed and the finance charge for each purchase is fully paid.

If the FINANCE CHARGE exceeds $5.00, the ANNUAL PERCENTAGE RATE is 20%, unless a different ANNUAL PERCENTAGE RATE is shown here ☒ %

Ownership of the merchandise remains in Sears until paid for in full. My installment payments shall be applied as follows: in the case of items purchased on different dates, the first purchased shall be deemed first paid for; in the case of items purchased on the same date, the lowest priced shall be deemed first paid for.

This agreement provides for a series of credit sales by Sears of merchandise and services for my personal, family or household use:

(1) On my subsequent purchases, you may charge a finance charge in accordance with your established terms. For **Easy Payment** purchases, I will pay a **FINANCE CHARGE** which will be an amount determined by applying an **ANNUAL PERCENTAGE RATE** of 20% to the first $450.00 of the amount financed (or part thereof), 16.50% to the next $550.00 of the amount financed (or part thereof) and 14.75% to any amount financed in excess of $1,000.00. For **Modernizing Credit Plan** purchases, I will pay a **FINANCE CHARGE** which will be an amount determined by applying an **ANNUAL PERCENTAGE RATE** of 14.75% to the amount financed.

(2) In accordance with Sears established terms, the finance charge will begin to accrue on my next billing cycle closing date and will be computed only on each new purchase, and the amount financed plus the finance charge of each new purchase will be added to my existing outstanding balance.

Until each item is fully paid for, I agree that: I have risk of loss or damage; I will not sell, transfer possession of, remove or encumber the property without your written consent; upon default on the terms of this agreement, you may declare my existing outstanding balance due and payable and you may repossess the property.

A delinquency charge of 5%, but not more than $2.50 may be assessed once on each installment in default for 16 days or more.

You are authorized to investigate my credit record and report to proper persons and bureaus my performance of this agreement.

NOTICE TO BUYER: (1) DO NOT SIGN THIS CONTRACT BEFORE YOU READ IT OR IF IT CONTAINS BLANKS. (2) YOU ARE ENTITLED TO A COPY OF THIS CONTRACT. KEEP IT TO PROTECT YOUR LEGAL RIGHTS. (3) UNDER CERTAIN CONDITIONS, YOU MAY REDEEM THE PROPERTY IF REPOSSESSED FOR A DEFAULT OR REQUIRE A RESALE OF THE REPOSSESSED PROPERTY. (4) SELLER MAY NOT USE UNLAWFUL METHODS TO REPOSSESS THE PROPERTY. (5) IF YOU PAY IN FULL IN ADVANCE, ANY UNEARNED FINANCE CHARGE WILL BE REBATED UNDER THE RULE OF 78.

RECEIPT OF A COPY OF THIS SECURITY AGREEMENT IS ACKNOWLEDGED:

CUSTOMER'S SIGNATURE _____
ADDRESS *123 Your Street*
CITY *Anywhere*   STATE *USA*   ZIP CODE *90101*
CUSTOMER'S NAME (PRINT) *John*   *Q.*   *Public*   WIFE'S NAME *Mary*
FIRST   INITIAL   LAST   FIRST

FIRST PAYMENT DUE _____
APPROVAL _____
DATE _____

F-10683-KS   Rev. 12/69

The customer who buys goods on credit is given the privilege of a 30-day charge account or may extend the payments on a monthly plan. Contracts, conditions, rates charged, amounts which can be purchased, and payment information are printed on the contract.

Interest and charge rates are regulated by state laws. Rates charged may vary from one company to another, but charges are under the maximum set by law. A number of states permit add-on rates of 17 percent to 20 percent a year. Study the "Sears Revolving Charge Account and Security Agreement," a sales contract used to familarize customers with conditions, rates, etc. of their revolving charge account.

Those who wish to take advantage of charge account purchases are required to make application and furnish the company with needed information. Study the example of an application form used for this purpose.

HOME LOANS

Many young men and women look forward to the time when they can own their own home. There has been a definite trend toward individual ownership for the last 20 years. Few families have the money to pay cash for a home; thus, a long-term loan is needed.

Housing loans are available from a number of financial institutions including banks, building and loan companies, insurance companies, mortgage companies, and private investors. The rates and contract terms offered by lending agencies differ to some extent, but operate under the laws of the state regulating sales of real estate.

Buying a home is a major financial step for a family and should be undertaken only after careful study and advice from knowledgeable people. Perhaps the most important thing to consider is the family's ability to take on such a financial obligation. Before considering anything else, it is necessary to make this decision. There is no one "pat" answer to this question. However, if a family is able to meet all present expenses and save money out of the present income, chances are good it will be possible to buy a home.

The size of the financial obligation a family should assume in buying a home is not easy to decide. A general guideline is to limit the debt to two times the family's yearly income or the monthly payment should be no larger than 25 percent of the take home pay of the head of the house. However, this figure may vary depending on the individual family situation.

A down payment is required, and the amount of the down payment will vary with the cost of the home and the institution making the loan.

The Federal Housing Administration, established in 1939, aids prospective home buyers by insuring mortgage loans made by approved private institutions. The financial protection provided to lending agencies makes it possible for them to finance home mortgages at a lower rate of interest and a lower down payment. The monthly payment is generally equal to rent for a comparable house, and maturity of the mortgage is long term. One of the main advantages of an FHA loan is the assistance the buyer gets in an inspection of the house and lot by experts in the field.

Before the contract to buy a home is signed, an attorney should be employed to examine the contract and deed for validity, back taxes, etc.

DATE	DIV.	CASH P.	. c/c	NEW BAL.	PMT.	CODE

SEARS REVOLVING CHARGE ACCOUNT AND SECURITY AGREEMENT

SEARS, ROEBUCK AND CO.

In consideration of your selling merchandise and services for personal, family or household purposes to me on my Sears Revolving Charge Account I agree to the following regarding all purchases made by me or on my Sears Revolving Charge Account Identification.

1. I have the privilege of a 30-day Charge Account, in which case I will pay the full amount of all purchases within 25 days from the date of each billing statement.

2. If I do not pay the full amount for all purchases within 25 days from the date of each billing statement, the following terms shall be in effect:
(A) I will pay the Deferred Payment Price for each item purchased consisting of:

   (1) The cash sale price, and

   (2) The **FINANCE CHARGE,** which will be the greater of (a) a minimum charge of 50¢ or (b) an amount determined by applying a periodic rate of 1.5% per month to the first $800.00 of previous balance or part thereof and an amount determined by applying a periodic rate of 1.0% per month to any part of the previous balance in excess of $800.00. If the **FINANCE CHARGE** exceeds 50¢, the **ANNUAL PERCENTAGE RATE** will be 18% on the first $800.00 of previous balance and 12% on that part of the previous balance in excess of $800.00.

(B) I will pay for all purchases in monthly installments which will be computed according to the following schedule:

If the unpaid balance is:	The scheduled monthly payment will be:	If the unpaid balance is:	The scheduled monthly payment will be:
$ .01 to $ 10.00	Balance	$300.01 to $350.00	$30.00
10.01 to 150.00	$10.00	350.01 to 400.00	35.00
150.01 to 200.00	15.00	400.01 to 450.00	40.00
200.01 to 250.00	20.00	450.01 to 500.00	45.00
250.01 to 300.00	25.00	Over $500.00	1/10 of account bal.

I will pay each monthly installment computed according to the schedule as stated above upon receipt of each statement. If I fail to pay any installment in full when due, you may, at your option, take back the merchandise or affirm the sale and hold me liable for the full balance on my account which shall be immediately due. Ownership of the merchandise purchased on this account shall remain in Sears until I have paid the purchase price in full. My installment payments shall be applied as follows: in the case of items purchased on different dates, the first purchased shall be deemed first paid for; in the case of items purchased on the same date, the lowest priced shall be deemed first paid for. I have risk of loss or damage to merchandise.

(C) You are to send me a statement each month which will show the unpaid balance for purchases, the Finance Charge, and the amount of the monthly installment coming due.

(D) I have the right to pay all or any portion of my account in advance.

3. You are authorized to investigate my credit record and report to proper persons and bureaus my performance of this agreement.

NOTICE TO BUYER: (1) DO NOT SIGN THIS CONTRACT BEFORE YOU READ IT OR IF IT CONTAINS BLANKS. (2) YOU ARE ENTITLED TO A COPY OF THIS CONTRACT. KEEP IT TO PROTECT YOUR LEGAL RIGHTS. (3) YOU HAVE THE RIGHT TO PAY IN ADVANCE THE FULL AMOUNT DUE. RECEIPT OF A COPY OF THIS SECURITY AGREEMENT IS ACKNOWLEDGED:

_____
(CUSTOMER'S SIGNATURE)

F15206-13 (REV. 7-1-69) DATE_____

The Revolving Charge Account Is Used by Department Stores — the Amount and Cost of Credit Is Agreed Upon at the Start of the Account

MR. MRS. MISS.	(PLEASE PRINT)				ACCOUNT NUMBER			LIMIT	DATE OPENED

MR. MRS. MISS. _John Q. Public_

ACCOUNT NUMBER 7

LIMIT _60_

DATE OPENED _3-13-70_

ADDRESS _123 Your Street_

INTERVIEWER

AUTHORIZER

PHONE NUMBER RES. _254-1198_

CITY _Anywhere, USA   90101_

DATE:

BUS. _235-1700_

AUTHORIZED PURCHASERS

E.P. ☐ OWN   ☒ MARRIED ☒

SRC ☒ RENT   ☐ SINGLE

MCP ☐ BOARD   ☐ WIDOWED ☐

AGE _36_

DEPENDENTS _w + 3_

WIFE'S NAME _Mary_

HOW LONG AT PRESENT ADDRESS _12 yrs_

1. _John Q. Public_
2. _Mary Public_
3. _____

EMPLOYER _Sheffield Steel Corp_   ADDRESS _Anywhere, USA_   HOW LONG _14 yrs_

OCCUPATION _Engineer_   TIME CARD OR BADGE NUMBER _7501_   EARNINGS $ _4200_   WK. ☐   MO. ☒

FORMER EMPLOYER (IF LESS THAN ONE YEAR WITH PRESENT EMPLOYER) _____   HOW LONG _____

NAME AND ADDRESS OF BANK _First National Bank, Anywhere, USA_   CHECKING ☒

EXPLAIN OTHER INCOME, IF ANY _Rental Property $ 100 per month_   SAVINGS ☒   LOAN

FORMER ADDRESS (IF LESS THAN TWO YEARS AT PRESENT ADDRESS) _____   HOW LONG _____

THE SPACES BELOW ARE TO BE FILLED IN WHEN THE MERCHANDISE ORDERED IS TO BE ATTACHED TO THE PROPERTY.

ADDRESS WHERE MATERIAL IS TO BE INSTALLED _____   COST OF PROPERTY $ _____   AMOUNT OF MORTGAGE $ _____

NAME OF PERSON HOLDING LEGAL TITLE _____   NAME AND ADDRESS OF MORTGAGE HOLDER _____

PREVIOUS SEARS ACCOUNTS				CREDIT REFERENCE	DATE OPENED	HIGH CREDIT	BALANCE DATE CLOSED	AMOUNT PAYMENTS	HOW PAID
E.P. ☐		S.R.C. ☐		1. _United Finance_ _Anywhere, USA_	9/65	1,500	5/68	46 00	I-1
DATE _____ LIMIT _____		DATE _____ LIMIT _____		2. _Boxer Furniture_ _Your City, USA_	2/62	700	1/65	19 50	I-1
STORE _____		ACCT. NO. _____		3. _First National Bank_ _Anywhere, USA_	1/60	3,000	500	50 00	I-1
	E.P.	S.R.C.		4. _Wilbur's Department Store_ _Anywhere, USA_	10/66	195	160	15 00	R-1
DATE OPENED				5.					
HIGH CREDIT									
PRESENT BALANCE DATE CLOSED									
MONTHLY PAYMENTS									
NO. PMTS. DELINQUENT									
HOW PAID									

WHEN YOU USE CONSUMER CREDIT

- Do you ask yourself this: "Is having this item **now** worth the added credit costs?"
- Do you know the sources of consumer credit in your community?
- Do you shop around to find where the credit rate is the lowest and most convenient?
- More important, do you have a credit rating that labels you as an outstanding credit risk?
- Do the items you buy on installment last far beyond the time the last payment is made?
- Do you make as large a down payment as possible without upsetting the family budget?
- Do you pay it off as quickly as possible without making the budget too tight?
- How does your decision fit into your family's budget and plans?
- Are you sure you can meet this payment, plus all other monthly expenses?

STUDY AIDS

NEW TERMS

annual interest rate	credit rating
asset	credit risk
balance	default
bankrupt	installment credit
borrower	per annum
charge account	percentage rate
collateral	principal

contract	repossession
credit	security agreement
creditor	truth-in-lending

STUDY QUESTIONS

1. How would you define the word "credit"?
2. Why is credit considered to be an economic tool?
3. How can different interest rates be justified?
4. When is it wise to get a collateral loan?
5. What should be used as a guide in determining the size of a home loan?
6. When should one consider installment credit for the purchase of an automobile?

DISCUSSION PROBLEMS

1. Why can the lowest interest rates for consumer credit usually be offered by the retail dealer?
2. Suppose that you plan to buy a stereo component system which costs $300. The dealer has agreed to accept $100 as down payment with the $200 balance to be paid in $25 per month payments plus a carrying charge of 18% per annum on the unpaid balance. What will be the total cost of the stereo in the eight-month payment period? Now suppose that the dealer offers you a 10 percent discount for cash sales; how much less would the stereo cost if you could pay cash?

CHAPTER THIRTEEN
AWARENESS OF LEGAL RESPONSIBILITIES

YOU AND THE LAW

Wherever people live together, they must develop rules of conduct. Without rules, there are no guidelines in dealing with one another. Laws are a set of rules that government enforces through the courts and other agencies. You have heard people say, "It is against the law." This means it is against the rules of the country or community to do certain acts. New laws are made, while others are repealed (revoked) to meet cultural needs each year. Laws make it possible for people to live together peacefully.

There are two major classifications of laws: public law and civil law. Public law includes constitutional law, international law, administrative law, and criminal law. **Public laws** are passed to regulate the relationships between individuals and the government. **Private law** and **civil law** include the rules that regulate the relationship among people and are concerned with contracts, real estate, and personal injury.

You probably have heard more about criminal law. However, more court action and lawyer's time is spent in civil law cases. Young people know it is against the law to steal or commit crimes of violence against other people, but they may not know much about the laws concerned with contracts, personal injury, or real estate.

Laws vary from state to state, but most states have adopted a uniform commercial code which deals with sales and contracts. The code standardizes laws, making them similar in all states. It is good business to secure the services of an attorney for legal advice on important problems. This is especially true where a complicated contract or will is to be written.

It must be remembered that questions given to a lawyer will be answered in the form of an opinion. It is not wise for a lawyer to give a definite statement, since all the circumstances may not be known, and a higher court may later reverse the lower court decision.

CONTRACTS

In our modern society, there is an increasing need to depend on others for the necessities of life. When dealing with people we often make promises that are legal obligations enforceable through court action. In fact, many of these promises are legal contracts. Thus, it is important for the young worker to understand the legal aspects of entering into a contract.

A contract is an agreement between two or more competent parties which makes an enforceable obligation. Should one party fail to keep the agreement, the other party may take the case to court for enforcement.

Contracts may result from informal or formal action. **Informal contracts** are made when you make purchases of clothing at the local store, have clothes cleaned at the dry

The Purchase of Clothing Is an Example of an Informal Contract

cleaner, or have your shoes repaired at the shoe shop. Other contracts, such as purchasing real estate, are **formal transactions** and may require legal assistance in drawing up the agreement and checking the accuracy of ownership. Some agreements relate to personal matters for practical purposes and are not enforceable by the courts.

Certain elements are necessary in order for a contract to be valid and enforceable by law. These essentials are as follows:

1. **MUTUAL ASSENT.** There must be an offer and acceptance.
2. **COMPETENT PARTIES.** All parties must be legally qualified to make enforceable contracts.
3. **LEGAL PURPOSE.** The agreement must be lawful.
4. **CONSIDERATION.** There must be something of value exchanged between the parties to make the contract binding.
5. **LEGAL FORM.** Most contracts must be in writing to be enforceable.

LEGAL QUESTIONS

The answer to each of these questions is "YES":

1. Is a contract binding if it is signed without being read?
2. Is a contract binding if you sign it just to get rid of a persistent salesperson?
3. Is a contract binding if you misunderstand part of it?
4. Is an installment sale agreement a contract?
5. Must a contract to purchase real estate be in writing?

The answer to each of these questions is "NO":

1. Is a contract binding if it involves breaking the law?
2. Is a contract binding if it is entered into under pressure or threat?
3. Is an agreement of a person that is younger than the recognized legal age to buy a contract item binding?
4. Is it necessary to sign a written agreement for the purchase of a suit of clothes for the contract to be binding?
5. Are you obligated to return or pay for merchandise sent to you that you did not order?

MUTUAL ASSENT

In every contract there is an **offer** and an **acceptance.** Mutual assent takes place between the parties when they are in complete agreement on the terms of the contract. In law, this is called "the meeting of the minds," meaning that both parties understand and are willing to enter into the agreement. Under the principles of law, a contract is not valid unless the parties freely and intentionally agree. Thus, to determine the validity of an offer, a three-item test can be used:

1. Is the offer made with the obvious intention of the first party (the offeror) to enter into legal agreement with the party accepting the offer?

The Price and the Terms of Sale Should Be Understood by Both Parties

2. Is the offer clear and definite?
3. Has the offer been properly communicated by words or actions to the party accepting?

Let's see how this test applies. Advertisements in newspapers have not been legally considered offers, since dealers may not be in a position to sell their products to everyone. It is apparent that dealers cannot be required or do not intend to enter into a purchase contract with everyone who may want to purchase their products. They may point out this fact in their advertisement with the words, "quantities limited," or "dealer reserves the right to limit sales."

An offer must be clear and definite in order to be considered a legal contract. For example, Mr. Jones, a farmer, had 50 riding horses for sale, and he told Mr. Smith that he would sell him a horse for $150. Mr. Jones had horses priced from $150 to $300. However, Mr. Smith understood he could take any one of the horses. This offer was not properly communicated and so was not a legal contract to sell a specific horse.

Terminating (ending) an offer can be accomplished in several ways. Most frequently, it is terminated in a stated length of time or at a given date. If no time to terminate the

offer is stated, it is good for a "reasonable period of time." An offer also is terminated upon the death of the offeror. The offer may be withdrawn at any announced time in cases of rewards. Withdrawal of any offer may be made if the offer has not been accepted in the specified or "reasonable" period of time.

Acceptance of an offer may be by direct communication or by mail. When an acceptance of an offer is made by mail, the contract is not made until the offeror receives the letter of acceptance from the offeree — except in the case where the offer was communicated by mail.[1]

COMPETENT PARTIES

For a contract to be valid, the parties making a contract must be considered competent. This means that the people involved must have the ability to fully understand the extent of their rights and obligations in the matter. Certain individuals are prevented by law from making enforceable contracts. The various state laws define who is competent to make contracts.

Among those considered not competent under the law are minors. A minor is a person who has not reached a specified age which is considered in the state to be the age of full maturity with the ability to make judgments. In most states anyone under the age of 18 is not considered competent and may not enter into legal contracts. Usually, contracts made by minors are voidable (may be broken) by the minor. However, when an agreement is made with an adult, the adult is required to fulfill the terms of the agreement if it is a legal contract. The privilege to cancel contracts is given only to the minor. The adult party of the contract must carry out his or her part of the contract.

[1]In this case, the U.S. Post Office is the offeror's "agent," and the contract is binding as soon as the acceptance is dropped in the mailbox.

> Bill Brown, a 14-year-old high school student, ordered a $36 radio kit through the Jones Appliance Store. When the kit finally arrived, the price had gone up to $46; and the dealer requested that Bill pay the $46 or return the kit. Legally, Mr. Jones was required to deliver the kit at the price stated in the contract. However, Bill could have refused to honor his agreement because he was a minor.

Although they may cancel many of their contracts, minors or their parents will be obligated on contracts for purchases of things minors actually need to sustain life. The law generally considers necessities to include food, clothing, shelter, and medical attention. Some exceptions will arise.

> Johnny, a 14-year-old freshman, purchased an expensive leather jacket from the local sports clothing store. Since Johnny's parents had already bought him several jackets, this jacket was not actually needed and it could not be considered a necessity. The store was forced to accept the return of the jacket and refund the full amount of the purchase.

The minor is responsible for medical attention. In an emergency case where a minor requires medical attention, the physician and hospital can collect any money due for services offered.

Contracts for luxuries are voidable by the minor, although the adult may be obligated by the contract. The problems arising from voidable contracts made by the minor have prompted merchants to ask parents of minors to countersign contracts for purchases. Many department stores have established charge accounts for minors countersigned by the parents. This practice reduces the problem of voidable contracts on the part of minors.

Many contract problems have been caused when minors deliberately misrepre-

sent their age to purchase a car or other articles. In such cases the adult may hold the minor liable for deceit and collect money and damages for the loss. Laws differ from state to state in dealing with this problem. Most merchants prevent these situations and protect themselves by demanding proof of age. Identification cards, driver's licenses, and draft cards are used for this purpose.

When people do not have the mental ability to understand the nature of contracts, they may be declared incompetent in a court of law. In addition to those who are mentally deficient, persons intoxicated when the contract was made, and insane persons may be declared incompetent by the court. Contracts made with such people are not enforceable.

THE LEGAL PURPOSE

To be valid, a contract must not be contrary to the law or to the interest of society. The terms of any agreement which are illegal or are harmful to the public health or morals are in fact not a contract because they are not enforceable. Examples of illegal agreements include those involving agreement to steal or to accept stolen goods. Agreements dealing with gambling or wagering are illegal in most states. Should you make a bet with someone and win, it is not possible to take legal action to collect the money won since the agreement is not legal. In a few states where betting on dog and horse racing have been legalized, winnings could be collected if the bets were made according to state law.

It is also illegal to enter into agreement to give false testimony or obstruct justice for a fee. Such agreements do not meet the requirements of being lawful.

In many cities and states certain business, craft, and professional men are licensed to practice or perform work. Contracts with individuals or firms without required licenses are not valid. For example, if an **unlicensed** electrician contracts to install the wiring in a house you are building,

Charging Interest on a Loan above the Maximum Legal Rate Is Called Usury

the contract is void because the city will not provide you service until the job is approved by an inspector. (The inspector will not approve work done by an unlicensed electrician.)

All states have established maximum interest rates which may be charged the borrower. Charging interest beyond the maximum contract rate is called **usury** and is illegal. Penalties for usury vary, but in some states the penalty may call for the forfeiture of both the principal and the interest of the contract loan.

Recent legislation passed by Congress, known as "truth in lending legislation," clarifies some of the problems concerned with usury laws.

CONSIDERATION

In order to be enforceable, a contract must be an agreement by which one party agrees to do something, and the other party agrees to do something of value in return. What either party agrees to do in return for the promise received is known as **consideration.** For example, Mr. Smith agreed to permit the electrical company to run a line across a part of his farm. When Mr. Smith signed the agreement (contract) to permit the erection of the power line, he received $1 as consideration. Although Mr. Smith would profit indirectly from having the power line installed, the consideration was necessary to make the contract legal. Consideration is not always in the form of money. It may include services, goods, or a promise to refrain from doing something one has the legal right to do.

LEGAL FORM

A contract may be **informal or formal.** Many contracts are simple and informal, and few of such contracts would involve the exchange of much money. Problems arising in making informal contracts may be resolved without court action. Other contracts, such as the purchase of real estate, must be formal, for they involve the exchange of large amounts of money for buildings and land.

Contracts may be either written or oral. In the sale of goods priced at less than $500, an oral agreement is enforceable. The nature of some transactions requires written contracts. A contract for labor and materials is not always in writing, but a written contract helps to avoid misunderstandings.

Certain contracts are required by law to be in writing. **Written contracts** include the following:

1. An installment credit or purchase contract.
2. A contract to sell or buy real estate, including buildings, land, mineral rights, and trees.
3. A contract to guarantee the debt of another person in case of default or ligation.
4. An agreement to sell personal property valued at over $500 (amount and

conditions may vary in different states).

5. An agreement that is not to be performed within a year from the date it is made.

Contracts are not required to be written in any particular form. However, to be legal, they should include:

1. The date and place of the agreement.
2. The names and addresses of the parties entering into the agreement.
3. A statement of the purpose.
4. A statement of the amount of money, goods, or services given in consideration of the agreement.
5. The signatures of parties or their legal agents.
6. Signatures of witnesses when required by law or in certain transactions.

PREPARING CONTRACTS

Problems result if people enter into an agreement when there is a misunderstanding on the part of one or both parties. Sometimes fraud is involved. In any event, when entering into an important contractual agreement, be extremely cautious in signing contracts. The following suggestions are made for making contracts:

1. When the contract is complex or of sufficient importance, it should be prepared by an attorney.
2. Read the contract carefully before signing. Be sure the terms and amounts of money listed are accurate.
3. If part of the contract is in small print and you are unable to understand, ask your attorney for help.
4. Always get a copy of what you sign with the signature of the other party, and file it in a safe place — preferably a bank box.
5. Any change made in the terms of the contract should be signed by both parties.

DEFECTIVE CONTRACTS

When a contract is found to be defective, it cannot be enforced. Such contracts are classified as **void** or **voidable** and may be broken by either party. A contract may be void under the following conditions:

1. When a contract is made by compulsion through threats or by violence.
2. When terms of the contracts are fraudulent, misrepresenting the actual situation.
3. When a clearly proven mistake has been made.

WHEN TO GET LEGAL ADVICE

Only a small percentage of our population breaks the law and requires an attorney for a court defense. Nevertheless, a family with honest intentions may get into legal difficulties. Almost everyone needs the services of a lawyer at some time. Here are some of the occasions **when you may need legal advice.**

A Contract Resulting from Threats of Violence Is Void and Not Enforceable

Just about every young family looks forward to buying a home. The purchase of real estate may be the first time you need a lawyer. Many real estate agents encourage the buyer to engage a lawyer to examine the legal papers that are involved in buying real estate. The contract and mortgage papers will need to be examined. Help is needed to determine if the property is free of back taxes and liens. How is the property ownership to be listed? You should ask your lawyer if you and your wife or husband should hold the property you purchase in **joint tenancy,** or **tenants in common,** or otherwise. Your lawyer must know the laws in the state in which you live and can explain the advantages and disadvantages for your transaction.

If you are not married, you may hold property in your own name and have none of the problems of joint holdings. Some may think that joint tenancy will take the place of a will. However, this may not be to the advantage of you or your family. A lawyer is needed to help you select the type of property holding best for your situation.

Suppose you have decided to buy a home and the real estate agent asks you to make a down payment. Be sure you have a written statement from the seller that the down payment will be returned to you if either of you fail to go through with the deal. Otherwise, you will probably have to forfeit your deposit.

Here are some considerations a buyer of real estate should carefully check:

1. Is the selling price **firmly fixed** in the terms of the contract? Contracts for new or remodeled houses may contain a clause that will permit the contractor to add increased cost. If such an escalator clause is accept-

able, be sure you can meet the additional costs.

2. Terms describing the down payment and remainder of the cost must be established **to your satisfaction.**

3. The contract should **state the date on which you may have possession** without a penalty or returning your money.

4. Be sure you have a **clear title** and learn **what restrictions** are placed on the property. Back taxes and any liens for work on the property should be paid by the seller before the contract is signed. **A lawyer's fee here may save you time, trouble, and money.**

5. The contract should state **who is responsible** for the property during the time between contract date and possession date.

6. Be sure the contract states the **seller's responsibility** for the function of heating, air conditioning, and plumbing — especially if you are buying a new house. The contract should also include the builder's responsibility for expected function of all parts of the house (roof, doors, walks, etc.) for a given length of time after occupancy.

7. If you are contracting for a new house, be sure you have **in writing** the conditions under which you or the builder can change plans or materials.

8. It is unwise to sign a contract with an **escape clause** for the builder.

9. Sign your contract **after your attorney has checked the terms** and given you an opinion.

People need legal protection and assistance in making important contracts.

Take the case of James Young, a recent technical school graduate, who was working for City Electric, a company located about two miles from James' home.

Since there was no bus service to the plant and little chance of James finding a ride with fellow workers, James decided he would need a reliable car. James couldn't afford to spend much for a car. After looking over his budget for the year, he decided $500 was all he could pay for a car.

James looked at several cars during the evenings and finally found a clean-looking car at "Jack's Quality Cars," a used car lot on Broadway. The price of the car seemed lower than others of the same brand, style, and age. The salesperson mentioned that he had just bought the car from a boy who needed the money to start college, and that he could sell the car to James at a lower price.

James should have been more cautious, but what appeared to be such a good deal was hard to pass up.

James started the car easily and drove it a few blocks. Everything seemed to be functioning except that the transmission seemed to slip slightly. He knew that the car should be checked by his friend, Roger, who was an expert mechanic at Westside Motors. However, it was Saturday afternoon, the service department was closed at Westside Motors, and Roger had gone to visit his brother in another city.

The salesperson had the contract ready for James to sign when he returned from the drive. James paid the $100 down and signed the contract which required 12 additional payments of $55 each. The payments included charges for credit, insurance, and taxes for the year.

The following Monday, James drove his car to work. The car ran smoothly.

James' trouble started on the way home. The car seemed to lose power when he tried to pass a truck. Something smelled hot. Then there was a **ripping** sound in the automatic transmission. James' car lost all power, and he was forced to pull off to the side of the road.

He called Roger, who drove out and looked at the car. It didn't take Roger long to see what the trouble was. The transmission was ruined.

The car was towed to the garage and the transmission was further examined. Roger estimated it would cost $225 to replace the transmission. James called Jack, the used car dealer, and was told that at the low price James paid for the car, he shouldn't expect any guarantee that the transmission wouldn't fail.

James didn't have $225 to replace the transmission. In desperation he called his father for advice. His father suggested that he bring the contract by for his lawyer to examine.

When Mr. Walker, the lawyer, read the contract, he knew that James had failed to read it in detail. The man at Jack's Quality Cars had typed in, "This vehicle sold as is." James had signed the contract which released the seller of any responsibility.

Mr. Walker called James' father and explained the mistake made in signing the contract in the first place. James had lost his rights as a buyer by signing a contract containing such a clause. James had given up his right to expect any warranty on the car. He was stuck with a $225 repair job and a $600 debt on the car. Things looked bad for James, who was 21 years old and could not disaffirm the contract on the basis of age.

Roger's discovery when he removed and disassembled the transmission saved James part of the loss. It was discovered that the transmission had been burned out recently and was patched up in order to function for a few more miles. When confronted with this information, Jack offered to give James a serviceable transmission to replace the ruined one. However, James still had to pay the labor cost for the repair job.

Practically everyone is involved in contracts each week. Most of our contracts involve only a small amount of money and are implied. For example, when you buy a can of tuna at the supermarket, the clerk checks your purchase and rings it up on the cash register. The contract is simple; you accept the offer to buy a can of tuna at 57¢ and pay for it. In return for the money you paid, the supermarket promises the tuna to be safe for edible purposes. Should the contents be spoiled, replacement or return of your money is expected.

When large sums of money are used in contracts, and formal procedures are used, you may need a lawyer to protect you. The small cost of legal assistance is a good investment and may save you considerable time and money.

STUDY AIDS

NEW TERMS

law
contract
consultation
voidable
countersign
usury
hazardous
commercial code
enforceable obligation
formal transaction
mutual assent

termination of offer
binding contract
ligation
reverse
legal opinion
competent
valid
communicated
necessity
consideration

STUDY QUESTIONS

1. What are the different classifications of laws?
2. What type of law requires the most legal consultation and court action?
3. When should legal advice be obtained?
4. What are the essential elements of a valid contract?
5. Who is considered incompetent and unable to enter into a contract agreement?
6. Is an advertisement considered to be a legal offer?
7. What items are considered necessities in a contract? What are luxuries?
8. Is a minor responsible for emergency medical attention costs?
9. Is it legal for minors to make purchases using their parents' credit card?
10. What are four steps of consideration that may be used in a contract?
11. Can a merchant legally collect a bill made by an intoxicated person?
12. Under what conditions can a gambling debt be legal?
13. What types of contracts are legally required to be in writing?
14. When can an unlicensed craftsman be refused payment for work performed?
15. What are five suggestions that can be made to persons preparing and/or signing a contract?
16. Under what conditions can a contract be declared defective?
17. Under what conditions can a sales contract be oral?

DISCUSSION PROBLEMS

1. It is necessary to revise laws occasionally because they are no longer appropriate. Can you think of a law that has been changed since the Constitution was written? Do you know of any law that has been changed in your town? Why were these changes made?
2. Imagine that you are a lawyer, and you have been asked if a certain contract is legal and can be enforced. What points will you study in the contract to help you decide if it is valid?
3. When should you ask a lawyer to examine a contract?
4. What can you do to avoid legal problems?

CHAPTER FOURTEEN
USING BANK SERVICES

Two hundred years ago, there were few people who needed to know much about banking. In the agricultural society of that day, most of the population lived on farms and paid for goods and services with cash or by the barter system. There was little need for substitutes for money, as there is today. In our modern, complex society practically everyone who earns or handles money will need the services of banks. Many payments of bills for goods and services cannot be paid over the counter; a check must be used. For example, if you wish to order a clock from a mail order business, you will need to use a substitute for money. You would probably use a personal check. The check would provide a means of safe transit for the money and also provide a receipt for your records.

Our national system of banks provides us with this service. Without such a system, it would be very difficult to operate our industries and businesses.

This unit will provide basic knowledge and information needed for using banking services.

BANKING INSTITUTIONS

Banks are business firms specializing in the transfer of money and credit. They are authorized by state or federal governments to perform a certain financial function, such as:

1. Receiving deposits of money subject to withdrawal by depositors.
2. Making loans to customers.
3. Paying interest to depositors.
4. Investing money.

There are several types of banks. However, one type is used by most people in managing their money. It is called a **commercial bank.** The main functions of a commercial bank are the following:

1. To receive deposits of money,
2. To loan money to individuals and businesses.

Another type of bank is the savings bank, known as a **savings and loan association.** A savings bank accepts deposits of money, and it loans or arranges credit to business, industry, and governments who borrow large amounts of money.

A **trust company** is authorized to administer trust funds and serve as administrators of the estates of deceased persons. Some banks are authorized to serve as trust companies and also to carry on regular banking functions. Present trends indicate that more banking institutions are being chartered as "full-service banks," giving them authority to perform commercial, savings, and trust functions.

BANK CLASSIFICATION

Banks are classified on the basis of their authorization either by state or federal government.

The Modern Bank Has Both Parking Facilities and Customer Convenience Windows

STATE BANK

A state bank is organized as a corporation and is chartered by the state in which it operates. A state bank may be a commercial bank, a savings bank, or a trust company. State banks may also be members of the Federal Reserve System.

NATIONAL BANK

A national bank is organized as a corporation and chartered by the federal government. National banks are subject to federal banking laws and regulations of the Federal Reserve System.

THE FEDERAL RESERVE SYSTEM

By 1913, the population and economy of the United States had grown so large that the Congress enacted a law to standardize banking practice and improve the banking service. This act was known as the **Federal Reserve Act.** This act established the Federal Reserve system which organized the country into 12 geographical banking districts. In each district there is a Federal Reserve bank. The functions of the 12 Federal Reserve banks are coordinated by a seven-member Board of Governors. The members of the Board of Governors are appointed by the President of the United States. Each district Federal Reserve bank is managed by a nine-member Board of Directors. Six members are elected by the member banks in the district, and three members are appointed by the Board of Governors.

The Federal Reserve system has the following five important functions:

The Interior of a Bank Is Pleasant and Convenient for the Customer

1. Holding reserves of member banks.
2. Supplying the needs of member banks for cash.
3. Controlling the volume of bank credit extended by banks in the United States.
4. Acting as a clearing house for checks of member banks.
5. Providing fiscal services for the United States Government.

FEDERAL DEPOSIT INSURANCE CORPORATION

Under provisions of the present Federal Deposit Insurance Corporation, all national and state banks that are members of the Federal Reserve System are required to insure their deposits with the Federal Deposit Insurance Corporation. The amount on deposit in each account is matched by insurance up to the maximum of $20,000; thus, the deposits of each customer's individual bank account are insured up to $20,000. In addition, the customer may share a joint account with another person — usually wife, husband, mother, or father — which is also insured to the maximum of $20,000 on deposit in that account. The size of the bank's assets makes little difference in the safety of deposits.

CHECK ENDORSEMENT AND CASHING

Bill Smith, a student enrolled in the high school work experience program, is employed by the Pittsburgh Machine Tool Company. He received a $24 check from the company for his first week of work. Before Bill cashed the check, he signed his name on the back of the check at the left end exactly as it appeared on the front of the check. By using this procedure, the company will know that Bill did cash his check and received cash for his work. This is called a **blank endorsement** of a check, and is necessary to cash it. It is not wise to make a blank endorsement until you are at the bank. If you are not known at the bank, it is best to endorse the check at the teller's window.

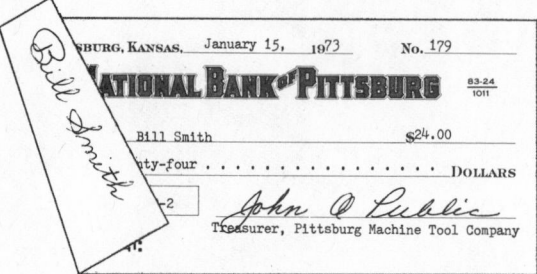

The Name Signed on the Back of the Check Is the Endorsement Signature and Should Match the Spelling of the Name on the Face of the Check

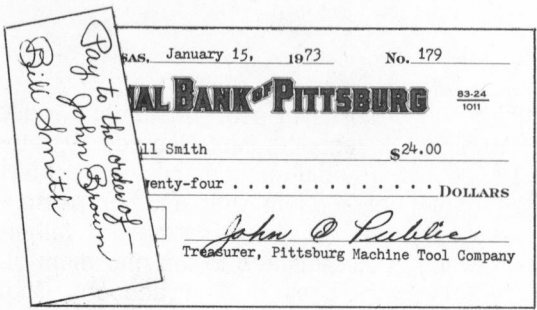

In addition to the blank endorsement, there are other endorsements. Should Bill wish to deposit the total amount of the check, he can use a **restrictive** endorsement by writing "For deposit only" above his signature. No one could cash and receive money from Bill's check; it can only be credited to his account. This is the best way to endorse a check which must be mailed to the bank. If Bill wishes to use the check to pay a debt to his friend John Brown, he can use the special endorsement by writing "Pay to the order of John Brown" and signing his name. Only John Brown can cash the check, by signing his name below

Bill's signature to receive money from the check.

Two considerations for use of checks are care of checks and promptness of depositing or cashing checks received. Checks from companies or individuals should not be held for an extended length of time. A delayed check makes bookkeeping much more difficult.

USE OF CHECKING ACCOUNT

One of the most useful and important functions provided by a bank is the checking service. This service provides you with a substitute for cash. Although it is possible to pay local bills and make local purchases with cash, most people must maintain a checking account to pay out-of-town bills and to keep their money in a safe place. It is not safe to send cash through the mail or to keep large amounts of cash in the home. Thus, maintaining a checking account is an important service to those managing money.

Most banks offer two different types of checking accounts. The depositor makes his or her choice according to the number of checks to be written and the minimum balance to be maintained each month.

The first type is commonly used by those who write many checks. The bank charges a service fee plus a charge for each check written. The total of the charges depends on the minimum monthly balance in the checking account.

The second type of checking account is the "low-volume account" in which only a few checks are written each month, and the balance may be quite low. The service charge is made when the depositor purchases the blank checks; and, if only a few checks are written each month, this type of account is less expensive. Students who have only a small amount of money in their checking accounts usually take advantage of the low-volume account.

OPENING A CHECKING ACCOUNT

Opening a checking account is a very simple procedure. First, you visit the bank of your choice and introduce yourself to an officer of the bank. You will probably be interviewed by the cashier or someone assigned to meet new depositors.

Checking accounts may be opened as **individual accounts** or **joint accounts,** depending on the needs of the person or persons starting the checking account. You will be required to sign a signature card using the signature you will use on all checks written on your account. You may also be assigned a depositor's number which is written on each check you write. You are now ready to deposit your money.

MAKING BANK WITHDRAWALS

You should be careful when you write a check. It is important to write clearly and to be sure the check is accurate before releasing it. All checks should be written in

ink which makes them more difficult to change. Each check is dated, and a check number may be inserted in the upper right corner of the check. The name of the person or company to whom the check is written should be carefully written on the second line from the top. You will notice in the illustration that the amount of the check is written twice. First, write the amount in figures, giving dollars and cents. Next, on the third line from the top, write the dollar amount spelled out and the cents amount of the check written as a fraction of one dollar. It is customary to draw a line to the end of the space. Most banks today require that you list your account number. Many checks have the account number and check number preprinted on them. These numbers provide ease in processing as well as a means of protecting the depositor. Then sign your name for identification exactly as written on the signature card.

THE CHECK STUB

The check stub provides the depositor with a space to record information about the transaction. It is wise to carefully complete the stub of the check first, otherwise it may be forgotten. The stub provides a place for deposits as well as withdrawals. When the records of all transactions have been recorded accurately, an up-to-date balance of the checking account is available to the writer.

In some cases, it may be wise to write the purpose of the check at the bottom, especially if the check is to be used as a receipt of payment. Some businesses assign a number to each charge account. When paying bills for which you have such a charge account number, you may help eliminate errors if you write that account number on the check.

A check may be used to withdraw cash from the bank. In this case, the check is written to "cash." However, a check for cash should be written at the bank and cashed immediately. If such a check is lost, it can be cashed by anyone.

Checking Accounts May Be Individual Accounts or Joint Checking Accounts — This Illustration Is an Individual Checking Account

DEPOSIT TICKET

FOR DEPOSIT TO THE ACCOUNT OF

ACCOUNT NUMBER

13-064-2

NAME *Bill Smith*

DATE *May 31* 19 *73*

ACKNOWLEDGE RECEIPT OF CASH RETURNED BY SIGNING ABOVE

The National Bank of Pittsburg

MEMBER FEDERAL RESERVE SYSTEM

Pittsburg, Kansas

⑈1011⑈0024⑈

CASH		
Check	125	00
TOTAL		
LESS CASH RECEIVED		
NET DEPOSIT	*125*	*00*

83-24
1011

In receiving items for deposit or collection, this bank acts only as depositor's collecting agent and assumes no responsibility beyond the exercise of due care. All items are credited subject to final payment in cash or solvent credits. This bank will not be liable for default or negligence of its duly selected correspondents nor for losses in transit, and each correspondent so selected shall not be liable except for its own negligence. This bank or its correspondents may send items directly or indirectly to any bank including the payor and accept its draft or credit as conditional payment in lieu of cash; it may charge back any item before final payment whether returned or not also any item drawn on this bank not good at close of business on day deposited.

Most Banks Provide a Deposit Slip Which You Prepare in Duplicate

CANCELLED CHECKS AND YOUR BANK STATEMENT

Checks which you write will be returned to you after payment. The checks are called **cancelled checks** and are useful to you as a receipt for payment and as a record of your bank account. Most banks return all cancelled checks to depositors each month. It is good business to file all the cancelled checks with the bank statement after you have made sure all the transactions are correct and the bank balance is accurate.

When you receive the cancelled checks from your bank, a bank statement will be included. The bank statement is an itemized list of checks that have been cancelled during the month. The statement will provide the balance at the start of the period and the balance at the end of the period.

The bank statement provides a record that can be used in checking your banking transactions for the month. Most of the checks will be returned to you with the bank statement.

No *10* $*13.50*

June 20, 19*73*

To *Speed Service*

FOR *Auto parts*

	DOLLARS	CENTS
BAL BROT FORD	84	90
AMT. DEPOSITED		
TOTAL		
AMT. THIS CHECK	13	50
BAL CARD FORD	71	40

PITTSBURG, KANSAS, *June 20,* 19*73*   No. *10*

The National Bank of Pittsburg

83-24
1011

PAY TO THE ORDER OF *Speed Service Garage* ———— $*13.50/100*

Thirteen and 50/100 ———————— DOLLARS

MEMBER FEDERAL RESERVE SYSTEM

ACCT. NO. *13-064-2*   *Bill Smith*

⑈1011⑈0024⑈ *For Auto Parts - Charge Acct. #62*

2-14-73

The Check Stub Provides a Space to Keep All Information Needed in Keeping an Accurate Record of Your Bank Account

THE NATIONAL BANK OF PITTSBURG

PITTSBURG, KANSAS 66762

BILL SMITH
66 ILLINOIS AVENUE
PITTSBURG, KANSAS 66762

ACCOUNT NUMBER
13-064-2

DATE OF STATEMENT
JUN 29 73

CHECKS AND OTHER DEBITS			DEPOSITS	DATE	BALANCE
			BALANCE FORWARD →		00.00
			125.00	MAY 31	125.00
4.97				JUN 01	120.03
2.00	13.22			JUN 04	104.81
11.25				JUN 07	93.56
17.95				JUN 11	75.61
6.51	3.00			JUN 13	66.10
9.00	4.50			JUN 14	52.60
			50.00	JUN 15	102.60
13.50				JUN 20	89.10
4.79				JUN 25	84.31

BALANCE PREVIOUS STATEMENT	NUMBER OF ENCLOSURES	CHECKS		DEPOSITS		SERVICE CHARGE	CLOSING BALANCE
		NUMBER	AMOUNT	NUMBER	AMOUNT		
00.00	11	11	90.69	2	175.00	.00	84.31

SC - Service Charge   LS - List   RI - Returned Items   DM - Debit Memo   OD - Overdraft Charge   IF - Insuf. Funds

The Bank Statement Includes All the Deposits Made to the Checking Account and Checks Paid by the Bank During the Period

HOW TO BALANCE YOUR CHECKBOOK

Many banks provide a printed form on the back of the statement which makes balancing an account much easier. In the illustration on page 200 you will see how to determine whether your balance and the balance on the bank statement agree. Any errors found in the bank statement should be reported at once.

The procedure for balancing your checking account each month is as follows:

1. **Sort your checks** numerically or by date issued.

2. **Check off in your checkbook** each of the checks paid by the bank, and list the numbers and amounts of those not paid in the space provided at the left. Be sure to include any check still outstanding from a previous statement.

3. **Enter and subtract** from your checkbook any other charge appearing on the statement.

4. **Reconcile your statement** in the space provided.

You Can Easily

BALANCE YOUR CHECK BOOK

FILL IN BELOW AMOUNTS FROM YOUR CHECK BOOK AND BANK STATEMENT

Balance Shown on
Bank Statement: $ _84.31_

Add Deposits
Not on Statement: $_____

_____

Total . . . $ _84.31_

Subtract Checks Issued but
Not on Statement:

$ _15.00_

_5.00_

_____

_____

_____

_____

_____

_____

Total . . . $ _20.00_

Balance . . . . . $ _64.31_

Balance Shown in
Your Check Book $ _64.31_

Add any Deposits Not
Already Entered in
Check Book: $_____

_____

_____

_____

Total . . . $ _64.31_

Subtract Service Charges
and other Bank Charges
Not in Check Book:

$ _00.00_

_____

_____

Total . . . $ _64.31_

Balance . . . . . $ _64.31_

These totals represent the correct amount of money you have in the bank and should agree.
Please examine your statement promptly and report any errors immediately.

It Is Necessary to Make a Reconciliation of the Bank Statement with Your Check Stubs

SUBSTITUTES FOR CASH

PERSONAL CHECKS

The advantages of using a personal checking account are many.

1. Checks are a substitute for money which may be safely sent through the mail. If the check is lost or stolen, it cannot easily be cashed.
2. A checking account makes it possible to keep only a small amount of cash in the home or on your person, reducing the chance of robbery.
3. Cancelled checks, endorsed by the person paid, furnish receipts of payment.
4. The record in the checkbook stub is a valuable record of money available for use.

BANK CARD SERVICE

A more recent type of banking service is the **Bank Card Service,** a type of credit provided by large organizations in cooperation with banks and business establishments. A special embossed plastic identification card is issued to those who desire the service. Each card has the name and serial number of the cardholder with a place for the cardholder's signature. Purchases may be made by the holder of a bank card at business establishments honoring the service. The issuer of the card furnishes the cardholder a monthly statement showing all purchases and cash advances made.

CERTIFIED CHECKS

A few companies today may refuse personal checks, especially if the amounts are

BankAmericard, Master Charge, and Bankmark Are Provided by Banking Institutions

large. Those who desire rapid service on orders may use a **certified check.** Your bank can provide this service. Money from your account will be withdrawn to cover the amount and held for payment. The certified check is stamped and signed by a bank official. The signature and the stamped information by the bank official make payment of the check guaranteed. The company will not have to wait to see if your check is good before delivering the merchandise you ordered.

CASHIER'S CHECK

For a small charge, it is possible to use a **cashier's check** to make payments. The cashier's check may be used for the same purpose as a certified check. However, a person need not have a checking account at the bank issuing a cashier's check. You pay the amount of the check, plus the charge, to the bank; and the bank writes the check.

MONEY ORDERS

A number of agencies furnish money orders for those making money transactions by mail. These include the American Express Company, the Railway Express Agency, and the United States Post Office. Postal money orders are most commonly used. They are sold at the post office for a

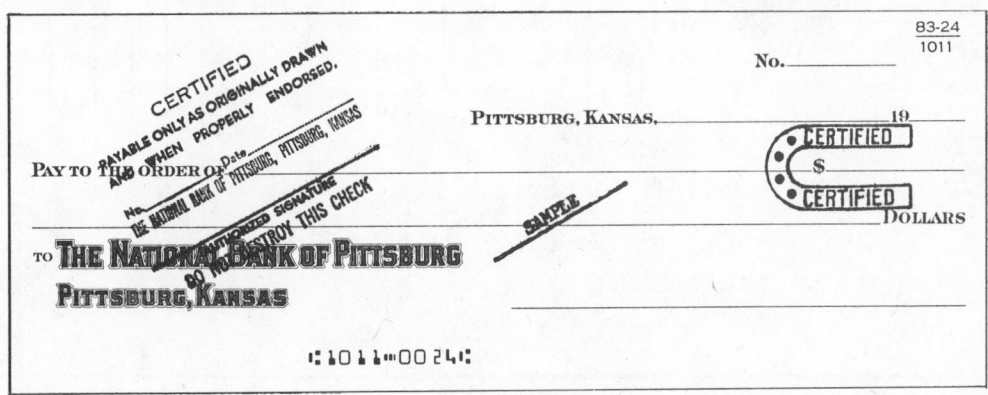

Many Companies Request Payment with a Certified Check for Goods or Services

YOUR MASTER CHARGE APPLICATION

651

P.O. Box 1611
Kansas City, Mo. 64141

PLEASE PRINT

master charge
THE INTERBANK CARD

FOR BANK USE ONLY

57 CPS _____ 06 CRL _____

07 CYL _____ 08 EXP _____

05 NO. CDS. _____

81	82	83	84	85	86	87	88	89

60 MR. ☐
   MRS./MISS ☐ _____ 74 AGE _____
   FIRST NAME   MIDDLE NAME   LAST NAME   DAY MO. YR.

51 SPOUSE NAME _____ 53 _____ 58 HOME PHONE (___) _____
                          CHECKING ACCT WITH   AREA CODE

02 ADDRESS _____ 03 _____ 04 _____
        (NUMBER AND STREET)   (CITY)   (STATE)   (ZIP CODE)

62 OWN HOME _____ RENT _____ PREVIOUS ADDRESS _____
                                      NUMBER & STREET   CITY   STATE

NEAREST RELATIVE _____
                NAME   ADDRESS   CITY   STATE

EMPLOYER
68 NAME _____ 65 POSITION _____ HOW LONG
                                                    EMPLOYED

EMPLOYER   EMPLOYER
69 ADDRESS _____ 70 PHONE (___) _____
                                      AREA CODE

WIFE'S EMPLOYER _____
                NAME   ADDRESS   PHONE NO.

CREDIT
66 REFERENCES _____ _____

_____ _____

_____ _____

_____ _____

APPLICANT'S SIGNATURE _____ SIGNATURE OF SPOUSE _____

DATE SIGNED _____

RULES FOR USE OF CARD AND TRUTH-IN-LENDING DISCLOSURES EFFECTIVE APRIL 1, 1973

These rules and agreement on reverse side of BankAmericard issued by Commerce Bank of Kansas City, N.A. (Issuer) constitute the contract governing the extension of credit by Issuer through use of BankAmericard(s) to each applicant (herein called "Holder") and any person using said card(s) with the express or implied permission of Holder, to which each such person severally expresses his consent and agreement by applying for, signing, using, or consenting to the use of, said card(s):

(1) Issuer agrees, pursuant to this BankAmericard contract, to pay (a) drafts drawn for purchase of goods and services sold by BankAmericard member merchants, and (b) drafts cashed by BankAmericard member banks ("cash advances"), to the extent of credit limit of account, as initially established by Issuer or as Issuer may, in its sole discretion, change at any time, and from time to time, at Holder's request or otherwise, so long as Holder shall not be in default hereunder.

(2) The periodic statement furnished by Issuer for the account shall set forth all charges and credits paid or received by Issuer during the preceding billing period and such statement shall be deemed conclusively correct and accepted by Holder unless Issuer is notified in writing of any errors therein within 14 days from the date of mailing of said statement.

(3) If total of payments, refunds and credits received by Issuer within one month of closing date is at least equal to amount of new balance shown on periodic statement, no FINANCE CHARGE will be imposed except on cash advances which incur FINANCE CHARGE from date the advance is posted to the account. A FINANCE CHARGE will be imposed on that portion of the Average Daily Balance not exceeding $900 at a periodic rate of 1½% per month (ANNUAL PERCENTAGE RATE 18%) and on that portion of the Average Daily Balance in excess of $900 at a periodic rate of ⅔ of 1% per month (ANNUAL PERCENTAGE RATE 8%).

(4) The Average Daily Balance for a billing period is determined by dividing the sum of the daily balances outstanding (excluding FINANCE CHARGES, drafts charged to account for purchases of goods or services in the billing period, and previous balance paid in full within one month of closing date; adding cash advances; and subtracting net payments and credits posted) for each day of the monthly billing period by the number of days in the monthly billing period.

(5) A charge of $3.00 will be made and added to the account of Holder for each check or other instrument for the payment of money sent to Issuer which is returned unpaid to Issuer.

(6) Holder agrees to pay to Issuer in accordance with billings all indebtedness incurred under this contract plus the applicable FINANCE CHARGES, and to make a minimum payment of $10 or 5% of the new balance shown on the periodic statement, whichever is greater, each month, and if new balance is less than $10, to pay such balance in full within one month of the statement date. All payments received by Issuer shall be applied first to FINANCE CHARGES previously billed, second to previous balance and then to other amounts owing.

(7) Credit extended by Issuer through use of BankAmericard is not a secured indebtedness; however, Issuer, pursuant to Missouri law, may exercise the right to set off property (including accounts) of a Holder which is in possession of Issuer against debts owed to Issuer by such Holder(s) and this right of setoff constitutes the only security interest which Issuer might acquire to secure indebtedness extended pursuant to use of BankAmericard.

(8) Issuer shall not be responsible for the refusal of anyone to honor BankAmericard and Issuer shall have no responsibility for merchandise purchased by or services rendered through use of BankAmericard, and all defenses, rights and claims relating to goods and/or services purchased through the use of BankAmericard shall be asserted only against the seller of such merchandise or services and not Issuer. Cash refunds will not be made on purchases made through use of BankAmericard and any refunds or adjustments will be effected through a credit to be granted by such seller.

(9) Holder agrees not to make or permit use of BankAmericard issued by Issuer for any purchase or cash advance which would exceed the limit Issuer has established as the credit limit for the account.

(10) Issuer reserves the right, at any time and without liability to Holder or any user and without affecting Holder's liability to Issuer, to revoke all credit available to Holder, to demand immediate payment of all amounts due, and to cancel the card(s) issued on such account. Holder agrees upon such demand to make such payment and to surrender to Issuer all cards issued on said account. Holder agrees to pay a reasonable attorney's fee in the event of suit.

(11) Credit extended through use of a BankAmericard issued by Issuer is pursuant to a credit card issued in Missouri, and this BankAmericard agreement is governed by Missouri law except to the extent governed by federal law. The invalidity of any term or condition of the rules or agreement pertaining to the use of BankAmericard shall not affect the validity of any other term or condition. Issuer reserves the right to amend this agreement in whole or in part at any time and from time to time.

BankAmericard Applcation

A B C

(Do Not Use This Space)

Mr. Mrs. Miss	Last Name (Please Print)		First Name		Initial	Age

Street Address		Spouse's First Name		Initial	Age

City	State	Zip Code	Telephone No.	Dependents	Social Security No.

TYPE:
1 2 3 4 5 6 7 8 9 0
C. L. 3 5 _____
NO. 1 2 3 4 _____
APPROVED BY: _____
DATE: _____

At Present Address Years Months	Own ☐ Rent ☐ With Parents ☐	If at above address less than 3 years, give former home address	Yrs.
		Zip	

Circle highest grade completed

High School	College	Graduate School
1 2 3 4 5 6 7 8 9 10 11 12	13 14 15 16	17 18 19 20

Applicant's Occupation	Monthly Income	Presently Employed By	Years	Months

Business Address: Street No.	City and State	Business Telephone
	Zip	

Previously Employed By	Occupation	Previous Business Address	Years	Months

Spouse's Occupation	Monthly Income	Spouse Employed By	Business Telephone	Years	Months

Automobile—Make	Year	Model	Financed By and Address	Balance Due	Driver's License No.

Name of Nearest Relative NOT Living with Me	Address	City	Relationship

Credit References (Banks, Stores, Credit Unions, Finance Co's, etc) and Complete List of All Debts Now Owing. Attach Additional Sheet if Necessary

Name	Address	Acct. No.	Balance Due

Home Financed By	Estimated Value	Loan Balance	Payment

Bank With: Checking	Bank	Account No.
Savings	Bank	Account No.

Number of Cards Needed [ ]

If a credit line of $1,000 or more is desired, please include a Financial Statement.

The above application is true and correct and applicant acknowledges receipt of and agrees to the contract and disclosures set forth to the left hereof and further agrees to pay all indebtedness incurred in accordance with such contract. Applicants authorize Commerce Bank of Kansas City, NA to offset any funds on deposit in the event of default. I have no other present indebtedness other than those listed above or attached hereto.

_____
Applicant's Signature   Date

_____
Signature of other applicant (spouse)   BAC 9401

NO ENVELOPE OR STAMP REQUIRED—JUST FOLD, SEAL, AND MAIL

Tear off along this perforation and retain contract terms for your records.

small charge. When you need a postal money order, you make the purchase at the post office. The money order clerk completes the order. The name of the purchaser and person to receive the money order are written in by the purchaser and mailed. The receiver must take the money order to the post office to cash it. The maximum amount of a postal money order is $100, which limits its use in sending large sums.

TELEGRAPHIC MONEY ORDERS

In emergencies, or when speed in sending is important, a Western Union Telegraphic Money Order can be used. The cost of sending money by wire depends on the amount but is more expensive than by mail. If desired, a message may be sent at the same time. For safety in sending money, a return reply may be requested to make sure the person intended is getting the money.

TRAVELER'S CHECKS

One of the most used and safest ways to take a substitute for cash on trips in the United States or to foreign countries is the use of traveler's checks. They can be purchased at banks, railroad offices or express offices in $10, $20, $50, or $100 denominations. The purchaser signs each check at the time of purchase and signs each check when it is cashed. Signatures must be identical before the check will be cashed. Traveler's checks can be replaced if lost or stolen, which makes this service a valuable one for the traveler. The cost of the service is low. The purchaser pays one dollar fee for each $100 in traveler's checks.

TO PURCHASER:

Need more Cheques and far fr...

Call at the nearest A...
press office. They will...
advise you how to m...
ments with your ban...
of additional Travele...

Or instruct your...
deliver additional...
through America...
of the world.

In countrie...
are required...
the cost of...
by the h...

MADE IN U.S.A.

AMERICAN EXPRESS TRAVELERS CHEQUES

The safe money that's spendable everywhere. Your signature is both your identification and your protection.

Sign here when you buy them

Sign here when you spend them

THE NATIONAL BAN...
OF PITTSBUR...
Pittsburg, K...

TO FINDER:

Please return these Cheques to an American Express office

...S DEPARTMENT, AMERICAN EXPRESS COMPANY
...NEW YORK, N. Y. 10006.

...em in the nearest U.S. Mail Box (return

...s a criminal offense to negotiate, or
...negotiate, Travelers Cheques which
...found, stolen or fraudulently obtained.

	LAST 3 FIGS. OF CHEQUE NO.	DATE SPENT	WHERE SPENT
PURCHASER AGREES TO TERMS AND CONDITIONS ON THE REVERSE SIDE			

WARNING TO PURCHASER

SIGN EACH CHEQUE <u>IMMEDIATELY</u> IN UPPER LEFT-HAND CORNER — YOU ARE NOT PROTECTED IN CASE OF LOSS OR THEFT UNTIL EACH CHEQUE IS SIGNED.

TOTAL AMOUNT $100.00	DATE PURCHASED 19

AMERICAN EXPRESS TRAVELERS CHEQUES
PURCHASER'S APPLICATION

THIS SALE CONSISTS OF 10 (TEN) TRAVELERS CHEQUES OF $10 DENOMINATION IN NUMERICAL SEQUENCE STARTING WITH ABOVE NUMBER.

NOTE: THIS RECORD SLIP SHOULD BE CARRIED SEPARATELY FROM CHEQUES.
Send a memorandum of the serial numbers to your home or other address for safekeeping, should both Cheques and this Record Slip be lost or destroyed.

PURCHASER'S COPY   SEE REVERSE SIDE

THE NATIONAL...
PITTSBURG
CORNER 4TH & BROADWAY
PITTSBURG, KANSAS

...ANKABLE
...FETY PAPER

BANK OF PITTSBURG
Pittsburg, Kansas

Traveler's Checks Must Be Signed When Purchased and Again When Cashed

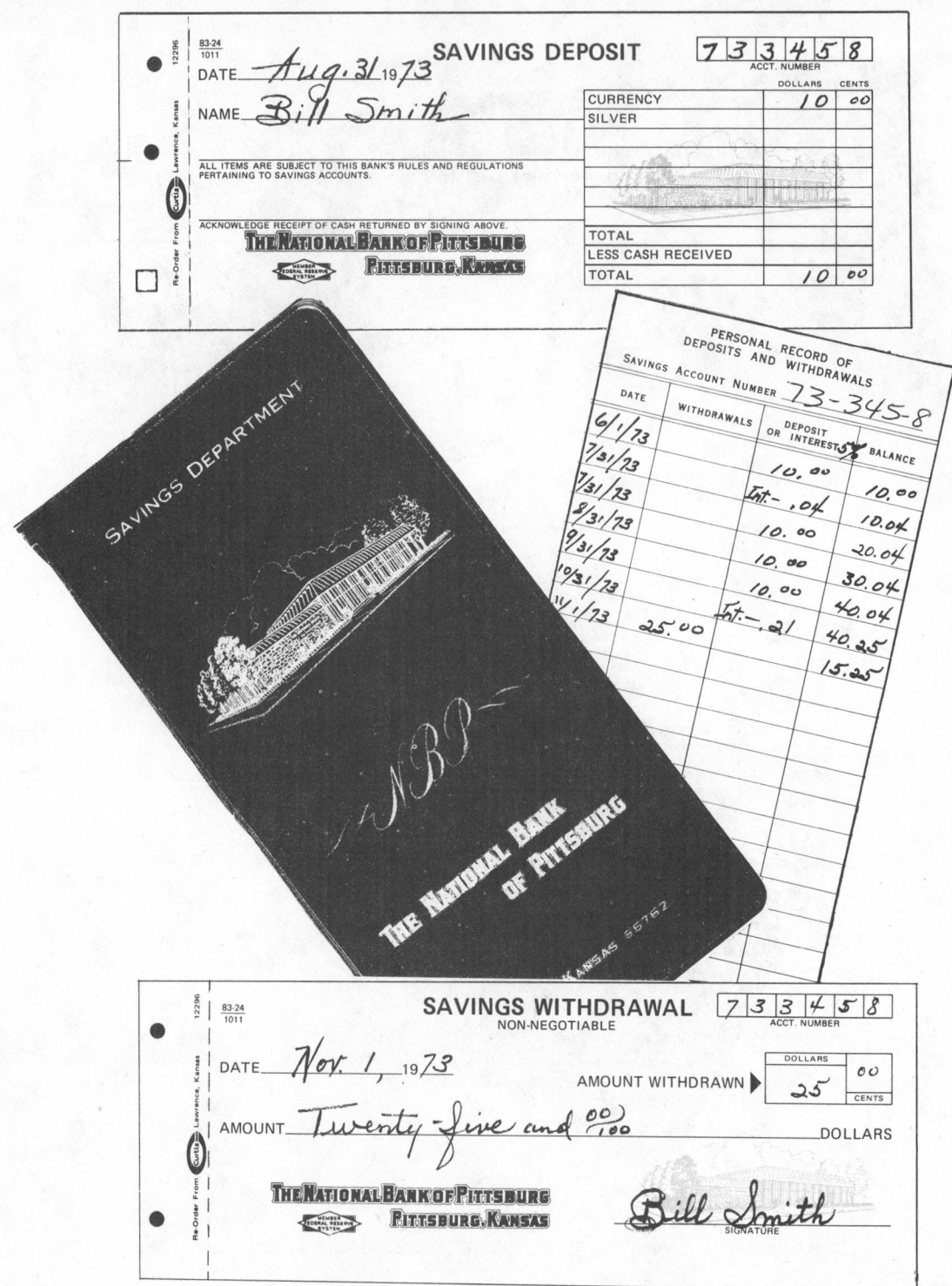

Both You and Your Bank Keep Records of Deposits, Withdrawals, and Interest Earned for Your Savings Account

THE SAVINGS ACCOUNT

Banks provide a savings account for their customers as well as a checking account. Several types of banks provide this service. Commercial banks accept savings of time deposits on which they pay interest. The interest rate paid on deposits may range from 4 to 8 percent and is compounded at different periods during the year. Banks have different rules and regulations on withdrawals. Some banks require at least 30 days notice before withdrawal. Special saving certificates may not be withdrawn for six months, while other certificates may not be withdrawn for one year.

Other types of banks accepting deposits for the purpose of saving and investments include savings banks, stock savings banks, and mutual savings banks.

It is a good idea to find out by asking your employer and other adults which types of savings banks are located in your community. Then ask at the banks what savings plans are available, what the interest is, how it is paid, and what rules govern savings deposits and withdrawals.

THE NATIONAL BANK OF PITTSBURG, KANSAS
RULES and REGULATIONS
GOVERNING SAVINGS ACCOUNTS

1. This contract is accepted and all deposits are made subject to the rules and regulations of the Bank as herein printed and made a part of this deposit contract.

2. Each person, at the time of opening a savings account, shall subscribe his or her name on the signature card provided for that purpose by the Bank. The signature of the depositor on said signature card and the making of the first deposit shall be deemed an agreement by such depositor to be governed by such rules and regulations as they shall then exist or be thereafter modified as herein provided.

3. The Bank reserves the right to return all or any part of the amount standing to the credit of any depositor and may at any time refuse to accept deposits from any person or may limit the amount thereof, in its absolute discretion. If the Bank shall elect to return any deposit, notice to that effect shall be mailed to the depositor at his address appearing on the books of the Bank and such deposit shall cease to bear interest from and after the date of mailing of such notice.

4. Withdrawals of deposits, and the interest thereon, may be made by a depositor personally or by any other person holding a written order or power of attorney, duly authenticated, of the depositor.

5. As a general rule depositors may withdraw their deposits at will but the Bank reserves the right to demand and have 60 days written notice of intention to withdraw the same. Such notice shall lapse and be considered canceled if the sum called for is not withdrawn within 5 days after the expiration thereof, and only one notice shall be in force at one time on any savings account. Any payment made by the Bank, without requiring notice, as herein provided, shall not be deemed a waiver of the right to require such notice as to future withdrawals.

6. Interest will be credited on all sums of $10.00 or more which have remained on deposit for one or more months next previous to interest paying dates and at such rate as the Board of Directors may establish.

Deposits made during the first 5 business days of each month will draw interest as if made on the first day of such month, but otherwise no interest will be credited for fractions of months or upon fractions of dollars. Interest will not be paid on average balances and all withdrawals between interest paying dates will be deducted from the first deposits. Interest credited but not withdrawn, will be added to the principal and thereafter draw interest the same as an original deposit.

No interest will be paid on accounts closed between interest paying dates.

7. Three withdrawals in any 3 months interest period will be allowed without charges; additional withdrawals will be permitted at 15c each.

If account is closed within 60 days after opening, a charge of One Dollar will be made to cover cost of stationery used.

8. In receiving items for deposit or collection, this Bank acts only as depositor's collecting agent and assumes no responsibility beyond the exercise of due care. All items are credited subject to final payment in cash or solvent credits. This Bank will not be liable for default or negligence of its duly selected correspondents nor for losses in transit, and each correspondent so selected shall not be liable except for its own negligence. This Bank or its correspondents may send items, directly or indirectly, to any bank, including the payor, and accept its draft or credit as conditional payment in lieu of cash; it may charge back any item at any time before final payment, whether returned or not, also any item drawn on this Bank not good at close of business on day deposited.

9. This Bank reserves the right to deduct from any deposit the amount of such claims as it may have against the original depositor.

10. The foregoing rules may be altered, amended, or rescinded, or new rules made by the Board of Directors at any time, upon posting a copy of such alterations, amendments, rescissions or new rules in the banking room of the Bank for 30 days and upon the expiration of such period of posting such alterations, amendments, recissions and new rules shall be binding upon all depositors as fully as if expressly assented to by them respectively.

Cards Enclosed in Savings Account Folders List Regulations Governing Such Accounts

You may find the interest rate varies from one bank to another and that banks also differ, depending on the type of savings account. After making sure that your account will be insured by the Federal Deposit Insurance Corporation or another reliable plan, you are in a position to look forward to achieving future goals.

The question you may ask is, "How much money should I save?" Some financial experts recommend that, as a reserve, you should have from three to six month's salary in your savings account to meet an emergency. Since each individual has special needs, there is no absolute amount to recommend. However, anything extra you may be able to save can be used for special goals that you have set.

The amount saved each month in relation to salary after taxes is shown in the chart below. The guide may be helpful to you in planning your savings.

If your monthly salary after taxes is . . .	You should save per month . . .
$200 to $300	$7 to $30
$300 to $400	$25 to $50
$400 to $500	$50 to $90
$500 to $600	$90 to $100
$600 to $700	$95 to $120
$700 to $800	$115 to $165
$800 to $900	$135 to $185
$900 to $1000	$150 to $220

STUDY AIDS

NEW TERMS

commercial bank	money order
savings bank	traveler's check
trust funds	promissory note
Federal Reserve	signature
certified check	depositor
cashier's check	withdrawal
bank card	transaction
checking account	endorsement
bank statement	check stub
bank balance	reconciliation

STUDY QUESTIONS

1. What are the different kinds of banks?
2. What are the two main functions of commercial banks?
3. What are the functions of the Federal Reserve System?
4. What is a bank deposit? A time deposit?
5. What is the procedure in starting a checking account?
6. How does a check stub help you to keep your checking account accurate?
7. How may a check be endorsed?
8. What procedures should be used in reconciling a bank statement with the check stubs?
9. What is the advantage of using a checking account?
10. Why do some companies request certified or cashier's checks for payment of goods and services?
11. Where can you purchase traveler's checks?
12. What is the FDIC, and how does it operate?

DISCUSSION PROBLEMS

1. Is your money "safer" in a state bank or a national bank? Why?
2. What advantage is there to you in being a depositor in a bank which is a member of the Federal Deposit Insurance Corporation?
3. List the steps required to open a checking account.
4. Pretend that you have just received your first paycheck. What would you do to get money from the check?
5. Rank the following according to which you think are the best ways of having money while on a vacation trip. Write (1) before the best choice, (2) before the next best way, (3) before the next choice, etc.
   _____ low denomination bills
   _____ personal checks
   _____ traveler's checks
   _____ bank card
   _____ money order
   _____ certified checks
6. Make up an imaginary food order. What should you do before and during payment of the bill?

CHAPTER FIFTEEN
TAXPAYER RESPONSIBILITIES

UNDERSTANDING TAXATION

Taxation is a process by which people pay the expenses of their government. Taxation is as old as government itself — historians indicate that even the earliest forms of government needed a method of financing the cost of government services. Many of them collected taxes in the form of goods and services, rather than in cash. This type of tax payment is called "payments in kind."

Taxation has been a problem to most governments. Deciding who shall pay taxes, how much to collect, and how to use the money has never been determined to the satisfaction of all the people.

The preamble of the Constitution of the United States sets forth the general function of our government as follows:

> We the People of the United States, in Order to form a more Perfect Union, establish Justice, insure domestic tranquility, provide for the common defense, promote the general welfare, and secure the Blessing of Liberty to ourselves and our posterity, do ordain and establish the Constitution of the United States of America.

Section 8 Article I of the Constitution establishes the responsibility and power of Congress in matters of taxation.

> The Congress shall have the power to lay and collect Taxes, Duties, Imposts and Excises, to pay the Debts and provide for the Common Defense and general Welfare of the United States: but all Duties, Imposts, and Excises shall be uniform throughout the United States.

The voters in the United States have a voice in the structure of the tax system. Our taxes are not imposed for the use of a dictator or a privileged few, but to pay for the goods and services we need and want. When you reach voting age in your state, it will not be possible for you as an individual to decide what taxes you will pay. Tax laws are designed to give equal justice to all citizens. In some cases, small groups may be hurt by laws passed for the general population. However, under our system individuals can vote for people to represent their interests. They can write and speak out against destructive practices. The important thing for young citizens to learn is that they have a responsibility as voters to know where each of the candidates for political office stands on tax issues and other financial problems of the country. The voter must be alert and informed on important questions which will affect everyone.

Our tax system is one in which taxpayers assess their own taxes. Basically our tax system is dependent upon a positive act of the citizen. At times, responsible taxpayers may lose faith in the tax system and become envious of those who cheat on tax returns. However, there is little reason for the honest taxpayer to feel envious of the tax evader. The chances of getting caught are high, and the penalties are severe for those who are convicted of tax evasion. Honesty in paying one's legally established share is not only an act of good citizenship, but one of pride and clear conscience.

TYPES OF TAXES

Many types of taxes have been used in the United States and other nations. Taxes may be classified in many ways. Important classifications are as follows:

DIRECT AND INDIRECT TAXES

Direct taxes are paid directly to the government by the taxpayer, hence the term "direct." The best example of a direct tax is our federal individual income tax which will be discussed later. Indirect taxes are taxes on goods and services. Such taxes include excise or sales taxes, cigarette stamp taxes, and duties on imports.

PROGRESSIVE AND REGRESSIVE TAXES

Taxes may be classified as progressive or regressive when considered in relation to the ability to pay. A tax is called progressive when the tax is levied proportionately to the ability of the person to pay. The graduated income tax is levied on the amount of income, and the person with a high income is taxed more than a person with a low income. A tax is classified as regressive when the taxation rate remains the same regardless of the so-called "ability to pay." Sales tax is considered to be a regressive tax, since the tax rate is the same for every purchase of goods without consideration of total purchase. Total purchase is assumed to reflect ability to pay. Taxes are not planned to be regressive, but in application they many

times are. A sales tax is considered regressive since a wealthy family pays less sales tax in proportion to its earnings than a poor family spending one half of their earnings on items on which sales tax is levied.

STATE AND LOCAL TAXES

To finance the operation of state and local government, several types of taxes are used today.

1. State and Local Tax Bases. State and local governments levy taxes because the people are in general agreement that it is best to pay collectively for public services that are needed by everyone. The elected officers of state and local government represent the taxpayers in establishing levies and assigning priorities for needs. Public services are important in developing and maintaining the kind of society we want. Tax money is needed to finance public education, build and maintain roads and highways, operate the welfare program, and carry on many other programs — such as public security, safety, conservation, and recreation.

To provide these services, taxes are levied on the basis of three general criteria:
1. What is owned (property).
2. What is earned (income tax).
3. What is spent (sales tax-users tax).

The percentage of taxes collected from each of the three measures listed may vary from state to state. Some economists argue that taxes should be progressive, or based on what is earned. However, property, income, and sales taxes are all used in most states.

2. Property Taxes. Property tax is levied on real estate. Each local tax district sets an annual rate which may vary widely with adjoining districts. The rate is based on the assessed valuation of the property. One of the problems is assessing property fairly. Property taxes are still the main source of revenue for operating schools.

Under average economic conditions, the property tax provides a stable source of school finance. In most districts the assessed valuation of property is only a part of the market value. New housing generally carries the highest assessment. The property tax assessment rates change slowly.

Personal property tax may be **tangible** or **intangible** which means that taxes on cars, trucks, machinery, equipment, and livestock are on "tangible" property. Taxes on bonds, saving accounts, and securities are personal "intangible" taxes.

3. Sales Taxes. Most states have started using sales tax to raise revenue for state and local expenses. The rates are as high as six percent in some states. Items on which sales tax is added differ among the states.

The sales tax was used to raise money for social welfare programs started in the 1930's when the country was in the depression. It is also used to finance other public programs. Schools and local units of government use sales tax as a source of revenue.

4. Highway and User Taxes. One of the chief sources of revenue for highway construction and maintenance is the tax on gasoline. Each state sets the rate in cents per gallon of gasoline. Another type of highway-user tax is the license fee for cars, trucks, buses, and trailers. Some cities also levy a tax on gasoline sold in the city. A federal tax is added to finance the interstate highway system.

Taxes on gasoline ranged from 5 cents to 10 cents per gallon in 1973. More than 7 billion dollars were collected by all states in 1971. This amount does not include the two cents per gallon federal tax on gasoline.[1] In some states about one-third of the consumer's cost for gasoline goes for user tax. User taxes are justified on the basis of benefit to the person using the roads. Taxes on rail, air or bus tickets also fall within this classification.

5. Payroll and Business Taxes. States and cities often require business organizations to buy a license for the privilege of operating a business. States also tax the net earnings of business establishments.

All states charge a percent on payrolls in occupations covered by Social Security. The revenue is used to finance unemployment compensation.

6. State Personal Income Taxes. About four-fifths of all states levy an income tax on individual earnings, but these rates differ from state to state. Some states base the state income tax on the federal income taxes paid by individuals. For example, Alaska has a rate of 16 percent of federal income tax. Other states set a percentage of federal income tax based on amount of federal income tax paid by the taxpayers. The rates vary from one to fifteen percent of federal taxes paid. Many states have reporting forms comparable to the federal reporting forms.[2]

The revenue derived from individual state income tax is used for a number of purposes. Education receives a large portion of the revenue in some states. The trend is that more states are turning to individual income tax, and the rates are going higher each year.

7. State Inheritance and Estate Taxes. The inheritance and estate tax is called a progressive tax, because more taxes are levied on the higher estates. All states have some type of estate tax, and thirty-eight states have inheritance tax laws.

Social reformers approve this type of tax to reduce the development of a powerful, wealthy group. However, trust laws and the right to make gifts makes it possible to transfer a part of estates to heirs without the high rate of estate tax being paid.

Estate tax revenues collected by the federal government are shared with the state if the state has passed an estate tax law. State estate tax laws vary widely.

FEDERAL INCOME TAX

The United States government's largest single source of revenue is through a graduated individual income tax. The Internal Revenue Service of the United States Treasury Department operates the nationwide collection service.

[1]Federal Highway Administration Department of Transportation, 1971.

[2]Federal Highway Administration Department of Transportation, 1971.

STATE GENERAL FUND

ESTIMATED EXPENDITURES
By Function of Government

Estimated expenditures from the State General Fund for fiscal year 1974 are $525.6 million, or 43.4% of total state expenditures from all funds. The chart below shows distribution of State General Fund expenditures by function of government for the fiscal year 1974. Amounts are in millions of dollars. No expenditures are made from the State General Fund for the Highways and Other Transportation Function.

ESTIMATED REVENUES BY SOURCE

State General Fund expenditures for fiscal year 1974 are estimated at $525.6 million and current receipts are estimated at $495.9 million. Sources of these revenues are shown below. (Amounts are in millions of dollars.)

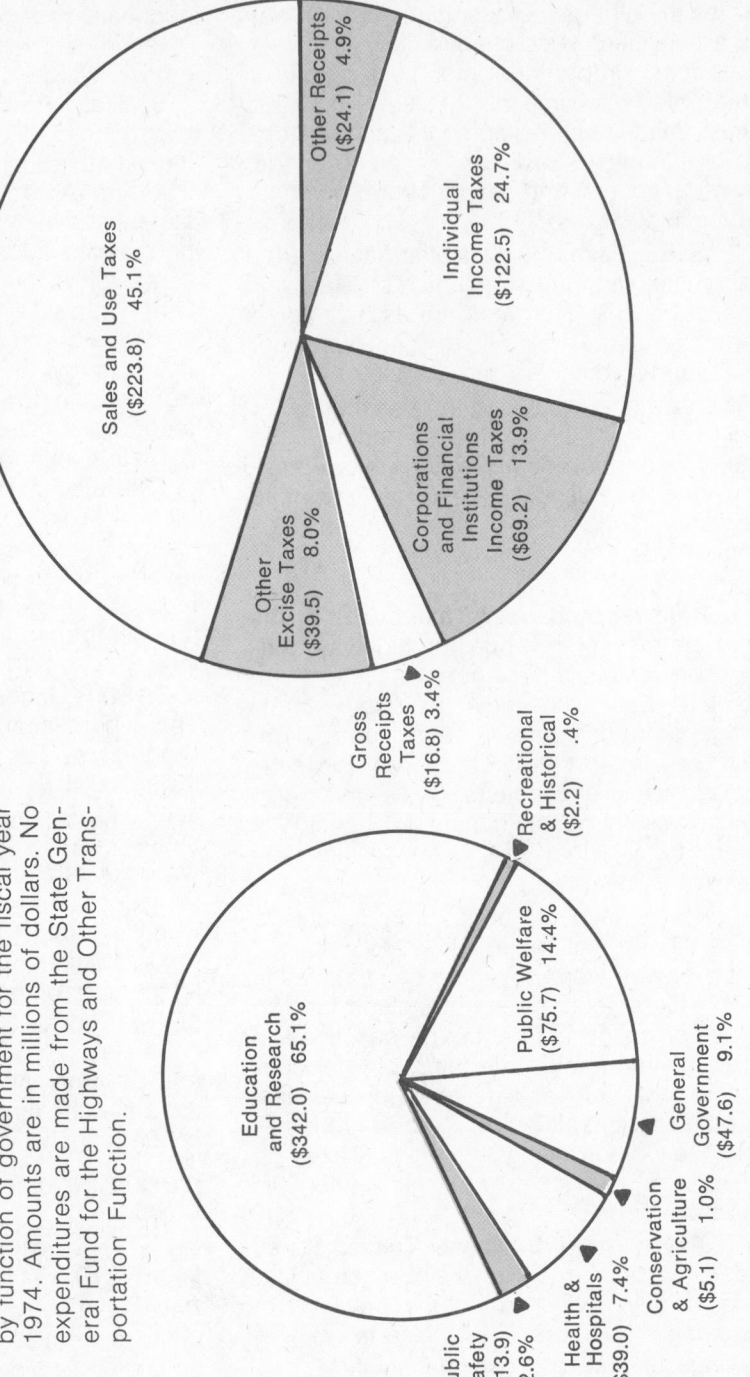

The State Government Uses Several Revenue Sources to Finance Governmental Functions

The history of taxation in our country is closely related to the history of the United States itself. One of the reasons we have the type of tax system we do is in part the result of bitter experiences with taxation during colonial times. Under the rule of the British Empire, taxation grew more oppressive. People were angry, because they had taxation without representation. Finally, after a number of tax schemes were tried by the British, the colonists rebelled in 1776 and declared their independence. One of the chief causes claimed for fighting the Revolutionary War was this taxation without representation. It was not until 1788 that the colonists were able to organize a constitution. Because of the experiences with unfair taxation, our Founding Fathers limited the federal government's power to tax.

After the war debts were paid, it was possible for President Jefferson and the Congress to abolish the whole system of collecting internal taxes. However, the War of 1812 was expensive, so the system of internal taxation was revised. Again, after the war was over, the federal government was able to pay the debts and abolish the excise tax, which was the same type of tax used to pay the war debts of the Revolution.

Taxes were raised again during the Civil War, when President Lincoln signed a comprehensive tax law to raise money to fight the war.

The law enacted in 1862 provided for taxation according to income. It also authorized the federal government to levy taxes on real estate, public utilities, and many consumer goods such as beer and tobacco. The law authorized a tax-collecting agency which was the forerunner of our present Internal Revenue Service. Agents were employed to collect taxes and special investigators were employed to detect fraud and to enforce the tax laws.

After the war was over and the debts were paid, the tax system was again repealed. By 1877 most of the levies had been removed and the federal government returned to tariff for operation expense rather than taxes.

During the last quarter of the 19th century (1875-1900), more attention was given to the need for a federal income tax system. The country experienced economic panic and depression during this period, causing hardship and suffering. The economic unrest during this period was partly responsible for the rise of a new political party called the "Populist Party." The members of the party included farmers and city labor groups who advocated a federal income tax to collect needed money and serve as a mechanism to regulate the economy, especially during depression and periods of expansion. The same group advocated public ownership of transportation and communication systems.

Because of the early experience with oppressive tax laws, most citizens of the United States had a strong feeling against taxes of any kind, especially federal. The Constitution, when adopted, specifically prohibited the levying of direct taxes. On several occasions the courts ruled tax laws unconstitutional because they were considered direct.

During the 1890's income tax laws were challenged in the federal courts. In 1895, the Supreme Court ruled that income tax was a form of direct tax and was therefore unconstitutional. The Income Tax Division in the Office of Internal Revenue was disbanded after that court ruling.

In order to enact an income tax law, it was necessary to change the Constitution. The increased need for money to operate the federal government and the need to reform the tax system of the country led to the proposal for an amendment to the Constitution. This amendment would give Congress the power to tax without apportionment among the States.

The 16th Amendment to the Constitution was passed by Congress in 1909, and was ratified by two-thirds of the states in February, 1913. Provisions of the amendment were as follows:

"The Congress shall have power to lay and collect taxes on incomes, from whatever sources derived, without apportionment among the several states, and without regard to any census or enumeration."

The cost of World War I was the greatest expenditure to the United States Government up to that time. The $35 billion cost of World War I was more than the cost of the federal government from 1791 to 1917. About one-third of the money was raised in taxes under the federal income tax system. The total income tax collection reached about $5½ billion per year in 1920.[3] The per capita cost of government was $178.

After the war, income tax was again reduced and the per capita cost of government fell to $28 under the Coolidge administration. However, when the great depression of 1929 hit the country and millions of people were unemployed, the country started a new economic practice of using federal money to revive the national economy. From 1933 to 1940, much social legislation was passed during the administration of President Franklin D. Roosevelt. The Bureau of Internal Revenue was given the responsibility for the collection of Social Security payroll taxes.

Only a small number of people paid federal income tax before World War II. The number has increased from 8,000,000 to more than 60,000,000 today.

Since the end of World War II, the personal income tax rate has remained at a high level. Cost of expensive programs, such as the Marshall Plan after the war, required billions of additional dollars. The Korean War, the Vietnam War, and the Cold War with Russia and China have required additional tax dollars. Today, the single largest ex-

[3]Department of the Treasury, Internal Revenue Service, "Understanding Taxes, Teaching Taxes Program," 1970 ed., pp. 2-4.

penditure in our national government is for national defense. Also, the cost of federal spending in health, education, and welfare continues to rise. The chart indicates how money is spent in relation to our gross national product.

During President Johnson's administration, Congress passed a new type of income tax law to assess a surcharge on the income tax one pays. The surcharge tax was added to income tax to raise additional revenue to finance the Vietnam War and to reduce inflation. The surcharge rates were about 10 percent, which was added to the income tax levied.

TAXES AND THE FEDERAL BUDGET

The Federal budget serves the same purpose as an individual's budget (to plan expenditures). The federal budget is prepared by the Bureau of the Budget under the direction of the President. It is a financial plan covering programs proposed by the President to meet the needs of the United States. The budget contains an estimate of income and expenses for one **fiscal year**, running from July 1 to June 30.

The budget is completed and sent to Congress in January before the fiscal year starts on July 1. Congress can make additions and deletions in the budget. The House of Representatives is responsible for appropriations to meet the expenses estimated in the budget.

The 1972 federal budget receipts reached a total of 208.6 billion compared to 188.4 billion for 1971. The total expenditures for 1972 were 230.5 billion, which resulted in a 21.9 billion deficit for the year. In 1971 total expenditures were 210.3 billion, which resulted in a deficit of 21.9 billion. The highest percentage of budget receipts comes from individual income tax, with Social Security (FIAC) taxes in second place. Corporate income tax is the third highest source of revenue. The budget outlay gives us significant indications of national priorities. In 1971, for the first time in twenty years the federal government spent a higher percent

The Government Dollar — Fiscal Year 1973

Where it comes from ...

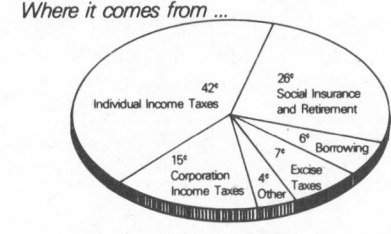

Where it goes ...

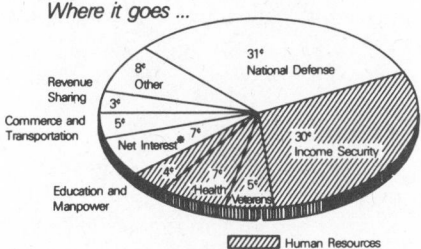

VZZZZZ Human Resources

* Excludes Interest Paid to Trust Funds

The following is a breakdown of how the Federal Government dollar was spent in 1973.

National defense: $76.1 billion. 31 cents of each dollar spent by the Government in 1973 went for maintaining our national security, for military assistance abroad, and for atomic energy programs.

International affairs: $3.2 billion. 1 cent of each dollar went for international programs, such as economic and technical assistance, Food for Peace, the operation of embassies abroad, and the Peace Corps.

Space research and technology: $3.3 billion. Manned space flight, space science, and technological and supporting activities, took about 1 cent of each Government dollar in 1973.

Agriculture and rural development: $6.2 billion. Almost 3 cents of each dollar spent were used for the stabilization of farm income, financing rural electrification and housing, soil conservation, research, and food inspection.

Natural resources and environment: $0.6 billion. Gross spending for pollution control, acquisition and maintenance of park lands, flood control, power projects, and related programs was over $5.7 billion. After deducting receipts of $5.1 billion for activities such as the leasing of mineral rights and timber sales, net spending for natural resources and environment was $0.6 billion in 1973.

Commerce and transportation: $12.4 billion. 5 cents of the 1973 Government dollar went for highway construction and mass transit; operation of the Federal airways, the Post Office, and the Coast

Guard; aids to economically-distressed areas and small business; and for related programs.

Community development and housing: $4.2 billion. The Federal Government helps provide loans and grants for public housing and community development. It also aids private housing through support of the mortgage market and rent supplements. These programs took 2 cents of the Government dollar.

Education and manpower: $10.8 billion. Programs to improve the quality of education at all levels, to assist science education and basic research, vocational education, and manpower training, took 4 cents of each dollar of the Federal budget.

Health: $18.4 billion. Through Medicare and Medicaid the Government helps pay the medical bills of the Nation's aged and poor. In addition, the Government provides funds for medical research, training health manpower, construction of health facilities, and the prevention and control of health problems. These programs took 7 cents of the Government dollar in 1973.

Income security: $72.8 billion. This category includes social security, unemployment and retirement benefits which are financed by taxes specifically levied for these programs. It also includes public assistance grants, food and nutrition programs, and vocational rehabilitation. These programs accounted for almost 30 cents of each Government dollar in 1973.

Veterans: $12.0 billion. Compensation and pensions, hospital care and medical treatment, education and training, life insurance benefits, and other veterans' programs took about 5 cents of the Government dollar.

Net interest: $17.4 billion. Interest payments on the debt held by the public required about 7 cents of each Government dollar in 1973.

General government: $5.6 billion. About 2 cents of each dollar went for law enforcement and justice, managing Government finances and property, and other general activities.

General revenue sharing: $6.6 billion. About 3 cents of each Federal dollar was given to State and local governments to spend according to their own needs and priorities subject to only minimal Federal restrictions.

Notes:

(1) The figures above add to more than total outlays because they include certain transactions which are entirely within the Government and thus deducted prior to arriving at the total.

(2) Detail may not add to totals due to rounding.

(3) More information on the budget is available in *The U.S. Budget in Brief,* which may be obtained for 60¢ from the Superintendent of Documents, U.S. Government Printing Office, Washington, D.C. 20402.

How the Federal Government Dollar Was Spent in 1973

of the budget on human resources than on national defense.

Human resources expenses were for income security, health, education, and veterans' benefits. The extension of social security was an area of expanding expense. In 1969 a budget surplus of 3.1 billion was used to reduce the national debt. In 1971 and 1972 a deficit of more than $21 billion occurred, which was in part the impact of inflation. The national debt was reported to be about $450 billion in 1973. The interest on the huge debt is about $25 billion a year which includes the interest as budgeted plus interest on money borrowed from government trust funds.

PREPARING INCOME TAX RETURNS

Under the provisions of our federal income tax law in 1973 every individual under the age of 65 with a gross income of $2,050 or more during the calendar year is required to file a federal income tax return. Anyone 65 years of age on the last day of the year is not required to file unless he or she has a gross income of $2,800 or more for the year. A gross income of in excess of $4,300 is necessary for married couples if both are over 65 years of age to file. However, it is necessary to file a return to get a refund for withholdings regardless of age or earnings.

Also, a person having less than the required gross income must file an income tax return and pay any tax due if they have uncollected Social Security tax on self-employed income of $400 or more.

ESTIMATED INCOME TAX

In a situation where taxpayers have sources of income above their salaries and withholdings are not made as a payroll deduction, estimated income tax must be paid four times a year. When total income tax exceeds withholdings by $100.00, declarations of estimated income tax are required. The chart below is used to illustrate who must file a declaration of estimated income tax.

Who Must File

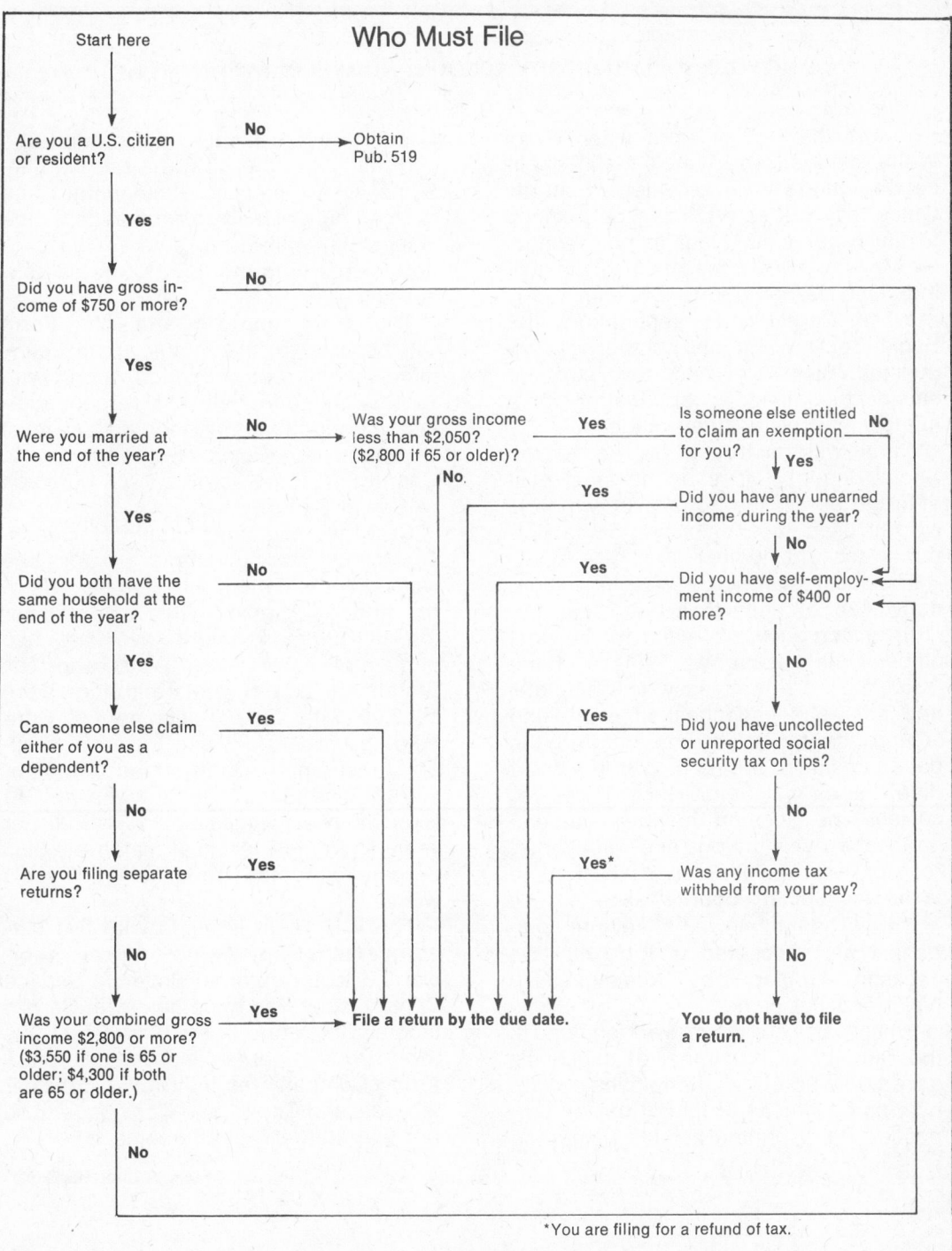

Start here

Are you a U.S. citizen or resident? — **No** → Obtain Pub. 519

Yes

Did you have gross income of $750 or more? — **No**

Yes

Were you married at the end of the year? — **No** → Was your gross income less than $2,050? ($2,800 if 65 or older)? — **Yes** → Is someone else entitled to claim an exemption for you? — **No**

No / **Yes**

Is someone else entitled to claim an exemption for you? **Yes** → Did you have any unearned income during the year? — **No**

Yes → Did you have self-employment income of $400 or more? — **No**

Did you both have the same household at the end of the year? — **No**

Yes

Did you have self-employment income of $400 or more? **No** → Did you have uncollected or unreported social security tax on tips? — **No**

Can someone else claim either of you as a dependent? — **Yes**

No

Did you have uncollected or unreported social security tax on tips? **Yes**

Are you filing separate returns? — **Yes**

No

Was any income tax withheld from your pay? — **Yes*** / **No**

Was your combined gross income $2,800 or more? ($3,550 if one is 65 or older; $4,300 if both are 65 or older.) — **Yes** → **File a return by the due date.**

No

You do not have to file a return.

*You are filing for a refund of tax.

This Chart Explains Who Must File Income Tax Returns

USING YOUR SOCIAL SECURITY ACCOUNT NUMBER IN TAX REPORTING

It was the first of April when Carol Wallis decided she would make application with the Employment Security Office for work as a typist. She planned to finish her junior year in high school on May 26, and wanted to use the typing skills learned during the year.

When Carol made application, her Social Securty account number was requested. Since she had never worked outside the home, an application for a number had never been made.

Carol was instructed to go to the Social Security office or the local post office to obtain the Form SS5, which is a form used to apply for a Social Security account number.

The local post office was in a more convenient location than the Social Security office, so Carol went to the post office, where she was given Form SS5. The card was easy to complete, and after she had checked everything entered on the card, she entered the date and signed the card. Within a short time, her Social Security card was received. The account number stamped on the card was the one she will use the rest of her life for reporting income taxes and Social Security taxes.

Carol was interviewed at several companies and accepted a job with the Jackson Manufacturing Company as a typist and file clerk.

When Carol started to work on June 4, the Director of Personnel at Jackson's gave her a Form W-4 (Employee's Withholding Certificate to fill out for tax purposes). Carol printed her full name and Social Security number on the first line and her full address on the second line. Since Carol had no dependents, she claimed only herself as a dependent. She signed her name and entered the date before returning the form to the personnel office.

The information on Carol's W-4 Form will be used by her employer to determine income tax deduction. Along with income tax deduction, 5.85 percent additional deduction from her wages must be made for Social Security tax. In Chapter 16 more attention will be given to Social Security tax.

Carol worked three months for Jackson Manufacturing Company before she went on a vacation with her parents at the end of August. When she left her job, the personnel clerk gave Carol two copies of Form W-2, "Wage and Tax Statement." Carol's total earnings were $960.00 with federal income tax withholdings of $101.73 and FICA tax (Federal Insurance Contributions tax) of $56.16. The Social Security tax (FICA) is payable on wages up to $13,200 per year. The employer must match the 5.85 percent deducted from the employee's wages.

The W-2 Form is made with five carbon copies. Copy A, the original, is forwarded to the Internal Revenue Service Center. Copy B is to be filed with Carol's income tax return Form 1040. Copy C is for Carol's records. Jackson Manufacturing Company retains Copy D for their records, and Copy 1 and Copy 2 are used in filing state or local income taxes.

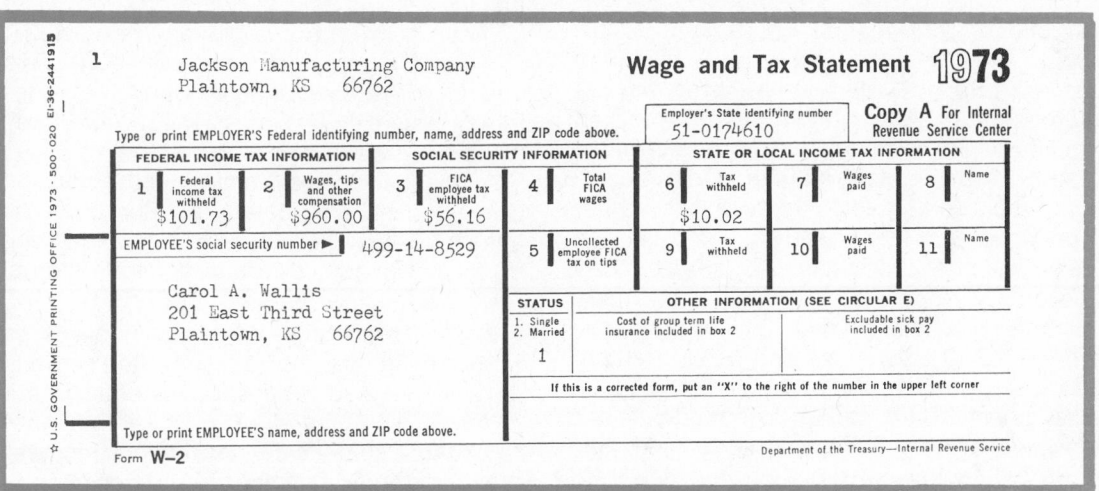

Form **W-4**
(Rev. Aug. 1972)
Department of the Treasury
Internal Revenue Service

Employee's Withholding Allowance Certificate
(This certificate is for income tax withholding purposes only; it will remain in effect until you change it.)

Type or print your full name: *Carol Annette Wallis*

Home address (Number and street or rural route): *201 East Third Street*

City or town, State and ZIP code: *Plaintown, Kansas 66762*

Your social security number: *499-14-8529*

Marital status
[X] Single   [ ] Married

(If married but legally separated, or wife (husband) is a nonresident alien, check the single block.)

1 Total number of allowances you are claiming *1*

2 Additional amount, if any, you want deducted from each pay (if your employer agrees) . . . . $

I certify that to the best of my knowledge and belief, the number of withholding allowances claimed on this certificate does not exceed the number to which I am entitled.

Signature ▶ *Carol A. Wallis*   Date ▶ *June 4*, 19 *73*

Employee's Withholding Allowance Certificate

---

1   Jackson Manufacturing Company
    Plaintown, KS 66762

Wage and Tax Statement 1973

Type or print EMPLOYER'S Federal identifying number, name, address and ZIP code above.

Employer's State identifying number: 51-0174610

Copy A For Internal Revenue Service Center

FEDERAL INCOME TAX INFORMATION		SOCIAL SECURITY INFORMATION		STATE OR LOCAL INCOME TAX INFORMATION		
1 Federal income tax withheld $101.73	2 Wages, tips and other compensation $960.00	3 FICA employee tax withheld $56.16	4 Total FICA wages	6 Tax withheld $10.02	7 Wages paid	8 Name
EMPLOYEE'S social security number ▶ 499-14-8529		5 Uncollected employee FICA tax on tips		9 Tax withheld	10 Wages paid	11 Name

Carol A. Wallis
201 East Third Street
Plaintown, KS 66762

STATUS	OTHER INFORMATION (SEE CIRCULAR E)	
1. Single 2. Married 1	Cost of group term life insurance included in box 2	Excludable sick pay included in box 2

If this is a corrected form, put an "X" to the right of the number in the upper left corner

Type or print EMPLOYEE'S name, address and ZIP code above.

Form **W-2**

Department of the Treasury—Internal Revenue Service

☆ U.S. GOVERNMENT PRINTING OFFICE 1973 · 500 · 020 EI-36-2441915

Wage and Tax Statement 1973, Form W-2

INCOME TAX REPORTING FORMS

In 1973, the forms used to file income tax returns were changed. The Short Form 1040A was authorized for those whose 1973 income was from wages, salaries, tips, other employee compensation, dividends or interest, and who did not itemize deductions. Those who had other sources of income or who wished to itemize deductions were required to use the standard Form 1040.

Since Carol's total income for 1973 was in the form of wages totaling $960.00, she used Form 1040A. As long as Carol's earnings for the year were less than $10,000 and she did not itemize deductions, the Internal Revenue Service would compute the tax. However, Carol had received instruction in computation of income tax returns; and she decided to complete the Form 1040A herself.

The example shown is a copy of the Form 1040A used by Carol. She followed the instructions for preparing Short Form 1040A which were made available by the Internal Revenue Service. She printed her name and address in the block of spaces provided on the form. She also printed the name of the county in which she lived; her Social Security number in the block on the right, and her occupation in the space provided. In the next section of space on line 1, she checked the box labeled "single." In the Exemptions section, she listed herself by checking the box under "Regular" on line 6a and entering 1 as the number of boxes checked under Exemptions. Carol had no dependents, so on line 7 the total exemptions claimed was 1. In the section for reporting income, lines 9 through 12, she entered the amount of $960.00 (from her copy of Form W-2 report filed by her employer) on line 9 and again on line 12.

The next two lines, preceded by dots, give her the choice of having her tax figured by the Internal Revenue Service or of computing it herself.

If she had wanted the IRS to figure her tax, she would have turned to page 2 of Form 1040A and complete lines 18, 20a, b, and c, and lines 21, 23, and 24 where she would have recorded the amount of tax withheld as shown on Form W-2.

Because Carol wanted to complete the income tax return herself, she checked Tax Table 1 and saw that income of $950-$975 was followed by zero. She wrote 0 in space number 17; 0 again in space number 18 because she had not contributed to any political organization; and 0 on line 19. On line 20a, she wrote $101.73 as amount of federal income tax withheld by her employer. Lines 20b and 20c did not apply, and on lines 21, 23, and 24, she again wrote $101.73. This amount will be refunded to Carol by the Internal Revenue Service, usually within thirty to ninety days.

After checking all entries for accuracy, Carol signed and dated the Form 1040A, attached Copy B of Form W-2, and mailed it in the envelope provided to the Internal Revenue Service Center in her region.

Carol found that completing the Short Form 1040A was not difficult after she had carefully studied the instructions and forms. However, filing income tax returns becomes much more complicated as earnings increase and come from a number of sources such as salaries, interest, rents, sale of property, and other business income.

Where to file

Use the envelope furnished you or the appropriate address shown on page 6.

Who May Use
Short Form 1040A

You may use Short Form 1040A if all your income in 1973 was from wages, salaries, tips, other employee compensation, dividends or interest and you do not itemize your deductions.

Who May NOT Use
Short Form 1040A

File Form 1040 instead of Short Form 1040A if:

● you had income other than wages, salaries, tips, dividends or interest

● you received $20 or more in tips in any one month, and you did not fully report these tips to your employer

● your Form W–2 shows uncollected employee tax (social security tax) on tips

● you have
    a retirement income credit
    an investment credit
    a foreign tax credit
    a credit for Federal tax on special fuels—nonhighway gasoline and lubricating oil, or
    a credit from a regulated investment company

● you choose the benefits of income averaging

● (1) you could be claimed as a dependent on your parent's return and (2) you had dividend or interest income AND (3a) your dividend and interest income was $750 or more, OR (3b) your total income (amount that would otherwise be shown on line 12, Short Form 1040A) is more than $8,666 ($4,333 if married and filing separately)

● your spouse files a separate return and itemizes deductions. Note: You may ignore this and still file Form 1040A if you don't consider yourself married for tax purposes because (1) you did not live with your spouse at any time during 1973, (2) you furnished more than half the cost of keeping up your home for 1973, and (3) your child or stepchild lived in your home for more than 6 months of 1973, and you can claim that child as a dependent

● you received capital gain dividends or nontaxable distributions (return of capital)

● you claim a deduction for business expenses as an outside salesman or for travel for your job

● you claim a sick pay exclusion

● you claim a moving expense deduction because you changed jobs or were transferred

● you are a railroad employee or employee representative and claim credit for excess hospital insurance benefits taxes paid

● you must file Form 2210 because line 22 is more than 20% of line 19. See instructions for Penalty for Not Paying Enough Tax During the Year on page 6.

● you had, at any time during the taxable year, an interest in or signature or other authority over a bank, securities, or other financial account in a foreign country (except in a U.S. military banking facility operated by a U.S. financial institution)

● you are required to file **Form 2555**, Exemption of Income Earned Abroad

● you were married to a nonresident alien at the end of 1973

● you are a nonresident alien (use **Form 1040NR**).

**Students Who Work in the Summer May Use
Short Form 1040A to Apply for Refund of Taxes
Withheld from Their Salaries**

Short Form 1040A   **U.S. Individual Income Tax Return**   Department of the Treasury / Internal Revenue Service   **1973**

Please print or type

Name (If joint return, give first names and initials of both)   Last name   **Carol A. Wallis**

Present home address (Number and street, including apartment number, or rural route)   **201 East Third Street**

City, town or post office, State and ZIP code   **Plaintown, KS 66762**

COUNTY OF RESIDENCE   **Jeff**

Your social security number   **490 14 8529**

Spouse's social security no.

Occupation   Yours ▶ **Typist**   Spouse's ▶

Filing Status—check only one:

1 ☒ Single
2 ☐ Married filing joint return (even if only one had income)
3 ☐ Married filing separately. If spouse is also filing, give spouse's social security number in designated space above and enter full name here ▶
4 ☐ Unmarried Head of Household
5 ☐ Widow(er) with dependent child (Year spouse died ▶ 19)

Exemptions   Regular / 65 or over / Blind

6a Yourself . . ☒ ☐ ☐   Enter number of boxes checked ▶ **1**
b Spouse . . ☐ ☐ ☐
c First names of your dependent children who lived with you _____   Enter number ▶
d Number of other dependents (from line 26) . . . ▶
7 Total exemptions claimed . . . . ▶ **1**

8 **Presidential Election Campaign Fund.**—Check ☐ if you wish to designate $1 of your taxes for this fund. If joint return, check ☐ if spouse wishes to designate $1. *Note: This will not increase your tax or reduce your refund.* **See note on back.**

Attach Copy B of Forms W-2 and Check or Money Order here

9 Wages, salaries, tips, and other employee compensation . . (Attach Forms W-2. If unavailable, attach explanation.)	9	960	00
10a Dividends (See instructions on page 3.) $............., 10b Less exclusion $ ...., Balance ▶	10c		
11 Interest income	11		
12 Total (add lines 9, 10c, and 11) (Adjusted Gross Income)	12	960	00

● If you want IRS to figure your tax, skip the rest of this page and see instructions on page 3.
● If line 12 is under $10,000 find tax in Tables 1–12 and enter on line 17. Skip lines 13 through 16.

13 If line 12 is $10,000 or more, enter 15% of line 12 but not more than $2,000 ($1,000 if line 3 checked) .	13		
14 Subtract line 13 from line 12	14		
15 Multiply total number of exemptions claimed on line 7 by $750	15		
16 Taxable income (subtract line 15 from line 14)	16		

(Figure tax on amount on line 16 using Tax Rate Schedule X, Y, or Z, and enter on line 17.)

16—82338-2

Form 1040A (1973)   Page **2**

17 Tax, check if from: ☒ Tax Tables 1–12 OR ☐ Tax Rate Schedule X, Y, or Z . .	17	0	
18 Credit for contributions to candidates for public office (see instructions on page 4)	18	0	
19 Income tax (subtract line 18 from line 17). If less than zero, enter zero	19	0	

20a Total Federal income tax withheld (attach Forms W–2 to front) . .   20a **101 73**
b Excess FICA tax withheld (two or more employers—see instructions on page 4)   b
c 1973 estimated tax payments (include amount allowed as credit from 1972 return)   c

21 Total (add lines 20a, b, and c)	21	101	73
22 If line 19 is larger than line 21, enter **BALANCE DUE IRS** Pay in full with return. Write social security number on check or money order and make payable to Internal Revenue Service ▶	22		
23 If line 21 is larger than line 19, enter amount **OVERPAID** . . . . ▶	23	101	73
24 Amount of line 23 to be **REFUNDED TO YOU** . . . . ▶	24	101	73

25 Amount of line 23 to be credited on 1974 estimated tax . . . ▶ 25

Other Dependents

(a) NAME	(b) Relationship	(c) Months lived in your home. If born or died during year, write B or D.	(d) Did dependent have income of $750 or more?	(e) Amount YOU furnished for dependent's support. If 100% write ALL.	(f) Amount furnished by OTHERS including dependent.
				$	$

26 Total number of dependents listed in column (a). Enter here and on line 6d . . . . ▶

Note: 1972 Presidential Election Campaign Fund Designation.—Check ☐ if you did not designate $1 of your taxes on your 1972 return, but now wish to do so. If joint return, check ☐ if spouse did not designate on 1972 return but now wishes to do so.

Under penalties of perjury, I declare that I have examined this return, including accompanying schedules and statements, and to the best of my knowledge and belief it is true, correct and complete. Declaration of preparer (other than taxpayer) is based on all information of which he has any knowledge.

Sign here ▶ *Carol A. Wallis*   Date **2/9/74**
Your signature

Spouse's signature (if filing jointly, BOTH must sign even if only one had income)

Preparer's signature (other than taxpayer)   Date

Address (and ZIP Code)   Preparer's Emp. Ident. or Soc. Sec. No.

☆ U.S. GOVERNMENT PRINTING OFFICE: 1973—O-500-056   16-82338-2

Form 1040A, Page 2

LEGAL REQUIREMENTS FOR TAXPAYERS

The law requires all taxpayers to keep records that will enable them to prepare complete and accurate income tax returns. The records should include accurate records on income, deductions, credits, and items required in filing income tax returns. Records for this purpose should include all receipts, cancelled checks, and other evidence to prove the amount claimed for deductions.

The taxpayer must also retain tax records on income and deductions until after the expiration of the statute of limitations, which is ordinarily three years from the date the return was due or filed.

April 15 of each year is the final date for filing income tax returns without penalty. When the last day for filing falls on Saturday, Sunday, or a legal holiday, the next succeeding day (which is not Saturday, Sunday, or a legal holiday) is considered the final day for filing. If the return is mailed, the postmark must show a date no later than the final filing date.

Under certain conditions, a person who is a resident of the United States may be granted an extension of time to file a return. Form 2688 is used for this purpose and may be obtained at the local Internal Revenue Office.

Taxpayers who discover mistakes after having filed tax returns before the final date of April 15, have a chance to rectify their error without penalty. "Form 1040X, Amended U.S. Individual Income Tax Return," is used for this purpose.

As young men and women earn more money and start families, it is good money management to become familiar with income tax matters. Many certified public accountants specialize in income tax service and can provide income tax filing assistance for a small fee.

CHARACTERISTICS OF A GOOD TAX SYSTEM

Few people enjoy paying taxes. Yet few of us would be willing to go without most of the services provided by local, state, and national governments. Since most young

As Earnings and Deductions Increase, Filing Income Tax Returns Becomes Much More Complicated

workers will be paying taxes for all their working lives, they should be interested in understanding what makes a good tax system.

One of the first questions to be asked is, "How much should I have to pay?" Everyone does not agree on this question. However, arguments of the past have centered on certain principles which should be considered in order to develop an equitable or "just" tax system. Adam Smith, a classical economist, presented guidelines for a good tax system before the Constitution of our nation was written. In his book titled, **Wealth of Nations**, he listed four principles of taxation. These principles are concerned with **equity, certainty, convenience,** and **economy.**

Equity is the idea that everyone should contribute to the support of his government according to his ability in the proportion to the revenue enjoyed as a citizen.

Certainty was a term used to describe the application of a tax law in respect to each individual. The amount assessed, the time of payment, and the manner of payment should be made clear and not applied arbitrarily.

Convenience means that taxes should be levied and collected at a time and place most convenient for the taxpayer.

Economy was a term used to indicate that no more tax money should be collected than

is necessary, and administrative costs should be kept at a minimum.

The principles of taxation are not discussed as much today as in the past. Most people recognize the merits of such principles as:

1. The ability to pay.
2. Benefits rendered from the taxes.
3. Sacrifice made by individuals.
4. Cost of service.

Economists still do not fully agree on what makes a good tax system. Arguments center on the following principles: cost of service rendered, ability of a person to pay, the sacrifices of individuals, and the benefits one derives from the taxes. All the above principles have merit as well as disadvantages. The ability to pay principle is in evidence when one studies the federal income system. However, we still depend on real estate tax to raise money on the local and state level. State and local governments are hard pressed to provide the services that are needed, especially in support of city services, such as police protection and street maintenance. Many believe the ability to pay principle is the most practical. A proportional tax system which can be made flexible is perhaps the least harmful tax. It does not kill business initiative, but can still supply money for the operations of the government and social and economic progress.

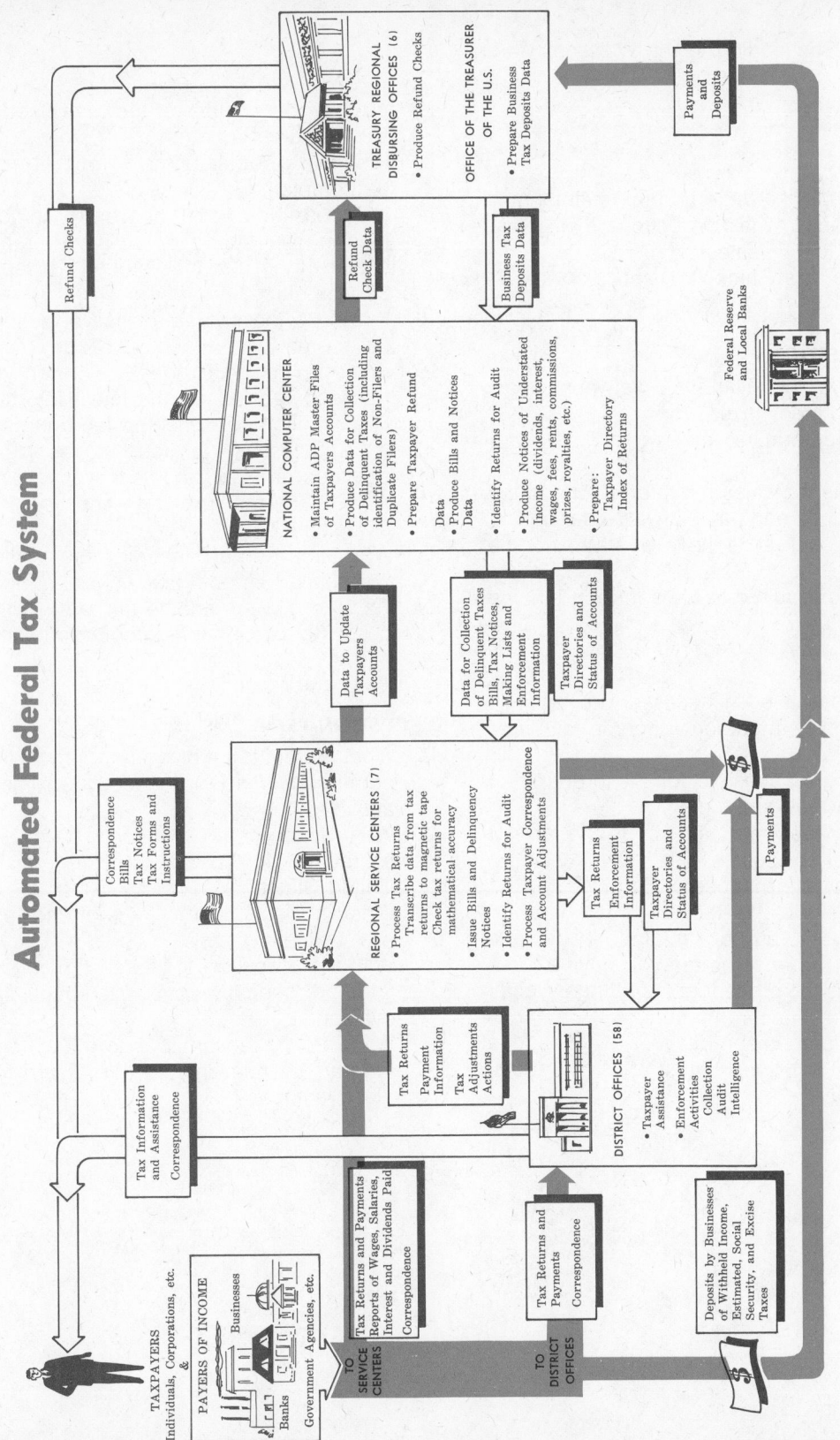

Automated Federal Tax System

An Automated Tax System Helps to Improve the Efficiency of Taxation

STUDY AIDS

NEW TERMS

direct taxes   wage and tax statements
excise taxes   tax deductions
federal budget   sales tax
inheritance taxes   highway-user tax
property taxes

STUDY QUESTIONS

1. What is the difference between direct and indirect taxes?
2. What determines the tax rate on property tax?
3. What is the sales tax rate in your state?
4. How does one pay highway-user tax?
5. Does your state have a state income tax?
6. Who is required to file a federal income tax return?
7. When was the federal income tax law enacted?
8. Why has it been necessary to retain a high level of personal income tax since 1940?
9. Who is responsible for the preparation of the federal budget?
10. What government agency is the largest user of tax dollars?
11. What is the purpose of Form W-2 in the tax system?
12. When you buy an automobile license, what type of taxes are you paying?
13. What is the procedure in getting a Social Security account number?
14. What percentage of your wages does your employer withhold for social security?
15. What is the number of the form used in filing income tax returns?
16. How many copies of the Form W-4 must be completed in your state?
17. Is it possible to correct an error in your income tax returns if you have already mailed them to the Internal Revenue Service office?
18. What are the characteristics of a good tax system?
19. Since tax laws change, where can you go each year to get the latest information on filing your income tax returns?
20. Is it necessary to keep a record of earnings and tax returns?
21. What is the tax surcharge and how is it completed?
22. Why is federal income tax called "graduated income tax"?
23. Can you file an income tax return without a Social Security account number?

DISCUSSION PROBLEMS

1. What percentage of your personal income should go to finance government activities?
2. What action can the voting citizen take in regard to the tax structure of the United States?
3. What is the argument for a strong federal taxing system?
4. Will an improved automated tax collector and checking system reduce tax evasion?
5. What are the advantages to the state in federal revenue sharing? What are the disadvantages?

CHAPTER SIXTEEN

USING SOCIAL SECURITY SERVICES

THE NEED FOR SOCIAL SECURITY

Most Americans want to be self-supporting throughout their lifetimes. Pioneers were taught the value of thrift and saving during childhood. Since most of the farmers depended on agriculture for an occupation, money was saved when crops and prices were good. The money they were able to save was invested in more land and livestock. Many were able to save enough to live comfortably during old age. If the farmer became disabled through accident or disease his family or friends took care of him.

With the change in America from a mainly agricultural economy to an urban industrial economy, problems developed for the people employed in business and industry. For many, it was not possible to make enough money during a lifetime to retire. Workers were required to take easier jobs and keep working as long as they were able. Many who were able to save money for retirement lost their savings and investments when economic depressions hit. During the great economic depression of the 1930's, farmers and most business people experienced great loss of money and property. The leaders of business, industry, and government started searching for ways in which economic security could be acquired for those reaching retirement age. Thus, in 1935, after the people of the United States had experienced the greatest economic panic in the history of the nation, Congress passed the Social Security Act and established the Social Security Administration.

Many workers in the United States were protected by private social insurance programs before 1930. These programs were established by labor unions and by the employees of some industries. Many of the insurance groups were financed by the contributions of the employees and their employers. Through these plans, the employees could have some of their monthly earnings deducted from their checks and invested in the pension fund. At age 65 or older, the workers who had worked for the company long enough were able to receive monthly checks for retirement. Some workers were also able to have health insurance

Private Retirement Plans Provide Good Benefits for Workers

227

as a part of their retirement. Many of the railroad companies, in cooperation with the workers and the union, were providing hospital care for the workers and retired workers.

While many private insurance and retirement plans provided good retirement benefits for their workers, most workers were unable to secure jobs with companies providing retirement plans. They were forced to live on the money they had saved. Most people felt that the only way to provide insurance coverage for the majority of the people was to establish a national social insurance program operated by a special agency of the federal government.

RECENT DEVELOPMENTS

The present United States program of social security is relatively new and many recent changes in the law have been made. Many countries in Europe developed some type of social security insurance long before the United States. Germany was a leader in social security legislation. It's workmen's compensation law and old age pension acts were enacted in 1880. Other countries in Europe established social security plans at a later date. Great Britain started a workmen's compensation program in 1897 and an old-age pension plan a short time later. Several other European countries started social security programs about 1900.

In the United States, Wisconsin was the first state to legislate and successfully implement a workmen's compensation law. The law was passed in 1911 and at about the same time the legislature passed the Wisconsin State Vocational Education Act.

THE SOCIAL SECURITY ACT OF 1935

In 1935 the United States Congress passed the first social security act, sponsored by Senator Robert F. Wagner of New York. The federal government was to provide a social security plan on a nationwide basis.

The major purpose of the act was to (1) provide unemployment insurance for persons out of work, and (2) to provide financial benefits for retired persons, the needy, aged, dependent children, the blind, and for the heirs in case of death. The unemployment insurance phase is handled primarily by the states with federal financial assistance. The second part of the act is directly under the control of the Social Security Administration, which is in the Department of Health, Education, and Welfare.

The basic idea on which the social security program was planned is a simple one. During the working years, employees, their employers, and self-employed persons are enrolled in the program and make social security contributions. The contributions are pooled in special trust funds. When earnings stop or are reduced because the worker retires, becomes disabled, or dies, monthly cash benefits are paid to replace part of the earnings the family has lost.

Part of the social security taxes contributed to the fund goes into a separate hospital insurance trust fund to provide the workers and dependents assistance in paying medical expenses. Medical insurance is financed by premiums paid by the people who have enrolled for this protection and by amounts contributed by the federal government.

WHO QUALIFIES FOR SOCIAL SECURITY

In 1973 more than nine out of ten jobs came under the coverage of social security. Persons enrolled in other retirement and social service insurance plans may **elect** to enroll and contribute to the social security program. The answer to the question "Who qualifies for social security?" is "Just about everyone in the United States." Thus, to be eligible to enroll in the social security program you must be employed in a "covered" occupation. Those not covered include employees in federal and state retirement plans. Farm and household workers whose earnings do not reach the minimum requirements, and self-employed persons whose net earnings are less than $400.00 a year over a period of years.

To qualify for retirement and other benefits requires contributions for a number of years by those enrolled. Other conditions for benefit eligibility will be noted under additional following topics on social security.

HOW IT WORKS

More than 9 out of 10 working people are building protection for themselves and their families under the social security program. To pay for this protection, workers make contributions based on their earnings covered by social security and their employers pay an equal contribution. A self-employed person pays contributions at a slightly lower rate than the combined employee-employer rate for retirement, survivors, and disability insurance. However, the hospital insurance contribution rate is the same for the employer, the employee, and the self-employed person.

The earnings covered by social security are reported, and a record of the covered earnings of each worker is kept by the Social Security Administration. The amount of the monthly retirement, survivors, or disability insurance payment is figured from the average monthly earnings in covered employment.

Social security contributions are placed in three special trust funds in the U.S. Treasury—one for retirement and survivors insurance, one for disability insurance, and the third for hospital insurance.

A fourth trust fund holds the assets of the medical insurance program. Into this trust fund go the premiums for medical insurance paid by the people enrolled and the matching amounts from the Federal Government.

Benefit payments and administrative expenses are paid from these funds. By law they can be used for no other purpose.

WHO GETS CASH BENEFITS

YOU

- As a retired worker (at 65, or in a permanently reduced amount beginning between 62 and 65)
- As a disabled worker at any age before 65

When you qualify for benefits at retirement or if you become disabled or at your death, certain of your dependents can receive benefits. Usually these are:

YOUR WIFE

- When 65 (permanently reduced amount as early as 62)
- At any age if caring for a child entitled to benefits, except student benefits

YOUR DEPENDENT HUSBAND

- At 65 (permanently reduced amount as early as 62)

YOUR UNMARRIED CHILDREN

- Under 18
- 18 and over if disabled before 18th birthday
- Between 18 and 22 if full-time students

YOUR WIDOW

- At 62 (permanently reduced amount as early as 60)
- At 50-60 in reduced amount if severely disabled
- At any age if caring for a child entitled to benefits, except student benefits

YOUR DEPENDENT WIDOWER

- At 62
- 50-62 in reduced amount if severely disabled

YOUR DEPENDENT PARENTS (after your death)

- At 62

LUMP-SUM DEATH BENEFIT

- Surviving spouse who was living in the same household
- If there is no spouse, to the person who paid the burial expenses or to the funeral home

Work Credit for Retirement Benefits

Year of Birth	Quarters Needed Men	Women	Year of Birth	Quarters Needed Men	Women
1892 or earlier	6	3	1911	24	22
1893	7	4	1912	24	23
1894	8	5	1913	24	24
1895	9	6	1914	25	25
1896	10	7	1915	26	26
1897	11	8	1916	27	27
1898	12	9	1917	28	28
1899	13	10	1918	29	29
1900	14	11	1919	30	30
1901	15	12	1920	31	31
1902	16	13	1921	32	32
1903	17	14	1922	33	33
1904	18	15	1923	34	34
1905	19	16	1924	35	35
1906	20	17	1925	36	36
1907	21	18	1926	37	37
1908	22	19	1927	38	38
1909	23	20	1928	39	39
1910	24	21	1929 or later	40	40

This table shows the quarters of coverage needed to get Social Security Act retirement checks. All quarters since Jan. 1, 1937, count.

RETIREMENT BENEFITS

One of the most important features of the Social Security Act is the retirement plan. Workers can move from job to job and the retirement plan remains in operation. This is not true in the retirement plans of most business and industrial concerns where workers will most likely lose retirement credit if they change jobs. While the social security retirement plan may not provide enough money to meet **all** expenses after retirement, it will provide a good financial base.

To qualify for the social security retirement plan, one must be enrolled and contribute to the plan for a number of years. The work year is divided into **quarters** for record keeping by the Social Security Administration. The number of quarters one must work to receive minimum financial benefits varies with the individual's age. Older persons will have fewer years to work, or fewer quarters to meet minimum requirements for retirement.

The table, titled "Work Credit for Retirement Benefits," is used to show the number of quarters needed in relation to date of birth. For a man or woman born in 1929 to qualify, 40 quarters are required. A person born in 1918 would need only 29 quarters to qualify.

The term "fully insured" is used to mean that a person has met the work time to meet minimum requirements. Under rules of the act in 1973, a person starting to work after 1973 would require 10 years or 40 quarters.

RETIREMENT BENEFITS

The dollar value of retirement benefits is based on the average earnings of the individual. How much an individual made and how many years he or she contributed will, in part, determine the amount of the monthly retirement check. The number of years used to determine the average is also based on the age of the worker. The table titled "Average Year Scale" is used to show how the age of the individual will establish the average number of years to be used in calculating the average earnings of the person retiring.

Social security taxes were collected on the basis of maximum amounts from 1937 to 1974. In figuring a person's retirement, the following amounts would be used to determine maximum average earnings per year. The amounts of earnings listed are the maximum amounts to be used and taxed for social security money, and individuals may have earned more or less, or perhaps no money during the years.

1930 - 1950	$ 3,000 per year
1951 - 1954	$ 3,600 per year
1955 - 1958	$ 4,200 per year
1959 - 1965	$ 4,800 per year
1966 - 1967	$ 6,600 per year
1968 - 1971	$ 9,000 per year
- 1973	$10,000 per year
- 1974	$12,000 per year

Since the scale for benefits is a "sliding" one after 1974, the rates will be automatically set by the **cost of living formula.** However, to get a general idea of benefits available for workers today, the table titled "Monthly Retirement Benefits" is used to show what monthly retirement benefits may be expected in 1973.

A number of retirement options and additional benefits were made available under the provisions of the 1972 Social Security law. Specific information may be obtained from your local Social Security Office.

SURVIVOR'S BENEFITS

The family of a young worker who dies can benefit financially from social security. The benefits will enable a young mother to keep her family together in the event of her husband's death. This part of the social security act is especially important to high school students contemplating marriage upon graduation.

Many young people think of social security as retirement and medicare. However, the "survivor's benefits" provide insurance for **them.** Many young fathers are killed in accidents, so for example, suppose the father of two small children under five is killed in an auto accident; social security benefits can provide for the children with financial assistance until they are eighteen. The widow is also entitled to financial benefits which will vary with the husband's earnings and quarters of credit.

Monthly Retirement Benefits

Average Yearly Earnings	Retired Worker	Retired Couple
$923 or less	$ 84.50	$126.80
$ 3,000	174.80	262.20
$ 4,200	213.30	320.00
$ 5,400	250.60	376.00
$ 6,600	288.40	432.60
$ 7,800	331.00	496.60
$ 9,000	354.50	531.80
$10,800	384.50	576.80
$12,000	404.50	606.80

These examples show how much you will draw in monthly retirement benefits at age 65, based on your average yearly earnings under the Social Security Act.

Average Year Scale

Year Worker Was Born	Years Counted Man	Woman	Year Worker Was Born	Years Counted Man	Woman
1896 or earlier	5	5	1913	19	19
			1914	20	20
1897	6	5	1915	21	21
1898	7	5	1916	22	22
1899	8	5	1917	23	23
1900	9	6	1918	24	24
1901	10	7	1919	25	25
1902	11	8	1920	26	26
1903	12	9	1921	27	27
1904	13	10	1922	28	28
1905	14	11	1923	29	29
1906	15	12	1924	30	30
1907	16	13	1925	31	31
1908	17	14	1926	32	32
1909	18	15	1927	33	33
1910	19	16	1928	34	34
1911	19	17	1929 or later	35	35
1912	19	18			

This table lists the number of years that must be counted in figuring a worker's average earnings on which all Social Security Act cash benefits are based.

DISABILITY BENEFITS

Disability insurance is very important to young workers and their families. In many situations it provides the only income when the worker is permanently disabled.

Since 1954, social security has provided protection at a low cost. Many improvements and wider coverage have been extended since that date. According to reports from the United States Office of Education, in 1972 more than 1.7 million disabled workers and more than 1.3 million of their dependents were receiving monthly social security benefits. Over 2.8 million children of deceased workers were also receiving financial assistance as well as 500,000 widows who were caring for their children.

The increase of disabling injuries, many permanent, makes social security insurance more important. About 11.5 million disabling injuries occurred in 1972 — an increase of 2 percent over 1971. In many situations, the social security benefit is the **only** source of income for the disabled and their dependents.

WHO IS ELIGIBLE?

Persons Disabled Before Age 22. If a son or daughter of fully insured parents is permanently disabled before reaching the age of 22, he or she is eligible. Persons disabled before age 22 need **no social security work credits** to get benefits. Their payments are based on the earning of the parents while enrolled in the social security program.

Examples of Monthly Cash Disability Benefits

	Average yearly earnings after 1950*							
	$923 or less	$1,800	$3,000	$4,200	$5,400	$6,600	$7,800	$9,000
Disabled worker	$ 84.50	$134.30	$174.80	$213.30	$250.60	$288.40	$331.00	$354.50
Disabled worker and wife at 62	116.30	184.70	240.40	293.40	344.60	396.60	455.20	487.50
Disabled widow at 50	51.30	67.30	87.50	106.80	125.50	144.30	165.60	215.40
Disabled worker, wife under 65 and one child (maximum family payment)	126.80	201.50	267.30	370.70	467.90	522.30	579.30	620.40

*The maximum earnings creditable for social security are $3,600 for 1951-54; $4,200 for 1955-58; $4,800 for 1959-65; $6,600 for 1966-67; $7,800 for 1968-71; $9,000 for 1972; $10,800 for 1973; and $12,000 for 1974. The maximum family benefit for a young disabled worker and his family in 1973 is $599.40 a month, based on average earnings of $8,400. The higher benefits shown, based on higher average earnings, will be payable in later years.

Disabled Worker Under 65. Workers who become severely disabled will be eligible for monthly payments if they have worked under social security long enough and recently enough to qualify. The work credits needed depend on the worker's age and date of disability. A person disabled before age 24 needs 1½ years in a three-year period. Those 24 through age 30 need credits for having worked one-half the time between age 21 and the date of disability. Those 31 and older need credits for at least five years out of the ten years ending when they became disabled. Some workers may need additional credits depending on their ages at time of disabilities.

Disabled Widows and Disabled Dependent Widows. A widow, dependent widower, and, under certain conditions, a surviving divorced wife of a worker who worked long enough under social security to qualify, may be able to get monthly payments as early as age 50.

Generally, a person is not eligible unless the disability started before the husband's or wife's death or within seven years after death. However, a number of exceptions exist that require special consideration by the Social Security Administration.

Special Provisions for the Blind. People who are considered blind under social security law and have worked long enough under social security are eligible for a "disability freeze" even if they are actually working. This means that the amount of their future benefits, based on average earnings, will not be reduced because they have low, or no earnings during the years they were disabled. Blind persons under 55 are eligible for benefits if they are unable to find substantial gainful employment.

HEALTH INSURANCE

Many of our older people living on fixed incomes are unable to meet all the costs of medical care that they need. Private companies have provided some insurance for the older group of citizens. However, insurance for those over 65 is expensive, and many cannot pay the high cost. In 1965, after much debate among different political

Requirements for Medicare

Birth Year	Quarters Needed Men	Women	Birth Year	Quarters Needed Men	Women
1903	3	3	1917	28	28
1904	6	6	1918	29	29
1905	9	9	1919	30	30
1906	12	12	1920	31	31
1907	15	15	1921	32	32
1908	18	18	1922	33	33
1909	21	20	1923	34	34
1910	24	21	1924	35	35
1911	24	22	1925	36	36
1912	24	23	1926	37	37
1913	24	24	1927	38	38
1914	25	25	1928	39	39
1915	26	26	1929		
1916	27	27	or later	40	40

This table shows how many quarters of coverage are needed to qualify for hospital insurance under the Social Security Act. Those born in 1902 or earlier need no quarters of coverage.

and professional groups, Congress passed an amendment to the Social Security Act to provide health insurance for those 65 and over.

Since 1965, health insurance has been broadened to cover more people needing assistance. Those under 65 with chronic kidney disease who needed hemodialysis treatments or kidney transplants were extended coverage. Eligibility for this assistance required that one work long enough under social security to be **fully insured** and also extended to those presently receiving certain social security benefits.

MEDICARE

Medicare was originally for persons over 65 who needed an inexpensive health insurance. However in 1973, medicare protection started for disabled persons under the age of 65.

The Medicare Program has two parts. One benefit is for **hospital insurance** to cover the expense while confined in a hospital, while the other part is to cover the cost of medical expenses which include **doctor bills** and other services not included in hospital expense.

Those born before 1903 can obtain medicare hospital benefits without having paid **any** social security taxes. In 1973, anyone under age 70 needed some work under social security to qualify. The work time varies and is based on age. Generally, the older a person is, the less work time is required. The work time requirement is from nine months to ten years. The table, titled "Requirements for Medicare," is used to show number of quarters of work credit required for coverage.

FINANCING SOCIAL SECURITY

The Social Security Act program is under the administration of the Department of Health, Education, and Welfare and is authorized to accept funds and make investments and disbursements. In 1972, the Agency reported assets of $43,794,938.[1]

The primary source of revenue to finance social security payments and administration is from social security taxes levied on salaries of workers, and contributions of

[1]Source: **Office of Research and Statistics, Social Security Administration, Department of Health, Education and Welfare. 1972.**

employers. Self-employed individuals must also pay a tax but at a higher rate than the individual. An examination of the data in the table titled "Social Security Taxes — Base and Rates" shows that the tax rates have increased from 1.00 percent in 1937 to 5.85 percent in 1974. The base on which taxes are levied has also increased from $3,000 in 1937 to $12,000 in 1974.[2]

The rate is scheduled to continue the upward climb with a rate of 6.05 percent for 1978-80, 6.15% for 1981-85, and 6.25% for 1986-1997.[3] The rate beyond that period is not definite, and the need for funds on which to operate will determine the rate. Many other factors will be considered by the year 2000 — the condition of the economy, the value of our money, the standard of living, and the average life span of those insured.

In 1972, more money was collected from social security taxes than was needed to meet expenditures; however, with the expanding programs and more coverage, projections for the year 2000 may be in error.

WHO WILL PAY?

The question is often asked, "Who will pay for the operation of this growing and costly system of social insurance?" Critics of the method of financing predict problems if wages do not increase during the next 25 years. Most likely, the law will be revised many times and automatic adjustments will be implemented. The social security tax may need to be made more **progressive.** Under the present tax base, those with higher incomes pay on only a part of their earnings. Remember that young workers can profit from social security, for if any young workers become disabled before reaching retirement age, the benefits will help them and their dependents. If they die, their families draw benefits.

The Social Security Act has been in oper-

ation since 1935, and since that time no effort has been made to discontinue the operation. Congress has continuously supported the system.

The value of social security to the young worker is reflected in the census statistics where it is reported that about five percent of the children are orphaned by loss of one or both parents. Social security benefits will be available to help them. The young worker can definitely profit from social security.

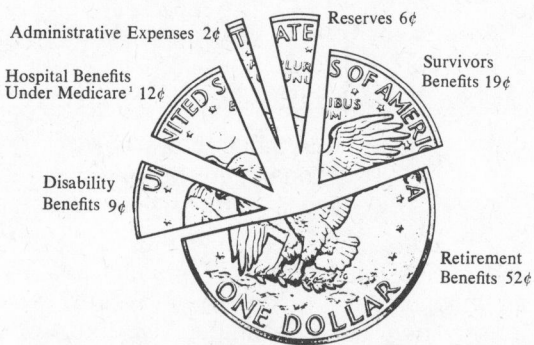

Administrative Expenses 2¢

Reserves 6¢

Hospital Benefits Under Medicare[1] 12¢

Survivors Benefits 19¢

Disability Benefits 9¢

Retirement Benefits 52¢

[1] The other part of Medicare, doctor-bill insurance, is financed by the monthly premiums paid by people who enroll in the program and by the Federal Government from general revenues.

What the Social Security Dollar Paid for in 1973

YOUR SOCIAL SECURITY CARD

Each of you should already have a Social Security card which indicates your Social Security number. If you do not have such a card, you should apply immediately to the Social Security Office in your area.

Our concern in this chapter has been with the financial benefits from the Social Security Act. There are a number of other uses for the number on your Social Security card.

Your Social Security number may be required for issuance of a public library card. Your application for employment requires a record of your Social Security number; this number and the wages paid to you are reported each year to the federal Internal Revenue Department as a verification for

[2]Source: U.S. Department of Health, Education and Welfare.
[3]Ibid.

Social Security Taxes Base and Rates

	Yearly Wage Subject To Tax	%	Maximum Tax on a Worker and Employer (Each pays this amount)	Self-Employed Person's Maximum Tax
1937-1949	$3,000	1.0	$30.00	None
1950	$3,000	1.5	$45.00	None
1951-1953	$3,600	1.5	$54.00	$81.00
1954	$3,600	2.0	$72.00	$108.00
1955-1956	$4,200	2.0	$84.00	$126.00
1957-1958	$4,200	2.2	$94.50	$141.75
1959	$4,800	2.5	$120.00	$180.00
1960-1961	$4,800	3.0	$144.00	$216.00
1962	$4,800	3.12	$150.00	$225.60
1963-1965	$4,800	3.6	$174.00	$259.20
1966	$6,600	4.2	$277.20	$405.90
1967	$6,600	4.4	$290.40	$422.40
1968	$7,800	4.4	$343.20	$499.20
1969-1970	$7,800	4.8	$374.40	$538.20
1971	$7,800	5.2	$405.60	$585.00
1972	$9,000	5.2	$468.00	$675.00
1973	$10,800	5.85	$631.80	$864.00
1974-1977	$12,000	5.8	$702.00	$960.00
1978-1980	$12,000	6.05	$726.00	$990.00
1981-1985	$12,000	6.15	$738.00	$1,002.00
1986-1997	$12,000	6.25	$750.00	$1,014.00
2011 and after	$12,000	7.3	$876.00	$1,014.00

Source: U. S. Dept. of Health, Education and Welfare

Tax figures for 1975 and later years exclude the impact of any increases resulting from rise in wages. Under recent changes in law, if benefits are increased because of a rise in consumer prices, the amount of wages subject to social security taxes also rises automatically.

federal withholding taxes. If you enter military service, your Social Security number becomes your military identification number. As you begin to save a part of your earnings, you will find that the bank requires a record of your Social Security number, for they, like your employer, must report annually to the federal government the amount of interest paid to you on your savings account.

You can easily see that your Social Security number is an important link between the government, your employer, and you. This number should be memorized in order that you will be able to write it without checking your Social Security card. To avoid loss of this number before it has been memorized, the Social Security Administration issues duplicate cards, one of which should be placed in a safety deposit box at the bank. The other card should be carried in your billfold. In case one card is lost, the Social Security Office will issue a duplicate if you can show one card; otherwise, a new number must be assigned. Remember — your Social Security card is one of your most vital possessions and you should make every effort not to lose it.

EMPLOYMENT SERVICES AND JOB INSURANCE

Two important parts of the Social Security Act are the divisions of Employment Service and Employment Security. The two programs are operated jointly by federal and state governments. Each state operates its

THE KEY TO YOUR SOCIAL SECURITY

Your social security number is your key to the benefits you have earned. You only need one number in your working lifetime, no matter how many jobs you have. And you keep the same number for life.

Your social security record is kept under the name and number on your social security card. You should always show your card to your employer. He needs the information on the card for his report of the amount of your earnings. Be sure his record of your number is correct.

If you are self-employed, copy the number directly from your social security card when you make out the self-employment part of your Federal personal income tax return.

Your social security number is also your tax number. Upon request, show it to anyone who pays you interest, dividends, or other income that must be reported.

individual plan, but is subject to the regulations of the Federal Social Security Act of 1935. The services provided under provisions of the two services have been improved in the various states over the years. In 1973 more than 2400 local offices were offering improved services.

The Employment Security Division has as its main goal the full utilization of the nation's "human resources." It assists those looking for jobs and employers in need of workers. Many states have recently organized computerized systems to increase efficiency of job referrals and job locations.

Service to returning veterans has been emphasized after recent wars. Vietnam veterans have received special employment services. In 1971, the President of the United States issued an executive order **requiring** government contractors to list all of their

If you have a

Social Security Card

Be sure to notify the

nearest social security office

when you change your name.

You'll get a social security card

with the same account number,

and the social security records

will be changed to show your

new name.

U.S. DEPARTMENT OF HEALTH, EDUCATION, AND WELFARE

Social Security Administration   SSI–69

openings with the employment service. All enlisted military personnel being discharged from the service were contacted for help in finding jobs.

The employment service has also been assigned some of the responsibility for training unemployed persons. Some minority groups, disadvantaged persons, and others benefited through training programs and job referrals.

Job insurance or unemployment insurance was also made a part of the Social Security Act of 1935. It is a program of short-term insurance for the payment of benefits to workers who are unemployed through no fault of their own. The provisions of laws vary among the states on the amount to be paid and the length of time payments are extended. Many states have recently increased payments and length of time payments can be paid. The table on the following page, "State Unemployment Compensations Maximums," lists maximum compensation paid in the states as of December, 1972.

CONDITIONS UNDER WHICH THE WORKER CAN COLLECT COMPENSATION

Some unemployment seems to be unavoidable in the work force of our modern industrial world. Many jobs are seasonal, and factories are forced to lay off employees during periods of retooling and model changes. Young workers who have little seniority may be the first to experience unemployment and need to understand the

State Unemployment Compensation Maximums — December 1, 1972

State	Maximum weekly benefit amount[1]	Maximum duration weeks	State	Maximum weekly benefit amount[1]	Maximum duration weeks
Alabama	$60	26	Montana	$52	26
Alaska	60-85	28	Nebraska	60	26
Arizona	60	26	Nevada	77	26
Arkansas	67	26	New Hampshire	75	26
California	75	26	New Jersey	76	26
Colorado	86	26	New Mexico	61	30
Connecticut	92-138	26	New York	75	26
Delaware	65	26	North Carolina	60	26
D. C.	105	34	North Dakota	62	26
Florida	64	26	Ohio	57-87	26
Georgia	55	26	Oklahoma	60	39
Hawaii	90	26	Oregon	62	26
Idaho	68	26	Pennsylvania	85-93	30
Illinois	51-97	26	Puerto-Rico	50	12
Indiana	45-65	26	Rhode Island	79-99	26
Iowa	68	26	South Carolina	59	26
Kansas	64	26	South Dakota	55	26
Kentucky	68	26	Tennessee	57	26
Louisiana	70	28	Texas	63	26
Maine	63	26	Utah	65	36
Maryland	78	26	Vermont	60	26
Massachusetts[2]	83-125	30	Virginia	54	26
Michigan	56-92	26	Washington	50	30
Minnesota	64	26	West Virginia	50	26
Mississippi	49	26	Wisconsin	60	34
Missouri	63	26	Wyoming	51	26

[1]Maximum amounts. When two amounts are shown, higher includes dependent's allowances.
[2]Amount limited only by average weekly wage.
Source: U. S. Department of Labor, Manpower Administration, Unemployment Insurance Service.

provisions of their state's unemployment compensation laws.

Workers may receive unemployment compensation benefits if they meet certain provisions of the state law. These provisions may include the following:

1. They have become unemployed through no fault of their own.
2. They must register at a public employment office for a job.
3. They must be willing to take a comparable job.
4. They must make a claim for benefits.
5. They earned a certain amount of money or worked a given length of time.
6. The job on which they worked is covered by state law.

Workers may **not** draw unemployment compensation under the following conditions:

1. If unemployed as a result of a labor dispute. (Some states have exceptions to this rule.)
2. If they quit a job without cause.
3. When discharged for misconduct. (The waiting period is usually longer with fewer payments for persons in this category.)
4. When they refuse to apply or take a suitable job.

5. When they misrepresent facts or make fraudulent claims.
6. If discharged for conviction of theft.
7. Other restrictions on payments include leaving the job for marriage or pregnancy, or to further education.

A Worker May Not Draw Unemployment Insurance If He Refuses to Take a Suitable Job

Unemployed workers are required to go to the local state employment service office and register for work. They may file for unemployment compensation in the same office. If a job which they can do is available, they must take the job or lose their unemployment benefits. When workers move to other states, they can still collect unemployment insurance at the new residence. The new state will act as their agent in most cases.

Benefits under the unemployment insurance program can be paid to unemployed workers who have recent employment or earnings in a job covered by the state law of the state in which they reside. The amount of earnings and the period of employment are used to calculate the amount of benefits workers may receive. The formula used varies from state to state. Generally, the benefits received are equal to one-half the worker's weekly salary. In a number of states the benefits the worker may receive are based on a prior 12-month period of work as well as a stated number of weeks.

To determine the weekly benefit amount of unemployment insurance, first find the amount of insured wages you were paid during the calendar quarter of the base period in which you received more wages than in any other quarter. Multiply this amount of wages by 4 percent. That amount is then rounded to the highest dollar. It is your determined weekly benefit amount. The highest weekly amount payable and the minimum weekly amount payable are established in accordance with the law. To find the total benefit amount, multiply your determined weekly amount by 26. Divide the total amount of wages you were paid during the base period by 3. Your total benefit amount is the lesser of the two calculations.

FINANCING UNEMPLOYMENT INSURANCE

Unemployment insurance is financed by both federal and state payroll taxes. Under the provisions of the Federal Unemployment Tax Act, as amended in 1970, the tax rate levied is 3.2 percent on the first $4,200 of annual earnings paid employees by employers of one or more workers on a specified day of 20 different weeks in a calendar year, or $1,500 payroll during the calendar quarter. A credit of up to 2.7 percent is allowed for taxes paid under state unemployment insurance laws that meet certain requirements, leaving the federal share at 0.5 percent of taxable wages, from which the federal government pays its share of costs.

OBJECTIVES OF UNEMPLOYMENT INSURANCE

Unemployment can cause a family many hardships. This is especially true of a young family that has little financial reserve to fall back on during periods of unemployment. The system provides some money while workers are temporarily unemployed or have lost their jobs and are seeking another. Thus, it is one of the "built-in" stabilizers which helps to protect the economic well-being of the individuals and their families. The system is also a built-in national economic stablizer. When workers are laid off their jobs, they start to receive payments from the unemployment insurance fund.

CLAIMANT: Do not write
in items 'A' or 'B'

UNEMPLOYMENT INSURANCE APPLICATION

☞ Read the instructions at the bottom of this form

A. Office No.	B. B. Y. E.	**1** PRINT—First Name, Initial, Last Name	**2** SOCIAL SECURITY NUMBER

3 1 ☐ Male
2 ☐ Female
4 Year Born

5 MAIL ADDRESS
Street and Number,
P. O. Box or RFD_____
City, State
and ZIP Code:

6 SHOW OTHER NAMES or Social
Security Numbers worked under during
past 18 months, if any

7 LAST JOB   Details of Job

EMPLOYERS' NAME AND PAYROLL ADDRESS			
LAST EMPLOYER (Regardless of state in which worked or size of firm)	Reason for Leaving Last Job 1 ☐ Quit 2 ☐ Fired 3 ☐ Lv. of Absence	Began Work	Last Day Worked
Firm Name of Employer_____	4 ☐ Laid off—Lack of Work	Mo. Day Year	Mo. Day Year
Street and Number_____	5 ☐ Labor Dispute	19	19
City, State and Zip Code	KIND OF WORK DONE (Job Title)	Rate of Pay on Last Job $ per	

8 NEXT TO LAST JOB (Omit if "next-to-last-job" ended more than 6 months ago)

NEXT TO LAST EMPLOYER			
Firm Name of Employer_____	Reason for Leaving Next to Last Job 1 ☐ Quit 2 ☐ Fired 3 ☐ Lv. of Absence	Began Work	Last Day Worked
Street and Number_____	4 ☐ Laid off—Lack of Work	Mo. Day Year	Mo. Day Year
City, State and Zip Code	5 ☐ Labor Dispute	19	19
	KIND OF WORK DONE	RATE OF PAY $ per	

9 HAVE YOU BEEN EMPLOYED by the Federal government in the past 18 months?... ☐ Yes ☐ No

10 HAVE YOU SERVED IN THE ARMED FORCES of the United States in the past 18 months?... ☐ Yes ☐ No

11 HAVE YOU BEEN EMPLOYED OUTSIDE the State of Kansas in the past 18 months?.. ☐ Yes ☐ No

12 HAVE YOU FILED A PREVIOUS CLAIM for Unemployment Insurance in the past 12 months?... ☐ Yes ☐ No

If "YES", Where?
(City & State)_____

When?
(Date)_____

Against what
State?_____

13 REMARKS:

14 CERTIFICATION: I register for work and apply for Unemployment Insurance benefits. All entries on this application are true and correct. I so certify knowing that
the law provides penalties if I make false statements or withhold material information to obtain benefits not due me.

CLAIM
ACCEPTED BY:_____

15 WRITE YOUR
NAME HERE X

CLAIMANT—Do Not Write in Boxes Below

C. Law(s)	D. B. Y. B.	E. Type	F. Claim Date	G. 1 2 3 4 5 6 7 8 9 0	H. BRE Today 1 ☐ Yes	I. Res. Code	J. To Report
K. Occ. Code		L. Industry	M. Suspense Effective		by:	N. K-Ben Atchd.	O.

INSTRUCTIONS TO CLAIMANT—READ CAREFULLY BEFORE COMPLETING

Complete items '1' through '12'. Use item '13', if needed. READ item '14'. WRITE your name in item '15' as it should appear in
item '1': first name, initial of middle name and last name.

Entry of your CORRECT Social Security Number is most important. A mistake will delay your claim.

Make NO entries in items lettered 'A' through 'O'.

PRINT all entries except your signature. Press hard enough to make a good carbon imprint on the three forms underneath.

K-Ben 10 (1-70) Unemployment Insurance Application—Kansas Employment Security Division   ROBERT R. (BOB) SANDERS, STATE PRINTER 1654-N

Applying for Unemployment Insurance

A. Office No.	B. Ben. yr. ends	1. Claimant's Name	2. Social Security Number

3. 1 ☐ Male	5. Claimant's Address	6. Other Names or Social Security Numbers used
2 ☐ Female		
4. Year Born		

7. This notice mailed Date	by:	NOTICE TO LAST EMPLOYER—ALLOWED CLAIM

8. Last Employer:	9. Reason for Separation (As furnished by the claimant)	10. Dates of Employment:
	1 ☐ Quit 2 ☐ Fired 3 ☐ Lv. of Absence	From: To:
	4 ☐ Laid off—Lack of Work	
	5 ☐ Labor Dispute	
	11. Kind of Work	12. Rate of Pay
		$ per

13. TO THE EMPLOYER: The claimant certifies that your firm is his most recent employer. As last employer you are an interested party to this claim.

VALID CLAIM: The claim is valid because the claimant was paid sufficient wages in insured work during the base period to qualify. He may receive benefits for any week of unemployment during the year ending on the date in Item "B" above, in which he is not disqualified, files a timely claim, has a balance in his benefit account and provides acceptable evidence that he is able to work, available for work and is trying to find a job.

NO REPLY to this notice is needed unless the reason for separation (Item 9), or last date worked (Item 10), as given by the claimant are incorrect or unless you now have or will have work for the claimant. Please use the handy "Employer Reply" below to submit this information.

IF YOU WISH TO PROTEST THE CLAIM because you believe the claimant should be disqualified or because you can furnish evidence that he is not able to work or is not available for work, please write us a letter. Be sure to indicate the claimant's CORRECT SOCIAL SECURITY NUMBER in your letter. Your protest, if any, should be made promptly since the determination conveyed by this notice is final 12 days after the date in Item '7'.

ADDRESS CLAIMS CORRESPONDENCE to the office servicing the claim. Note the first 2 digits in the Office Number, Item 'A' above. A directory of office addresses by office numbers is on the other side.

IF YOU ARE A BASE PERIOD EMPLOYER as well as the last employer on this claim, you will receive a Base Period Employer Notice in addition to this Last Employer Notice, unless a determination has been stamped in Item 14, below. If you receive a Base Period Employer Notice, it will explain what action you may take. We emphasize that such action must be *in addition* to any response to the Last Employer Notice.

14.	15. ☐ If checked, the claimant presented a Notice of Partial Unemployment from your firm. Please see enclosed instructions. Weekly Benefit Amount $_____	**BENEFIT DEPARTMENT** Kansas Employment Security Division 401 Topeka Avenue Topeka, Kansas 66603

EMPLOYER REPLY

(Reply needed only if one or both answers in item 1 is "No" or there are entries in item 2 and/or 3)

1. Are these entries on this form correct?

Item 9, Reason for separation ☐ Yes ☐ No
Item 10, Last date worked ☐ Yes ☐ No

If "NO" to either, please enter corrected information:_____

2. Check, if applicable: ☐ We have work for this claimant now.
☐ We will have work for this claimant about _____ 19___

3. REMARKS OR OTHER INFORMATION:_____

Date_____ Firm Name_____ by:_____

K-Ben 44 (6-70) Notice to Last Employer—Allowed Claim

1654-N

Computation of Benefit Amount

BASE PERIOD: First four of last five completed calendar quarter preceding claim effective date.

File valid claim Feb. 10, 1972, Benefit Year begins on Sunday, Feb. 6, 1972.

Benefit year begins ..... Feb. 6, 1972
Benefit year ends .... Feb. 5, 1973

BASE PERIOD

LAG QUARTER

FILING QUARTER

BENEFIT YEAR

1970 Oct-Nov-Dec	1971 Jan-Feb-Mar	1971 Apr-May-June	1971 July-Aug-Sept	1971 Oct-Nov-Dec	1972 Jan-Feb-Mar	1972 Apr-May-June	1972 July-Aug-Sept	1972 Oct-Nov-Dec	1973 Jan-Feb-Mar
WAGES $750	WAGES $800	WAGES $700	WAGES $450	(Wages in this quarter not used)					

WEEKLY BENEFIT AMOUNT
The insured had the highest earnings ($800) in the Jan-Mar Qtr of 1971 ...... $800 × 4% = $32 WBA

QUALIFYING EARNINGS
To qualify for benefits the Insured must have been paid wages from insured employment in at least two quarters with total wages of at least 30 times his Weekly Benefit Amount .... 30 × $32 = $960 (The Insured, in this example, qualifies.)

TOTAL BENEFIT AMOUNT
$750 + $800 + $700 + $450 = $2,700 = Total Base Period Earnings.
1/3 of $2,700 = $900
26 × $32 (Weekly Benefit Amount) = $832.00
$832.00 is the Total Benefit Amount since it is less than $900.00

How to Determine Your Weekly Unemployment Benefit Amount

REQUEST FOR STATEMENT OF EARNINGS

ACCOUNT NUMBER ➤ | 000 | 00 | 0000

DATE OF BIRTH ➤ | MONTH January | DAY 1 | YEAR 1970

Please send me a statement of the amount of earnings recorded in my social security account.

NAME { MISS MRS. MR. }   John Q. Public

Print Name and Address In Ink Or Use Typewriter

STREET & NUMBER _____

CITY & STATE _____   ZIP CODE _____

SIGN YOUR NAME AS YOU USUALLY WRITE IT   *John Q. Public*

Sign your own name only. Under the law, information in your social security record is confidential and anyone who signs someone else's name can be prosecuted.

If your name has been changed from that shown on your social security account number card, please copy your name below exactly as it appears on that card.

When they return to work, payments stop, and reserves are again collected for the next period of unemployment. When unemployment is high, funds go into circulation again. When unemployment is low, funds will build up. Multiply this process by millions of unemployed persons and you will find a sizeable amount of money going into the economy.

WORKMEN'S COMPENSATION

Industrial workers of 75 years ago faced many dangers from the crude machinery with which they worked and the unsafe methods used. Accidents killed or injured workers at an alarming rate. Accidents were considered a normal part of a worker's risk, and some employers were rather lax in practicing safety in industry. When workers were injured in an industrial accident, they had difficulty getting compensation for injuries. In many cases, only expensive lawsuits allowed injured workers to get payment for their injuries.

As the number of industrial workers increased and accidents increased, attention to the problem was brought to the general public. Gradually the philosophy of accident responsibility changed, placing a larger part on the employer rather than the employee.

Laws were passed to protect the worker in case of accidents on the job. The laws are called "Workmen's Compensation Laws." There are different responsibilities on the part of employers and employees in reporting accidents and action taken in accidents.

The cost of industrial accidents is very high, not only in money lost, but in suffering by the workers and their families. Claims of injured workers have increased tremendously.

Compensation claims reached near $1,800,000,000 in 1965 compared with $500,000,000 in 1950. The increase in 15 years represents a larger work force and a higher rate of compensation. However, the workers of today have many other sources of social insurance to protect them, while the early workers had only workmen's compensation for protecton.

One important thing for young workers to remember if injured on the job is that it is most important to report the injury to the employer. The requirement that the employee report an injury is for the protection of both employee and employer. A delay in reporting an injury creates doubt about the accident. A prompt notice protects the employee and also protects the employer against a fraudulent claim.

The time limits in reporting accidents and occupational diseases vary from state to state. All reports are processed, numbered, and coded. A screening process is involved, and the accident is analyzed. From reports and analysis, safety experts can study the data and hopefully prevent other such accidents, thereby reducing the cost to the worker and employer.

Those disabled by industrial accidents may become productive citizens again through rehabilitation programs. Here again, state programs are different. It is important for workers to learn of the rehabilitation programs available in the state in which they live.

STUDY AIDS

NEW TERMS

social legislation	Social Security
economic depression	Administration
Medicare	Social Security Act
Old Age and	compensation
Survivors Insurance	disability
benefits	Medicaid
retirement	eligibility
contributions	major risks

STUDY QUESTIONS

1. Why do we need state and federal insurance programs?
2. How is the social security plan financed?
3. When was the Federal Social Security Act implemented?
4. At what age can a disabled worker qualify for Social Security Act benefits?
5. How may you check your Social Security contributions?
6. At what age can a healthy worker start drawing social security retirement benefits?
7. What is the basis for calculating a person's monthly cash benefits for retirement?
8. Will a widow over 65 lose her Social Security Act benefits if she remarries?
9. Are farmers covered under the provision of the Social Security Act?
10. What is the use of Form SS-5?
11. Under Social Security Act laws, are cash benefits paid by the federal government?

DISCUSSION PROBLEMS

1. List as many reasons as possible why social insurance is needed today.
2. What are the advantages and disadvantages of operating a federally controlled social insurance program?
3. What are the three major risks for which protection is provided in the Social Security Act? Which one is most important to a high school student?
4. What is the maximum amount of cash benefits available to a worker upon retirement? Is the amount adequate?
5. Under what conditions can workers between the ages of 18 and 65 claim Social Security Act benefits?
6. Is it wise for a young worker to invest in other retirement plans?

CHAPTER SEVENTEEN
USING INSURANCE FOR PROTECTION

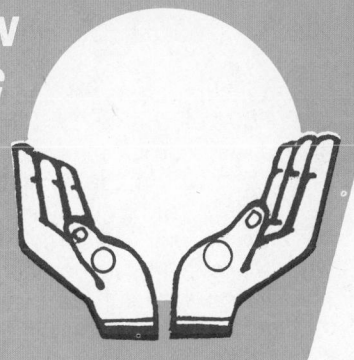

SHARING ECONOMIC LOSSES

The Indians who roamed the plains and woodlands many years ago had little need for the types of insurance available to us today. Their way of life was simple in comparison to ours. However, the Indians did need a form of insurance which they supplied for themselves. The basic idea in insurance is to have many people share the risk of economic loss. The Indians pooled their labor and time to ensure the health and safety of all members of the tribe. They lived off the land and had little interest in individual ownership of real estate. The braves hunted wild game to provide meat while the squaws and children raised corn and other grains to ensure the food supply for the winter. In case of injury or death to the parents, other members of the tribe cared for the family. This was a simple form of insurance.

Ever since the dawn of history, people have banded together to share economic loss and other hazards. As early as 900 B.C., sea-going people who lived on the islands of Rhodes in the Mediterranean Sea organized a plan to share the loss or damages to their ships and cargos. Like the Indians banding together for mutual protection, this illustrates the insurance principle of sharing economic loss. The Romans organized a type of life insurance for their soldiers during the 7th century. They also organized burial societies to share the cost of funerals. Members of guilds banded together and organized insurance plans for the protection of members and their families.

Marine insurance to protect ship owners and shippers developed rapidly in England during the 17th Century when a new method of insuring ships and cargos evolved. Those who had the money and were willing to share the risk of a shipment would sign a contract to underwrite, or guarantee, a percentage of loss in case the ship and cargo were lost. Should the ship reach port and sell the cargo, the underwriter would profit. However, in case of shipwreck, the underwriter would lose.

Indians Banded Together to Insure the Health and Safety of the Members of Their Tribe

Life insurance as we know it today started over 300 years ago. The first policies probably grew out of marine insurance where protection was made available to the ship's passengers during a voyage.

There are early records of an Englishman who wrote a life insurance policy in 1583. The first successful life insurance company in America was founded in Philadelphia and was called "A Corporation for the Relief of Poor and Distressed Presbyterian Ministers and of the Poor and Distressed Widows and Children of Presbyterian Ministers."[1] A mutual fire insurance company was founded in Philadelphia by Benjamin Franklin.

INSURANCE NEEDS OF YOUNG WORKERS

The insurance needs of single young workers are quite different from the needs of those workers who have families. John Smith is working on his first job since graduating from high school. He lives in a furnished apartment and has little personal property other than his wardrobe and an old car. His insurance needs are different from his sister Mary's who operates a beauty shop with an inventory of $10,000 and a mortgage of $5,000 on the equipment. The risks are different in these two situations, but both need insurance for protection against economic loss.

As a worker, you face risks every day. You may become ill and need hospitalization, or you may be injured on the highway or on the job. The young worker faces other risks, too. Should Mary's beauty shop be destroyed by fire or by a wind storm, a property insurance policy would protect her from a disastrous loss. Mary could be sued if a patron was injured in her shop. Liability insurance would protect her and the patron in case of an accident of this kind.

[1] R. Wilfred Kelsey and Arthur C. Daniels. **Handbook of Life Insurance**, Institute of Life Insurance, New York. pp. 8-9.

Many kinds of insurance are needed. As a single young man or woman with few responsibilities and little property, a life insurance policy plus a health and disability policy may be all the insurance you need. If you own a car, it will be necessary for you to buy car insurance. Many states require liability insurance before licensing a driver. For those owning business or real estate, property insurance will protect them from loss.

When young people marry and start families, a larger percentage of their insurance budgets may be needed for life insurance. Mary will need to continue liability insurance for herself and her employees in the beauty shop. Retirement is probably not a big worry for young workers. However, it is wise to start saving through an insurance policy or a savings plan at an early age for retirement.

A large percentage of your insurance budget should go for life insurance. People who buy insurance protect themselves by sharing economic loss with their fellow workers and friends.

PLANNING FOR PERSONAL INSURANCE

In planning your insurance program, it is necessary to first determine the risk you face at home, on the highway, and on the job. List all the risks which you may encounter in groups under headings of (1) property, (2) liability, (3) life, and (4) health insurance. Secondly, you must determine which risk you cannot afford to take without the protection of insurance. It will not be economically possible to protect yourself from all risks. Also, in planning you must consider the insurance protection furnished by your employer. A few people actually buy more insurance than they can afford and are pressed to meet all the other expenses. Such a person may be called "insurance poor."

Many large insurance companies furnish guidelines to assist persons in deciding how much to budget for insurance. The services of a good insurance agent from a recog-

INSURANCE POOR?

Now have all you need with one easy monthly payment—through State Farm!

nized company are important. The young worker should select the agent and company carefully. One important check to make is to learn if the agent and his or her company have a state license to operate. The reputation of agents may be determined by recommendations from their policyholders. The premium (payments) on insurance policies may vary with the company. It is wise to compare the cost of insurance in different companies before buying.

Few young workers will have the experience or knowledge to buy insurance without cautious consideration and help from their parents, employers, and friends. Thus, in the remainder of this unit we will consider the different types of insurance available and suggest pointers for buying insurance.

TYPES OF INSURANCE

Although there are other kinds of insurance, we will discuss the basic four types

If a Home Is Damaged or Destroyed by Fire, Insurance Makes Rebuilding Possible

here. The four most common are Property, Auto, Life, and Health.

PROPERTY INSURANCE

Many large insurance companies in the United States are licensed to sell property insurance. For a small premium payment each year, policyholders can protect their investments in a home or other property. A family investment in a home built with savings over a 20-year period may be lost in minutes in a fire or tornado. Insurance makes it possible to rebuild.

The homeowner policy provides insurance coverage for owner and occupants of one- and two-family private residences. Many homeowners buy a comprehensive insurance policy which includes protection against many perils. The chart shows the basic coverage included in a comparative homeowner policy.

An inventory of personal property should be made and a copy placed in your bank safety deposit box. If a claim is made, it is easier to settle when a complete inventory is available.

Liability insurance may also be included under the homeowner's policy. The liability insurance part of the homeowner's policy protects against claims in areas of personal liability, medical payments, and damage to the property of others. This coverage will protect persons injured on the homeowner's property or cover property damage.

AUTOMOBILE INSURANCE

The owners and operators of automobiles must assume a great deal of responsibility. The National Safety Council estimated that more than 56,000 persons were killed in accidents in 1972 and billions in property loss result from accidents each year. The rise in accidents is a great problem both to the insured and to the insurer. Cost of automobile insurance accident claims are increasing each year at an alarming rate. No driver can afford to drive without adequate protection.

Those who own or operate a motor vehicle should have a complete understanding of automobile insurance and should consider the following types of coverage.

First, bodily injury liability coverage is very important, since those riding in the car or injured by the car can be protected. The driver can also be protected against lawsuits of persons injured or killed by the insured's vehicle. Different amounts of coverage may be purchased. It is possible to carry as much as $100,000 for one person or a total of $300,000, should more than one person be injured in an accident.

IN CASE OF ACCIDENT

1. Call the city police or highway patrol.
2. Obtain the names and addresses of driver, persons injured, passengers, and witnesses of the accident.
3. Write a brief description of injuries and property damage.
4. Write a description of the accident, time of day, visibility, road conditions, and other observed information.
5. Check the accident area for skid marks and tire marks.
6. Notify your insurance company representatives.
7. Your insurance company prefers that you not discuss the accident with other persons, but remember remarks and discussion by those at the scene of the accident.

Bodily Injury Liability Insurance Is a Must

Insurance Covers Loss from All These Perils

INSURANCE INVENTORY

HOMEOWNERS*

DWELLING (Including Garage)	VALUES
Replacement Cost (Estimate)	$_____
Actual Value (Replacement cost Less Depreciation) (Estimate)	$_____
Present Insurance (Amount)	$_____
Premium (Present Insurance)	$_____

PRESENT COVERAGE

- Fire and Extended Coverage ☐
- Broad Form ☐
- Dwelling & Special Form ☐

_____ ☐

Other Forms

EXPIRATION DATE _____

PERSONAL PROPERTY

(Replacement Cost, Less Depreciation)	Actual Value
Furniture (Living Room, Dining and Bedrooms)	$_____
Appliances	$_____
Clothing	$_____
Linens, Rugs, Etc.	$_____
China, Silverware	$_____
Other Articles (Books, Sports Equipment, Etc.)	$_____
TOTAL	$_____
Present Insurance (Amount)	$_____
Premium (Present Insurance)	$_____
EXPIRATION DATE _____	

FORM NO(s). _____

	Expiration Date

COVERAGE: AMOUNTS

A DWELLING . . . . . _____

B PRIVATE STRUCTURES . . _____
Detached Garage, Etc.

C UNSCHEDULED PERSONAL PROPERTY
On Premises . . . . . . _____

Off Premises . . . . . . _____

D ADDITIONAL LIVING EXPENSE . . . . . . _____

E COMPREHENSIVE PERSONAL LIABILITY . . _____

F MEDICAL PAYMENTS . . _____
(Per Person)

G PROPERTY DAMAGE . . _____

ADDED COVERAGES:

End. No. _____

End. No. _____

End. No. _____

Premium: 1st Year $_____

2nd Year $_____

3rd Year $_____

TOTAL $_____

If Paid In Advance . . TOTAL $_____

*COVERAGE SUBJECT TO POLICY TERMS.

It Is Important to Have an Inventory of All Property Insured

Second, medical payment coverage is also available. This coverage is similar to the protection offered in a homeowner's policy. It will pay medical expenses for a person who may be injured while a passenger in your car. You should consider this type of insurance if you transport persons to work or children to school.

Third, collision insurance is available. If you have a large investment in your car, collision insurance is recommended. Complete coverage is very expensive. A $50 or $100 deductible policy is less expensive. The owner pays the first $50 or $100 of the damage.

Fourth, property damage liability insurance protects you and the owner of another car or property from loss when your vehicle causes the damage. Property damage liability insurance is available in amounts of $5000 to $100,000. This coverage is generally purchased with bodily injury liability insurance and is equally important. In many states the law requires all drivers to carry these two types of insurance.

Fifth, comprehensive insurance protects

you against loss due to damage to your automobile from fire, lightning, flood, and windstorm. Glass breakage is also covered under this section of a policy. You also have protection against theft of your car or parts of the car under comprehensive coverage.

Sixth is protection against uninsured drivers who may involve you in an accident. This type of coverage is limited to the amount of liability required under the laws of the various states.

Automobile insurance is expensive, so we should buy only the insurance necessary for protecting ourselves and others. No one should drive a car without liability insurance. Both bodily injury and property damage coverage are needed unless a person has the wealth to pay damages resulting from accidents which may be his or her fault. Most young people should also buy insurance for medical payments to protect others riding in their cars. Collision insurance is rather expensive. Individual circumstances must be considered in deciding whether this type of insurance is necessary. For example, if your car is old and has little value, you should probably not carry collision insurance. On the other hand, if you use your car in sales work, and have most of your money invested in the car, it would be wise to purchase collision insurance. If your car is essential for your job, you may carry insurance to provide transportation while your auto is being repaired.

Auto Insurance Rates. There are many factors affecting the rates of the insurance charged by different companies.

1. The rates set by an insurance company reflect the cost of claims over a three-year period of time, and companies who are selective in choosing drivers they insure will probably have lower rates. Therefore, drivers who have good records should buy from selective companies.

2. The area where you live is a second factor. Congested urban areas have a higher rate of accidents than rural areas, thus a higher rate must be charged the policyholder.

3. The cost of car repair affects insurance rates. Charges are higher in some areas and some cars are more expensive to repair.

4. A fourth factor in determining rates is the classification of the driver. The young male driver under 25 years of age has a greater accident claim rate than any other group. Since statistics show that persons in this classification have more accidents, a much higher rate is charged.

25% OFF Good Student Discount

STATE FARM INSURANCE
Auto Life Fire

car insurance-wise

Some companies give special discounts for students who have high grades in high school or college. Drivers must remember that insurance rates are based on accidents and claims over the last three years of the company's experience. The more money a company must spend for accident claims, the higher insurance rates will go.

Automobile owners and drivers should familiarize themselves with the rules and regulations of their respective insurance companies and state laws. The local and state procedures should be observed in reporting accidents when there is bodily injury and/or damages of $50 or more.

No-Fault Auto Insurance. Under the present and past automobile liability insurance system in the United States, the basic premise established was that the person responsible should pay for damages to the individual and for property damage. The driver who was at fault paid for the damages. In actual practice, the driver's insurance company compensated the injured person. The amount of compensation depends on the limits of the guilty parties and on the agreement between the parties on the extent of damages.

In many cases, the injured person wants more compensation than the insurance company is willing to pay, and the only recourse is to settle the claim through a lawsuit in the civil court.

The fault system leads to costly litigation and is criticized as being inequitable and very slow in getting claims settled. In many large cities the court docket is jammed with such cases. Not only is the system slow; it is also very expensive. Legal expenses are reported to cost about 2.2 billion dollars annually, which is one dollar out of every three dollars the motorist pays in premiums.

To reduce delays and cost in automobile insurance, some states have enacted "no-fault automobile insurance." Under provisions of a truly no-fault insurance, insurance companies would pay for damages without naming a guilty party. The victims would be guaranteed standard compensation

for injuries and damages without a lawsuit. Under the no-fault insurance law the individual would be unable to take the case to court.

Most states have been slow in moving into the no-fault insurance plan. Many legal groups, especially trial lawyers, fight the no-fault idea in state legislatures. The chief argument is that the individual should not give up the right to sue for damages. Insurance companies indicate the soaring cost of auto insurance can be reduced if costly litigation can be discontinued. The insurance companies have been successful in getting governmental assistance in developing safer cars, so perhaps all states will have no-fault insurance by 1980.

LIFE INSURANCE

When you start your first full-time job, you may have little interest in buying life insurance. However, in a few years you may be married and have children. Life insurance will then be of real interest. First, life insurance will give economic protection to the family if one or both parents die as a result of accident or disease. Second, life insurance will provide a way to save money for some future use such as education for the children or income for retirement years. Life insurance will also help to meet financial emergencies, should they arise. Third, life insurance is a good method to save during working years.

Life insurance is especially important to young people who have dependents. If they should die or become disabled, the family could be left without any income. The risk is greatest when the family is young and expenses are largest. Little or no money has been saved; but with life insurance, the dependents can be protected. First, insurance can provide cash for immediate expenses such as payments on furniture, an automobile, a home, or funeral debts. Large, long-term debts, such as home mortgages, may be covered by a mortgage-cancellation clause in the policy. Second, insurance can provide money for the family to live on while

DAMAGE by your automobile

  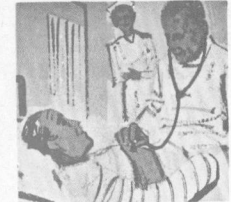

☐ Bodily Injury and Property Damage Liability —including bailbond expense, attorney fees and court costs.

Medical Payments— reimbursement for medical expenses arising out of an auto accident.
☐ Major Medical
☐ Standard Form

DAMAGE to your automobile

 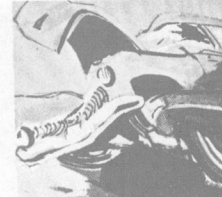 

Comprehensive . . . accidental loss or damage* including theft rental.

☐ 100% Coverage
☐ $50 Deductible

Collision or Upset
☐ 80% Collision
☐ Deductible

☐ Emergency Road Service
service expense for mechanical first aid.

*luggage and wearing apparel for certain listed perils.

PLUS these special coverages

☐ Uninsured Automobiles—bodily injuries caused by a legally liable but uninsured or unknown driver.

☐ Rental Reimbursement— Car rental (up to a specified amount) while insured auto is being repaired.

☐ Automobile Death Indemnity, a scheduled amount payable if caused by an automobile accident

☐ Total Disability— Weekly payments for total disability caused by an automobile.

☐ Personal and residence liability, including medical payments

NOTE: These are brief explanations of coverages, but not a contract. Your legal contract is contained only in your policy. If you have any questions, please contact your State Farm agent. Some coverages (or certain features of some coverages) may not be available in your state.

Automobile Insurance Is Needed to Protect Your Investment and Persons Who May Be Injured by Your Automobile

adjustments are being made. Life insurance combined with federal Social Security benefits will generally provide enough money to keep the family together until the children are through school and able to provide for themselves.

Thus, life insurance provides economic protection for a young worker's family in case of death. It also provides certain benefits for the insured. Several types of policies have cash or loan values which may be used by the policyholder in case of a financial emergency. A policy with adequate value can be used in securing a loan in case of an immediate need for cash.

Kinds of Life Insurance. Most young people will not have to wait long after taking their first jobs before they are contacted by an insurance agent who wants to sell them a life insurance policy. Young persons graduating from colleges and technical schools are often the prime target for sales prospects. In 1972, about 145 million people in the United States were insured by one or more life insurance policies with an estimated $206 billion coverage. Total benefits were expected to reach $19 billion in 1973. Premium receipts, which were three-fourths of insurance companies' total income, were expected to be near $48 billion for the year.[2]

Insurance is big business with over 1½ million employers of which 180,000 are life insurance sales personnel.[3] It is very important that a young person learn all possible information about life insurance before the salesperson arrives. The decision one makes on the purchase of life insurance is of the utmost importance. No one should sign a sales agreement with an insurance agent until a complete unbiased study is made of goals and economic expectations.

Term Insurance. Term Insurance, as the name suggests, is a kind of insurance issued for a set period of time of one to twenty years. Usually a policy is for five years and

may be renewed at 5-, 10-, 15-, and 20-year periods. The cost of term insurance is low for young people. The purpose is to provide the beneficiaries economic protection in the event of the insured person's death.

Term policies are of two types; **participating** and **nonparticipating**. Term policies issued by mutual or policyholder-owned companies, are called participating, since they pay a dividend to the policy holder. This dividend is to return the money not used for benefits during the preceding year. The nonparticipating policies pay no dividends; however, the premium may be lower for the nonparticipating policies.

Term insurance can be used by young workers to provide economic protection for their families when the children are young. There is no saving or investments involved. The cost of a term policy increases with the age of the insured.

The costs of term policies will vary from company to company. Persons contemplating using term insurance should shop for the best price. Many employers and professional groups make term insurance available at a very low rate.

Whole Life Insurance. The purpose of **whole life insurance** is to provide lifetime insurance protection. The premium costs remain the same throughout one's life. Several types of policies are available under whole life.

Straight life, or ordinary life is the most popular type of life insurance. It is generally recommended for the head of a young family because of the low average cost and because straight life can provide death benefits when the family is young. It can also be used for emergency collateral should the policyholder need to borrow money, and it has a cash value which is a good investment. The premiums are payable for life.

Limited pay life is a modification of whole life and differs from straight life in three important ways. First, the premium payments are set for a given period of time, generally from 10 to 30 years. Protection is for life but premiums are compressed into shorter

[2]U.S. Department of Commerce, U.S. Industrial Outlook, 1973, pp. 419-420.
[3]Ibid.

payment time, making them higher. Cash value is reached at an earlier time. Limited pay life is designed for persons who enjoy high earnings for a shorter period of time than the ordinary worker. Professional athletes, writers, and performers may desire to purchase limited pay life insurance policies.

Before you decide to buy whole life insurance, it is wise to get professional help. A number of publications can also be useful. One is published by the Consumers Union, titled **Life Insurance**.

Endowment Insurance. An endowment insurance policy enables a person to accumulate a sum of money in a set time by paying high premium rates. This type of insurance provides an opportunity to invest for retirement and at the same time have economic protection for the family of the insured in the event of death. There are many variations in endowment insurance plans.

Straight endowments have provisions for a person to buy protection and at the same time make investments in the form of premium payments for a period of 10 to 30 years.

The insurance endowments can be used for future family economic goals. Many policies are planned and sold to provide an educational fund when the children reach college age. The sums of endowments vary, and the premiums match the total investments and the number of years premiums are to be paid. Premium payments usually have a high rate of payment.

Another type of endowment insurance is **retirement** income endowments. This plan is designed for the insured to accumulate a cash value of several thousand dollars when the insured person reaches 65 years of age. Monthly payments are promised by the insurance company for a specified number of years. In some plans a lump sum may be paid when the policyholder reaches 65.

Modified Policies. Many insurance companies offer modified life insurance policies by combining some of the features of term, whole life, and endowment insurance plans. Some take advantage of the policyholder's ability to pay. When the person is young, the term policy with low rates can be converted into other types of policies when the person's earnings are higher. This type of a policy is sometimes referred to as the family plan.

In addition to a number of plans that are available, other options known as "clauses" can be written into individual policies. Double indemnity may be written into a policy which provides two times the face amount of the policy to be paid to the beneficiary when the policyholder meets accidental death. Another clause may be written which provides a waiver of all future premiums in the event that the policyholder becomes disabled.

Industrial Insurance. Industrial insurance is a special type of insurance offered to industrial workers. Premiums are collected by the worker's employer usually as payroll deductions. For a few cents each week, the worker can purchase a small policy of $1000 or less through payroll deduction. Industrial insurance is the only insurance some workers can afford. Medical examinations are usually not required. The policies generally include death and disability features.

Group Insurance. This insurance is available at special rates to workers of some employers. In most instances, the insurance company will accept the company's health records, and no individual examinations are required of the workers. Rates are usually low and are based on the group's age, environmental conditions, hazards, etc. Many companies pay part of the premiums.

Group insurance may be purchased as group term insurance or group permanent life insurance, which does accumulate a cash value. Group term insurance rates increase as the age of the employee increases, and they are expensive for the older worker.

Savings Bank Insurance. Savings bank insurance has been authorized by a few states. The savings banks accept the premium payments for insurance just as they accept savings deposits. Insurance policies sold by savings banks are limited in amount by state regulations.

Savings bank insurance was intended for wage earners as a convenient method of paying for insurance and to take the place of industrial life insurance which is being discontinued in many places.

How Much Life Insurance Should One Buy? Many factors must be considered if one is to answer the question, "How much life insurance is enough?" The answer to the question is an individual family matter, and there is no sure formula to guarantee accuracy of decision. The responsibility of the worker; the number of children; the family income; and the general condition of the family's economic situation must be considered.

Some life insurance agents may suggest spending 6 percent of the family's gross income, plus 1 percent for each dependent. For a family with a $12,000 gross income and three dependents, $1,080 per year would be too much of a burden and might result in the family's being deprived of a number of other needs. When a whole life policy is economically unfeasible for a family, the next consideration should probably be a combination of term insurance, social security, and other alternatives. Careful study is needed before one becomes obligated to make higher premium payments.

To decide what kind of life insurance is right for you, you should decide what you want your life insurance to do for you and your dependents.

First:

How much money do you want to leave your dependents if you should die this year? Will you require more insurance to provide for them?

Second:

What are your retirement plans? Will insurance be needed or will other investments and pension plans provide the money you will need?

Third:

How much can you afford for insurance premiums? Will your income increase during the coming years in relation to increased expenses?

When you have arrived at answers to these three questions you are ready to consult with insurance agents, study their literature, and select an insurance company and agent.

HEALTH INSURANCE

Needs for Health Insurance. Medical knowledge and skill have developed rapidly in the last 25 years. People today enjoy better health and have better medical care than ever before. However, more and more people need medical care, and the problem of financing the cost of sickness and accidents is a major one for many people. A lengthy period in the hospital would impoverish most families. To avoid financial disaster, most families carry health and accident insurance.

Three types of organizations provide health and accident insurance on a voluntary basis. These include **insurance companies** which pay cash benefits to policyholders and their families in case of sickness or accident. Benefits are paid for loss of income and for hospital, surgical, and medical cost. **Nonprofit organizations** provide service benefits to members of the plan. For example, Blue Cross is a nonprofit company paying for hospital costs and Blue Shield covers doctors' fees and other medical costs. Another plan is the **consumer-sponsored plan** which provides full hospital and medical costs. Under this plan, an industry may own its own hospitals and employ a medical staff to serve those covered.

Under the Social Security Act, most U.S. citizens age 65 and over become eligible for hospital insurance. Those eligible could also elect to take the voluntary medical insurance. The medicare and medical programs provide health insurance for the aged that would not be possible otherwise. The program is financed through the social security taxes paid by employers and their employees and the self-employed person. Benefit payments under the program were about $2.3 billion for fiscal year 1972.

Types of Health Insurance. There are five basic types of commercial health insurance other than that sponsored by the Social Security Organization. They are: hospitalization, medical-surgical, major medical, comprehensive and income protection or disability insurance.

1. Hospitalization insurance pays for all or a part of the expenses that occur during a hospital confinement. It may include, in addition to a hospital room, the cost of X-rays, use of operating rooms, anesthetics, and laboratory expenses. Most policies have limitations on expense per day and total expenses the company will pay should be well defined and studied carefully by the policyholder.
2. Medical-surgical insurance pays the cost of the surgeon and surgical bills. The list of expenses covered should be lengthy and cover a wide range of illnesses. The maximum amount paid for each operation should be listed in the policy.
3. Major medical is a type of policy to cover all the expenses of hospital care, including doctor bills, surgical fees, drugs, and tests. Many of the policies have a deductible clause which means that the policyholder pays the first $100 or more expense.
4. Comprehensive health insurance is a new plan for persons living in large metropolitan areas. The members of this plan pay a fixed yearly sum. When the member of the group needs health care, the cost of medical care is covered by the insurance plan. One objective of the plan is to provide preventative medicine.
5. Income protection is also available to purchase individually as salary protection or disability insurance. For a given premium amount, the insurance company agrees to pay the policyholder an agreed-upon monthly salary until recovery. In some cases there is a limitation of the number of months salary to be protected. Others are for life in the case of disability.

Evaluation of Health Insurance Services. Although health insurance companies are regulated by state and federal laws, the cost-benefits of companies vary. Large companies such as Aetna, Blue Cross, and Mutual of Omaha provide most of the services. However, many small mail order companies also offer health insurance. In recent years sales of these companies have been increasing. Recently, complaints from policyholders have increased. It is wise to be very careful in purchasing insurance from such companies. An evaluation of the mail order company is important. Some questions to ask are as follows:

1. Does the policy guarantee the non-variable premium rate? Some companies raise the premiums substantially as the age of the person increases.
2. What percent of the premium dollar is returned in benefits? Some companies return as little as 36 percent for individual policies, while others return as much as 67 percent. Some companies are not licensed in all states and the state insurance departments cannot help you collect from these companies.
3. What are the benefits to be expected in the event of accident or illness?

SUGGESTIONS FOR BUYING INSURANCE

Buying life insurance is more important than buying automobile insurance, because life insurance continues year after year.

The following suggestions are made for life insurance specifically. However, they may apply to most types of insurance.

1. Select a good company and a reliable agent. Both can be recognized by a little investigation of past service to their customers and rates charged.

2. Analyze your needs. Too many buyers don't study their needs enough to make a wise decision. Buyers should be careful not to buy more insurance than they can afford. A few make real sacrifices to pay insurance premiums.

3. Program your insurance purchases. Your insurance needs will change and your income will most likely increase. Purchase a policy that can be adjusted to fit your needs.

4. Don't drop one policy to buy another. In most situations it is not wise to change policies or companies. You will lose a part of the cash loan value, and rates go higher as the policyholder gets older.

5. Arrange the best terms for payment of premiums. The least expensive plan to pay premiums is on an annual basis. Semiannual or monthly premium pay-

---

6 WAYS YOU CAN STRETCH YOUR HEALTH CARE DOLLARS

1. HAVE A REGULAR FAMILY DOCTOR

The doctor who sees you regularly knows you best. Generally, he is able to diagnose your illness quicker with more certainty than a physician who is seeing you for the first time without the benefit of your past medical history. And because a regular family doctor does have your complete medical record, he may be able to avoid duplication of many expensive, time-consuming tests.

2. IF POSSIBLE, VISIT THE DOCTOR IN HIS OFFICE

Office calls are far less expensive since they don't involve the travel time required to make a house call. The doctor is better able to treat you at the office, too, where he has a vast array of medical equipment and trained personnel to assist him.

3. BE SURE TO HAVE REGULAR CHECKUPS

Oftentimes a routine physical checkup will reveal an unsuspected illness that might otherwise go undetected until it has reached a serious or incurable state. The small fee charged for a physical examination may save you an expensive bill later on. It could even save your life!

4. CHOOSE A SEMIPRIVATE HOSPITAL ROOM

Unless your doctor feels a private room is absolutely necessary, consider the semiprivate room when you are hospitalized. It can cut your hospital bill considerably and, unless you're seriously ill, it's nice to have someone to talk to during the long hours you'll spend in bed.

5. MAKE CERTAIN YOU TAKE ALL YOUR TAX DEDUCTIONS

You're allowed to deduct all medical expenses that exceed 3% of your income as well as drugs and medicines that exceed 1% of your income. Keep accurate records of all your medical expenses to make sure you don't overlook any deduction to which you are rightfully entitled.

6. MOST IMPORTANT, KEEP YOUR PRESENT HEALTH INSURANCE IN FORCE

Over the past few years, medical care costs have increased at a faster pace than any other kind of personal expense. Since the 1957-1959 base period, the Consumer Price Index for medical care has risen more than 31%. The chart below graphically portrays the spiraling cost of medical care in relation to other items in your family budget.

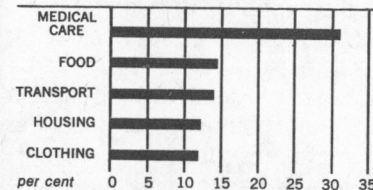

Percentage Increase in Consumer Prices (1957-1959) — 1966

MEDICAL CARE / FOOD / TRANSPORT / HOUSING / CLOTHING — per cent 0 5 10 15 20 25 30 35

Even greater increases have occurred in the area of hospitalization. Since 1960, hospital expense each patient-day has risen from $32.00 to $46.00—a 44% increase!

Because of this steadily increasing cost of medical care, it is more important than ever before that you retain the fine protection you now carry with Mutual of Omaha. There's no substitute for the feeling of financial security this coverage can offer you. when you're sick or hurt . . . security that can play an important role in your ability to get well.

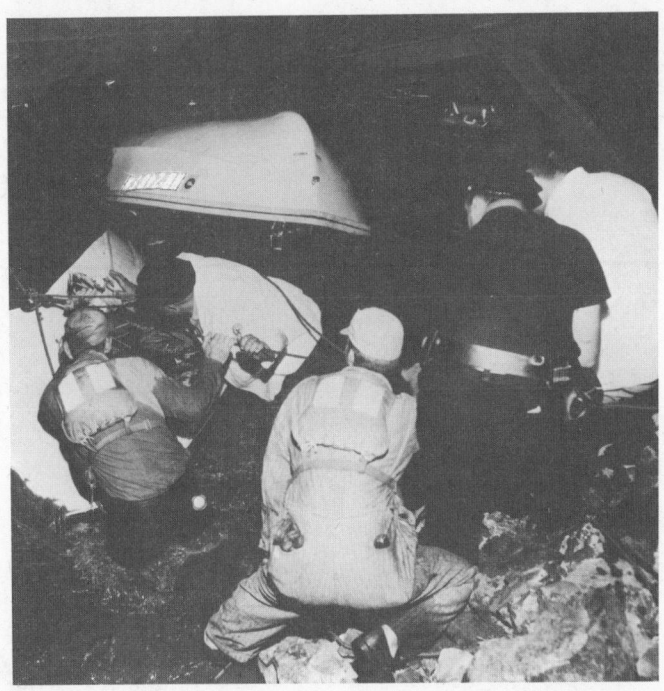

Accident Photographs

ments cost the company more book-keeping time and therefore must cost more.

6. Keep your policy in a safe place. Your insurance policy and other valuable papers should be placed in a safe place. It is good planning to have members of your family or close relatives know where the policy is located.

Life insurance is complicated, so all the information you need to select an insurance policy cannot be discussed here. It is, therefore, very important for the young worker to study carefully all the facets of a policy before entering into a contract.

STUDY AIDS

NEW TERMS

property insurance
liability insurance
comprehensive
  insurance
personal property
bodily injury
term policy
group insurance
coverage
protection
deductible
endowment

annuity
premium
benefits
collision insurance
homeowner's policy
insurance claim
savings bank
  insurance
straight life
limited payment
industrial insurance

STUDY QUESTIONS

1. What nationality groups had a form of insurance during ancient times?
2. What type of insurance was the forerunner of life insurance?
3. What is meant by the term, "liability insurance?"
4. Why should every homeowner maintain a homeowner's insurance policy?
5. What six types of insurance should be carried by everyone who operates a motor vehicle?
6. What are the factors which determine insurance rates?
7. What kinds of life insurance could you buy?

8. What types of organizations provide health and accident insurance?
9. What coverage provisions should be included in a health insurance policy?
10. Why should a young, healthy wage-earner pay for health insurance?

DISCUSSION PROBLEMS

1. Study each of the accident photos on the following pages.
   a. Make an imaginary report of the personal injury resulting from each accident. What would you estimate each injured person will pay for medical care? What kind of insurance protection should the person have to pay the doctor and hospital charges?
   b. Make an imaginary report of the property damage in each accident. What kinds of insurance protection are needed?
   c. In which of the photos of accidents is there an obvious need for liability insurance?
   d. Which of the following insurance plans could be needed by the accident victims in the photo?

life	accidental death
property	legal defense cost
collision	accident-income
theft	major medical
liability	accident-income
hospital-surgical	mortgage-pay

2. Why is there greater need for insurance protection today than there was in 1670?
3. What is the difference between property and liability insurance? Should you have both types of insurance?
4. Give some imaginary examples of use of property and liability insurance. Do you think the premium payment required was "worth it" in these cases?
5. Take the role of the person who has just had an auto accident while driving a friend's car and tell what you would do.

PART FOUR
PLANNING YOUR FUTURE RESPONSIBILITIES

INTRODUCTION

From the time we begin kindergarten until the time we retire from an active working life at age 65 or 70, society expects us to assume certain responsibilities. These change throughout life. If we are to meet these responsibilities in such a way as to make the greatest contribution to the good of society and to our own happiness, we must go through certain stages of career development. If we miss a stage, we cannot successfully go on to the next stage.

As we move toward the year 2000, our lives will surely be affected by these expected changes.[1]

[1]**America's Next 30 Years—Business and The Future**. Council on Trends and Perspective Economic Analysis and Study Group, Chamber of Commerce of the United States, Washington, D.C., 1970.

The 1970's and 1980's will bring —
1. A great era of invention, discovery, and social change.
2. A great increase in technological advances.
3. More money to spend by most — although there will be a growing gap between the wealthy and the poor. More will be spent for education, recreation, and travel.
4. A learning society. Education will not stop for most people when they graduate from high school — or even college. They will continue their education throughout their lifetime.

The way in which you can move through the stages of career development in order to successfully fulfill your responsibilities is discussed in Part IV. Much of this development depends upon a plan of continuous education. The means of getting this education is brought into focus for you too, perhaps for the first time.

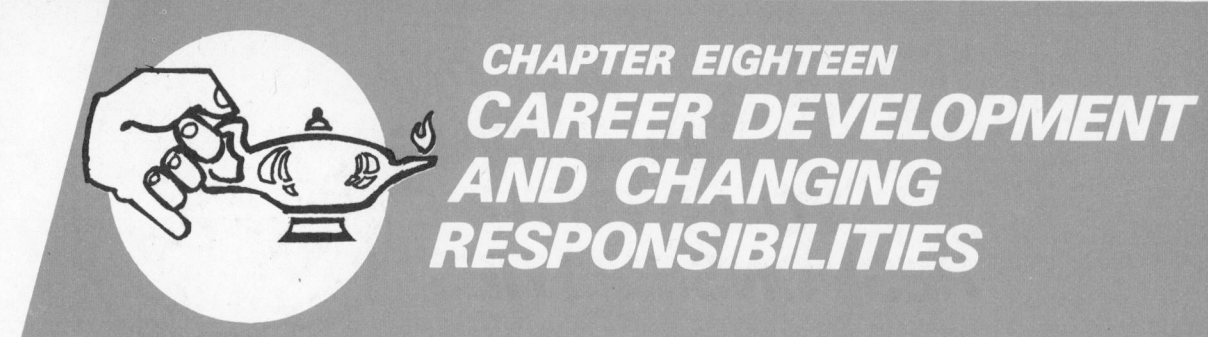

CHAPTER EIGHTEEN
CAREER DEVELOPMENT AND CHANGING RESPONSIBILITIES

AVERAGE PERSON'S CAREER AND RESPONSIBILITY GROWTH

Even though we do not know how long we will live or exactly how many years we will work, we make plans based on what we know about the **average** person.

We have discussed the importance of satisfying work for a satisfying life — the work you do largely determines your **way of life**. Because of this, psychologists have recognized certain stages through which each person passes in career development. With each stage there are certain responsibilities; and as we move from one stage of career development to the next, our responsibilities change. The stages of career development and responsibility may be identified according to the following chart.

STAGE 1 — 5 TO 10 YEARS OLD

The things we do and learn before **stage 1** in the chart are of great importance but are not directly related to our career development. Often the child who receives a great deal of attention and direction during learning activities, finds learning easier and more fun than the child who is neglected. The more interest people take in us, and the more active we (and they) keep our mind,

Stages of Vocational Development and Life Responsibility

Stage	Age	Career Development	Life Responsibilities
1	5-10	Learns to identify workers by parents' work, TV.	Personal cleanliness, closely supervised household chores, school responsibilities.
2	10-15	Develops work habits.	Organize school assignments, added household chores not so closely supervised.
3	15-25	Learns about self and how to fit into the world, selects and prepares for career, begins work.	To succeed on job, manage money; if married, responsibility to family.
4	25-55	Growth and productivity.	Family and home responsibilities, education for children; may need larger home, two cars.
5	55-65	Preparing for retirement.	Children grown and establishing own homes, need for smaller home, saving for retirement.
6	65-	Relaxing and contemplating.	Little or no responsibility to job, free to travel.

The Child Who Receives Attention and Direction During Learning Activities at Home Often Places a Higher Value on Learning

the easier it will be for us to succeed in the next stages of our lives.

Stage 1 in our career development takes place between the ages of 5 and 10. It is at this time that we begin to notice that people are identified by the kind of work they do. We learn this mainly by seeing how closely our parents are identified with their work, and by watching television. The responsibilities which we should assume during stage 1 are limited to our school assignments, some supervised household chores, and the responsibility for our own cleanliness.

STAGE 2 — 10 TO 15 YEARS OLD

In **Stage 2,** we develop work habits which will be with us for a long time. Those who have developed good work habits by the time they are about 15 years old will find little difficulty succeeding in stage 3. Responsibilities in stage 2 include school assignments and added household chores which are not so closely supervised.

STAGE 3 — 15 TO 25 YEARS OLD

Stage 3 takes place mainly between the ages of 15 and 25. This book deals mainly with what happens to you during these years. We have discussed selecting appropriate career goals, locating job vacancies, applying for a job, and improving your chances of being successful on the job. These responsibilities — along with getting the appropriate educational preparation necessary to reach your long-range career goal — are critical. They are critical because you cannot successfully move on to stages 4, 5, and 6 unless you have been at least fairly successful in stage 3. Success in each stage depends upon how successful you were in the previous stage. Our main life responsibilities during stage 3 are job success, management of money, and — if married — responsibility to family.

STAGE 4 — 25 TO 55 YEARS OLD

Someone has said that the success you achieve by age 25 is of no great credit to you, but is due mainly to the education provided by your parents and society. That is, if we have equal education and ability, we are all at about the same level of success at age 25. What happens after we are 25 is due mainly to our own efforts. Career development in **Stage 4** is growth and increased productivity. It occurs between the ages of 25 and 55, and it is a chance to continue to improve ourselves through our efforts on the job and through a continuing educational program. This continuing education may take many forms. You may take courses in adult evening school or through university extension — or you may continue your study through selective reading. Thus, our responsibilities to ourselves and to our work has changed from what it was in stage 3. Our responsibilities to others have changed too. It is during these years, age 25 to 55, that we raise children and provide encouragement for their success in each of the first three stages of career development and life responsibilities. The more successful we have been in each stage, the more guidance we can give our children as they pass through these same stages.

STAGE 5 — 55 TO 65 YEARS OLD

When we reach **Stage 5**, our children are probably grown and have established their own homes. Thus, our responsibilities change again. We may no longer need such a large home. Perhaps one car will do instead of two. Living expenses may be less during stage 5 than they were while children were home and in school, but we will need to save some money for retirement, travel, and possible medical expenses.

STAGE 6 — OVER 65 YEARS OLD

Stage 6 is retirement. It is a time to relax, and it is also a chance to pursue hobbies and activities which you have always wanted to do. If you have been successful in each of the stages up to retirement, you will look back over life with satisfaction. You will feel that you have made a contribution to society.

Success in each stage depends upon success in the previous stage. Because of this, many people are frustrated by a feeling that they are not as successful in their work, or in life, as they should be. Often, it is because they did not get all they should have out of their experiences in stages 2 and 3. If you feel that your own career development is not keeping pace with your life responsibilities, talk it over with your school counselor. People who are successful in one stage move on to the next stage knowing they will succeed in the experiences appropriate for the new stage.

CASE STUDIES

The four cases which follow were based upon studies conducted by Dr. Robert J. Havighurst of the University of Chicago. They were previously reported in **Man In A World At Work,** Houghton Mifflin Company, Boston, 1964. These are presented here to illustrate the significance of success in the various stages of career development.

Joseph's father is a high school teacher. The boy went through elementary school and high school with a good record. In high school he got credit for four years of mathematics and four years of science, partly through studying by himself with the assistance and encouragement of a science teacher in high school. When he entered the state university, he was given advanced standing and encouraged to begin sophomore work in science and math. Upon graduation with honors in physics, Joseph had his choice of several scholarships for graduate study; he decided to apply for one of the NASA awards, which he won.

Joseph is one of many people for whom a career is the axis of life. His thoughts and aspirations have centered on his occupation since he was 12 years old, when he began to study algebra by himself, having finished his seventh-grade arithmetic textbook by Christmas of that school year. Indeed, some of his teachers feel that he is too narrowly devoted to a career, and that such concentration and single-mindedness have cost him something. He has had very little interest in girls, and his male friends think of him as one who fails to enjoy social events, music, or a good conversation . . .

Joseph identified with his father when he was a young boy, and in this way the concept of himself as a worker became a part of his ideal self. From the age of 10 he could not see himself in the future except as a man who worked and supported a family. Then, from about the age of 10 to 15, he formed a set of basic work habits which he has maintained all his life. He learned to do a job which was clearly his responsibility, whether this meant doing chores at home or getting his school lessons done as soon as they were assigned, and not putting them off in favor of seeing a movie or watching television.

His next step was to decide to become a scientist and to prepare for this career by his choice of studies in high school and college. As he progressed through college, he decided to pursue graduate work in the field of physics. During his senior year in college he examined the possibilities. When he heard of the NASA fellowship program, he applied for it.

For what will follow in Joseph's life, we can predict some such course as the following: He will work on a government assignment in space science for a few years, then find himself in a responsible position in this area, with younger men working on his team. By the time he is 40, he will be one of the outstanding men in space science. He will choose between research and administration in a university or a government science agency. For the next twenty years he will be at the peak of his productivity and influence.

During this period, Joseph will be helping his own children get started in their careers, and he will probably take a leading position on committees of scientists for the recruiting and training of young scientists. He will also become active as a citizen, serving on advisory boards to the President or to Congress. Eventually, in his 60's, Joseph will slowly reduce his work load. He will lecture frequently, advise frequently, and publish less than he did in earlier years. At about the age of 70, he will retire from his formal position but remain active as a kind of elder statesman of science. Perhaps he will write and publish his memoirs as a pioneer in space science.

More than thirty years ago, Anderson and Davidson said, "The work a man does to earn his livelihood stamps him with mental and physical traits characteristic of the form and level of his labor, defines his circle of friends and acquaintances, affects his use of leisure, influences his political affiliations, limits his interests and the attainment of his aspirations, and tends to set the boundaries of his culture."[1] This is true of Joseph. It is also true of two other boys who grew up in the same town and attended the same schools as Joseph — but their vocational development was different from Joseph's, and different from that of each other.

[1] H. D. Anderson and P. E. Davidson, **Occupational Trends in the United States** (Stanford, California: Stanford University Press, 1940), p. 1.

PHIL

Phil was a very bright boy with an I.Q. of 140. He learned rapidly in school. At home he had a variety of interests, mainly pet animals and games which he played with neighborhood children. His father was in charge of canned goods and packaged food at a supermarket. Neither of his parents read much beyond looking at the daily papers. They were active in their church and were constantly working on committees in preparation for a church dinner or some similar activity.

Phil identified with his father as a worker and a man who did things with and for other people. Phil's own energy was largely used in active play in the neighborhood. At home he early developed the habit of reading comic books, of which he always had a stack of twenty or thirty on hand. When he had finished reading them, he traded them with other boys for books he had not read. In school, Phil got his assigned lessons quickly and usually had everything finished in class so that he had little or no homework to do. However, he did not develop the kind of intellectual curiosity that Joseph had. Thus, when Phil finished his arithmetic lesson for the day, he used the rest of his time "fooling around" and bothering other children until the teacher had a talk with him about it; they agreed that Phil could read comic books whenever he had finished his school work for the day. Joseph, on the other hand, worked ahead in his arithmetic and soon finished the book. He then went on to study an algebra book while Phil read his comic books.

In spite of this apparent waste of time, Phil learned the basic habits of industry in two ways. First, he went to work selling newspapers . . . His ability to put work ahead of other things is illustrated by an incident which occurred when he was in the sixth grade. Phil sprained his ankle. The doctor put a plaster cast around it, telling Phil's mother that he could go around normally except when it rained, for he was not to get the cast wet. Phil went to school and to his newspaper business on dry days. On rainy days, he stayed home from school; but he always went to his job, rain or shine.

By the time Phil was 15 years old, he was working on Saturdays in a shoe store. The summer he was 16 he practically ran the store while his employer played golf. His employer came to rely more and more on Phil, and he began to talk of the time when Phil would be through high school and would work full time. Meanwhile, Phil attracted customers with his affective sales personality; and he committed himself more and more to the business. His school grades dropped from A's to B's, and one or two of his teachers spoke to him about his apparent loss of interest in school. Phil remarked that he was getting what he needed from school. He was the senior class president and a popular boy, well regarded in the school as well as the community.

In spite of urging by some of his teachers, Phil did not go to college. Instead, he entered the shoe business where, by the time he was 25, he was a minor partner. We can see Phil growing into the mastery of his business, becoming sole owner before he is 40, and becoming a leader in the chamber of commerce and in his service club. He may serve on the school board and take an active interest in the vocational education program of schools. His own children will be given the best education he can get for them in local schools, and he will encourage them to go to college "to take advantage of things I didn't have time for," as he will perhaps put it.

From the age of 40 to perhaps 70, Phil will be one of the leading local merchants, generally pleased with himself though occasionally wondering whether he made the right choice when he decided to go into business locally rather than to college. This choice, he will see, both made possible his rapid rise to local business success and also denied him the opportunity of getting into a broader sphere of work, possibly a position in a large business where he might have gained statewide or national fame.

Ray had a very different career from that of Joseph and Phil, though work was for him also a central axis. His father, an unskilled worker on a construction gang, managed to keep fairly steady work, although there were slack times when he supplemented his unemployment compensation with a part-time commercial fishing on the big river that ran by the city. Ray's mother also worked at times, in a laundry, when money was needed and she could get away from home without neglecting her four children. Ray's identification was with a hardworking man who kept busy at one thing or another.

In school, Ray did not do at all well. He had a reading disability that began to handicap him seriously by the time he reached the fifth grade. His mother took him out of a parochial school and put him in a public school where she was told by neighbors that Ray might get special help. But there was very little improvement and Ray made less and less effort to master his school work. A "tough" lad, he took the leadership among a small group of boys who were failing in school. They became quite unruly, sometimes openly defiant of the assistant principal of the school. They also began to miss school regularly. Ray's parents tried punishing him when poor reports cards and complaints about his behavior came home. But Ray became stubborn at such times, and his mother and father said privately that perhaps there was not much to be done. Neither of them had gone beyond the eighth grade in school.

Ray learned something about work through delivering papers after school in the afternoons, and through chores at home which his father insisted on his doing. By the time he was 14, he was actively looking for odd jobs and for such seasonal work as berry picking.

School was less and less attractive to Ray, and when he dropped out a month before his sixteenth birthday, the principal made no effort to call him back. Ray immediately went to work in the laundry where his mother was employed, and in a few months he had a job on a construction crew. He worked steadily, got along well with foremen and his fellow workers, and learned the essentials of his job quickly.

When he was about 17 years of age, Ray married a girl a year younger, and by the time he was 20 they had two children. They lived in a very small house with low rent, but they had not gone into debt and were slowly accumulating furniture that would last them a long time. Ray's wages increased slowly, and when he was 21 he became assistant foreman of a road-working crew. At 25, he was regarded by the road contractor who employed him as one of his most responsible men and was told that the next vacancy in a foreman's job would go to him.

This is probably as good a job as Ray will ever have. He may be able to keep this type of job until he is 60. He will raise his children and send them through high school, urging them to get more education than he was able to get. He is likely to buy a house on the edge of the city and to do a good deal of work on it, adding a room when his growing family needs it, and keep a vegetable garden. Perhaps he will buy a motor boat to use on the river for fishing.

As he gets on into his 60's, he may have to give way to a younger man as foreman, a man who knows the newer road-building methods and can read technical journals. Ray probably will take a less responsible job and then retire willingly on his Social Security pension at 65. He may do what work he can find in the neighborhood for a few years, helping younger men who are repairing their homes. In any case, he will regard himself as a man who did his share of work in life and who enjoyed his family and friends.

"All three of these boys reached manhood in 1960, but their stories could have been matched many times in any year during the preceding 60 years of the 20th century. However, before the advent of space science, it is likely that Joseph would have become a chemist or an engineer. There would be a growing number of boys like Joseph as the century wore on, while life stories like those of Phil and Ray would grow less frequent."[2] Meanwhile, the story of Kenny will likely become more frequent.

[2]Robert J. Havighurst, "Youth in Exploration and Man Emergent," **Man In A World At Work**. Edited by Henry Borow, National Vocational Guidance Association, c1964 (printed by Houghton Mifflin Co., Boston), p. 220.

Kenny grew up in the poorest part of the same city where the other three boys lived. He never knew his father. His mother had two later husbands. The one with whom she lived when Kenny was 5 to 10 years old was a truck driver who spent much time away from home, except when he was not working, when he loafed around home, drinking a good deal and beating Kenny for little or no reason. Kenny probably never identified with this man, or with any man who set an example of regular work and a regular life. When Kenny was about 10, his stepfather deserted his mother, leaving her with two younger children. She then received Aid for Dependent Children for about four years, when she married again. This husband was a fairly steady worker but paid very little attention to his stepchildren. He was a silent, gloomy man who worked in a factory.

Kenny was at least average in intelligence and got average grades in the first few years of school. But as school work grew harder and more demanding, Kenny lost interest. There was no one at home to show an interest in the lessons, and he soon quit doing homework. He and several boys in the neighborhood spent their free time playing exciting games together. Their first contact with the police came when Kenny was 10 years old and the gang walked barefoot one night along a strip of freshly laid cement sidewalk. From this time on, Kenny and his gang were always dodging the police as a result of one escapade or another. By the time Kenny was 16, he had been arrested several times and brought to court twice, both times for stealing.

At school Kenny made little or no effort to do his work. He was known to teachers as a bright, mischievous boy who had to be watched constantly. By the time he was 14, his behavior was so bad that he was expelled from one class after another. At 15, he had only two regular classes, being consigned to study hall the rest of the time. To the relief of everybody, he left school the day he was 16.

During the next year, Kenny worked at eight or ten jobs briefly. They were not good jobs by his standards, and his work was seldom satisfactory by the standards of his employers. He was arrested twice . . . and placed on probation both times. When he reached 17, he volunteered for the Navy. In six months he was discharged because he did not work satisfactorily at anything.

Back at home, Kenny loafed a while, then was arrested and sent to prison briefly for burglary. At the age of 19, he married a 17-year-old girl and began to hold jobs for longer periods of time. By the time he was 25, he was working as long as a year at a time at one or another factory job, but he was still a marginal worker, likely to be laid off when work was slack or to quit a job when he did not like the foreman or his fellow workers. He was learning to live on a combination of unemployment compensation, as long as it lasted, and wages for unsteady work.

It is a question whether Kenny will ever become a steady, responsible worker. Automation may push him out of work, and he does not seem to care much about what happens as long as there is income from one or another government source. He is in danger of becoming permanently unemployed. One cannot see him at 30, or 40, or 50 as maintaining a responsible role as a worker and citizen and provider for his family.

STUDY HELPS

STUDY QUESTIONS

1. How do you expect your responsibilities to change between now and a year from now? Two years from now? Five years from now?

2. What kind of planning do you think might help you to assume your new responsibilities?

CHAPTER NINETEEN
IMPLEMENTING YOUR PLAN FOR SUCCESS

THE NATURE OF WORK TODAY

We live in an age characterized by a high rate of change. Those who retire during this decade have witnessed the greatest technological advances in history. Perhaps one of the best illustrations of change is in the area of air travel. Through the ages, people have been interested in flight, but it was necessary to wait until this century for progress. In 1903 the Wright brothers flew the first ''heavier-than-air'' plane at Kitty Hawk, North Carolina. Charles A. Lindberg made his famous solo flight from New York to Paris in 1927. Commercial airlines started flying across the oceans in the next decade. Interplanetary travel started in 1969 when Neil Armstrong and his crew made the first moon landing. In practically all technical areas we see evidence of amazing changes. Radio, telephone, and television have all been developed for practical use in this century. Color television has been developed in the last few years. The use of nuclear energy has increased considerably since 1950. Computers have revolutionized the business world.

Technology has advanced so far that most of the unskilled jobs are no longer available. Automation is rapidly replacing machine operators in manufacturing. Production has increased greatly with less manpower needed. Business and industry have be-

Automation Is Rapidly Eliminating the Need for Unskilled Workers

come so complex today that workers must be educated if they expect to be employed and must continue learning to advance in their jobs.

Education and training are greatly needed by the work force of today. Young people should take advantage of every possible opportunity to learn the skills and knowledge for their future work.

THE SOCIAL IMPACT OF CHANGE

The rapid change in our work role has an impact on our social role. Perhaps the shock of social change (which accompanies occupational change) has greater impact upon the individual and society in general.

Many will agree that technological change has accelerated at a greater pace than social or cultural change. The imbalance of the two ratios of acceleration is reflected in the general behavior and dissatisfaction of people today.

As mentioned in previous chapters, work is a powerful force in shaping your identity as an individual and as a member of society. Thus, the importance of carefully selecting education or training after completing high school is increased. First, when you select and complete a program of instruction, you are most likely to spend a number of years in that occupation. Second, if the occupation for which you train and work does not provide the satisfaction you desire, it will be necessary to prepare for another occu-

Many People Are Unhappy in Their Work, Although the Economic Returns Are Good

pation or be unhappy in the first one selected. Recent studies provide evidence that many people are unhappy in their work, although the economic returns are good. Work problems carry over from the job into the worker's home life and cause many social problems.

MATCHING PERSONAL CHARACTERISTICS TO JOB REQUIREMENTS

In 1973, about 85 million people were working in about 40 thousand different types of jobs. During the 1970's it is estimated that nearly 34 million young men and women will join the labor force to replace people in existing jobs or to fill new job openings. Making a wise career choice is not only important to the happiness of the young worker but also to the nation's economic, social, and political stability as well. Your career decision can mean the difference between a meaningful occupational experience or an unhappy job-hopping ordeal.

People are different, so it is only natural that they will select different types of jobs. The most important thing is to find the right job for **you.** The matching process of person to job is not easy. First, the availability of jobs may not be sufficient for everyone desiring to do that type of work. Second, the ability, temperament, and interest of the person may limit him or her to certain occupations. Third, the geographical location of the work may not be acceptable to the individual. Fourth, the opportunity to prepare for the occupation of one's choice may not be available because of expenses and limited schools.

However, with 40 thousand different types of jobs, many places to prepare, and a number of professional guidance and counselor personnel to assist a young person, perhaps it will be possible to reduce many of the poor career choices. It is wise to consider several options for training.

1. Education and Earning. The economic and societal values of work have dominated our thoughts of its meaning for generations, since a function of work is to produce and

The Education You Have and the Skills You Learn Are Closely Related to the Money You Will Earn During Your Lifetime

distribute goods and services to serve the people's needs and desires. However, work must also contribute to a person's self-esteem, identity, and sense of order.

The education you have and the skills you use are closely related to the money you will earn during your lifetime. In 1966 it was estimated by the United States Department of Labor that those who quit school at the eighth grade could expect a lifetime earnings of $154,000. High school graduates of 1966 could expect total earnings of $282,000 during their lifetimes, and the expected average earning for college graduates would be $451,000.

Practically all surveys made on lifetime earnings of workers indicate that there is a close relationship between education and earnings. Some say that an individual's lifetime earnings depend more on willingness to work hard and save money for investment. This may be partly true, but education and training will give the individual an advantage over the person who has equal initiative and ability.

2. Education and Job Security. The importance of education and job security cannot be overlooked. The Labor Department Survey, made in 1968, clearly reveals a relationship between the unemployment rate of 18- and 19-year-old men and women and the level of their educational attainments. The survey report indicated that of all the unemployed in the United States in March, 1968, 22 percent were from the 18- to 19-year-old group who had only 5 to 7 years of elementary education. Fourteen percent of the unemployed in this age range had attended high school. Persons who had completed high school had the lowest unemployment and accounted for 8.6 percent of the unemployed.

It was also noted that 40 percent of the male workers were employed in the lowest paid occupations. Workers who failed to finish high school represented a total of 76.8 percent, and the occupations offered little opportunity for advancement.

The jobs for which those without training can qualify are decreasing each year. For example, farm employment has continued to drop since World War II. Three million jobs were lost in agriculture between 1947 and 1962. It appears that job loss will continue among farm workers for several years. Those with little training who have worked in this occupational area are forced to prepare for other employment or be among the unemployed.

The best job security is found in the jobs that require the most education and training. Employment in the professional, technical, and related occupational groups has increased rapidly since 1950. Employment in these areas will continue to increase for some time, especially in the technical areas. Thus, young people who desire employment in these areas must prepare through additional education and training.

WORK OPPORTUNITIES FOR YOUNG PEOPLE

In recent years the United States Department of Labor has provided much information on the labor force. The Bureau of Labor Statistics has organized occupations into categories and collected data on the number of people working in the occupations. The total labor force projected by 1980 was 100.7 million available workers, with 2.7 million members of the labor force in the Armed Forces and 98 million in the civilian work force.

The following information is based on information and statistics furnished by the Department of Labor.

CLERICAL AND RELATED OCCUPATIONS OUTLOOK

1. Opportunities. Clerical occupations offer work for more than 13 million people and the number of jobs is increasing in several areas of the occupation. The work requires all levels of skill and training. Many high school graduates get their first jobs in clerical work. More jobs are reported for secretaries and stenographers than in any other clerical line of work. The information provided by the Bureau of Labor Statistics is reported in the graph below for eleven occupational areas.

2. Training Required. It is possible to qualify for a clerical occupation with a minimum of time and money invested for training. Many high school graduates who take typing, shorthand, bookkeeping and office

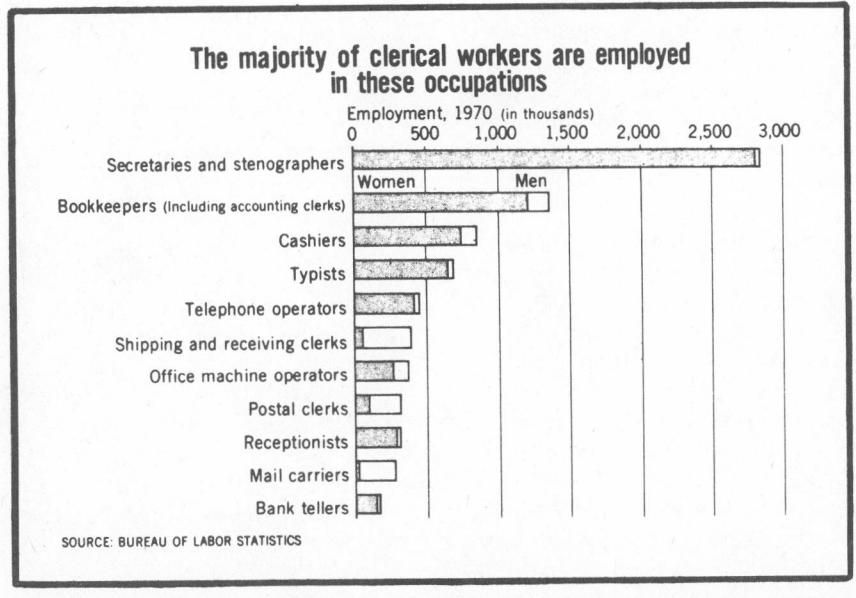

The majority of clerical workers are employed in these occupations

Employment, 1970 (in thousands)

SOURCE: BUREAU OF LABOR STATISTICS

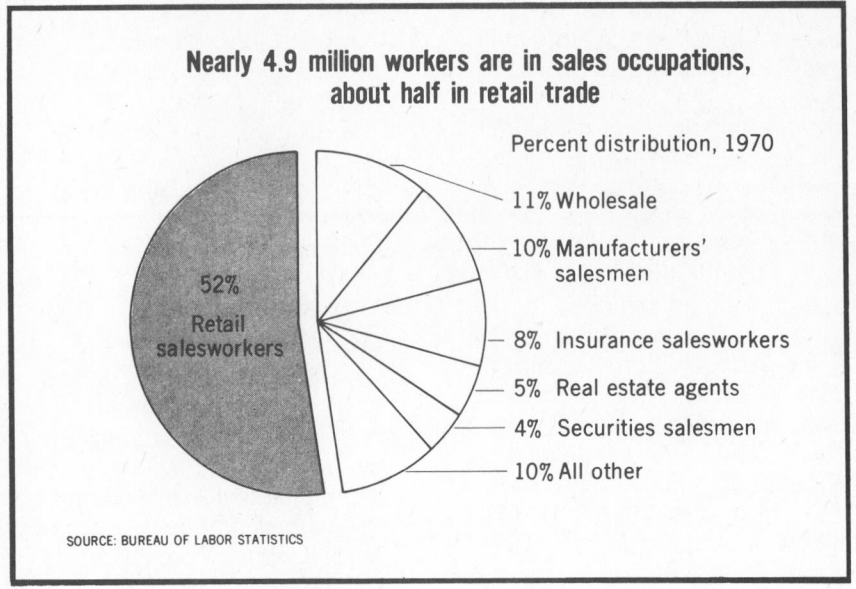

Nearly 4.9 million workers are in sales occupations, about half in retail trade

Percent distribution, 1970

52% Retail salesworkers

11% Wholesale

10% Manufacturers' salesmen

8% Insurance salesworkers

5% Real estate agents

4% Securities salesmen

10% All other

SOURCE: BUREAU OF LABOR STATISTICS

practice enter work upon graduation. Preparation for electronic computing may be done in a vocational school, junior college or four-year college. Many learn by on-the-job training. Practically all the skills needed for clerical work can be learned in evening adult classes.

OPPORTUNITIES IN SALES

1. Outlook. Many opportunities are available for young people in sales. In 1970 about 4.9 million workers were employed in sales with 52 percent employed in retail sales. Sales work provides opportunities for those who wish to work only part time. The percent of jobs in the various areas of sales is reported in the graph above.

2. Training and Qualifications. The education and training one needs to enter sales work varies from a few days of on-the-job training to a college degree. Many sales-personnel need very little training to sell a standard item in the marketplace.

The salesperson who sells products that require the application of engineering or business skills are required to have considerable education at the college level. Many times these sales personnel are ex-

pected to serve as consultants and write specifications for engineering equipment or insurance policies for large industrial firms.

Instruction in both human relations and public speaking is also needed in sales work and may be acquired in evening schools.

SERVICE OCCUPATIONS

1. Outlook. Service occupations such as sales occupations include a wide range of work with about ten million workers employed in the various occupational groups listed in these categories.

The larger numbers of jobs are in the food preparation and the service areas. Nearly two million people are employed in hotels, restaurants, hospitals, rest homes, schools, plant cafeterias, and clubs. Service workers are also employed in building cleaning and servicing. Two million workers held jobs in this area of service work in 1970.

Private household workers are the third largest group of service workers. Those employed in this area of work perform household tasks of cooking, cleaning, serving meals, and other needed household tasks.

More than a million people are employed in health service occupations which include nurse's aides and hospital attendants. A majority of those in this group are employed in hospitals.

Protective service work provides jobs for nearly another million. The majority of these workers are employed by city governments and include occupations of police officers, fire fighters, security guards, and constables. Others in this area are welfare workers, homemaker aides, sheriffs, and lawyers.

Also classified as workers in the service area are personal service workers which include barbers, cosmetologists, and other personal service workers.

2. Training Requirements. The training requirements for service workers vary widely among the various groups. Many in the food preparation service area learn on the job. However, increased attention is being given to training more of these workers. Special schools and programs are available for chefs, cooks, waiters, and waitresses in public and private vocational programs.

Police work may be learned in special junior college programs or in programs operated by large metropolitan police departments. There are also opportunities to learn on the job and in special evening schools. During the last ten years, the Fed-

eral government has been involved in operating special Manpower Development Training Programs for those desiring work in the service occupations.

The graph below is used to show employment in the various areas of the service occupations.

SKILLED AND MANUAL OCCUPATIONS

1. Outlook. Young people who have mechanical ability and who enjoy working with tools and machines will find many opportunities for good jobs in skilled and manual occupations. About 27.8 million people worked in this area in 1970. The blue collar workers, as this group is called, filled about one-third of all jobs in the labor force. The range of jobs includes construction; manufacturing; and servicing, operating, and repairing most of the equipment used today. Hundreds of occupations are listed in this category.

The number of skilled and semiskilled workers is expected to increase during the next ten years, but at a rate of about one-half the growth of the total labor force. However, replacements for the people who retire or change jobs will provide more than

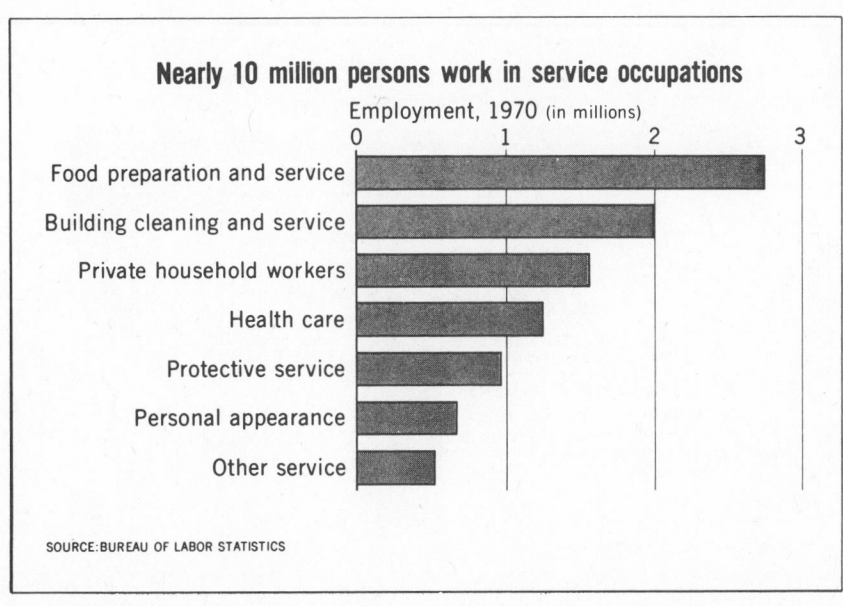

Nearly 10 million persons work in service occupations

Employment, 1970 (in millions)

SOURCE: BUREAU OF LABOR STATISTICS

600,000 job openings each year providing many opportunities for young people entering the labor market.

The percent of distribution of the 10 million workers employed as machinist and supervisors is presented in the first graph below. Mechanics and repair workers comprise the largest group of workers in this category. Construction workers make up the second largest group with about 2.7 million employed.

The statistics presented in the second graph below provide information on the number of persons employed in various skilled occupations in 1970. Persons working in these occupations are employed by

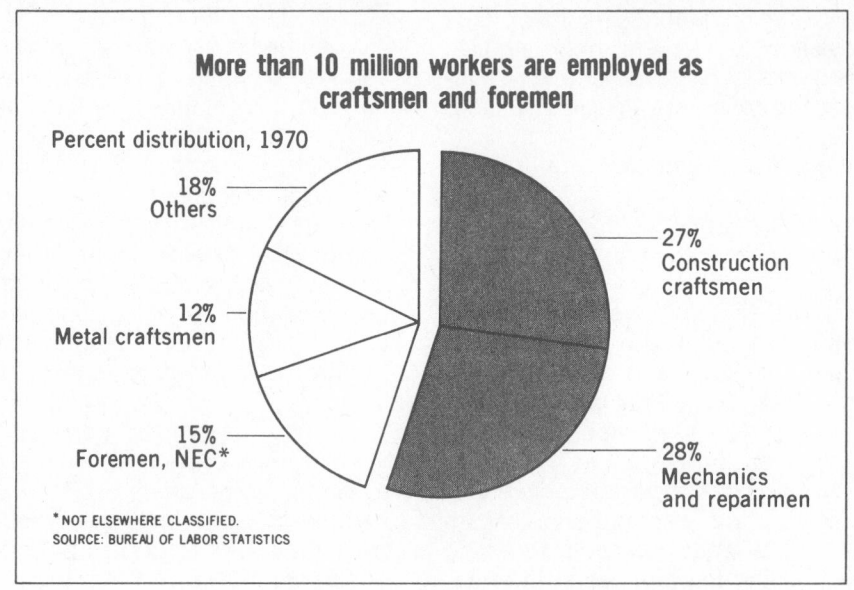

More than 10 million workers are employed as craftsmen and foremen

Percent distribution, 1970

18% Others

12% Metal craftsmen

15% Foremen, NEC*

27% Construction craftsmen

28% Mechanics and repairmen

* NOT ELSEWHERE CLASSIFIED.
SOURCE: BUREAU OF LABOR STATISTICS

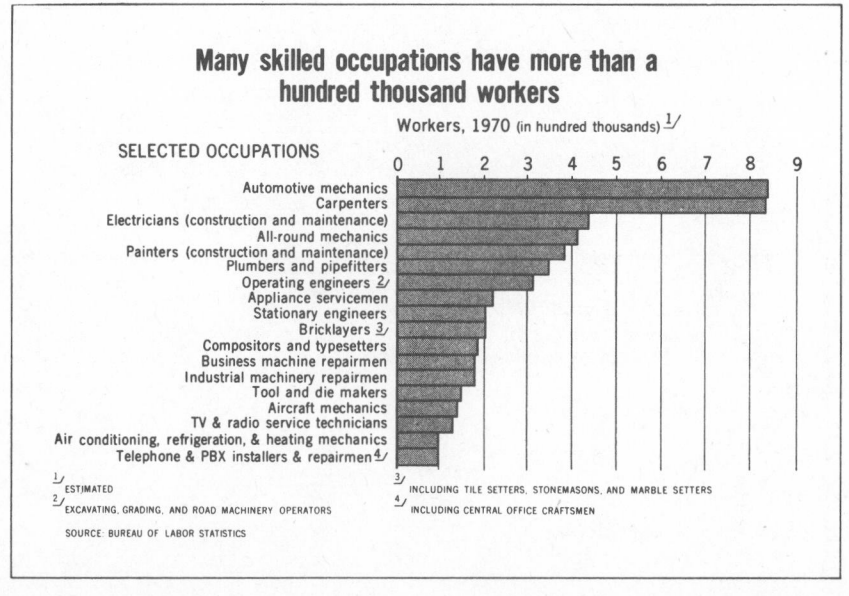

Many skilled occupations have more than a hundred thousand workers

Workers, 1970 (in hundred thousands) [1]

SELECTED OCCUPATIONS

Automotive mechanics
Carpenters
Electricians (construction and maintenance)
All-round mechanics
Painters (construction and maintenance)
Plumbers and pipefitters
Operating engineers [2]
Appliance servicemen
Stationary engineers
Bricklayers [3]
Compositors and typesetters
Business machine repairmen
Industrial machinery repairmen
Tool and die makers
Aircraft mechanics
TV & radio service technicians
Air conditioning, refrigeration, & heating mechanics
Telephone & PBX installers & repairmen [4]

[1] ESTIMATED
[2] EXCAVATING, GRADING, AND ROAD MACHINERY OPERATORS
[3] INCLUDING TILE SETTERS, STONEMASONS, AND MARBLE SETTERS
[4] INCLUDING CENTRAL OFFICE CRAFTSMEN

SOURCE: BUREAU OF LABOR STATISTICS

large corporations, governmental agencies, or small organizations, and many operate their own businesses. Most of the workers are located in industrial states, but some of the jobs are available in all states.

Semiskilled work provides jobs for about 13.9 million people. Or e worker in every six can be classified as a member of this group. The broad field of semiskilled will provide a large number of employment opportunities for young persons in the years ahead. Truck drivers make up the largest single group in the semiskilled area of work. Large numbers of workers operate machines in industry and assemble manufactured products.

2. Training and Qualifications Needed. Persons qualified to do skilled work must have a thorough knowledge of the processes involved in their work. Skilled trade workers must know how to interpret the plans of engineers and architects in the construction of buildings, bridges, roads, factories, and machines. The best way to learn most of the skilled trades is through a good apprenticeship program. However, many people learn the occupation by attending vocational-technical schools or by on-the-job training provided by many large companies. Preparation for the semiskilled operative jobs may require a two-year specialized training program. Opportunities are available for training, but it may take considerable effort to find the type of training program desired. A good high school preparation is very helpful in most of the skilled and semiskilled occupations. Many young persons have gone directly from a high school vocational program into a skilled or semiskilled job.

PROFESSIONAL AND RELATED OCCUPATIONS

1. Opportunities. Professional occupations are classified in two major types. The largest group includes occupations requiring graduation from college and specialized study. Such professional occupations include architects, engineers, physicians, dentists, teachers, and lawyers. The second group includes artists and athletes — a high level of skill and creative ability is needed to qualify for these positions. Academic preparation in higher education is useful but not necessary to be employed.

Professional occupations offer many opportunities for interesting and responsible

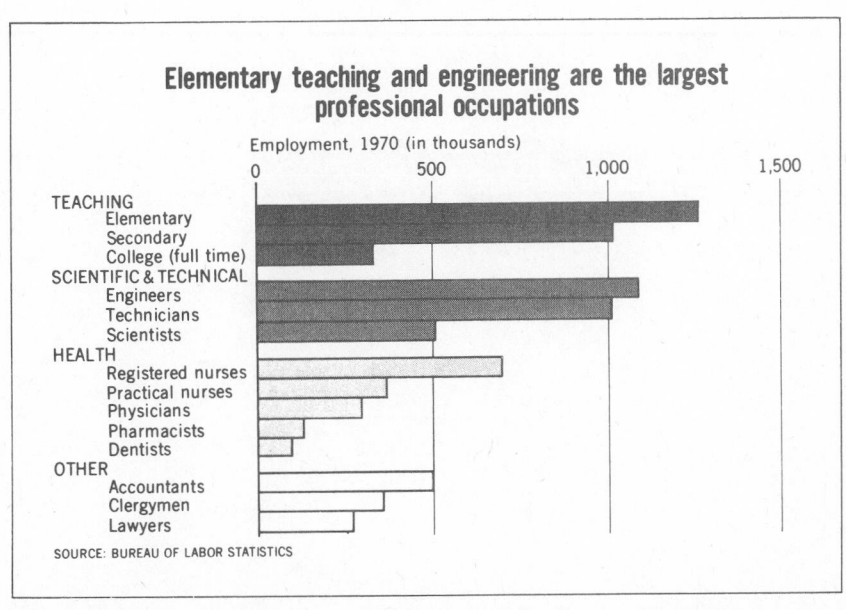

Elementary teaching and engineering are the largest professional occupations

Employment, 1970 (in thousands)

SOURCE: BUREAU OF LABOR STATISTICS

work. Some provide high earnings after a few years of experience. In 1970 about 11.1 million people were employed in all professional occupations — this is about one out of every seven persons in the labor force.

The rate of employment increase was higher in the professional and related occupations than in any other occupational classification during the decade of the 60's. Some areas in the professional and related occupations are predicted to have continued growth during the 70's. The demand for elementary and secondary public school teachers will not be as great as in the 60's. The number of students entering school is not increasing at as high a rate, and the shortage of money in public schools has caused some reduction in the number of teachers for special activities.

The rapid increase in engineering jobs has also levelled since the space program has been cut back. Employment for persons holding advanced degrees in some areas of physical and social science has also levelled. In 1973, there was an indication that supply had caught up with demand for many professional occupations requiring the Ph.D. degree.

The growth in need for health services is expected to continue for several years. More doctors and nurses will be needed for new job requirements as well as for replacements.

The largest professional and related occupational areas are shown in the graph on page 281.

2. Educational Requirement for Professional Work. Professional occupations attract many young persons each year. To enter the professions, it is necessary to compete with many talented individuals, and the educational requirements are quite high. For example, the educational requirement for architects is generally five or six years of college work in a prescribed curriculum and three years of professional work experience followed by a competitive examination which must be passed to get a license. Most engineering curriculums require at least four years of college. To enter a professional school in medicine, dentistry, or veterinary medicine, one must complete a baccalaureate degree and three or four years in a specialized area of study. The trend seems to be to increase the college work for preparation.

In the related professional occupations of management, it is possible to be em-

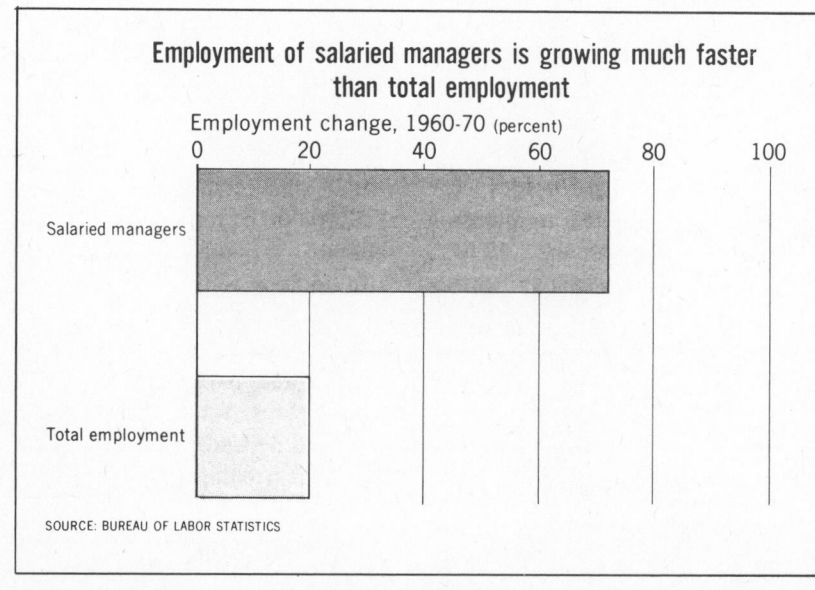

Employment of salaried managers is growing much faster than total employment

Employment change, 1960-70 (percent)

Salaried managers

Total employment

SOURCE: BUREAU OF LABOR STATISTICS

ployed after years of work in the supporting areas. However, employers increasingly require beginning managers to have completed college. College degrees in business administration, technology, and some of the social sciences are good for management. This area of employment is expected to continue in its growth rate. The graph on page 282 is used to describe employment in the managerial occupations.

PREPARATION FOR WORK

Most jobs available to young men and women require some specialized training. The training needed may vary from a few days on the job to several years of college preparation. In deciding what career you wish to make your life work, you must carefully evaluate your own interests and abilities and match them with job data available,

Preparation for Skilled or Technical Jobs in Printing Includes Completion of an Apprenticeship or a Program in a Vocational School or College

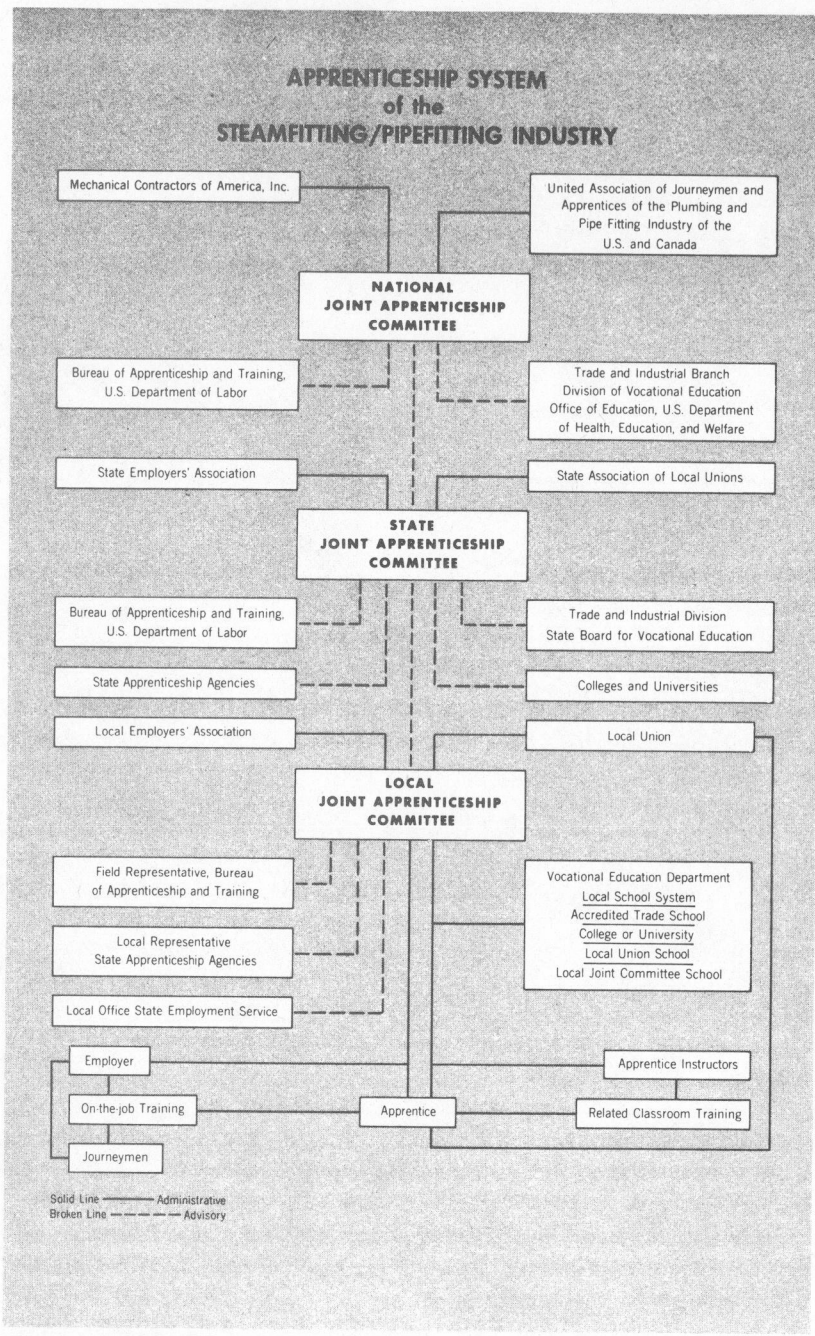

Industry and Labor Work Together to Form Apprenticeship Standards in the Crafts and Trades

Certificate of Completion of Apprenticeship

United States Department of Labor

Bureau of Apprenticeship and Training

This is to certify that

has completed an apprenticeship in the trade of

under sponsorship of

in accordance with the standards recommended by the

Federal Committee on Apprenticeship

PRESENTED

Certificate of Completion of Apprenticeship

training required, and training opportunities.

There are many opportunities in the world of work today. Of course, it is wise to remain in high school and graduate if possible. Your efforts in high school studies will provide you with a background needed for further preparation and open the door to many training programs. However, if it isn't possible for you to remain in high school, there are many opportunities available to learn on the job.

APPRENTICESHIP

High school graduation is preferred but not essential to enter many of the occupations that may be learned through on-the-job training or apprenticeship. In fact, many skilled trade workers learned their trades through an apprenticeship.

Apprenticeship has many important advantages for young people starting out in the world of work. It offers an efficient way to learn skills and job-related information in an organized program. It also makes it possible to earn as you learn with no great investment of money required for tuition and fees. Upon completion of an agreed number of hours of work experience (6,000 to 8,000 in most of the construction crafts) and attending 144 hours of formal instruction each year, the apprentice is advanced to a union classification called journeyman. A journeyman classification in a union pays well. Journeymen can work in almost any geographical area chosen.

The apprenticeship program is offered cooperatively between the employer, the employee (apprentice), and an apprenticeship committee. The Bureau of Apprenticeship and Training is responsible for supervision and registration. About 350 occupations may be learned through apprenticeship training. Almost 300,000 people were

APPRENTICESHIP APPLICATION FORM

Application for .... apprentice

(Trade)

Under the .... Apprenticeship Standards

Name .... Date ....

Address .... Telephone ....

(Street)   (City)

Age ...... Date of Birth ...... Single? ...... Married? ...... Number of Dependents ......

Indicate by   G.I.   Re-hab.   Non-   Length and Branch of

(x) whether: Veteran ..... Veteran ..... Veteran ..... Military Service ......

EDUCATIONAL HISTORY:

No. years in Grammar School? .... No. years in High School? ....

College .... Years .... Major Courses ....

(Name)

Other training ....

WORK HISTORY: (List latest employment first, include trade experience in armed forces)

1. Employer .... Address ....
   From .... To .... Duties ....

2. Employer .... Address ....
   From .... To .... Duties ....

3. Employer .... Address ....
   From .... To .... Duties ....

I believe that my past work experience should entitle me to credit on my term of apprenticeship. (If credit is requested, attach detailed statement on a separate sheet giving reasons for this claim)

Have you read the Apprenticeship Standards for this trade? .... If a minor, have your parents or guardians read these Standards? ....

If accepted and indentured, will you willingly carry out your part of the agreement? .... If a veteran, do you have your Certificate of Eligibility? ....

Reason for choosing this trade ....

....

REFERENCES: (Not to include relatives)

Name .... Address ....

Name .... Address ....

Name .... Address ....

Social Security No. .... Signature of Applicant ....

APPRENTICESHIP AGREEMENT
Between Apprentice and Employer

The employer and apprentice whose signatures appear below agree to these terms of apprenticeship:

The employer agrees to the nondiscriminatory selection and training of apprentices in accordance with the Equal Opportunity Standards stated in Section 30.3 of Title 29, Code of Federal Regulations, Part 30; and in accordance with the terms and

conditions of the .... which are
(Name of Apprenticeship Standards)
made a part of this agreement.

The apprentice agrees to apply himself diligently and faithfully to learning the trade in accordance with this agreement.

Trade .... Term of apprenticeship ....
(Hours or Years)

Probationary period .... Credit for previous experience ....

Term remaining .... Date the apprenticeship begins ....

This agreement may be terminated by mutual consent of the parties, citing cause(s), with notification to the Registration Agency.

....
(Name of Apprentice–Type or Print)

....
(Signature of Apprentice)

....
(Address)

....
(Parent or Guardian)

....
(Name of Employer-Company)

....
(Address)

....
(Signature of Authorized Official)

TO BE COMPLETED BY THE APPRENTICE:

Date of birth ....
Month   Day   Year

Check: Male ...... Female ......

If you consider yourself a member of one of the ethnic groups listed, please check:

Negro ....

Oriental ....

American Indian ....

Spanish American ....

Approved by ...., Apprenticeship Committee.

Date .... by ....
(Signature of Chairman or Secretary)

Registered by ....
(Name of Registration Agency)

Date .... by ....
(Signature of Authorized Official)

working as apprentices in 1973, and interest in apprenticeship is increasing.

Young men and women who are interested in apprenticeships should consult their high school counselor or the State Department of Labor. To apply, one must be between 16 and 28 years of age. The recruitment, selection, employment, and training of apprenticeship is to be made under guidelines of the Equal Opportunity Act, and all applicants receive equal opportunity to qualify.

Any person interested in apprenticeship should complete an application form and submit it to the Apprenticeship Committee in his or her district. The apprentice signs an agreement to follow apprenticeship rules and regulations. The apprentice's wage scale is based on the journeyman's rate and is developed on the number of hours worked.

ON-THE-JOB TRAINING

Many companies offer young people on-the-job training. The length of time for training varies from a few days to two or three years. The starting pay for on-the-job training is low, but it is gradually increased. Some industries offer in-plant training programs which include formal classroom instruction. Other companies depend upon schools and colleges to assist with the instruction.

To find the type of on-the-job training employment desired, apply to the Area Job Opportunity Center of the State Employment Security Division or directly to company personnel offices or private employment agencies.

VOCATIONAL SCHOOLS

Following the enactment of the Vocational Education Act of 1963, the local, state, and federal agencies have cooperated in establishing a system of area vocational-technical schools. These schools, in most states, offer a broad program for high school and post-high school students in addition to evening courses for adults.

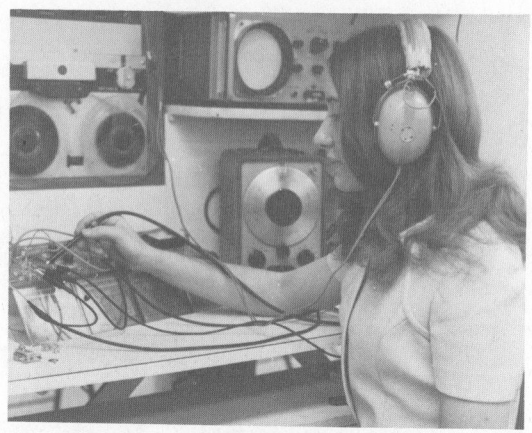

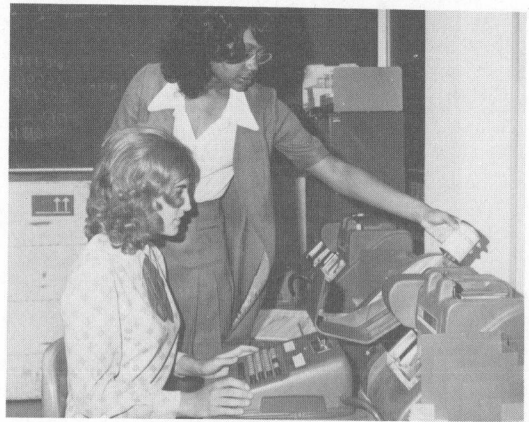

Many Opportunities Are Available to People in the Technical Areas

Vocational-technical schools have a two-fold purpose. First, programs are offered to help meet the manpower needs of the communities by providing skilled persons to take the available jobs; secondly, they provide students with opportunities to learn salable skills which will prepare them for employment in many varied skilled occupations.

These schools are quite inexpensive for qualified applicants. Some schools charge as little as $16 per year for basic fees. Class fees for tools and materials depend upon the course, but such fees are modest for most schools. Instruction is very broad and students may prepare themselves in the occupational areas of business, health, industrial-technical, and agriculture-related occupations. Instruction in over forty industrial occupations may be available in the larger schools.

High school students interested in employment immediately after graduation can profit from vocational education. Many students use the skills learned in high school vocational courses to finance advanced instruction in college. The vocational skills learned in high school may also be useful in obtaining military ratings or apprenticeship credit. The low cost of instruction may be very important to many students, and all high school students should have a knowledge of what vocational education opportunities are available in their communities.

COMMUNITY JUNIOR COLLEGE

In the last few years, the enrollment in community junior colleges has increased and the curriculum expanded to offer more vocational, technical, and adult education. Traditionally, the junior college was organized to offer only transfer credit to a four-year college or university program. In 1973, there were more than 1,100 community two-year colleges operating in the United States with an enrollment of 2½ million students. Many community colleges offer extensive evening adult programs. It is possible to learn a new occupation at night school in a number of the junior colleges located in the larger cities.

The two-year community colleges offer opportunities to young people who would not attend college otherwise. One advantage of attending the community college is that a student may live at home and earn the first two years of college at a greatly reduced cost. The adjustment from high school to a local community college may also be easier than adjusting to a large university.

Many academic fields of study are offered in the community junior colleges as well as the two-year technical programs. The community colleges offer instruction in more than 60 occupations in agriculture, trades

and industry, machinists, drafting artists, mechanic, restaurant, business, health, home economics, industry, and service occupations.

It has been estimated that 50 percent of our future manpower will be given instruction on the post-high school level in area vocational schools and community colleges. In many areas, a community junior college or an area vocational-technical school is within commuting distance of persons who desire additional instruction.

FOUR-YEAR COLLEGES AND UNIVERSITIES

Young men and women who plan to enter professional work are generally expected to prepare in a college or university. Over 2,000 colleges and universities offer professional and highly technical training for those qualified after high school graduation. About 22 percent of the young people graduating from high school earned a bachelor degree from a college in 1973. This percent is about equal to the percent of the labor force working in professional and technical occupations.

Many professional occupations require at least four years of college. A few require six to eight years of college preparation for entry. A number of professions may be entered without a college degree, but related experience and education are required to enter work.

Planning a college education should be started while you are in high school, and all aspects of planning should be completed before actually enrolling in college. Public institutions of higher learning have been organized in each state. However, each state follows an individual plan with individual requirements. Generally, the more expensive programs, such as medicine and law are offered in the state university, while the less expensive and less lengthy programs are offered in state colleges.

In selecting a college or university, it is wise to make a study of those offering the program you desire. A comparison of the costs, convenience, reputation, and entry

If You Wish to Prepare for a Profession, You Should Begin Planning Your College Education While You Are Still in High School

requirements would be useful. In many of the areas of study, the institution can accept a limited number of students each year; thus, it is wise to make application at several institutions.

Colleges and universities publish catalogs which give most of the information you need. Additional information may be obtained by writing to the college or university.

Estimating the cost of college training is important — especially if you are on a close budget. Costs vary from school to school. Private colleges are usually more expensive. Public universities charge higher fees than state colleges. In 1973, estimated cost of attending college varied from $1500 to several thousand dollars a year. If you live at home while attending college, you will save several hundred dollars each year.

Financial aid is available to deserving students. Both private and public schools offer scholarships and fellowships to a num-

ber of students each year. Students who hope to qualify for financial awards should apply early. Students may borrow money for their educational expenses. National Defense Student Loans have been available for several years. Students may borrow up to $5,000 in a four-year period and repay the money after finishing college. Most students work to pay part of their educational expenses. Some students work enough to pay all of their expenses. However, it may take an additional year or two to finish a four-year program. Recent research indicates that students' grades are not drastically affected when they work part time while attending college.

Many students who start to college do not finish. Latest statistics indicate that only one-half of those attending earn a degree. It is therefore important to carefully plan for college before enrollment. Students, parents, and guidance counselors should work

The Construction Industry Provides Many Jobs for Skilled Trade Workers, Architects, Engineers, Supervisors, and Managers

together in answering the question, "Should I go to college?" A few questions you should answer:

1. Do I really want to make the sacrifice of time, effort, and money to complete a college degree?
2. Do I have the ability to master the knowledge and skill involved to per-

form effectively after graduation?
3. Am I really interested in the work for which I am preparing?
4. Can my parents afford to pay for my college education?

Perhaps many other questions concerning a college education should be asked. College study is rigorous and success requires interest, maturity, and self-discipline.

The interest in higher education is expected to continue through 1980 with a projection of over one million bachelor degrees earned per year by 1980. The graph below is used to describe the growth in the number of college graduates by year between 1960 and 1970 with estimated number for 1980.

ADULT EDUCATION

College education is not the only road to a successful career. One avenue for success is through adult or continuing education. This route takes longer, but the satisfaction may be greater. More attention is being given to informal adult education today. Most city high schools offer evening courses in business and industrial subjects. Private schools offer evening programs for those

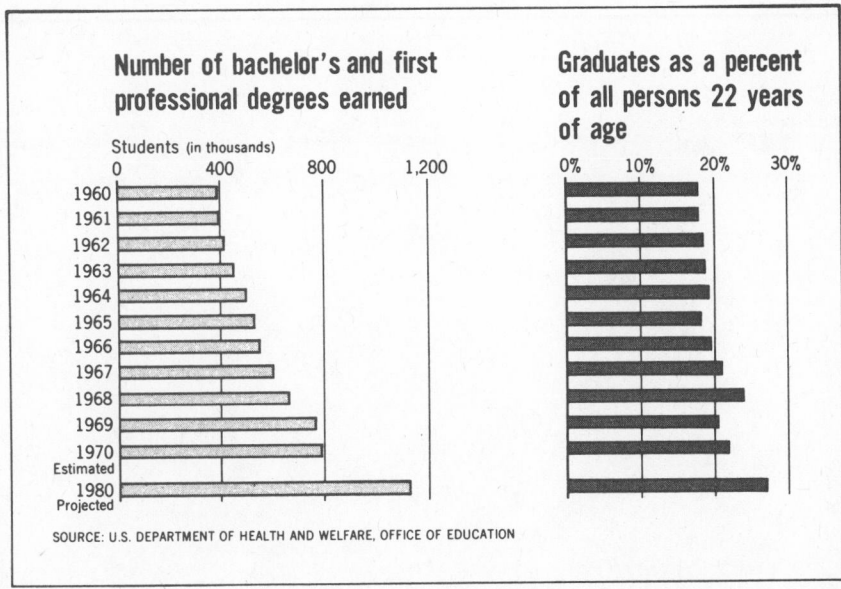

SOURCE: U.S. DEPARTMENT OF HEALTH AND WELFARE, OFFICE OF EDUCATION

who work during the day. Correspondence courses are offered in many subjects. Those interested in learning have numerous opportunities.

Many have developed into successful professionals through adult education. The adult who has been self-reliant for a number of years approaches educational opportunities realistically and with a determination to succeed.

MILITARY TRAINING

Education and training offered by the military services have provided many opportunities for young men and women during the last thirty years. Many of the skills learned in the Air Force, Army, Navy, and Marine Corps have civilian application. Much of the training would have been very expensive to acquire in civilian life.

Military personnel operate and maintain some of the most complicated equipment available in communications and transportation. Many former military pilots and maintenance personnel learned their work using the most modern airplanes, computers, and electronic equipment. Industry has employed many of those completing military service.

There are many advantages for young men and women in military service. The pay is good and opportunity for travel is excellent. Additional education is available. Those who elect to make the military service a career can expect a good retirement at the end of twenty or thirty years.

To enlist in the service, one should have a high school education and courses related to the military occupational specialty. A good background in high school science or business may be helpful.

Young men and women interested in becoming commissioned officers in one of the branches of the military service may take advantage of the Reserve Officer Training Corps program (ROTC) by making this program a part of their baccalaureate degree curriculums. Many colleges and universities offer military science which leads to a commission upon graduation. Students admitted to the military science program take required courses and receive compensation during advanced training.

Those who have specialized college training needed by the military service may qualify for a direct commission. Information may be obtained at a local recruiting office.

The Air Force. For young men on the way up.

QUALIFICATIONS

- Be at least 17 and not over 27 years old. (Under 18 requires consent of your parents.)
- Pass the aptitude test.
- Meet required physical standards.

Women Officers in the United States Air Force

HERE'S WHAT IT TAKES

- Be a U. S. Citizen
- Have a baccalaureate degree
- Meet specific physical and mental requirements
- Be between 20½ and 29½ years of age

The Military Offers Many Opportunities for Education and Travel

HELP OTHERS. HELP YOURSELF. IN THE COAST GUARD.

WHO CAN JOIN?

You can if you're between 17 and 26 and a U.S. citizen (or have filed a declaration of intent to become one). You can even have two dependents.

All we ask is that you meet certain physical standards, be of good moral character and pass the Armed Forces Qualification Test.

For more details— without obligation—contact your Coast Guard recruiter.

Government Careers Offer Training and Challenging Experiences for Many Young Men and Women

DON'T FOOL WITH YOUR FUTURE...
PLAN IT ... WITH THE MARINES.

AVIATION TECHNOLOGY

UNIVAC 1500 Operator/Programmer
UNIVAC 1500 Systems Technician
Aviation Support Equipment Technician
Aircraft Ordnance Man
Avionics Technician
Aviation Electrician
Air Controlman
Airborne Radio Operator
Aerial Navigator
Aerographer (Weatherman)

AIRCRAFT
MAINTENANCE/ORDNANCE

Aviation Machinist (Jet Engines)
Aviation Machinist (Reciprocating
  Engines)
Aviation Structural Mechanic
  (Safety Equipment)
Aviation Structural Mechanic
  (Hydraulics)
Aviation Structural Mechanic
  (Structurals)
Aviation Support Equipment Man
  (Mechanical)
Aviation Support Equipment Man
  (Hydraulics)
Aircrew Survival Equipment Man
Cyrogenics Equipment Technician
Basic Helicopter Man
Aviation Munitions Man
Aircraft Ordnance Technician

AVIATION ADMINISTRATION

Aviation Supply Man
Aviation Maintenance Administrative
  Man
Aviation Operations Clerical Man
Aviation Crash Crewman
Aircraft Launch and Recovery
  Equipment Man

MILITARY POLICE

Military Policeman
Corrections Specialist

ELECTRICAL, MECHANICAL

Plumber and Water Supply Man
Electrician
Electrical Equipment Man
Refrigeration Mechanic
Metal Worker
Engineer Equipment Mechanic
Engineer Equipment Operator
Small Arms Repairman
Artillery Repairman
Tracked Vehicle Repairman
Machinist
Fire Control Instrument Repairman
Ammunition Storage Man
Field Wireman
Office Machine Repairman
Metal Body Repairman
Automotive Maintenance Man
Motor Vehicle Operator

COMMUNICATIONS

Field Radio Operator
Communications Technicians

ELECTRONICS

Electronics Man
Field Communications Repairman

FOOD SERVICES

Baker
Food Services Man

COMPUTER OPERATOR

Systems 360 Technician
Systems 360 Disk Technician
Operations Man
Programmer

COMBAT AND COMBAT ARMS

Infantryman
Field Artillery Batteryman
Field Artillery Scout
Short Party Fire Control Man
Tank Crewman
Field Artillery Fire Control Man
Counter Battery/Mortar Control Man
Artillery Ballistics Meteorology Man
Combat Engineer
Bulk Fuel Man
Amphibian Vehicle Crewman
Air Control/Anti-Air Warfare Man
Redeye Gunner/Operator
Hawk Missile Fire Control Crewman

ADMINISTRATIVE

Basic Clerical Man
Postal Clerk
Intelligence Man
Communications Center Man
Card Punch Operator
Electric Accounting Machine Operator
Legal Clerk/Court. Reporter

SUPPLY, LOGISTICS, DISBURSING

Embarkation Man
Logistics Man
Supply Man
Warehouseman
Subsistence Supply Man
Procurement Supply Man
Freight Operations Man
Freight Transportation Clerk
Passenger Transportation Clerk
Disbursing Man

Skills Learned in the Military Can Be Used in Civilian Life

PLANNING FOR YOUR SUCCESS
IN THE WORLD OF WORK

Some people are surprised to learn that many people are employed in their jobs by chance rather than as the result of careful planning. Some small and seemingly insignificant event sent the person in one career direction. The person may have been in the right place at the right time to get the job. Often little planning was done before receiving training or before taking the job. In many situations, the events made success possible. However, for some, the right chance or that good opportunity never came, and these people lead a life of frustration and disappointment.

There is no substitute for planning, whether it is in business, industry, or **life.** Thus, it is very important for young persons to study the possible results of alternatives they may find available. Good planning does not **ensure** succeeding in the world of work, but it increases the options that may be available. Implementing your **plan for success** in your work and in life should start early and be continuously reviewed as you grow older.

The Navy's New Career Training Programs

The New Vocational School Graduate Enlistment Program

The skills required for many Navy jobs are comparable with related civilian occupational skills. Consequently, many civilian high school and post high school vocational and technical schools offer courses that are comparable with the training provided in Navy Class "A" schools.

Qualified men and women who have satisfactorily completed acceptable civilian courses of instruction, either during high school or in post high school institutions, may be eligible to enlist in the Vocational School Graduate Enlistment Program.

Men and women who have completed a minimum of 1000 hours or one year of formal vocational training may be eligible to be enlisted in pay grade E-2. Those who have completed a minimum of 2000 hours or 2 years of vocational training may be eligible to be enlisted in pay grade E-3.

Men and women enlisted in this program will be termed what the Navy calls "strikers"—that is, apprentices working in the Navy rating which is the most compatible with their civilian training and background.

Young Men and Women Graduates of Vocational-Technical Schools May Be Eligible for Advanced Ratings in a Military Career

STUDY AIDS

NEW TERMS

ability tests
apprenticeship
committee
aptitudes

automation
job opportunity center
labor projections
lifetime earnings

STUDY QUESTIONS

1. What are some of the technological changes that have caused occupational changes? How have these changes affected your preparation for work?
2. Based on the lifetime earnings estimated by the United States Department of Labor, how much more money will a college graduate earn than a high school graduate?
3. In 1973, approximately how many people were employed in the United States? How many different types of jobs were represented?
4. What are some of the problems in matching the worker and the job?
5. What is the employment outlook in the clerical occupations?
6. What percent of the labor force engaged in sales work was involved in retail sales in 1970?
7. What types of jobs are included in the service occupations?
8. In 1970, how many persons were employed in the skilled and manual occupations? What is the outlook for skilled trade workers and supervisors?
9. What is the procedure in making application for apprenticeship?
10. How many hours of skill work and related instruction are needed for an apprentice to reach journeyman status?
11. What are the factors to be considered in making the decision to attend or not to attend college?
12. What are the opportunities and advantages of military service?

DISCUSSION PROBLEMS

1. Suppose your best friend wants to quit school at the end of the 10th grade. Think of as many reasons as you can to persuade your friend that staying in school is the better thing to do.
2. At the present time, what occupation do you plan to enter? What influenced you to select this occupation? Why do you think you will be successful in this job? Is it the only occupation which interests you?
3. Study the graphs used by the United States Labor Department to describe employment opportunities. What occupations appear to offer the best chances for challenging employment?

APPENDIX ONE
PARLIAMENTARY PROCEDURE

I. THE NEED FOR PARLIAMENTARY PROCEDURE

Members of a democratic society need a set of rules to obtain group concensus in solving problems and making decisions. To arrive at decisions, a group of people must have a leader skilled in rules of discussion and debate. The parliamentary procedure is a logical method of working with groups and has been used for this purpose for many years. The English Parliament used the procedure to conduct its business. This became known as parliamentary law. Many modifications have been made to fit the needs of different groups. However, the purpose is still the same — to carry on orderly group meetings conducted on the basis of democratic principles.

A. DEMOCRATIC PRINCIPLES

Parliamentary procedure is based upon a number of democratic principles which are as follows:

1. Debate of the group must be fair to all present.
2. All entitled members of the group are free to debate under the rules established.
3. The majority has the right to decide the issues.
4. The minority is also guaranteed the right to express its opinion with protection from the majority provided through parliamentary law.
5. The minority members are expected to abide with the decision when made by the majority.

B. PARLIAMENTARY TERMS

In order to participate in groups using parliamentary procedure, members need to learn the terms used. When persons participating know the terms and the rules, the organization can move ahead with efficiency.

1. **The chair:** Means the office or dignity of one who presides. A President, Chairman, Speaker, Moderator, etc.
2. **The House:** The members, group or body assembled.
3. **The Meetings:** A gathering of members.
4. **A Quorum:** The number of entitled members who must be present to legally transact business and make decisions.
5. **Minutes:** The official record of the proceedings of an organization.
6. **Proxy:** A signed statement by a member authorizing another member to vote in his absence.
7. **Pro tem:** Acting during the absence of another officer.
8. **Pro and Con:** Means for or against a motion or rule.

C. OTHER TERMS USED IN PARLIAMENTARY PROCEDURE

1. **The Motion:** Is a proposal by a member of the house that certain action be taken by the organization.
2. **Second the Motion:** Is stated when a second member of the house approved the motion.
3. **Amending a Motion:** To change the first motion.
4. **The Question:** Means for the presiding officer to call for a vote by the members.
5. **New Business:** Business brought before the house for the first time.
6. **Unfinished Business:** Old business brought before the house for the second or more times.
7. **Table the Question:** To delay decision on the motion.
8. **To Adjourn:** To officially close the meeting by a majority vote of those present.

II. CONDUCTING A BUSINESS MEETING

It is not the purpose of this guide to give the rules of parliamentary procedure in detail. Persons who are elected to office, or who serve as the group's parliamentarian, should study Rules of Order by H. M. Robert, published by Scott, Foresman and Company, Glenview, Illinois.

A. STEPS IN HOLDING A MEETING

No business can legally be transacted at a meeting of any organization unless a quorum is present. Usually a quorum is a majority of members. However, it may be a number fixed by the rules of the organization.

When a quorum is present the usual conduct of the meeting is as follows:

1. The presiding officer takes the chair and calls the meeting to order.
2. He or she presents the order of business as prescribed by the rules of the organization. If the organization has not adopted an order of business, it may follow a play similar to the one described in B, conducting a meeting.

B. CONDUCTING A TYPICAL CLUB MEETING

Many high school organizations have adopted national order of business with ceremonies for meeting. The Future Farmers, Future Homemakers, Distributive Education Clubs, and the Vocational Industrial Clubs of America have adopted general procedures for their meetings.

The meeting described here will be typical of many organizations.

1. President: takes the chair, rises, raps the gavel on wood block and calls, "Meeting will come to order."
2. President: "Bill Smith will lead us in the pledge of allegiance to the Flag."
3. President: "Carol Wallis will lead us in singing America."
4. President: "Marie Smith, the secretary, will read the minutes of the previous meeting."
5. President: "Are there corrections to the minutes?" If no corrections are made from the house, the president says, "The minutes are approved as read." If corrections are necessary, the president will ask the secretary to correct the report and say, "Are there any other corrections?" "The minutes stand approved as corrected."
6. President: "The next order of business is the reports of other officers." (May include corresponding secretary, treasurer's report, and other officer reports).
7. President: "The next order of business is the reports of standing committees."
   a. Report of the membership committee
   b. Report of the finance committee
   c. Report of the program committee
   d. Report of other committees
8. President: "The next order of business

is reports from the special committees.''

    a. Report of the picnic committee

    b. Report of other committees

9. President: ''Is there any unfinished business to act upon today?'' (If no unfinished business, the next order of business is new business.)

10. President: ''Is there any new business to be considered today?'' (Under new business a number of actions are considered, such as communications, presenting of bills for payment, future plans, settings dates for other activities, etc.)

11. President: ''The program committee will now present the program.'' (The president presents the program chairman who introduces the speaker or whoever presents the program. When the program is concluded, the program chairman returns the meeting to the chair after thanking the participants.)

12. President: ''Is there future business or any announcement to come before the meeting?'' (After announcement, etc., the president may ask for a motion to adjourn. After a motion, a second to the motion, and a majority voting in favor of adjournment.) President: The meeting is adjourned.''

III. CLASSIFICATION OF MOTIONS

Motions are classified as to their importance. The rank of importance is called the order of precedence. For the purpose of this guide in parliamentary procedure, main motions and secondary motions will be considered.

A main motion is used to introduce a proposal for action by the organization while a secondary motion may be made while the main motion is pending. Only one main motion may be before the organization at one time. Secondary motions made while the main motion is pending must be disposed of before voting on the main motion.

A. STEPS IN MAKING A MOTION

1. Any member who desires to make a motion to introduce an item of business should rise and request recognition from the chair (presiding officer). The proper address is call out, ''Mr. President,'' ''Madam President,'' ''Mr. Chairman,'' etc. When the chair has recognized the member by name, the member may present his or her motion to the organization. A main motion must have a second. After the second is made the motion may be debated. The final vote is taken after the discussion is ended. A majority rules. A simple majority is one more than one half of the members present.

    a. Example in Using a Main Motion.

    John Smith: (Rising) ''Mr. President.''

    President: ''Mr. Smith.''

    John Smith: ''I move that the club purchase a new ceremonial emblem before the state contest in April.''

    Carol Wallis: ''I second the motion.''

    President: ''It is moved by John Smith and seconded that the club purchase a new ceremonial emblem before the state contest.''

    Members: Discussion.

    President: ''Is there further discussion? (a pause) Are you ready for the question?'' Unless there is a response the president continues. ''All in favor of the motion say Aye.'' ''Those opposed say No.'' ''The ayes have it.'' The motion to purchase a new ceremonial emblem before the state contest has passed.

    b. Amending a Motion

    Many times it is desirable to amend a main motion to make improvements or to make passage of the main motion possible. Suppose for example that Joan Adams thinks new ceremonial flags should also be purchased. To amend the pending motion she followed the following procedure:

Joan Adams: "Mr. President."

President: "Miss Adams."

Joan Adams: "I move to substitute for the pending motion that we purchase ceremonial flags and ceremonial emblem before the state contest in April."

Mike Taylor: "I second it."

Members: Discussion.

President: "It has been moved by Miss Adams and seconded to amend the pending motion by adding ceremonial flags to the motion to purchase a ceremonial emblem." "Are you ready for the question?" "All who are in favor of amending the main motion say Aye." All opposed to amending the main motion say No." "The ayes have it, the amendment to the motion carried." "Are there other amendments?" (pause) "If there are no other amendments the question on the main motion is before the assembly." "All in favor of the motion say Aye." "All opposed say No." "The ayes have it." "Motion carried."

c. Table a Motion

When the main motion is pending, it may be necessary to make a secondary motion to delay or postpone action on the pending motion until a more favorable time.

An example of using the secondary motion is to lay a question on the table. This can be illustrated by going back to the main motion after it was amended again. Suppose the treasurer of the club was concerned about the purchase of a ceremonial flag and ceremonial emblem since adequate money was not available at the time of the meeting but would probably be before the next meeting a month later.

Bill Brown: "Mr. President."

President: "Mr. Brown."

Bill Brown: "I move that the pending motion to purchase a ceremonial emblem be tabled until next meeting in order to better know our financial situation."

Roy Hays "I second it."

President: "It has been moved and seconded to table the motion to purchase a ceremonial emblem before the state contest next April." "The motion is undebatable, unamendable, and requires a majority vote of members present." "Those in favor of the motion say Aye." "Those opposed say No." "The ayes have it, and the motion for the club to purchase a new ceremonial emblem before the state contest in April is tabled."

To lay a question on the table is one of seven motions called subsidiary motions, which should all be learned and practiced by club members.

IV. ELECTION OF OFFICERS

The democratic process requires that persons in leadership positions be nominated and elected to the position by their fellow club members.

Nominations are made by a committee, from the floor, and through a nominating ballot.

In many clubs new officers are nominated by a committee which is appointed by the president. The committee should be named with adequate time to make selections and contact persons selected to be nominated. Some clubs instruct the nominating committee to select two persons for each office. Other clubs require the nominating committee to select only one officer for each office.

On the date set for election of officers, the president requests a report from the chairmen of the nominating committee.

Chairman: "Mr. President, the nominating committee submits the following nominations:

For President — Mr. James Thompson
For Vice-President — Miss Jane Green
For Secretary — Miss Katherine Mills
For Treasurer — Mr. Jon Teel"

President: "Are there other nominations from the floor?" If no additional nominations are made from the floor, the following is correct practice.

Bill Smith: "Mr. President, I move that nominations close."

Carol Wallis: "Mr. President, I second the motion."

President: "It has been moved and seconded that nominations for officers be closed." "Are you ready for the question?" (pause) "Those in favor please stand." (A two-thirds majority is needed to close nominations.) "There being a two-thirds majority, the motion is carried, and nominations are closed."

After nominations have been closed with one person nominated for each office, a motion for election of officers by acclamation is in order.

Member: "Mr. President, I move that we accept the nominations of the nominating committee and elect the new officers by acclamation."

OPPRESSIVE CHILD LABOR IS DEFINED AS EMPLOYMENT OF CHILDREN UNDER THE LEGAL MINIMUM AGES [1]

AGE STANDARDS

16—BASIC MINIMUM AGE FOR EMPLOYMENT

At 16 years of age young people **may be employed in any occupation** other than a nonagricultural occupation declared hazardous by the Secretary of Labor. There are no other restrictions. If not contrary to State or local law, young people of this age may be employed during school hours, for any number of hours, and during any periods of time.

18—MINIMUM AGE FOR EMPLOYMENT IN NONAGRICULTURAL OCCUPATIONS DECLARED HAZARDOUS BY THE SECRETARY OF LABOR

16—MINIMUM AGE FOR EMPLOYMENT IN AN AGRICULTURAL OCCUPATION DECLARED HAZARDOUS BY THE SECRETARY OF LABOR AT ANY TIME AND FOR EMPLOYMENT IN AGRICULTURE DURING THE HOURS SCHOOLS ARE IN SESSION IN THE DISTRICT WHERE THE MINOR LIVES WHILE WORKING. (See Child Labor Bulletin No. 102.)

[1]**Child Labor Provisions of the Fair Labor Standards Act** (United States Department of Labor WHPC Publication 1258), Jan. 1969, pp. 5-30.

14—MINIMUM AGE FOR SPECIFIED OCCUPATIONS OUTSIDE SCHOOL HOURS

Employment of 14- and 15-year-old youths is limited to certain occupations outside school hours only and under specified conditions of work as set forth in Child Labor Regulation No. 3 (see p. 26).

COVERAGE OF THE CHILD LABOR PROVISION

EMPLOYMENT

IN COMMERCE

Employees engaged in interstate or foreign commerce are covered. This includes, among others, workers in the telephone, telegraph, radio, television, importing, exporting, and transportation industries; employees in distributing industries, such as wholesaling, who handle goods moving in interstate or foreign commerce, as well as workers who order, receive, or keep records of such goods; and clerical and other workers who regularly use the mails, telephone, and telegraph for interstate or foreign communication.

IN THE PRODUCTION OF GOODS FOR COMMERCE

Employees who work in places that produce goods for interstate or foreign commerce, such as manufacturing establishments, oil fields, mines; or in occupations that are closely related or directly essential to the production of such goods are covered.

IN AN ENTERPRISE ENGAGED IN COMMERCE

Employees employed in certain enterprises, as that term is defined in the act, which are engaged in interstate or foreign commerce or in the production of goods for such commerce are covered. Included in this category are such establishments as hotels, motels, restaurants, hospitals, laundries and dry cleaning establishments, institutions for the resident care of the sick or aged, other retail and service establishments, and schools.

The child labor provisions apply to an enterprise even though a business unit of such establishment is exempt under section 13 from the monetary provisions of the act.

IN OR ABOUT AN ESTABLISHMENT PRODUCING GOODS FOR COMMERCE

Producers, manufacturers, or dealers are prohibited from shipping or delivering for shipment in interstate or foreign commerce any goods produced in an establishment in or about which oppressive child labor has been employed within 30 days prior to the removal of the goods. It is not necessary for the employee to be working on the goods that are removed for shipment in order to be covered.

EXEMPTIONS FROM THE CHILD LABOR PROVISIONS OF THE ACT

THE CHILD LABOR PROVISIONS DO NOT APPLY TO:

Children under 16 years of age employed by their parents in **agriculture** or in non-agricultural occupations **other than** manufacturing or mining occupations or occupations declared hazardous for minors under 18.

Children under 16 years of age employed by other than their parents in **agriculture,** if the occupation has **not** been declared hazardous and the employment is **outside the hours schools are in session** in the district where the minor lives while working. Children employed as **actors** or **performers** in motion picture, theatrical, radio, or television productions.

Children engaged in the **delivery of newspapers** to the consumer. **Homeworkers** engaged in the **making of wreaths** composed principally of natural holly, pine, cedar, or other evergreens (including the harvesting of the evergreens).

HAZARDOUS OCCUPATIONS

The Fair Labor Standards Act provides a minimum age of 18 years for any **nonagricultural** occupation which the Secretary of Labor "shall find and by order declare" to be particularly hazardous for 16- and 17-year-old persons, or detrimental to their health and well-being.

A 16-year minimum age applies to any agricultural occupation that the Secretary of Labor "finds and declares" to be particularly hazardous for the employment of children under 16.

Determination of hazardous occupations is made after careful investigation by the U. S. Department of Labor's Bureau of Labor Standards of the occupations to be included within the scope of the investigation. During such an investigation, trained personnel gather statistical data on industrial injuries, visit typical plants to observe the occupations and their hazards under actual operating conditions, and seek the opinion and advice of safety engineers, plant supervisors, trade association officials, union leaders, and State factory inspectors, as well as experts from industrial accident commissions and agencies of the Federal Government. A preliminary report is prepared on the basis of the investigation and is submitted for comment and suggestion to a technical advisory committee appointed from the ranks of employers, associations, trade unions, and experts in the particular field under consideration. After comments and suggestions have been received from the advisory committee, the report is revised and a proposed finding and order, if justified, is prepared.

Upon issuance and publication of the proposed finding and order, opportunity is given for any interested party to make objection to or to suggest revisions in the order at a public hearing. Objections and suggested revisions are carefully considered and, if they are found to be justified, the proposed order is revised. Thereafter, if warranted, the order is adopted and issued by the Secretary of Labor. Once issued, the orders have the force of law, and a violation of their provisions constitutes a violation of the child labor provisions of the Fair Labor Standards Act.

The 17 hazardous occupations orders now in effect apply either on an industry basis, specifying the occupations in the industry that are not covered, or on an occupational basis irrespective of the industry in which found. Investigations and procedures followed in determining hazardous occupations in agricultural employment are similar to those described in connection with industry.

EXEMPTIONS:

Nonagricultural Hazardous Occupations Orders Nos. 5, 8, 10, 12, 14, 16 and 17 contain exemptions for apprentices and student-learners provided they are employed under the following conditions:

I. **Apprentices:** (1) The apprentice is employed in a craft recognized as an apprenticeable trade; (2) the work of the apprentice in the occupations declared particularly hazardous is incidental to his training; (3) such work is intermittent and for short periods of time and is under the direct and close supervision of a journeyman as a necessary part of such apprentice training; and (4) the apprentice is registered by the Bureau

of Apprenticeship and Training of the U. S. Department of Labor as employed in accordance with the standards established by that Bureau, or is registered by a State agency as employed in accordance with the standards of the State apprenticeship agency recognized by the Bureau of Apprenticeship and Training, or is employed under a written apprenticeship agreement and conditions which are found by the Secretary of Labor to conform substantially with such Federal or State standards.

II. **Student-Leaners:** (1) The student-learner is enrolled in a course of study and training in a cooperative vocational training program under a recognized State or local educational authority or in a course of study in a substantially similar program conducted by a private school; and (2) such student-learner is employed under a written agreement which provides: (i) That the work of the student-learner in the occupations declared particularly hazardous shall be incidental to his training; (ii) that such work shall be intermittent and for short periods of time, and under the direct and close supervision of a qualified and experienced person; (iii) that safety instructions shall be given by the school and correlated by the employer with on-the-job training; and (iv) that a schedule of organized and progressive work processes to be performed on the job shall have been prepared. Each such written agreement shall contain the name of the student-learner, and shall be signed by the employer and the school coordinator or principal. Copies of each agreement shall be kept on file by both the school and the employer. This exemption for the employment of student-learners may be revoked in any individual situation where it is found that reasonable precautions have not been observed for the safety of minors employed thereunder.

A high school graduate may be employed in an occupation in which he has completed training as provided in this paragraph as a student-learner, even though he is not 18 years of age.

HAZARDOUS OCCUPATIONS ORDERS IN NONAGRICULTURAL OCCUPATIONS

Those occupations declared to be particularly hazardous for minors between 16 and 18 years of age (also for minors 14 and 15) are included in the seventeen Hazardous Occupations Orders listed on following pages:

(1) Occupations in or about plants or establishments manufacturing or storing explosives or articles containing explosive components.
(2) Occupations of motor-vehicle driver and outside helper.
(3) Coal-mine occupations.
(4) Logging occupations and occupations in the operation of any sawmill, lath mill, shingle mill, or cooperage-stock mill.
(5) Occupations involved in the operation of power-driven woodworking machines.
(6) Occupations involving exposure to radioactive substances and to ionizing radiations.
(7) Occupations involved in the operation of elevators and other power-driven hoisting apparatus.
(8) Occupations involved in the operation of power-driven metal forming, punching, and shearing machines.
(9) Occupations in connection with mining, other than coal.
(10) Occupations involving slaughtering, meat-packing or processing, or rendering.
(11) Occupations involved in the operation of certain power-driven bakery machines.
(12) Occupations involved in the operation of certain power-driven paper-products machines.
(13) Occupations involved in the manufacture of brick, tile, and kindred products.
(14) Occupations involved in the operation of circular saws, band saws, and guillotine shears.
(15) Occupations involved in wrecking, demolition, and shipbreaking operations.
(16) Occupations involved in roofing operations.
(17) Occupations in excavation operations.

TEXT OF THE HAZARDOUS OCCUPATIONS ORDERS IN NONAGRICULTURAL OCCUPATIONS

MANUFACTURING OR STORAGE OCCUPATIONS INVOLVING EXPLOSIVES (ORDER NO. 1)

The following occupations in or about plants or establishments manufacturing or storing explosives or articles containing explosive components:

(1) All occupations in or about any plant or establishment (other than retail establishments or plants or establishments of the type described in subparagraph (2) of this paragraph) manufacturing components except where the occupation is performed in a "non-explosive" area as defined in subparagraph (3) of this section.
(2) The following occupations in or about any plant or establishment manufacturing or storing small arms ammunition not exceeding .60 caliber in size, shotgun shells, or blasting caps when manufactured or stored in conjunction with the manufacture of small-arms ammunition:
(a) All occupations involved in the manufacturing, mixing, transporting, or handling of explosive compounds in the manufacture of small-arms ammunition and all other occupations requiring the performance of any duties in the explosives area in which explosive compounds are manufactured or mixed.

(b) All occupations involved in the manufacturing, transporting, or handling of primers and all other occupations requiring the performance of any duties in the same building in which primers are manufactured.

(c) All occupations involved in the priming of cartridges and all other occupations requiring the performance of any duties in the same workroom in which rim-fire cartridges are primed.

(d) All occupations involved in the plate loading of cartridges and in the operation of automatic loading machines.

(e) All occupations involved in the loading, inspecting, packing, shipping and storage of blasting caps.

DEFINITIONS

(1) The term "plant or establishment manufacturing or storing explosives or articles containing explosive components" means the land with all the buildings and other structures thereon used in connection with the manufacturing or processing or storing of explosives or articles containing explosive components.

(2) The terms "explosives" and "articles containing explosive components" mean and include ammunition, black powder, blasting caps, fireworks, high explosives, primers, smokeless powder, and all goods classified and defined as explosives by the Interstate Commerce Commission in regulations for the transportation of explosives and other dangerous substances by common carriers (49 CFR Parts 71-78) issued pursuant to the Act of June 25, 1948 (62 Stat. 739; 18 U.S.C. 835).

(3) An area meeting all of the following criteria shall be deemed a "nonexplosive area":

(a) None of the work performed in the area involves the handling or use of explosives;

(b) The area is separated from the explosives area by a distance not less than that prescribed in the American Table of Distances for the protection of inhabited buildings;

(c) The area is separated from the explosives area by a fence or is otherwise located so that it constitutes a definite designated area; and

(d) Satisfactory controls have been established to prevent employees under 18 years of age within the area from entering any area in or about the plant which does not meet criteria (a) through (c).

(Effective July 1, 1939. Amended February 13, 1943, and June 12, 1952.)

MOTOR VEHICLE OCCUPATIONS (ORDER NO. 2)

(a) **Except as provided in paragraph** (b). The occupations of motor vehicle driver and outside helper on any public road, highway, in or about any mine (including open pit mine or quarry), place where logging or sawmill operations are in progress, or in any excavation of the type identified in § 1500.68 (a) are particularly hazardous for the employment of minors between 16 and 18 years of age.

(b) **Exemptions**

(1) **Incidental and occasional driving.** The finding and declaration in paragraph (a) shall not apply to the operation of automobiles or trucks not exceeding 6,000 pounds gross vehicle weight if such driving is restricted to daylight hours; **provided,** such operation is only occasional and incidental to the child's employment; that the child holds a State license valid for the type of driving involved in the job which he performs and has completed a State approved driver education course; and **provided further,** that the vehicle is equipped with a seat belt or similar device for the driver and for each helper, and the employer

has instructed each child that such belts or other devices must be used. This subparagraph shall not be applicable to any occupation of motor-vehicle driver which involves the towing of vehicles.

(2) **School bus driving.** The finding and declaration in paragraph (a) shall not apply to driving a school bus during the period of any exemption which has been granted in the discretion of the Secretary of Labor on the basis of an application filed and approved by the Governor of the State in which the vehicle is registered. The Secretary will notify any State which inquires of the information to be furnished in the application. Neither shall the finding and declaration in paragraph (a) apply in a particular State during a period not to exceed the first 40 days after this amendment is effective while application for such exemption is being formulated by such State seeking merely to continue in effect unchanged its current program using such drivers, nor while such application is pending action by the Secretary.

(c) **Definitions.**

(1) The term "motor vehicle" shall mean any automobile, truck, truck-tractor, trailer, semitrailer, motorcycle, or similar vehicle propelled or drawn by mechanical power and designed for use as a means of transportation but shall not include any vehicle operated exclusively on rails.

(2) The term "driver" shall mean any individual who, in the course of his employment, drives a motor vehicle at any time.

(3) The term "outside helper" shall mean any individual, other than a driver, whose work includes riding on a motor vehicle outside the cab for the purpose of assisting in transporting or delivering goods.

(4) The term "gross weight" includes the truck chassis with lubricants, water and full tank or tanks of fuel, plus the weight of the cab or driver's compartment, body and special chassis and body equipment, and payload. (Eff. Jan. 1, 1940, amended May 6, 1955; Nov. 1, 1967; and Sept. 5, 1968.)

COAL MINE OCCUPATIONS (ORDER NO. 3)

All occupations in or about any coal mine, except the occupation of slate or other refuse picking at a picking table or picking chute in a tipple or breaker and occupations requiring the performance of duties solely in offices or in repair or maintenance shops located in the surface part of any coal-mining plant.

DEFINITIONS

The term "coal" shall mean any rank of coal, including lignite, bituminous, and anthracite coals.

The term "all occupations in or about any coal mine" shall mean all types of work performed in any underground working, open pit, or surface part of any coal-mining plant that contributes to the extraction, grading, cleaning, or other handling of coal. (Effective September 1, 1940.)

LOGGING AND SAWMILLING OCCUPATIONS (ORDER NO. 4)

All occupations in logging and all occupations in the operation of any sawmill, lath mill, shingle mill, or cooperage-stock mill except the following:

(1) Exceptions applying to logging:

(a) Work in offices or in repair or maintenance shops.

(b) Work in the construction, operation, repair, or maintenance of living and administrative quarters of logging camps.

(c) Work in timber cruising, surveying, or logging-engineering parties; work in the repair or maintenance of roads, railroads, or flumes; work in forest protection, such as clearing fire trails or roads, piling and burning slash, maintaining fire-fighting equipment, constructing and maintaining telephone lines, or acting as fire lookout or fire patrolman away from the actual logging operations: **Provided,** that the provisions of this paragraph shall not apply to the felling or bucking of timber, the collecting or transporting of logs, the operation of power-driven machinery, the handling or use of explosives and work on trestles.

(d) Peeling of fence posts, pulpwood, chemical wood, excelsior wood, cordwood, or similar products, when not done in conjunction with and at the same time and place as other logging occupations declared hazardous by this section.

(e) Work in the feeding or care of animals.

(2) Exceptions applying to the operation of any permanent sawmill or the operation of any lath mill, shingle mill, or cooperage-stock mill: **Provided,** that these exceptions do not apply to a portable sawmill the lumber yard of which is used only for the temporary storage of green lumber and in connection with which no office or repair or maintenance shop is ordinarily maintained: and **Further provided,** that these exceptions do not apply to work which entails entering the sawmill building:

(a) Work in offices or in repair or maintenance shops.

(b) Straightening, marking, or tallying lumber on the dry chain or the dry drop sorter.

(c) Pulling lumber from the dry chain.

(d) Clean-up in the lumberyard.

(e) Piling, handling, or shipping of cooperage stock in yards or storage sheds, other than operating or assisting in the operation of power-driven equipment.

(f) Clerical work in yards or shipping sheds, such as done by ordermen, tallymen, and shipping clerks.

(g) Clean-up work outside shake and shingle mills, except when the mill is in operation.

(h) Splitting shakes manually from pre-cut and split blocks with a froe and mallet, except inside the mill building or cover.

(i) Packing shakes into bundles when done in conjunction with splitting shakes manually with a froe and mallet, except inside the mill building or cover.

(j) Manual loading of bundles of shingles or shakes into trucks or railroad cars, provided that the employer has on file a statement from a licensed doctor of medicine or ostepathy certifying the minor capable of performing this work without injury to himself.

DEFINITIONS

The term "all occupations in logging" shall mean all work performed in connection with the felling of timber; the bucking or converting of timber into logs, poles, ties, pulpwood, chemical wood, excelsior wood, cordwood, fence posts, or similar products; the collecting, skidding, yarding, loading, transporting, and unloading of such products in connection with logging; the constructing, repairing, and maintenance of roads, railroads, flumes, or camps used in connection with logging; the moving, installing, rigging, and maintenance of machinery or equipment used in logging; and other work performed in connection with logging. The term shall not apply to work performed in timber culture, timber-stand improvement, or in emergency firefighting.

The term "all occupations in the operation of any sawmill, lath mill, shingle mill, or cooperage-stock mill" shall mean all work performed in or about any such mill in connection with storing of logs and bolts; converting logs or bolts into sawn lumber, laths, shingles, or cooperage stock; storing, drying, and shipping lumber, laths, shingles, cooperage stock, or other products of such mills; and other work performed in connection with the operation of any saw mill, lath mill, shingle mill, or cooperage-stock mill. The term shall not include work performed in the planing-mill department or other remanufacturing departments of any sawmill, or in any planing mill or remanufacturing plant not a part of a sawmill.

(Effective August 1, 1941. Amended September 12, 1942; June 25, 1943; October 18, 1944; September 11, 1946; February 2, 1948; and April 15, 1967.)

POWER-DRIVEN WOODWORKING MACHINE OCCUPATIONS (ORDER NO. 5)

The following occupations involved in the operation of power-driven woodworking machines:

(1) The occupation of operating power-driven woodworking machines including supervising or controlling the operation of such machines, feeding material into such machines, and helping the operator to feed material into such machines, but not including the placing of material on a moving chain or in a hopper or slide for automatic feeding.

(2) The occupations of setting up, adjusting, repairing, oiling, or cleaning power-driven woodworking machines.

(3) The operation of off-bearing from circular saws and from guillotine-action veneer clippers.

DEFINITIONS

(1) The term "power-driven woodworking machines" shall mean all fixed or portable machines or tools driven by power and used or designed for cutting, shaping, forming, surfacing, nailing, stapling, wire stitching, fastening, or otherwise assembling, pressing, or printing wood or veneer.

(2) The term "off-bearing" shall mean the removal of material or refuse directly from a saw table or from the point of operation. Operations not considered as off-bearing within the intent of this section include: (a) The removal of material or refuse from a circular saw or guillotine-action veneer clipper where the material or refuse has been conveyed away from the saw table or point of operation by a gravity chute or by some mechanical means such as a moving belt or expulsion roller, and (b) the following operations when they do not involve the removal of material or refuse directly from a saw table or from the point of operation: the carrying, moving, or transporting of materials from one machine to another or from one part of a plant to another; the piling, stacking, or arranging of materials for feeding into a machine by another person; and the sorting, tying, bundling, or loading of materials.

EXEMPTIONS

The exemptions for apprentices and student-learners discussed on page 304 apply to this Order.

(Effective August 1, 1941. Amended November 13, 1942; February 18, 1944; July 12, 1944; October 31, 1945; September 27, 1946; November 24, 1951; and September 23, 1958).

OCCUPATIONS INVOLVING EXPOSURE TO RADIOACTIVE SUBSTANCES AND TO IONIZING RADIATIONS (ORDER NO. 6)

Any work in any workroom in which (a) radium is stored or used in the manufacture of self-luminous compound; (b) self-luminous compound is made, processed, or packaged; (c) self-luminous compound is stored, used, or worked upon; (d) incandescent mantles are made from fabric and solutions containing thorium salts, or are processed or packaged; (e) other radioactive substances are present in the air in average concentrations exceeding 10 percent of the maximum permissible concentrations in the air recommended for occupational exposure by the National Committee on Radiation Protection, as set forth in the 40-hour week column of Table One of the National Bureau of Standards Handbook No. 69 entitled "Maximum Permissible Body Burdens and Maximum Permissible Concentrations of Radionuclides in Air and in Water for Occupational Exposure," issued June 5, 1959.

Any other work which involves exposure to ionizing radiations in excess of 0.5 rem per year.

DEFINITIONS

As used in this section: the term "self-luminous compound" shall mean any mixture of phosphorescent material and radium, mesothorium, or other radioactive element; the term "workroom" shall include the entire area bounded by walls of solid material and extending from floor to ceiling; the term "ionizing radiations" shall mean alpha and beta particles, electrons, protons, neutrons, gamma, and X-ray and all other radiations which produce ionizations directly or indirectly, but does not include electromagnetic radiations other than gamma and X-ray.

(Effective May 1, 1942. Amended July 9, 1949; June 23, 1957; August 14, 1958; and October 21, 1961).

POWER-DRIVEN HOISTING APPARATUS OCCUPATIONS (ORDER NO. 7)

The following occupations involved in the operation of power-driven hoisting apparatus:

(1) Work of operating an elevator, crane, derrick, hoist, or high-lift truck, except operating an unattended automatic operation passenger elevator* or an electric or air-operated hoist not exceeding 1 ton capacity.

(2) Work which involves riding on a man-lift or on a freight elevator, except a freight elevator operated by an assigned operator.

(3) Work of assisting in the operation of a crank, derrick, or hoist performed by crane hookers, crane chasers, hookers-on, riggers, rigger helpers, and like occupations.

DEFINITIONS

The term "elevator" shall mean any power-driven hoisting or lowering mechanism equipped with a car or platform which moves or guides in a substantially vertical direction. The term shall include both passenger and freight elevators, (including portable elevators or tiering machines) but shall not include dumbwaiters.

The term "crane" shall mean a power-driven machine for lifting and lowering a load and moving it horizontally, in which the hoisting mechanism is an integral part of the machine. The term shall include all types of cranes, such as cantilever gantry, crawler, gantry, hammer-head, ingot-pouring, jib, locomotive, motor truck, overhead traveling, pillar jib, pintle, portal, semi-gantry, semi-portal, storage bridge, tower, walking jib, and wall cranes.

The term "derrick" shall mean a power-driven apparatus consisting of a mast or equivalent members held at the top by guys or braces, with or without a boom, for use with a hoisting mechanism and operating ropes. The term shall include all types of derricks, such as A-frame, breast, Chicago boom, gin-pole, guy, and stiff-leg derricks.

The term "hoist" shall mean a power-driven apparatus for raising or lowering a load by the application of a pulling force that does not include a car or platform running in guides. The term shall include all types of hoists, such as base-mounted electric, clevis suspension, hook suspension, monorail, overhead electric, simple drum, and trolley suspension hoists.

*Note: See "Exception" (p. 311)

The term "high-lift truck" shall mean a power-driven industrial type of truck used for lateral transportation that is equipped with a power-operated lifting device usually in the form of a fork or platform capable of tiering loaded pallets or skids one above the other. Instead of a fork, or platform, the lifting device may consist of a ram, scoop, shovel, crane, revolving fork, or other attachments for handling specific loads. The term shall mean and include high-lift trucks known under such names as forklifts, fork trucks, forklift trucks, tiering trucks, or stacking trucks, but shall not mean low-lift trucks or low-lift platform trucks that are designed for the transportation of, but not the tiering of, material.

The term, "manlift" shall mean a device intended for the conveyance of persons which consists of platforms or brackets mounted on, or attached to, an endless belt, cable, chain or similar method of suspension; such belt, cable, or chain operating in a substantially vertical direction and being supported by and driven through pulleys, sheaves or sprockets at the top or bottom.

EXCEPTION

This section shall not prohibit the operation of an automatic elevator and an automatic signal elevator provided that the exposed portion of the car interior (exclusive of vents and other necessary small openings), the car door, and the hoistway doors are constructed of solid surfaces without any opening through which a part of the body may extend; all hoistway openings at floor level have doors which are interlocked with the car door so as to prevent the car from starting until all such doors are closed and locked; the elevator (other than hydraulic elevators) is equipped with a device which will stop and hold the car in case of overspeed or if the cable slackens or breaks; and the elevator is equipped with upper and lower travel limit devices which will normally bring the car to rest at either terminal and a final limit switch which will prevent

the movement in either direction and will open in case of excessive over travel by the car.

DEFINITIONS

As used in this exception:

For the purpose of this exception the term "automatic elevator" shall mean a passenger elevator, a freight elevator, or a combination passenger-freight elevator, the operation of which is controlled by pushbuttons in such a manner that the starting, going to the landing selected, leveling and holding, and the opening and closing of the car and hoistway doors are entirely automatic.

For the purpose of this exception, the term "automatic signal operation elevator" shall mean an elevator which is started in response to the operation of a switch (such as a lever or pushbutton) in the car which when operated by the operator actuates a starting device that automatically closes the car and hoistway doors — from this point on, the movement of the car to the landing selected, leveling and holding when it gets there, and the opening of the car and hoistway doors are entirely automatic.

(Eff. Sept. 1, 1946, Amended Sept. 30, 1950; Sept. 1, 1955; and Nov. 7, 1967.)

POWER-DRIVEN METAL FORMING, PUNCHING, AND SHEARING MACHINE OCCUPATIONS (ORDER NO. 8)

The occupations of operator of or helper on the following power-driven metal forming, punching, and shearing machines:

(1) All rolling machines, such as beading, straightening, corrugating, flanging, or bending rolls; and hot or cold rolling mills.

(2) All pressing or punching machines, such as punch presses, except those provided with full automatic feed and ejection and with a fixed barrier guard to prevent the hands or fingers of the operator from entering the area between the dies; power presses; and plate punches.

(3) All bending machines, such as apron brakes and press brakes.

(4) All hammering machines, such as drop hammers and power hammers.

(5) All shearing machines, such as guillotine or squaring shears; alligator shears; and rotary shears.

The occupations of setting up, adjusting, repairing, oiling, or cleaning these machines including those with automatic feed and ejection.

DEFINITIONS

The term "operator" shall mean a person who operates a machine covered by this Order by performing such functions as starting or stopping the machine, placing materials into or removing them from the machine, or any other function directly involved in operation of the machine.

The term "helper" shall mean a person who assists in the operation of a machine covered by this Order by helping place materials into or remove them from the machine.

The term "forming, punching, and shearing machines" shall mean power-driven metal-working machines, other than machine tools, which change the shape of or cut metal by means of tools, such as dies, rolls, or knives which are mounted on rams, plungers, or other moving parts. Types of forming, punching, and shearing machines, enumerated in this section are the machines to which the designation is by custom applied.

EXEMPTIONS

The exemptions for apprentices and student-learners discussed on page 304 apply to this Order.

(Effective October 30, 1950. Amended September 23, 1958, and November 15, 1960.)

Note: This order does **not** apply to a very large group of metal-working machines known as machine tools. Machine tools are defined as "power-driven complete metalworking machines having one or more tool- or work-holding devices, and used for progressively removing metal in the form of chips." Since the Order does not apply to machine tools, the 18-year age minimum does not apply. They are classified below so that they can be readily identified.

Milling function machines

Horizontal Milling Machines
Vertical Milling Machines
Universal Milling Machines
Planer-type Milling Machines
Gear Hobbing Machines
Profilers
Routers
**Circular Saws

Planning function machines

Planers
Shapers
Slotters
Broaches
Keycasters
Hack Saws
**Band Saws

Grinding function machines

Grinders
Abrasive Wheels
Abrasive Belts
Abrasive Disks
Abrasive Points
Buffing Wheels
Polishing Wheels
Stroppers
Lapping Machines

Boring function machines

Vertical Boring Mills
Horizontal Boring Mills
Jig Borers
Pedestal Drills
Radial Drills
Gang Drills
Upright Drills
Centering Machines
Reamers
Honers

**See HO 14

Turning function machines

Engine Lathes
Turret Lathes
Hollow Spindle Lathes
Automatic Lathes
Automatic Screw Machines

OCCUPATIONS IN CONNECTION WITH MINING, OTHER THAN COAL (ORDER NO. 9)

All occupations in connection with mining, other than coal, except the following:

(1) Work in offices, in the warehouse or supply house, in the change house, in the laboratory, and in repair or maintenance shops not located underground.

(2) Work in the operation and maintenance of living quarters.

(3) Work outside the mine in surveying, in the repair and maintenance of roads, and in general clean-up about the mine property such as clearing brush and digging drainage ditches.

(4) Work of track crews in the building and maintaining of sections of railroad track located in those areas of open-cut metal mines where mining and haulage activities are not being conducted at the time and place that such building and maintaining work is being done.

(5) Work in or about surface placer mining operations other than placer dredging operations and hydraulic placer mining operations.

(6) The following work in metal mills other than in mercury-recovery mills or mills using the cyanide process:

   (a) Work involving the operation of jigs, sludge tables, flotation cells, or drier-filters.

   (b) Work of hand sorting at picking table or picking belt.

   (c) General cleanup work.

Provided, however, that nothing in this section shall be construed as permitting employment of minors in any occupation prohibited by any other hazardous occupations order issued by the Secretary of Labor.

DEFINITIONS

As used in this section: The term "all occupations in connection with mining, other than coal" shall mean all work performed underground in mines and quarries; on the surface at underground mines and underground quarries; in or about open-cut mines, open quarries, clay pits, and sand and gravel operations; at or about placer mining operations; at or about dredging operations for clay, sand or gravel; at or about bore-hole mining operations; in or about all metal mills, washer plants, or grinding mills reducing the bulk of the extracted minerals; and at or about any other crushing, grinding, screening, sizing, washing or cleaning operations performed upon the extracted minerals except where such operations are performed as a part of a manufacturing process. The term shall not include work performed in subsequent manufacturing or processing operations, such as work performed in smelters, electro-metallurgical plants, refineries, reduction plants, cement mills, plants where quarried stone is cut, sanded and further processed, or plants manufacturing clay, glass, or ceramic products. Neither shall the term include work performed in connection with coal mining, in petroleum production, in natural-gas production, nor in dredging operations which are not a part of mining operations, such as dredging for construction or navigation purposes.

(Effective January 6, 1951.)

OCCUPATIONS INVOLVING SLAUGHTERING, MEAT-PACKING OR PROCESSING, OR RENDERING (ORDER NO. 10)

The following occupations in or about slaughtering and meat-packing establishments, rendering plants, or wholesale, retail or service establishments:

(1) All occupations on the killing floor, in curing cellars, and in hide cellars, except the work of messengers, runners, handtruckers, and similar occupations which require entering such work-

rooms or workplaces infrequently and for short periods of time.

(2) All occupations involved in the recovery of lard and oils, except packaging and shipping of such products and the operation of lard-roll machines.

(3) All occupations involved in tankage or rendering of dead animals, animal offal, animal fats, scrap meats, blood, and bones into stock feeds, tallow, inedible greases, fertilizer ingredients, and similar products.

(4) All occupations involved in the operation or feeding of the following power-driven meat-processing machines, including the occupation of setting up, adjusting, repairing, oiling, or cleaning such machines: meat patty forming machines, meat and bone cutting saws, knives (*except bacon-slicing machines), head splitters, and guillotine cutters; snout pullers and jaw pullers; skinning machines; horizontal rotary washing machines; casing-cleaning machines such as crushing, stripping, and finishing machines; grinding, mixing, chopping, and hashing machines; and presses (except belly-rolling machines).

(5) All boning occupations.

(6) All occupations that involve the pushing or dropping of any suspended carcass, half carcass, or quarter carcass.

*Note: The term "bacon-slicing machine" as used in this Order refers to those machines which are designed solely for the purpose of slicing bacon and are equipped with enclosure or barrier guards that prevent the operator from coming in contact with the blade or blades, and with devices for automatic feeding, slicing, shingling, stacking, and conveying the sliced bacon away from the point of operation.

(7) All occupations involving hand-lifting or hand-carrying any carcass or half carcass of beef, pork, or horse, or any quarter carcass of beef or horse.

DEFINITIONS

The term "slaughtering and meat-packing establishments" shall mean places in or about which cattle, calves, hogs, sheep, lambs, goats, or horses are killed, butchered, or processed. The term shall also include establishments which manufacture or process meat products or sausage casings from such animals.

The term "rendering plants" shall mean establishments engaged in the conversion of dead animals, animal offal, animal fats, scrap meats, blood, and bones into stock feeds, tallow, inedible greases, fertilizer ingredients, and similar products.

The term "killing floor" shall include that workroom or workplace where cattle, calves, hogs, sheep, lambs, goats, or horses are immobilized, shackled, or killed, and the carcasses are dressed prior to chilling.

The term "curing cellar" shall include that workroom or workplace which is primarily devoted to the preservation and flavoring of meat by curing materials. It does not include that workroom or workplace where meats are smoked.

The term "hide cellar" shall include that workroom or workplace where hides are graded, trimmed, salted, and otherwise cured.

The term "boning occupations" shall mean the removal of bones from meat cuts. It shall not include work that involves cutting, scraping, or trimming meat from cuts containing bones.

EXEMPTIONS

This Order shall not apply to the killing and processing of poultry, rabbits, or small game in areas physically separated from the killing floor.

The exemptions for apprentices and student-learners discussed on page 304 apply to this Order.

(Eff. May 8, 1952; Amended Nov. 15, 1960; Dec. 22, 1962, and Dec. 30, 1963.)

POWER-DRIVEN BAKERY MACHINE OCCUPATIONS (ORDER NO. 11)

The following occupations involved in the operation of power-driven bakery machines:

(1) The occupations of operating, assisting to operate, or setting up, adjusting, repairing, oiling, or cleaning any horizontal or vertical dough mixer; batter mixer; bread dividing, rounding, or molding machine; dough brake; dough sheeter; combination bread slicing and wrapping machine; or cake cutting band saw.

(Effective July 21, 1952. Amended November 15, 1960.)

POWER-DRIVEN PAPER-PRODUCTS MACHINE OCCUPATIONS (ORDER NO. 12)

The occupations of operating or assisting to operate any of the following power-driven paper-products machines:

(1) Arm-type wire stitcher or stapler, circular or band saw, corner cutter or mitering machine, corrugating and single- or double-facing machine, envelope die-cutting press, guillotine paper cutter or shear, horizontal bar scorer, laminating or combining machine, sheeting machine, scrap-paper baler, or vertical slotter.

(2) Platen die-cutting press, platen printing press, or punch press which involves hand feeding of the machine.

The occupations of setting up, adjusting, repairing, oiling, or cleaning these machines including those which do not involve hand feeding.

DEFINITIONS

The term "operating or assisting to operate" shall mean all work which involves starting or stopping a machine covered by this Order, placing materials into or removing them from the machine, or any other work directly involved in operating the machine.

The term "paper-products machine" shall mean power-driven machines used in the remanufacture or conversion of paper or pulp into a finished product. The term is understood to apply to such machines whether they are used in establishments that manufacture converted paper or pulp products, or in any other type of manufacturing or nonmanufacturing establishment.

EXEMPTIONS

The exemptions for apprentices and student-learners discussed on page 304 apply to this Order.

(Effective September 11, 1954. Amended September 23, 1958, and November 15, 1960).

OCCUPATIONS INVOLVED IN THE MANUFACTURE OF BRICK, TILE, AND KINDRED PRODUCTS (ORDER NO. 13)

The following occupations involved in the manufacture of clay construction products and of silica refractory products:

(1) All work in or about establishments in which clay construction products are manufactured, except (a) work in storage and shipping; (b) work in offices, laboratories, and storerooms; and (c) work in the drying departments of plants manufacturing sewer pipe.

(2) All work in or about establishments in which silica brick or other silica refractories are manufactured, except work in offices.

(3) Nothing in this section shall be construed as permitting employment of minors in any occupation prohibited by any other hazardous occupations order issued by the Secretary of Labor.

DEFINITIONS

The term "clay construction products" shall mean the following clay products: Brick, hollow structural tile, sewer pipe and kindred products, refractories, and other clay products such as architectural terra cotta, glazed structural tile, roofing tile, stove lining, chimney pipes and tops, wall coping, and drain tile. The term shall not include the following non-structural-bearing clay products: Ceramic floor and wall tile, mosaic tile, glazed and enameled tile, faience, and similar tile, nor shall the term include non-clay construction products such as sand-lime brick, glass brick, or nonclay refractories.

The term "silica brick or other silica refractories" shall mean refractory products from raw materials containing free silica as their main constituent.

(Effective September 1, 1956.)

OCCUPATIONS INVOLVED IN THE OPERATION OF POWER-DRIVEN CIRCULAR SAWS, BAND SAWS, AND GUILLOTINE SHEARS (ORDER NO. 14)

The occupations of operator or of helper on the following power-driven fixed or portable machines equipped with full automatic feed and ejection:

(1) Circular saws.
(2) Band saws.
(3) Guillotine shears.

The occupations of setting up, adjusting, repairing, oiling, or cleaning circular saws, band saws, and guillotine shears.

DEFINITIONS

The term "operator" shall mean a person who operates a machine covered by this Order by performing such functions as starting or stopping the machine, placing materials into or removing them from the machine, or any other function directly involved in operation of the machine.

The term "helper" shall mean a person who assists in the operation of a machine covered by this Order by helping place materials into or remove them from the machine.

The term "machines equipped with full automatic feed and ejection" shall mean machines covered by this Order which are equipped with devices for full automatic

feeding and ejection and with a fixed barrier guard to prevent completely the operator or helper from placing any part of his body in the point-of-operation area.

The term "circular saw" shall mean a machine equipped with a thin steel disc having a continuous series of notches or teeth on the periphery, mounted on shafting, and used for sawing materials.

The term "bandsaw" shall mean a machine equipped with an endless steel band having a continuous series of notches or teeth, running over wheels or pulleys, and for sawing materials.

The term "guillotine shear" shall mean a machine equipped with a moveable blade operated vertically and used to shear materials. The term shall not include other types of shearing machines, using a different form of shearing action, such as alligator shears or circular shears.

EXEMPTIONS

The exemptions for apprentices and student-learners discussed on page 304 apply to this Order.

(Effective November 15, 1960.)

OCCUPATIONS INVOLVED IN WRECKING, DEMOLITION, AND SHIPBREAKING OPERATIONS (ORDER NO. 15)

All occupations in wrecking, demolition, and shipbreaking operations.

DEFINITIONS

The term "wrecking, demolition, and shipbreaking operations" shall mean all work, including cleanup and salvage work, performed at the site of the total or partial razing, demolishing, or dismantling of a building, bridge, steeple, tower, chimney, other structure, ship or other vessel.

(Effective November 15, 1960.)

OCCUPATIONS IN ROOFING OPERATIONS (ORDER NO. 16)

All occupations in roofing operations.

DEFINITIONS

The term "roofing operations" shall mean all work performed in connection with the application of weatherproofing materials and substances (such as tar or pitch, asphalt prepared paper, tile, slate, metal, translucent materials, and shingles of asbestos, asphalt or wood) to roofs of buildings or other structures. The term shall also include all work performed in connection with: (1) The installation of roofs, including related metal work such as flashing and (2) alterations, additions, maintenance, and repair, including painting and coating, of existing roofs. The term shall not include gutter and downspout work; the construction of the sheathing or base of roofs; or the installation of television antennas, air conditioners, exhaust and ventilating equipment, or similar appliances attached to roofs.

EXEMPTIONS

The exemptions for apprentices and student-learners discussed on page 304 apply to this Order.
(Effective February 5, 1962.)

OCCUPATIONS IN EXCAVATION OPERATIONS (ORDER NO. 17)

The following occupations in excavation operations:
(1) Excavating, working in, or backfilling (refilling) trenches, except (a) manually excavating or manually backfilling trenches that do not exceed four feet in depth at any point, or (b) working in trenches that do not exceed four feet in depth at any point.
(2) Excavating for buildings or other structures or working in such excavations, except (a) manually excavating to a depth not exceeding four feet below any ground surface adjoining the excavation, or (b) working in an excavation not exceeding such depth, or (c) working in an excavation where the side

walls are shored or sloped to the angle of repose.
(3) Working within tunnels prior to the completion of all driving and shoring operations.
(4) Working within shafts prior to the completion of all sinking and shoring operations.

EXEMPTIONS

The exemptions for apprentices and student-learners discussed on page 304 apply to this Order.
(Effective May 9, 1963.)

CHILD LABOR REGULATION NO. 3

EMPLOYMENT OF 14- AND 15-YEAR-OLD MINORS IS LIMITED

to certain occupations under conditions which do not interfere with their schooling, health, or well-being.

(a) **14- AND 15-YEAR-OLD MINORS MAY NOT BE EMPLOYED:**
(1) DURING SCHOOL HOURS, except as provided in paragraph (b).
(2) BEFORE 7 a.m. or AFTER 7 p.m. except 9 p.m. from June 1 through Labor Day (time depends on local standards).
(3) MORE THAN 3 HOURS A DAY — on school days.
(4) MORE THAN 18 HOURS A WEEK — in school weeks.
(5) MORE THAN 8 HOURS A DAY — on nonschool days.
(6) MORE THAN 40 HOURS A WEEK — in nonschool weeks.

(b) In the case of enrollees in work training programs conducted under Part B of Title I of the Economic Opportunity Act of 1964, there is an exception to the requirement of paragraph (a) (1) of this section if the employer has on file with his records kept pursuant to Part 516 of this title an unrevoked written statement of the Administrator of the Bureau of Work Programs or his representative setting out the periods which the minor will work and certifying that his health and well-being, countersigned by the principal of the school which the minor is attending with his certificate that such employment will not interfere with the minor's schooling.

PERMITTED OCCUPATIONS FOR 14- AND 15-YEAR-OLD MINORS IN RETAIL, FOOD SERVICE, AND GASOLINE SERVICE ESTABLISHMENTS

14- AND 15-YEAR-OLD MINORS MAY BE EMPLOYED IN —

(1) OFFICE and CLERICAL WORK (including operation of office machines).

(2) CASHIERING, SELLING, MODELING, ART WORK, WORK IN ADVERTISING DEPARTMENTS, WINDOW TRIMMING and COMPARATIVE SHOPPING.

(3) PRICE MARKING and TAGGING by hand or by machine, ASSEMBLING ORDERS, PACKING and SHELVING.

(4) BAGGING and CARRYING OUT CUSTOMERS' ORDERS.

(5) ERRAND and DELIVERY WORK by foot, bicycle, and public transportation.

(6) CLEAN UP WORK, including the use of vacuum cleaners and floor waxers, and MAINTENANCE of GROUNDS, but not including the use of power-driven mowers or cutters.

(7) KITCHEN WORK and other work involved in preparing and serving food and beverages, including the operation of machines and devices used in the performance of such work, such as, but not limited to, dishwashers, toasters, dumbwaiters, popcorn poppers, milk shake blenders, and coffee grinders.

(8) WORK IN CONNECTION WITH CARS and TRUCKS if confined to the following:

Dispensing gasoline and oil.
Courtesy service.
Car cleaning, washing and polishing.
Other occupations permitted by this section.

BUT NOT INCLUDING WORK:
Involving the use of pits, racks or lifting apparatus or involving the inflation of any tire mounted on a rim equipped with a removable retaining ring.

(9) CLEANING VEGETABLES and FRUITS, and WRAPPING, SEALING, LABELING, WEIGHING, PRICING and STOCKING GOODS when performed in areas physically separate from areas where meat is prepared for sale and outside freezers or meat coolers.

IN ANY OTHER PLACE OF EMPLOYMENT

14- AND 15-YEAR-OLD MINORS MAY BE EMPLOYED IN — any occupation EXCEPT the excluded occupations listed below:

14- AND 15-YEAR-OLD MINORS MAY NOT BE EMPLOYED IN —

(1) Any MANUFACTURING occupation.

(2) Any MINING occupation.

(3) PROCESSING occupations (except in a retail, food service, or gasoline service establishment in those specific occupations expressly permitted there in accordance with the foregoing list).

(4) Occupations requiring the performance of any duties IN WORKROOMS OR WORKPLACES WHERE GOODS ARE MANUFACTURED, MINED, OR OTHERWISE PROCESSED (except to the extent expressly permitted in retail, food service, or gasoline service establishments in accordance with the foregoing list).

(5) PUBLIC MESSENGER SERVICE.

(6) OPERATION OR TENDING or HOISTING APPARATUS or of ANY POWER-DRIVEN MACHINERY (other than office machines and machines in retail, food service, and gasoline service establishments which are specified in the fore-

going list as machines which such minors may operate in such establishments).

(7) ANY OCCUPATIONS FOUND AND DECLARED TO BE HAZARDOUS.

(8) OCCUPATIONS IN CONNECTION WITH:

(a) TRANSPORTATION of persons or property by rail, highway, air, on water, pipeline or other means.

(b) WAREHOUSING and STORAGE

(c) COMMUNICATIONS and PUBLIC UTILITIES

(d) CONSTRUCTION (including repair) Except Office or Sales Work in connection with these Occupations (not performed on transportation media or at the actual construction site).

(9) ANY OF THE FOLLOWING OCCUPATIONS IN A RETAIL, FOOD SERVICE, OR GASOLINE SERVICE ESTABLISHMENT:

(a) WORK performed IN or ABOUT BOILER or ENGINE ROOMS.

(b) Work in connection with MAINTENANCE or REPAIR OF THE ESTABLISHMENT, MACHINES or EQUIPMENT.

(c) OUTSIDE WINDOW WASHING that involves working from window sills, and all work requiring the use of LADDERS, SCAFFOLDS or their substitutes.

(d) COOKING (except at soda fountains, lunch counters, snack bars, or cafeteria serving counters) and BAKING.

(e) Occupations which involve OPERATING, SETTING UP, ADJUSTING, CLEANING, OILING, or REPAIRING power-driven FOOD SLICERS and GRINDERS, FOOD CHOPPERS and CUTTERS, and BAKERY-TYPE MIXERS.

(f) Work in FREEZERS and MEAT COOLERS and all work in PREPARATION OF MEATS for sale (except wrapping, sealing, labeling, weighing, pricing and stocking when performed in other areas).

(g) LOADING and UNLOADING GOODS to and from trucks, railroad cars or conveyors.

(h) All occupations in WAREHOUSES except office and clerical work.

AGE CERTIFICATES

An employer can protect himself from unintentional violation of the minimum age provisions by obtaining and keeping on file an AGE OR EMPLOYMENT CERTIFICATE for each minor employed, showing the minor to be of the age established for the occupation in which he is employed. Employers should obtain such a certificate and have it on file before the minor starts work.

Age or employment certificates, sometimes called work permits or working papers, issued under State child labor laws are accepted as proof of age in 45 States, the District of Columbia, and Puerto Rico. Special arrangements for proof of age have been made in Alaska. In 4 States — Idaho, Mississippi, South Carolina, and Texas — Federal certificates of age are issued by the Wage and Hour and Public Contracts Divisions.

Age certificates have the twofold purpose of (1) protecting minors from harmful employment as defined by the child labor provisions of the act; and (2) protecting employers from unintentional violation of the minimum age provisions of the act by furnishing them with reliable proof of age for minors employed in their establishment. This protection is specifically authorized by the act.

To make sure that the minors in their employ are of legal age under the act, employers are urged to obtain an age certificate for every minor claiming to be under 18 years of age before employing him in any occupation, and for every minor claiming to be 18 or 19 years of age before employing him in any of the nonagricultural occupations declared hazardous.

The age certificate protects the employer only if it shows the minor to be of the legal age for the occupation in which he is employed.

If an employer has any difficulty in obtaining age certificates for minors he wishes to employ, he should notify the nearest office of the Wage and Hour and Public Contracts Divisions (see pp. 31 and 32) or the Bureau of Labor Standards, U. S. Department of Labor, Washington, D. C. 20210.

PENALTIES FOR VIOLATION

The act provides, in the case of willful violation, for a fine up to $10,000; or, for a second offense committed after the conviction of such person for a similar offense, for a fine of not more than $10,000; or imprisonment for not more than 6 months, or both. The Secretary of Labor may also ask a Federal district court to restrain future violations of the child labor provisions of the act by injunction.

STATE CHILD LABOR LAWS

Every State has a child labor law and all but one has a compulsory school attendance law. Whenever a State standard differs from a Federal standard, the higher standard must be observed.

ADDITIONAL INFORMATION

Inquiries about the Fair Labor Standards Act will be answered by mail, telephone, or personal interview at any office of the Wage and Hour and Public Contracts Division of the U. S. Department of Labor. Offices are listed in the telephone directory under the U. S. Department of Labor in the U. S. Government listing. These offices also supply publications free of charge.

Offices listed in **boldface** are staffed by investigation personnel whose duties frequently require them to be away from the office. Telephone messages and requests for information may be left at these offices

when regular personnel are not on duty. Personnel appointments may be arranged by either telephone or mail.

Alabama: **Anniston**, Birmingham, **Dothan**, **Florence**, **Huntsville**, Mobile, Montgomery, **Opelika**, **Selma**, **Tuscaloosa**

Alaska: **Anchorage**

Arizona: Phoenix, **Tucson**

Arkansas: **El Dorado**, **Fayetteville**, **Fort Smith**, **Hope**, Little Rock, **Pine Bluff**

California: **Bakersfield**, **Fresno**, Hollywood, Long Beach, Los Angeles, **Modesto**, **Monterey**, Oakland, **Redding**, **Riverside**, Sacramento, **San Diego**, San Francisco, **San Jose**, **San Mateo**, **Santa Ana**, **Santa Rosa**, **Stockton**, **West Covina**, Whittier

Colorado: Denver, **Pueblo**

Connecticut: **Bridgeport**, Hartford, **New Haven**, **New London**

Delaware: **Wilmington**

District of Columbia: College Park

Florida: **Clearwater**, **Cocoa**, **Fort Lauderdale**, **Fort Myers**, Jacksonville, **Lakeland**, **Leesburg**, Miami, North Miami, **Orlando**, **Ormond Beach**, **Panama City**, **Pensacola**, St. Petersburg, Tampa, **West Palm Beach**

Georgia: **Albany**, **Athens**, Atlanta, **Augusta**, **Brunswick**, Columbus, **Gainesville**, Hapeville, **Macon**, **Rome**, Savannah, **Thomasville**, **Valdosta**

Hawaii: Honolulu

Idaho: **Boise**

Illinois: Chicago, Springfield

Indiana: **Evansville**, Indianapolis, South Bend

Iowa: **Burlington**, **Cedar Rapids**, **Davenport**, Des Moines, **Fort Dodge**, **Mason City**, **Sioux City**, **Waterloo**

Kansas: **Great Bend**, **Pittsburg**, **Salina**, **Topeka**, Wichita

Kentucky: **Ashland**, Lexington, Louisville, **Middlesboro**, **Pikeville**

Louisiana: **Alexandria**, Baton Rouge, **Hammond**, **Houma**, **Lafayette**, **Lake Charles**, **Monroe**, New Orleans, Shreveport

Maine: Portland

Maryland: Baltimore, College Park, **Hagerstown**, **Salisbury**

Massachusetts: Boston, **Lowell**, Springfield, **Worcester**

Michigan: Detroit, Grand Rapids, **Lansing**
Minnesota: Minneapolis
Mississippi: **Columbus, Clarksdale, Greenville, Greenwood, Hattiesburg,** Jackson, **Meridian, Tupelo**
Missouri: **Cape Girardeau, Columbia, Joplin,** Kansas City, **St. Joseph,** St. Louis, **Springfield**
Montana: **Great Falls**
Nebraska: **Grand Island, Lincoln,** Omaha
Nevada: **Reno**
New Hampshire: Manchester, **Laconia**
New Jersey: **Camden,** Newark, Paterson, Trenton
New Mexico: Albuquerque, **Las Cruces, Roswell**
New York: **Albany,** Bronx, Brooklyn, Buffalo, Hempstead, New York, **Rochester,** Syracuse
North Carolina: **Asheville,** Charlotte, **Durham, Fayetteville, Goldsboro,** Greensboro, **Hickory, High Point,** Raleigh, **Wilmington, Winston-Salem**
North Dakota: **Bismarck**
Ohio: Cincinnati, Cleveland, Columbus
Oklahoma: **Ardmore, Enid, Lawton, Muskogee,** Oklahoma City, Tulsa
Oregon: **Eugene, Medford,** Portland, **Salem**
Pennsylvania: **Allentown, Altoona, Chester, Hazelton, Indiana, Johnstown, Lancaster, Lewistown,** McKeesport, **New Castle,** Philadelphia, Pittsburgh, **Reading, Scranton, Uniontown, Washington,** Wilkes-Barre

Rhode Island: Providence
South Carolina: **Charleston,** Columbia, **Florence, Greenville, Spartanburg**
South Dakota: **Aberdeen, Rapid City,** Sioux Falls
Tennessee: **Bristol, Chattanooga, Columbia, Jackson, Johnson City,** Knoxville, Memphis, Nashville
Texas: **Abilene, Amarillo, Austin, Beaumont,** Corpus Christi, Dallas, El Paso, Forth Worth, **Galveston,** Harlingen, Houston, **Laredo, Longview, Lubbock, Lufkin, Midland,** Odessa, **Paris,** San Antonio, **Texarkana, Tyler, Victoria,** Waco, **Wichita Falls**
Utah: **Ogden,** Salt Lake City
Vermont: **Burlington, Montpelier**
Virginia: **Alexandria, Norfolk,** Richmond, Roanoke, **Waynesboro**
Washington: Seattle, **Spokane, Tacoma**
West Virginia: **Bluefield,** Charleston, Clarksburg, **Huntington, Logan**
Wisconsin: Madison, Milwaukee, **Oshkosh**
Wyoming: **Casper, Cheyenne**

Puerto Rico: **Arecibo, Caguas,** Hato Rey, Mayaguez, **Ponce,** Santurce
Canal Zone, Virgin Islands: Santurce, Puerto Rico

American Samoa, Eniwetok Atoll, Guam, Johnston Island, Kwajalein Atoll, Wake Island: Honolulu, Hawaii

REGIONAL OFFICES
BUREAU OF APPRENTICESHIP AND TRAINING

Location	States Served	
Region I John F. Kennedy Federal Bldg., Room 1703-A Government Center Boston, Mass. 02203	Connecticut Maine Massachusetts	New Hampshire Rhode Island Vermont
Region II 1515 Broadway, 37th Floor New York, N.Y. 10036	New Jersey New York	Puerto Rico Virgin Islands
Region III P.O. Box 8796 Philadelphia, Pa. 19101	Delaware Maryland Pennsylvania	Virginia West Virginia
Region IV 1317 Peachtree Street, NE., Room 700 Atlanta, Ga. 30309	Alabama Florida Georgia Kentucky	Mississippi North Carolina South Carolina Tennessee
Region V 300 South Wacker Drive, 13th Floor Chicago, Ill. 60606	Illinois Indiana Michigan	Minnesota Ohio Wisconsin
Region VI 1512 Commerce Street, Room 704 Dallas, Tex. 75201	Arkansas Louisiana New Mexico	Oklahoma Texas
Region VII Federal Office Bldg., Room 2107 911 Walnut Street Kansas City, Mo. 64106	Iowa Kansas	Missouri Nebraska
Region VIII Republic Bldg., Room 232A 1612 Tremont Place Denver, Colo. 80202	Colorado Montana North Dakota	South Dakota Utah Wyoming
Region IX 450 Golden Gate Avenue, Room 9001 P.O. Box 36017 San Francisco, Calif. 94102	Arizona California	Hawaii Nevada
Region X Arcade Plaza Bldg., Room 2055 1321 Second Avenue Seattle, Wash. 98101	Alaska Idaho	Oregon Washington

This Information Is Provided for Students, Teachers, and Guidance Personnel Who Wish to Contact the Federal or State Apprenticeship Office in the Local Region

INDEX